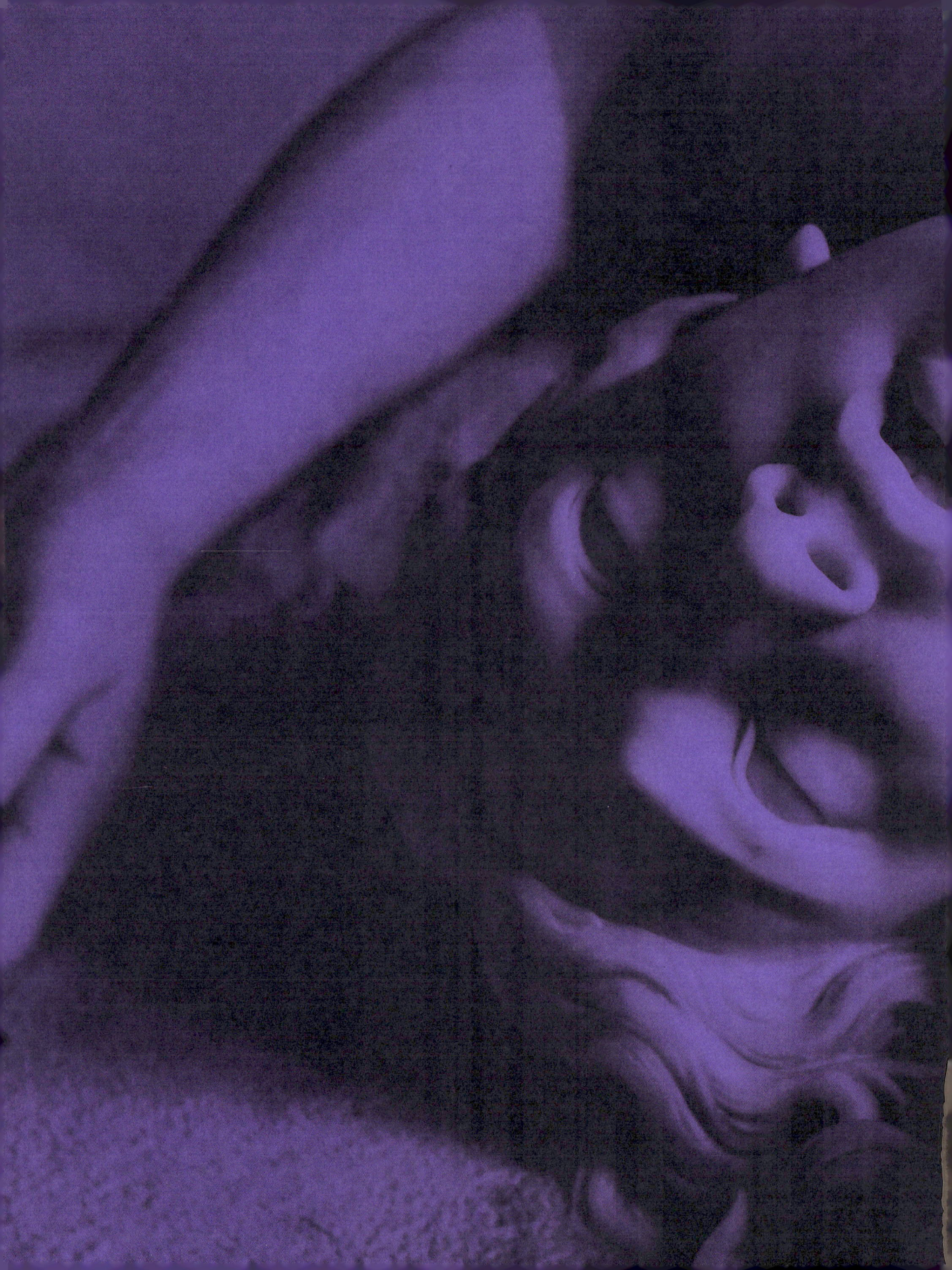

W

THE SECOND COMING

BEING A LAVISHLY ILLUSTRATED
COMPENDIUM OF HITHERTO UNPUBLISHED
MUSINGS PERTAINING TO DARK CULTURE

Print is

Undead

Misery Index

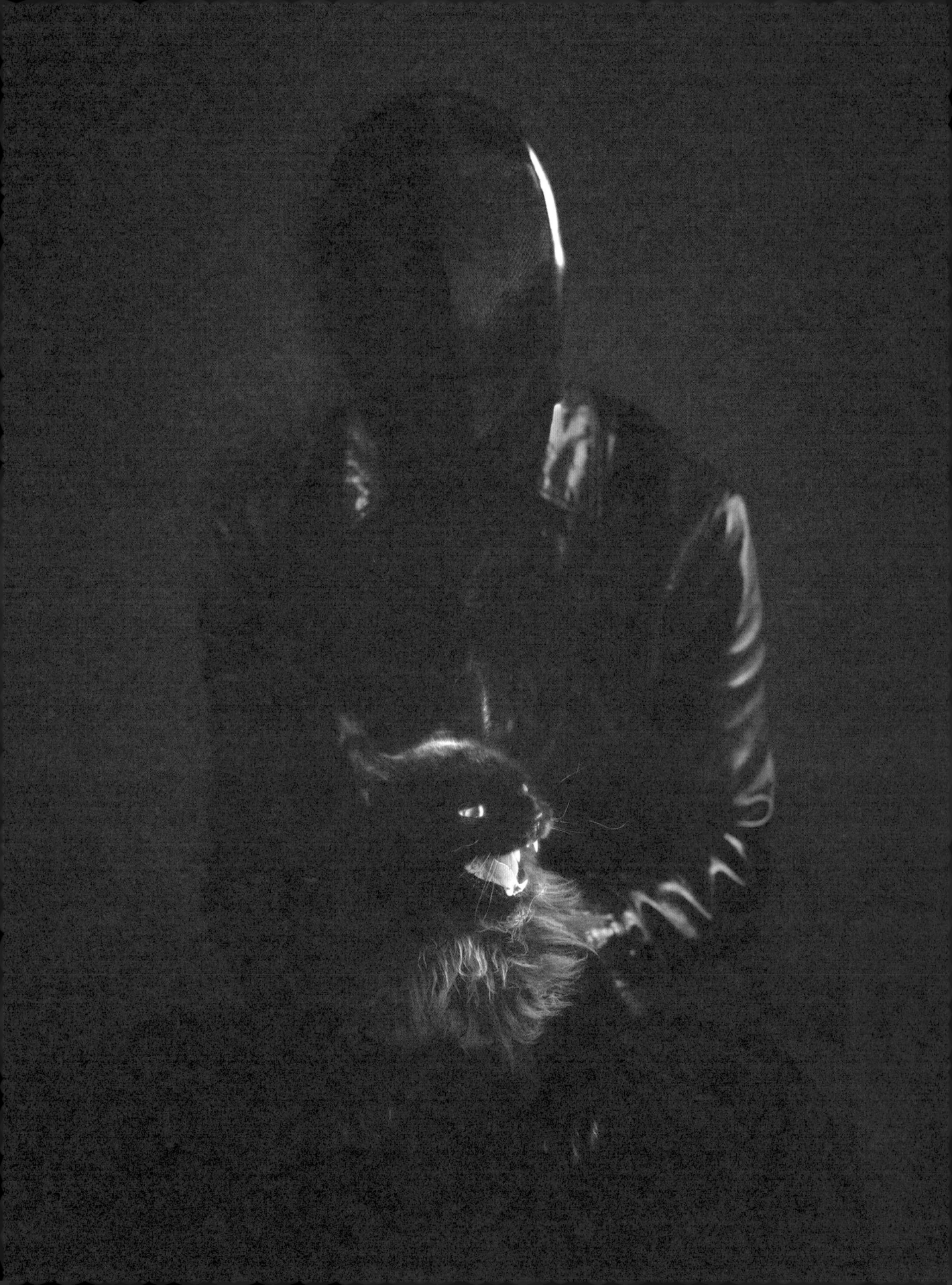

"What a great time to be alive if you love the theater of the absurd."

— David Lynch

So, you like it dark, do you? You've come to the right planet. Earth circa 2025 is one big Hieronymus Bosch painting, surreal and disconcerting, crawling with peculiar creatures in precarious situations. Grotesque figures in power glower over their subjects; neighbor defiles neighbor. Overhead, mysterious objects fly with impunity. One hopes they are benevolent aliens here to save us from ourselves.

Our plight recalls the famous poem "The Second Coming" by William Butler Yeats, written shortly after the First World War and during the 1918–19 flu pandemic:

Things fall apart; the centre cannot hold;
Mere anarchy is loosed upon the world,
The blood-dimmed tide is loosed, and everywhere
The ceremony of innocence is drowned;
The best lack all conviction, while the worst
Are full of passionate intensity.

Part of the allure of dark culture is the feeling of liberation that comes with acknowledging the realities of life—its horrors as well as its pleasures—and the acceptance of the inevitability of death. There is defiance in wearing black, dancing our asses off while staring into the abyss. *Wednesday* was created to explore darkness as a catalyst for creative expression, so, it's go time for us. Buckle up! We won't go quietly, that much is certain. And as always, we look to the artists, the poets, the makers, and the misfits for the sustenance needed to keep moving forward. Even here, even now, there is so much beauty to be found.

Welcome to *Wednesday No. 2: The Second Coming.*

Black Plastic, Founder
blackplasticmusic.com

Photograph
Heather McGrath

The Second Coming

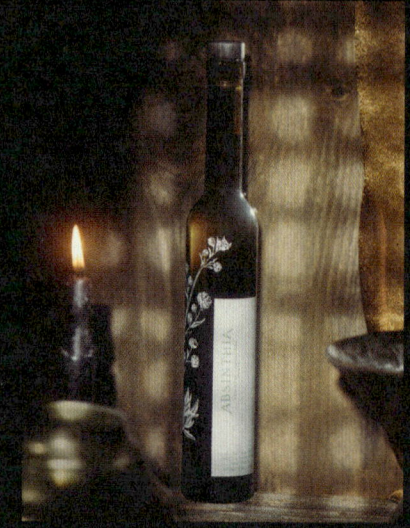

The town's clock struck midnight when Theodore left the pub where he worked and trudged to his dorm. It was a crisp Friday evening, February 1862, in England. Theodore lived in the attic of Canterbury Music Hall, where he was a custodian. His heart still mourned the loss of his fiancée Annita, who had held the leading role at the theatre. He lit a half-candle and perused the note a sailor had given him at the pub, until it was memorized:

The Second Coming: Absinthe, to rekindle the ardour of the soul; butterfly pea gin, to restore the variegated hues of one's essence; cassis liqueur, to sweeten the darker inclinations; Champagne, to honour life's fleeting splendour; and six drops of lemon, to mirror life's trials. With each sip, those whom you have lost may be rediscovered—though take heed, for the mind may stray into peril.

At 2 AM, he snuck into the pub, repeating the formula under his breath. With two bottles of Second Coming, he returned home. For the next fourteen years, Annita's falsetto resounded in the theater at random hours. Eventually, manager Charles Morton couldn't take it any longer and turned over management to R.E. Villiers, who displaced Theodore and enlarged the theater.

Ingredients:
¾ oz. Absinthia Absinthe Verte
¾ oz. cassis liqueur
¾ oz. butterfly pea gin of your choice
½ oz. fresh lemon juice
1 oz. Champagne
6 drops of water
Crushed ice to fill
Lemon twist

Method:
Combine absinthe, cassis, gin, lemon juice, Champagne, and 6 drops of water in a shaker.

Add ice and shake again until well chilled. Strain over crushed ice into a rocks glass.

Garnish with a lemon twist to evoke light piercing through darkness.

Words *Dylan Wolfram* / **Photographs** *Heather McGrath* / **Recipe** *De'Qustay Johnson*
Cocktail Stylist *Mia Andreoli* / **Hand model** *Christian Restrepo wearing Rick Owens*

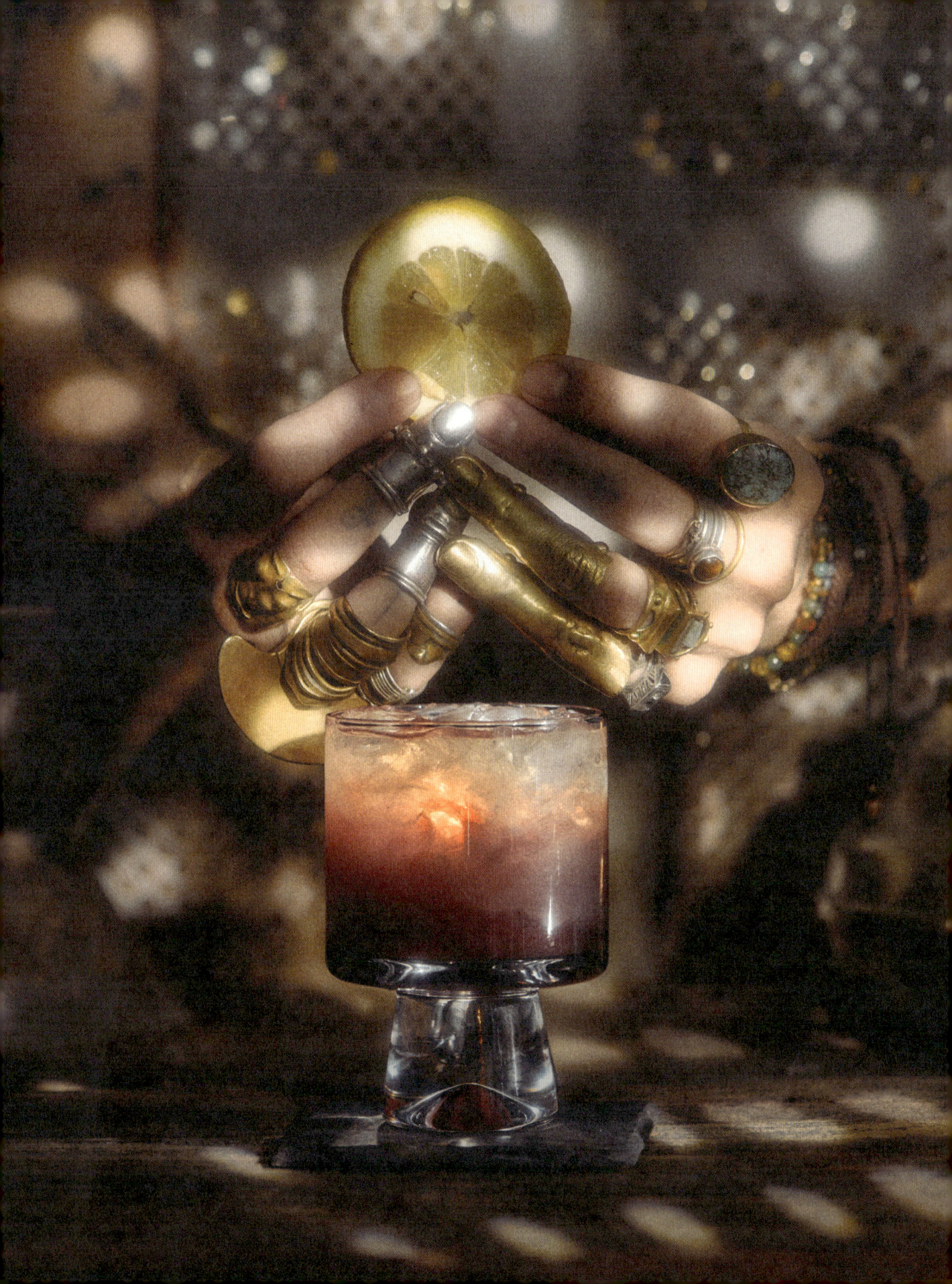

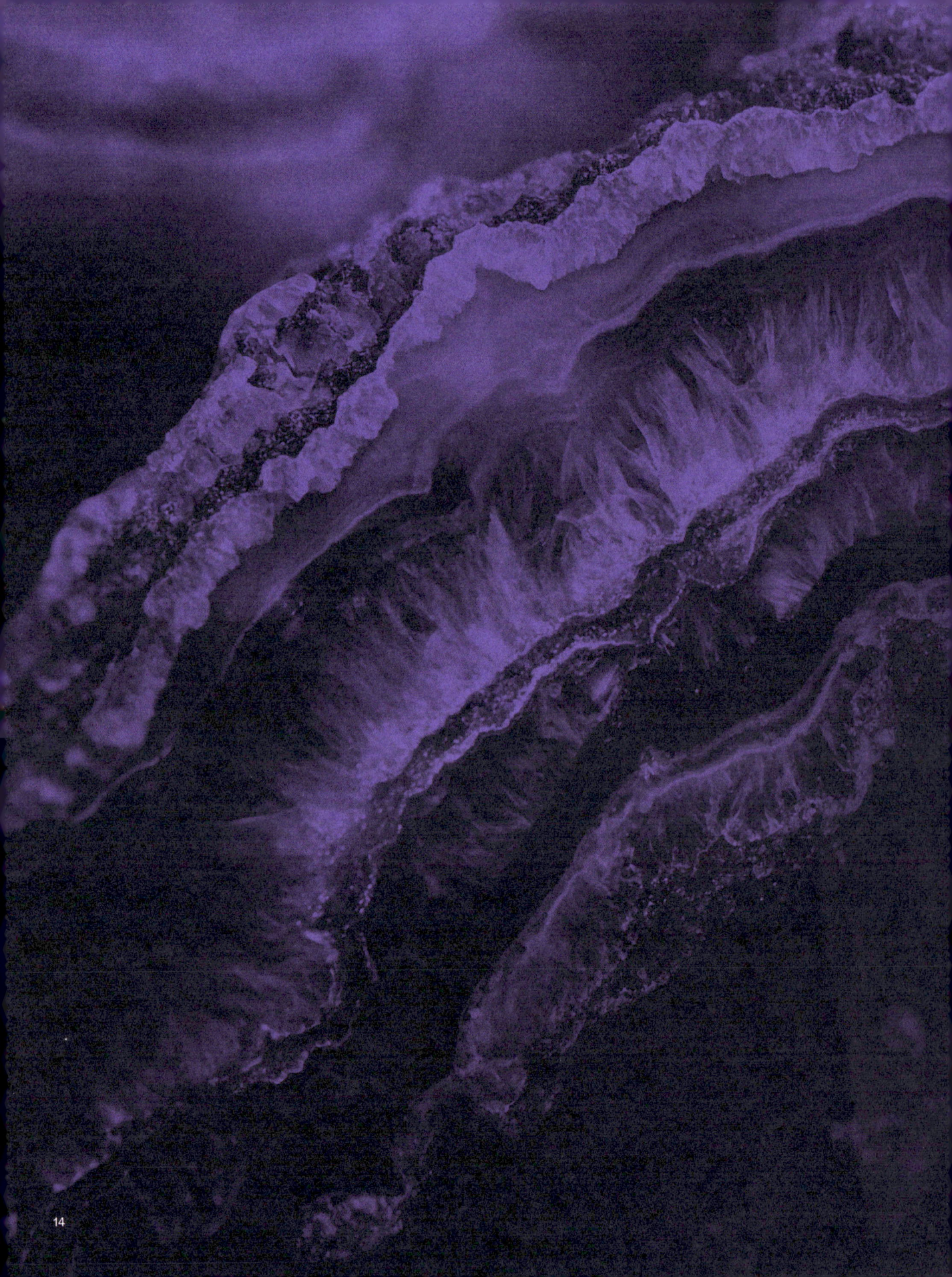

I

A bevy of dark delights awaits to be coveted. / An engrossing edition elicits unexpected emotions. / Sad dolls long for children to wipe away their eternal tears. / A century-old visage is resurrected in resin. / The sweet smell of self-immolation is now available to those who prefer to live. / The hand of a hanged murderer is expressed in marble. / Cats, like chaos, are currently having a moment. / An acrostic nursery rhyme is reinterpreted for our caustic, cursory times.

16 — 37

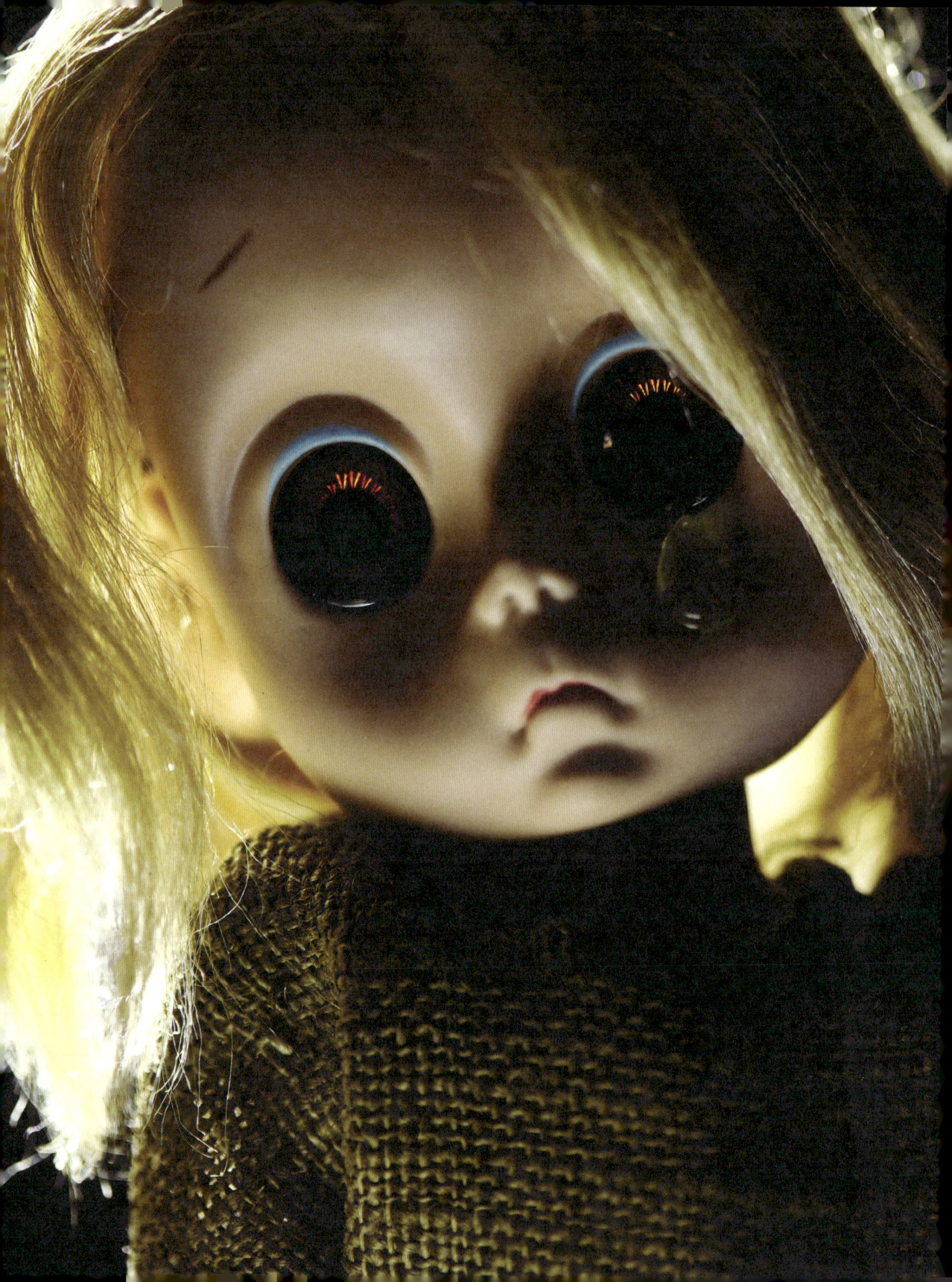

CABINET OF CURIOSITIES

For your edification and entertainment, we are proud to unlock the doors
of the *Wednesday* Wunderkabinett and invite you to view the strange and beautiful
assortment of anomalies, oddities, and artistic incomparables contained therein.

Words *Christopher Stella* / Curation *Kevin Grady*
Photographs *Mitch Tobias*

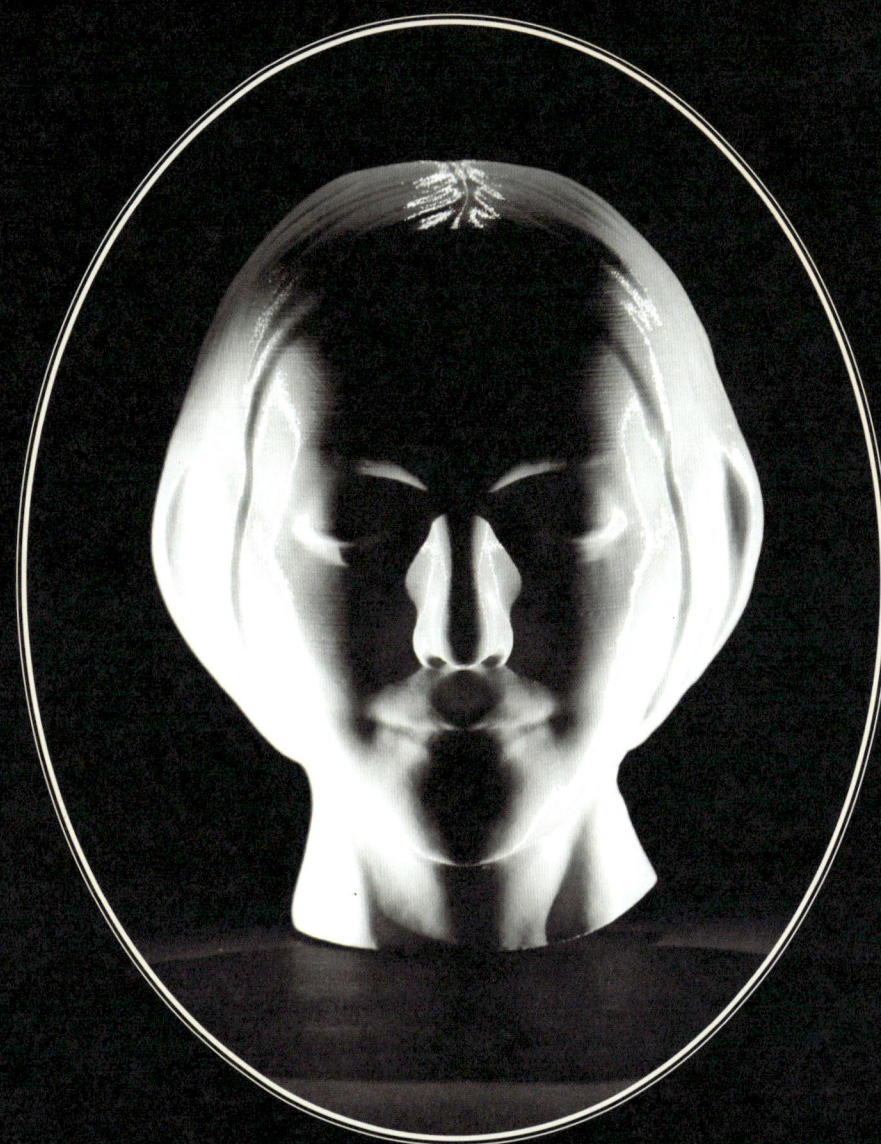

3D L'Inconnue de la Seine Death Mask

—

Nameless young ladies appear to enjoy a certain vogue in this present issue of *Wednesday*. Tradition relates that, in the closing years of the 19th century, the unmarred body of an unknown maiden was pulled from the Seine near the Quai du Louvre in Paris. So entranced was the attending mortician by her tranquil and delicate beauty that he cast her death mask and—being a man of enterprise—sold duplicates of it to many a Parisian household. Thus did the fair mask adorn innumerable parlors of the Belle Époque, stirring the fancies of poets and philosophers from Rilke to Camus. This most enduring and enigmatic countenance may now be yours, faithfully rendered in splendid three dimensions by TTPrinting and offered for acquisition through the esteemed emporium of Etsy. Properly suspended upon the wall behind one's person, it shall assuredly stir the curiosity of colleagues in any modern parlor of telegraphic discourse.

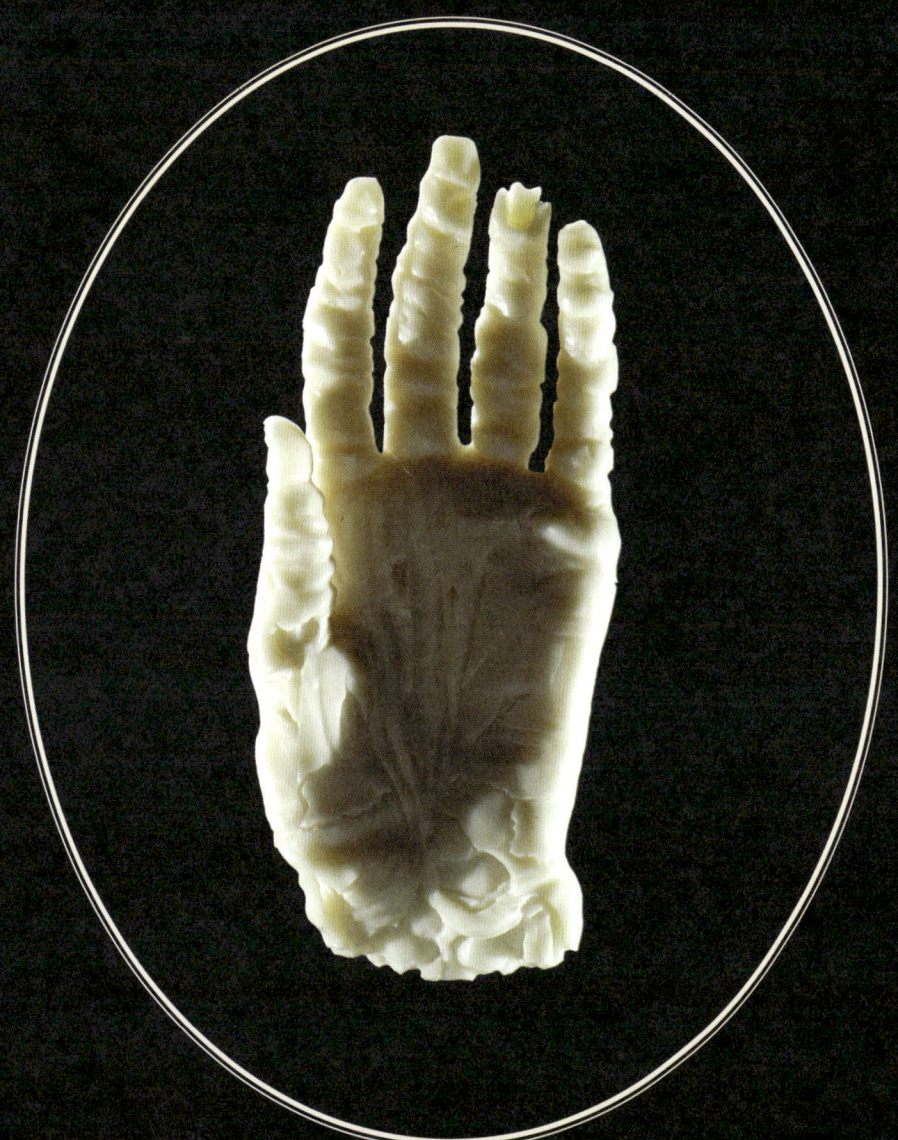

Hand of Glory by Ossua Et Acroamata

—

While it's a common presumption that vintage originals hold the upper hand over modern reproductions, one may safely entertain the notion that this marble replica—crafted by the sinister artisans of Ossua et Acroamata—offers greater resilience and, happily, a more agreeable scent than its forebears. Among 18th-century Europeans, the "Hand of Glory" was believed to harbor arcane powers, its origin shrouded in macabre ritual: Severed from the limb of a hanged murderer, it was meticulously pickled, salted, and sun-dried. An extra measure of grisly ingenuity involved fashioning a candle from the rendered fat of the executed, affixed between the fingers. Legend whispers that, when set ablaze, the ghastly light would paralyze any beholder. Employed by criminals seeking to evade capture, such practices likely fostered a vicious cycle of further "glories" production. Yet, those were 18th-century problems. Today, you possess the refined luxury of acquiring a superior, premade hand—devoid of grime and mortal toil.

The Raven

Once upon a midnight dreary, while I pondered, w...
Over many a quaint and curious volume of forgo...
While I nodded, nearly napping, suddenly there came a t...
As of someone gently rapping, rapping at my chamber d...
"'Tis some visitor," I muttered, "tapping at my chamber...
Only this a...

Ah, distinctly I remember it was in the bleak December;
And each separate dying ember wrought its ghost upon...
Eagerly I wished the morrow;—vainly I had sought to b...
From my books surcease of sorrow—sorrow for the lost...
For the rare and radiant maiden whom the angels name...
Nameless...

Poe's Phantasia

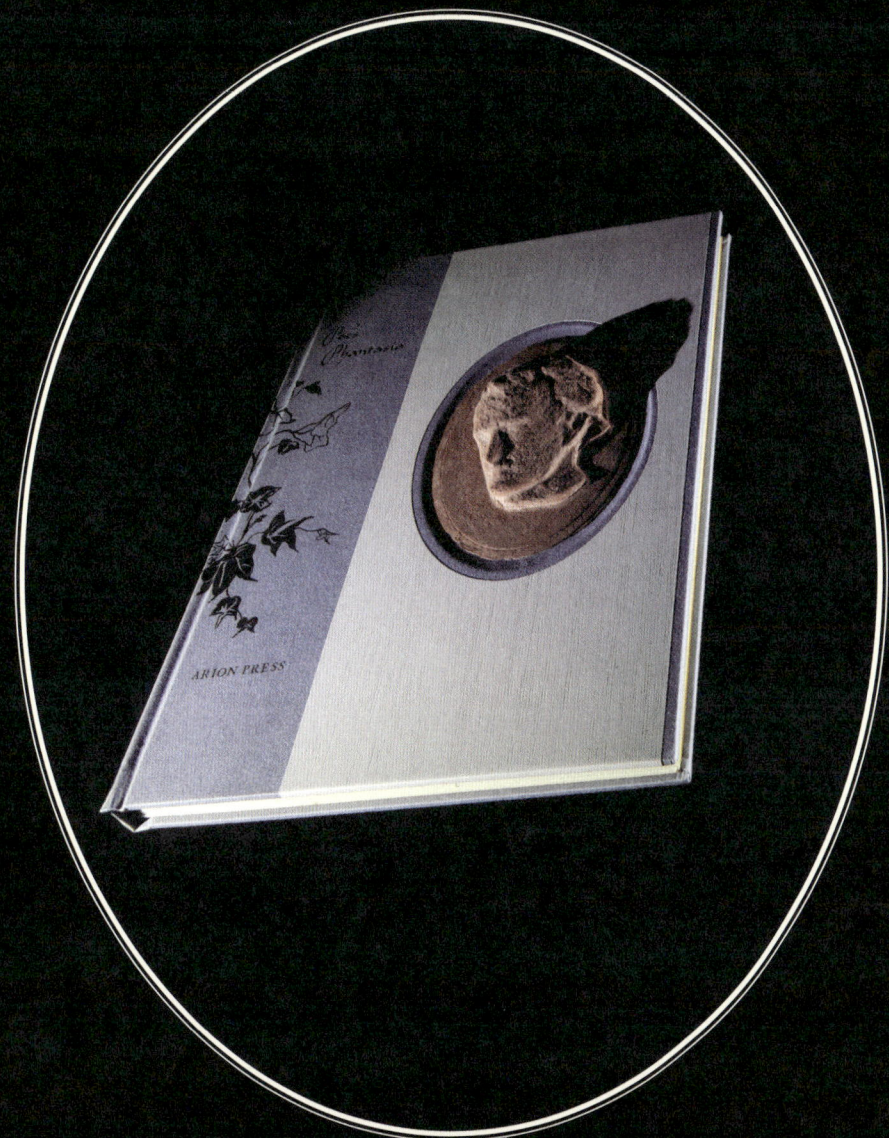

Poe's Phantasia (Arion Press)

—

Edgar Allan Poe once declared that the demise of a fair and tender young lady constituted the most poetical theme the human mind might contemplate. In these sumptuous twin volumes—made entirely by hand by Arion Press in San Francisco—the reader is invited anew to traverse the shadowed corridors of his imagination. The first tome presents fourteen tales and sundry verses, while the second is devoted wholly to "The Raven"—featuring perhaps the most celebrated of literature's departed maidens, Lenore. Both are gorgeously illuminated by artist Natalie Frank, whose phantasmagoric illustrations of passion and of violence are as fit a mirror to Poe's preoccupations as any brush might contrive. And though most *Wednesday* readers, we suspect, have not revisited the Master since the enforced studies of youthful scholarship, let it be known that his narratives—encountered in the fuller measure of one's years—resound with a poignancy, a terror, and a strange beauty more affecting than ever.

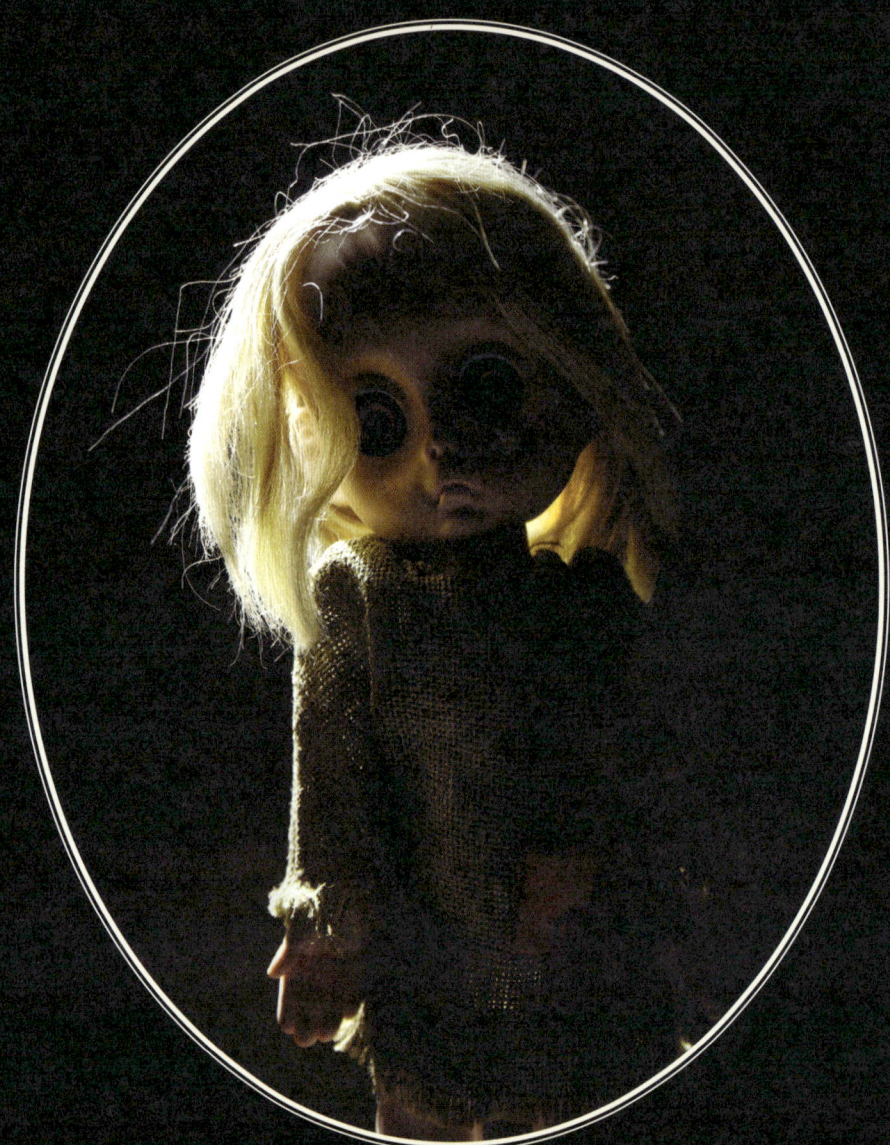

Little Miss No Name

—

Pray, who in all of Soho's alleyways could have conceived such a creation, save perhaps Charles Dickens himself? Direct from a tempest-torn back lane to the nursery of your young charge, here is a miniature ragamuffin—artfully crafted to soothe and solace. Born in the year of our Lord 1965 by the esteemed Hasbro, this diminutive sentinel, Little Miss No Name—complete with a detachable teardrop—was alas discontinued shortly thereafter. Presently, in pristine mint condition, she is available for auction across various noted outlets. What better method to imprint the virtues of altruism and charity than by bestowing upon a child their very own doe-eyed Jane Doe to cherish and tend? Do not omit to behold the original televised advertisement, wherein she is immortalized by the poignant refrain: "She has no one to talk to, she just sits, and she stares." Verily, one wonders—was it the Quaaludes?

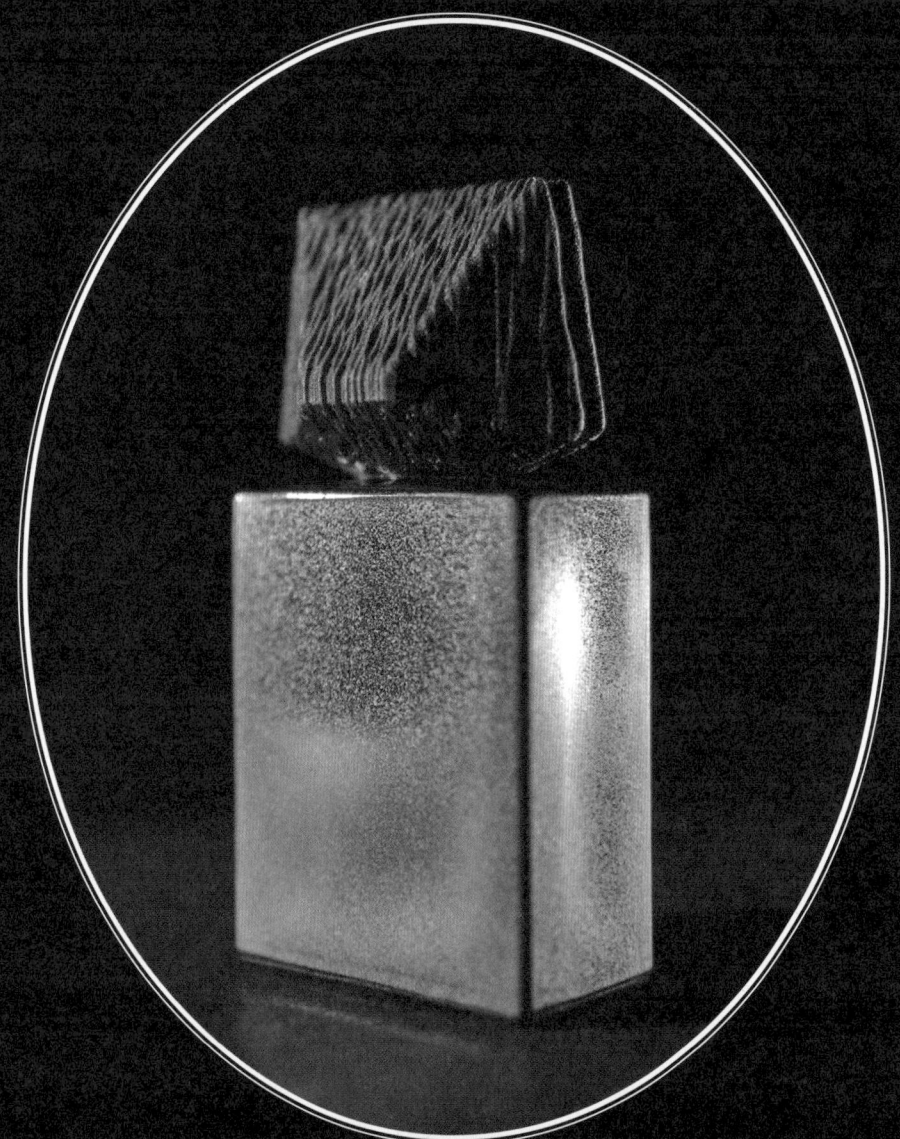

MASS Perfume By Sruli Recht

—

How is one to describe a fragrance its very creator has called indescribable? Permit us to commence with some context: MASS was initially part of artist/designer Sruli Recht's "Luxury of Choice" collection—nineteen objets d'art devised to lend an air of ceremony and refinement to the solemn act of euthanasia. Amongst these curiosities: a crystal bowl, designed for self-drowning; a pillow-mask of the finest lamb-shearling, designed to smother with all the tenderness of a mother's embrace; and, under the austere title "Who by Fire," a self-immolation set complete with a most elegant ignition apparatus of glass, flint, and steel, accompanied by a flammable body spray—MASS. Happily for those of a more combustible temperament, the fragrance—composed of cumin, orris, cashmere wood, and ambergris—may now be procured wholly divorced from its more incendiary consort, though prudence might yet suggest abstaining from its application in the near society of cigars, candles, or the domestic hearth.

Goth's Best Friend

Words *Britt Collins* / Photograph of Robert Smith *Steve Rapport, Getty Images*

Cats are having a moment, blazing across international headlines, hot in Hollywood, on the cover of *The New Yorker,* and dominating the cat-lady-crazed American politics. There's even a new 'Cats About Town' walking tour, a romp across New York that captures the city's history from a feline's perspective over the centuries.

Cats, with their punky attitude and capricious ways, tread the fine line between domestication and wildness. The ancient Egyptians thought cats were divine and their gleaming full-moon eyes were portals to other realms. They were elevated into the pantheon of cat-headed gods, and the most famous goddess was Bastet, a black feline. Similarly, in many cultures, black cats in particular were associated with magic and the supernatural, believed to exist between the earthly and spirit world.

The fabulousness of these gothic beauties, made of inky velvet that shimmers in the right light, runs deep. Black felines blazed through literature, from Edgar Allan Poe's spooky gem *The Black Cat* to the walking, talking, smoking, vodka-guzzling devil's apostle cat Behemoth in Bulgakov's *The Master and Margarita*. As a cat person who's rescued and raised dozens of cats of every stripe, anything with cats intrigued me. The charming little black rebel kitten with one white paw, blue eyes, and magic whiskers, who performed spells in *Gobbolino the Witch's Cat*, always stayed with me.

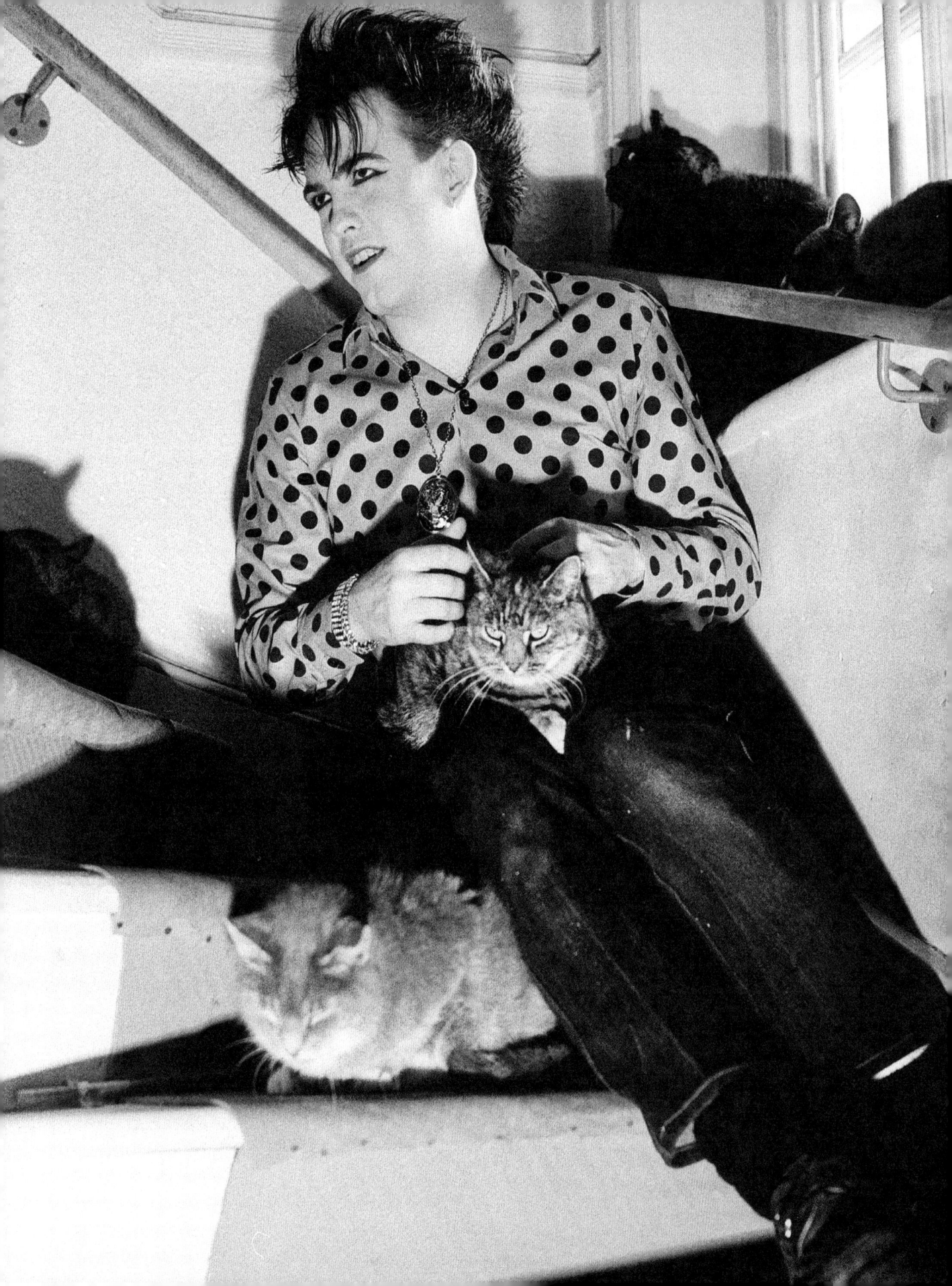

But cats haven't always had a good rep. Black cats have long been misunderstood and maligned, accused through the ages of bringing bad luck, sinking ships, consorting with witches and the devil. It was thought that witches turned into black cats at nightfall, and their reflective eyes glowed with the fires of hell. The witch hunt, sanctioned by the Roman Catholic church, raged for over 300 years and swept across the Atlantic with the Puritans, killing and burning millions of innocent women and their "familiars."

In recent times, cats have become symbols of defiance. The Industrial Workers of the World use a black cat as their icon of wildcat strike action, while the Black Panthers named their party after the beautiful black animal to signify freedom and strength. Journalist and activist Gloria Steinem, who has had many cats over the decades, credits her favorite late gray Persian Magritte as her teacher "when it comes to a strong will and self-authority." When Steinem was asked how to raise the next generation of feminists in the climate of pervasive misogyny and sexual harassment, she suggested raising them like cats. "Cats don't let you touch them. Cats tell you what they're going to do, and that's that."

Cats are sensualists, things of beauty, that have in-spired artists for centuries. Leonardo da Vinci thought 'the smallest feline is nature's masterpiece." Klimt's love of cats was legendary. He took whole colonies of strays, many of them feral, into his multiple studios, where they often caused chaos, ripping and peeing on his artworks. Louis Wain, the crazy-cat lady of the art world, whose obsession with his furry friends and quirky illustrations and paintings of big-eyed moggies and kittens, dressed up and doing human things, turned him into a sensation. Andy Warhol spent his entire life surrounded by cats and filled his five-story Manhattan brownstone into a multi-generational cat colony. He published a book *25 Cats Name Sam and One Blue Pussy*, a series of vivid ink-wash portraits, as a tribute to his 26 treasured companions.

Many of the greatest writers found solace and inspiration among cats. Mark Twain doted on his tribe of 19 beloved felines. His rapport and reverence for them was so profound that he couldn't bear to be without them. He rented kittens for company when he traveled. Baudelaire was enchanted by the beauty and otherness of these elegant creatures. The only thing William Burroughs loved more than drugs were his cats, whom he considered his spiritual guides and credits for restoring his humanity. Charles Bukowski lived very much like the rescued waifs and strays he adored because they were themselves, they do what they want and don't give a damn. "In my next life I want to be a cat," he wrote. "To sleep 20 hours a day and wait to be fed. To sit around licking my ass."

Musicians, too, have a special kinship with cats and share similar traits, with nocturnal habits and being fiercely independent, wilful spirits who are pure emotion. Keith Richards once said that cats are musicians without instruments. He's rescued many moggies, including a stray kitten found in a storm while recording in Barbados. He named him Voodoo, and he inspired the Grammy-winning album *Voodoo Lounge*. Jazz musicians often called each other "cat" as a sign of respect because cats are smooth and cool. Abbey Road Studios famously became a drop-off for boxes of unwanted kittens. The prevailing wisdom on the streets of London was that they would always find homes among musicians. All four of the Beatles were cat fanatics, especially John Lennon. From childhood until his final days, he lived with seven to ten cats at any one time and was besotted with them. Paul McCartney also maintained a lively multi-feline household with a dozen or so cats and kittens. McCartney told me in an interview that the death of John's favorite cat Alice, who'd fallen out the window of the Dakota, had brought him and John back together after their long fall-out. Behind every great rock star is a great cat or several. Bowie, himself a feline in human form with sphinx-like eyes and vampire teeth even named one of his songs "Cat People." Bob Dylan, Frank Zappa, Debbie Harry, and Patti Smith were all mad about cats, with a preference for black ones.

However, black kitties sadly are spurned in favor of gingers, tabbies, calicos, and their more colorful counterparts. Just like black dogs, black cats languish in shelters and are the last to be adopted or, worse still, are abandoned by their owners, due to lingering superstitions. Now these mini panthers are facing another setback and being rejected because supposedly dark-furred animals don't look as good in selfies.

By adopting a black cat or kitten you might be saving their lives. They won't steal your soul, but they'll definitely steal your heart. As French novelist Colette, the original cat woman, said, "Time spent with cats is never wasted," and they only make our lives richer. ∎

Britt Collins is the author of

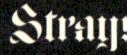

A LOST CAT, A HOMELESS MAN AND THEIR JOURNEY ACROSS AMERICA

(Simon & Schuster)

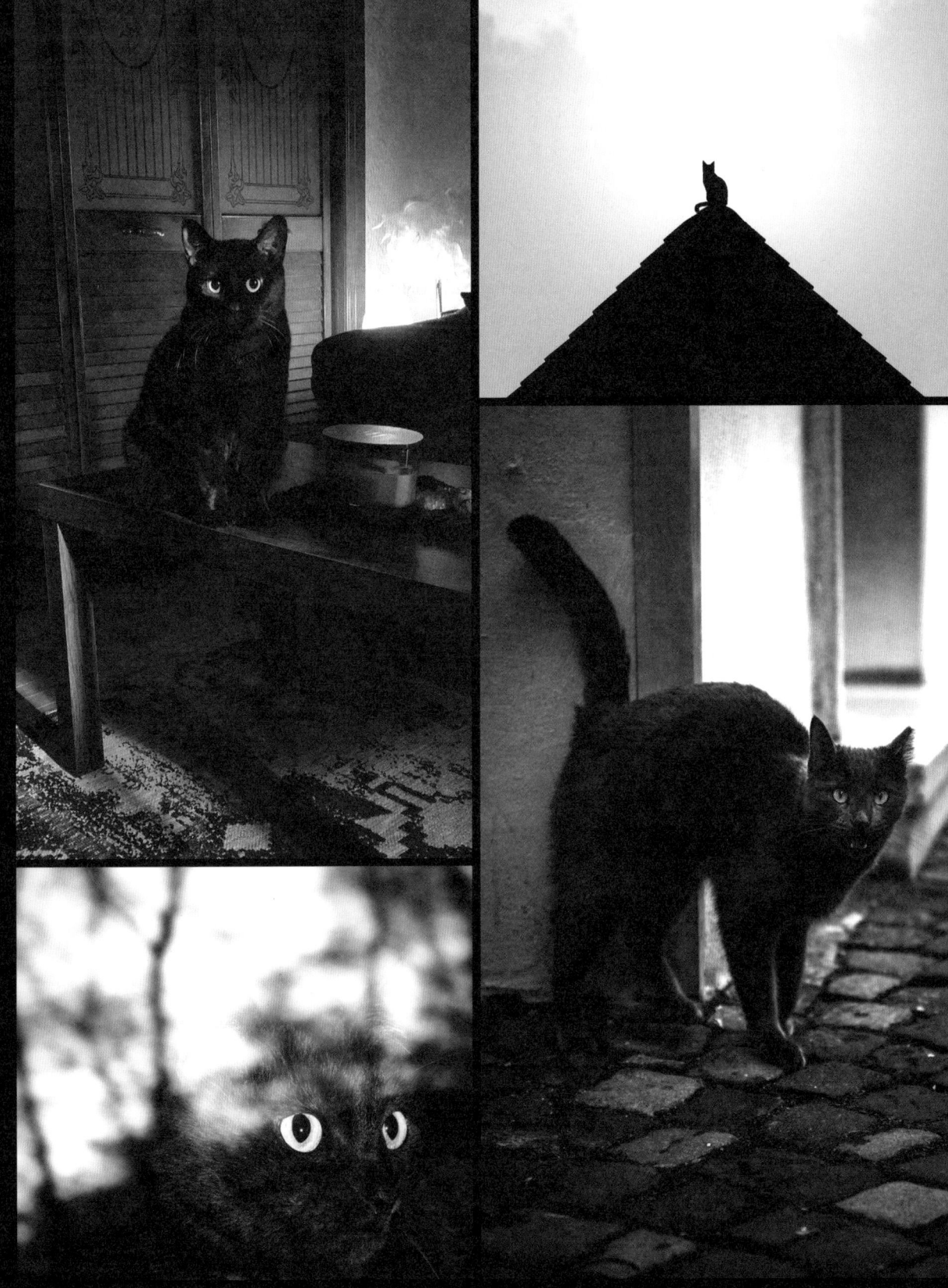

A LITTLE GOREY

—

A is for Anika, who picked all the threads.

B is for bats in your belfries (your heads).

C is for cats who do just what they want.

D is for Dracula, out on the hunt.

E is for Edgar, let's give him a shout.

F is for Frankenstein, feeling left out.

G is for Grady, directing the art.

H is for Pleasant Home, who get a heart.

I is for Isla, playing with snakes.

J is for jumping off stairs without breaks.

K is for Karen, who styled the hair.

L is for lice—luckily, none were found there.

M is for Michael, whose assistance was phat.

N is for Nina, who lent us her cat.

O is for "Oh my! We can't kill the tots!"

P is for Piper, who took all the shots.

Q is for Quinn, whose jumping was hype.

R is for raccoon, the two-headed type.

S is for Stump, in Ed Gorey mode.

T is for tarantulas, and a toad.

U is for you there, looking so dapper.

V is for Victoria, the beautiful flapper.

W is for Woolly Mammoth, providing the props.

X is for marking the spot for Quinn's hops.

Y is for Yes, we had a great time.

Z is quite lousy for ending this rhyme.

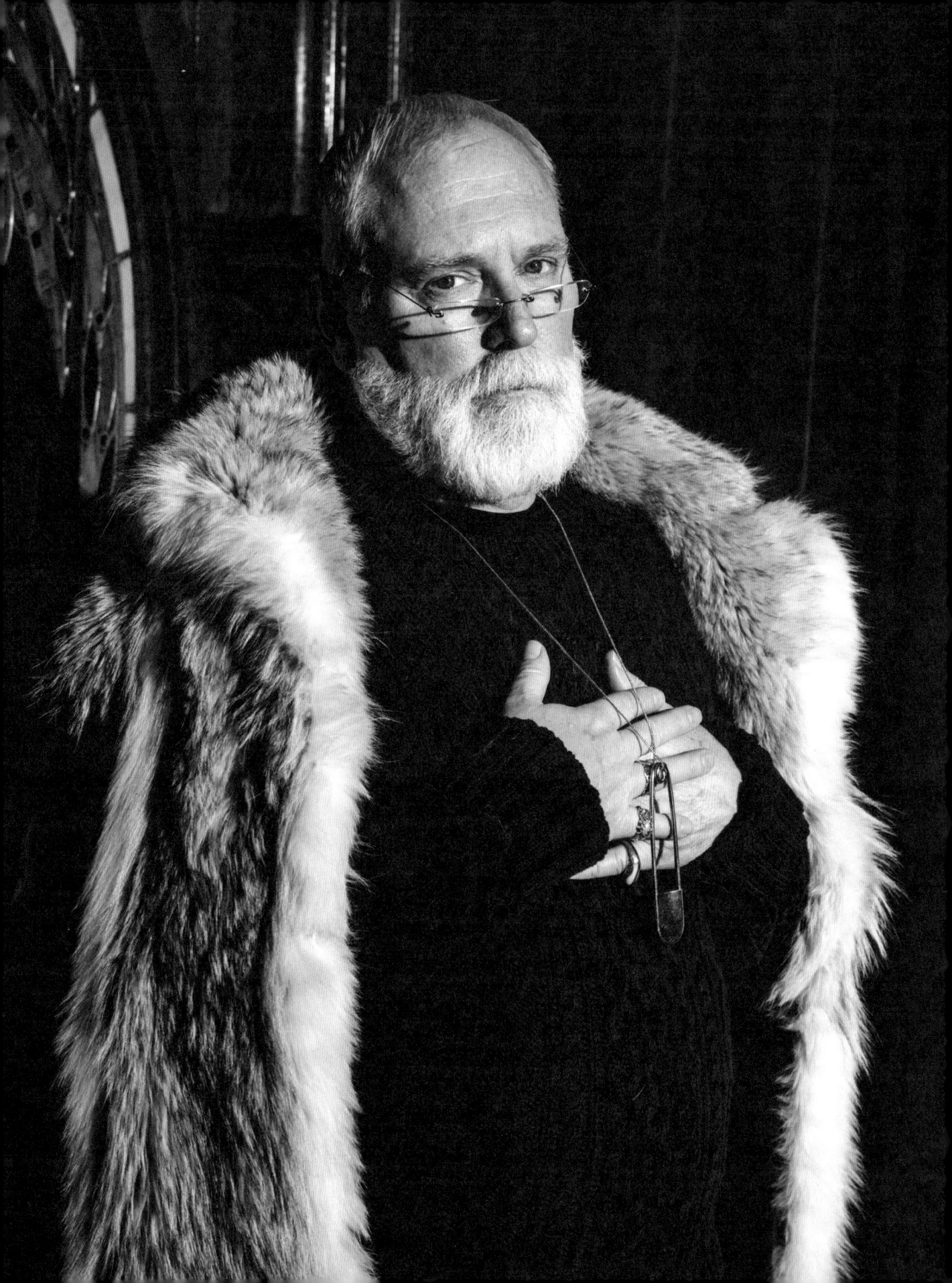

Photographs *Steven Piper* / **Models** *Stump Mahoney, Victoria Happ, Isla Wojtonik, Quinn Wojtonik*
Stylist *Anika Ladero* / **HMU** *Karen Jiménez* / **Photo Assist** *Michael Brandt* / **Location** *Pleasant Home Foundation*
Props *Woolly Mammoth Antiques & Oddities* / **Cat** *Nina Clevinger's*

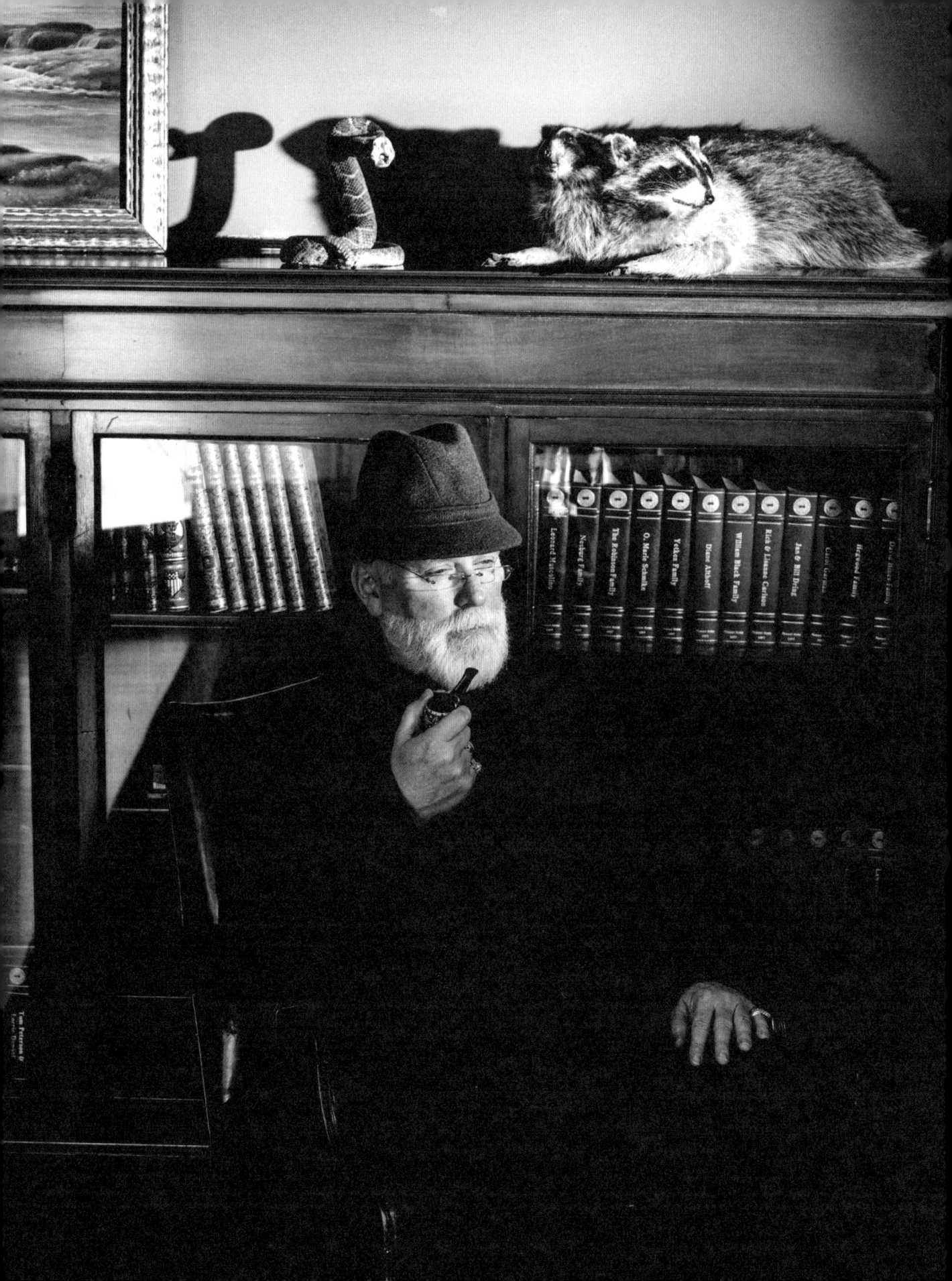

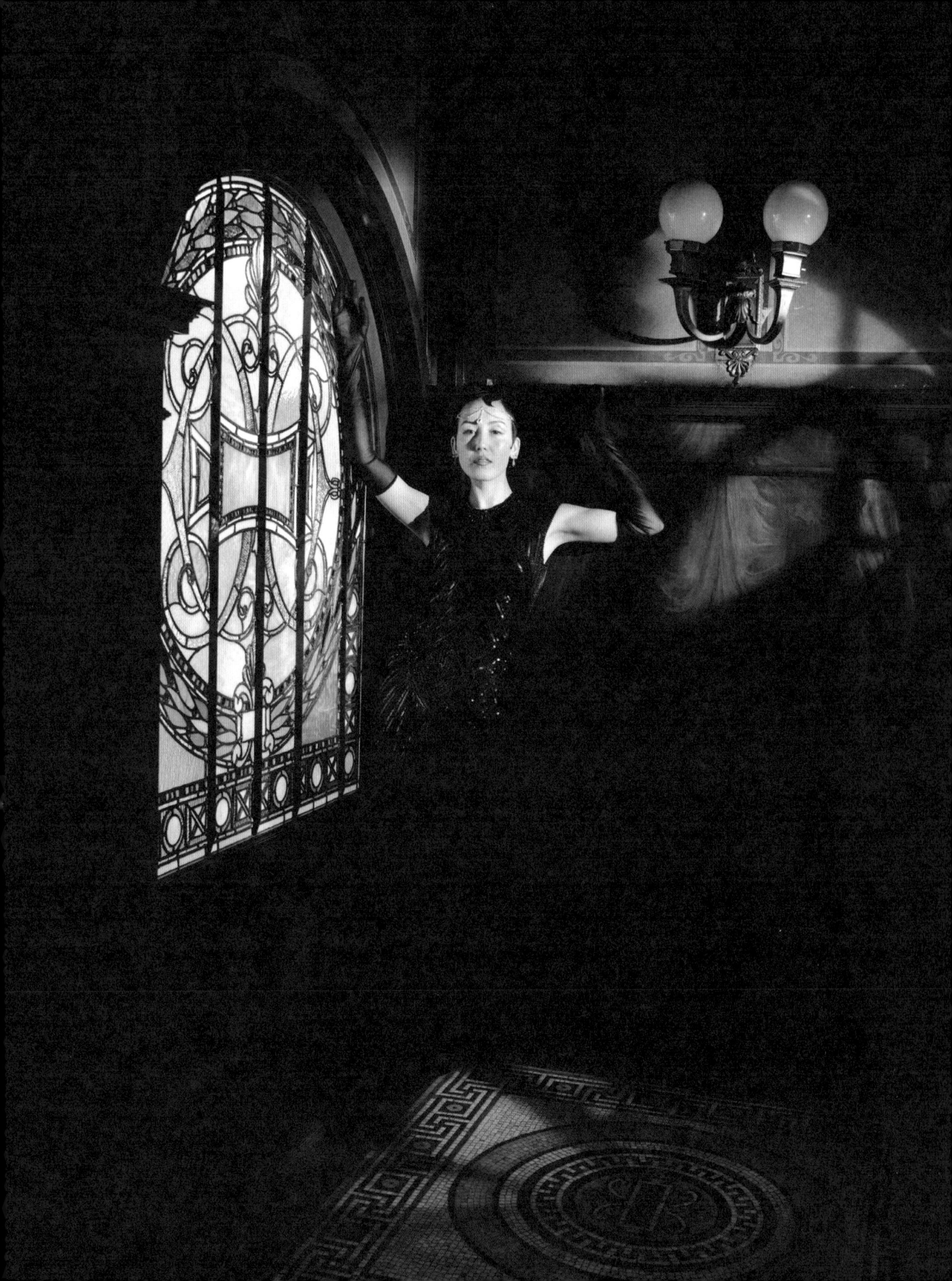

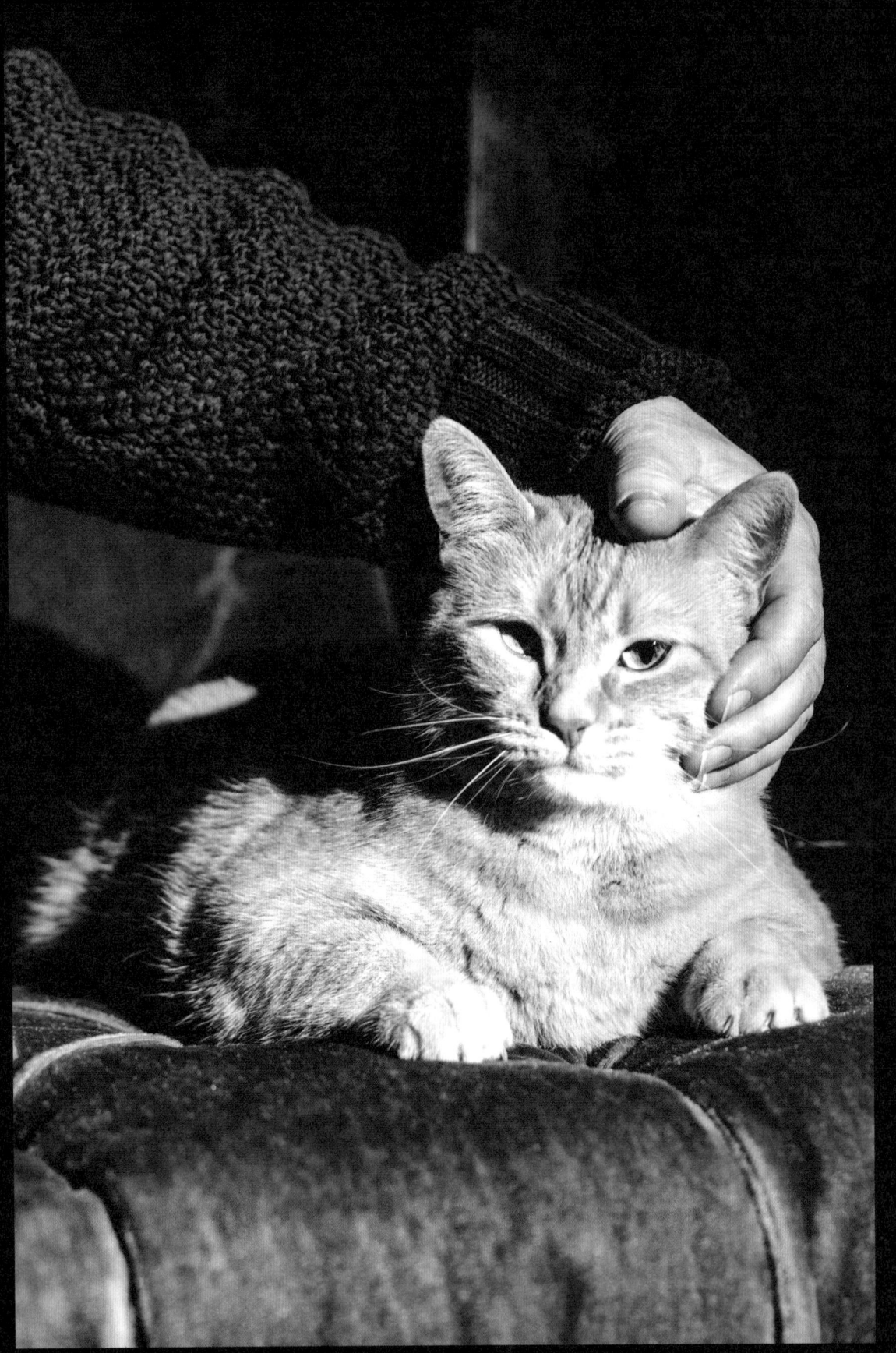

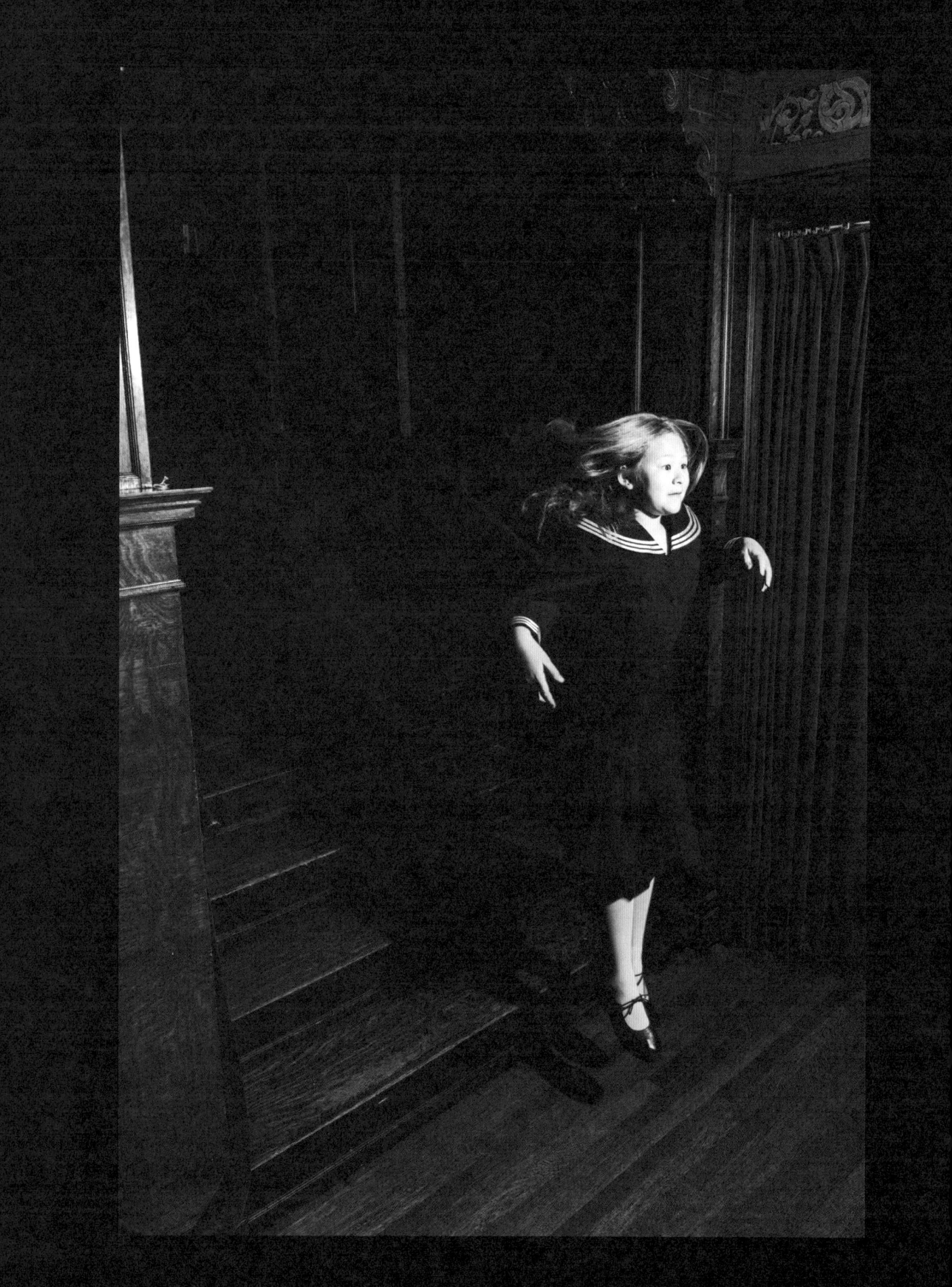

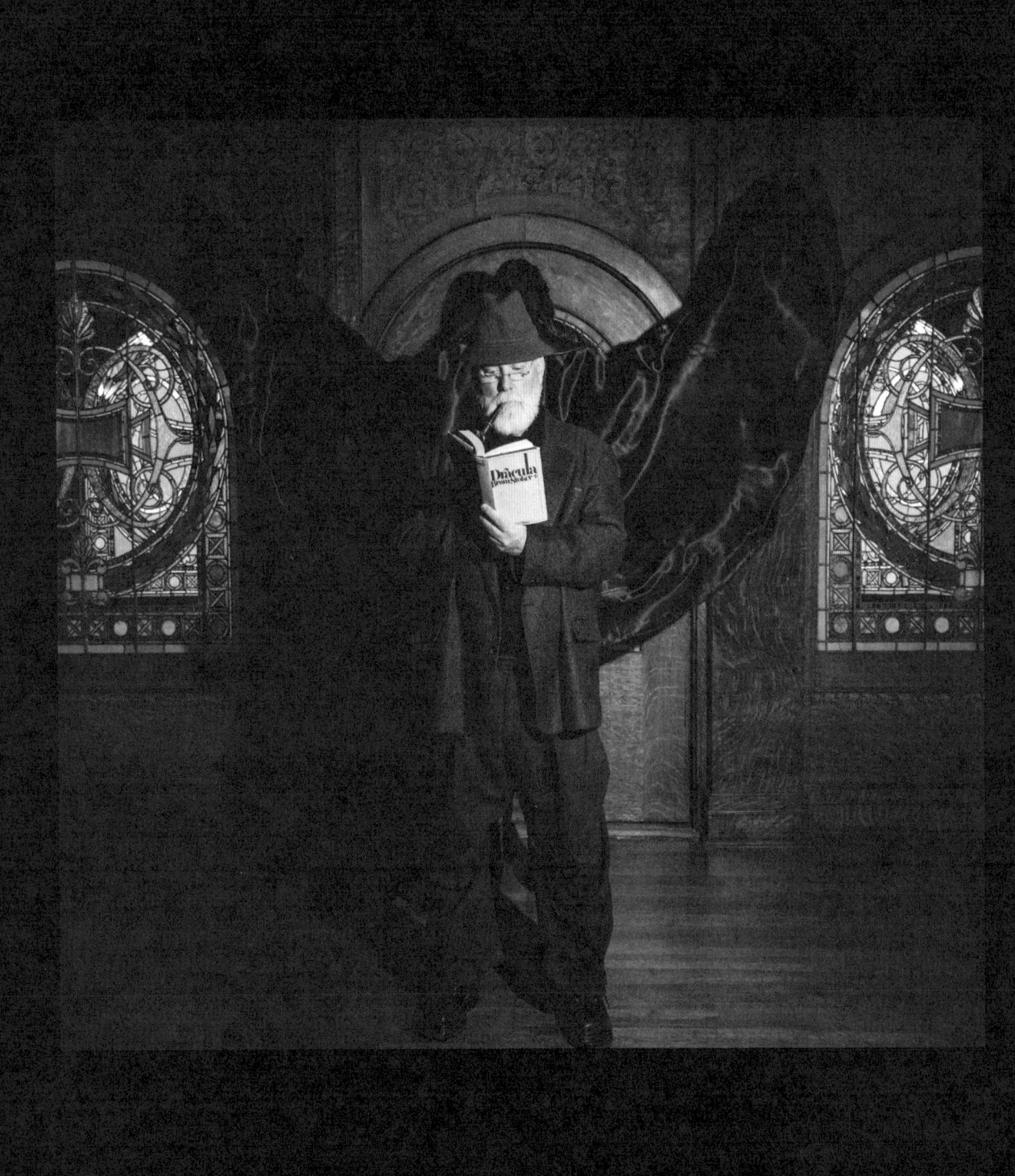

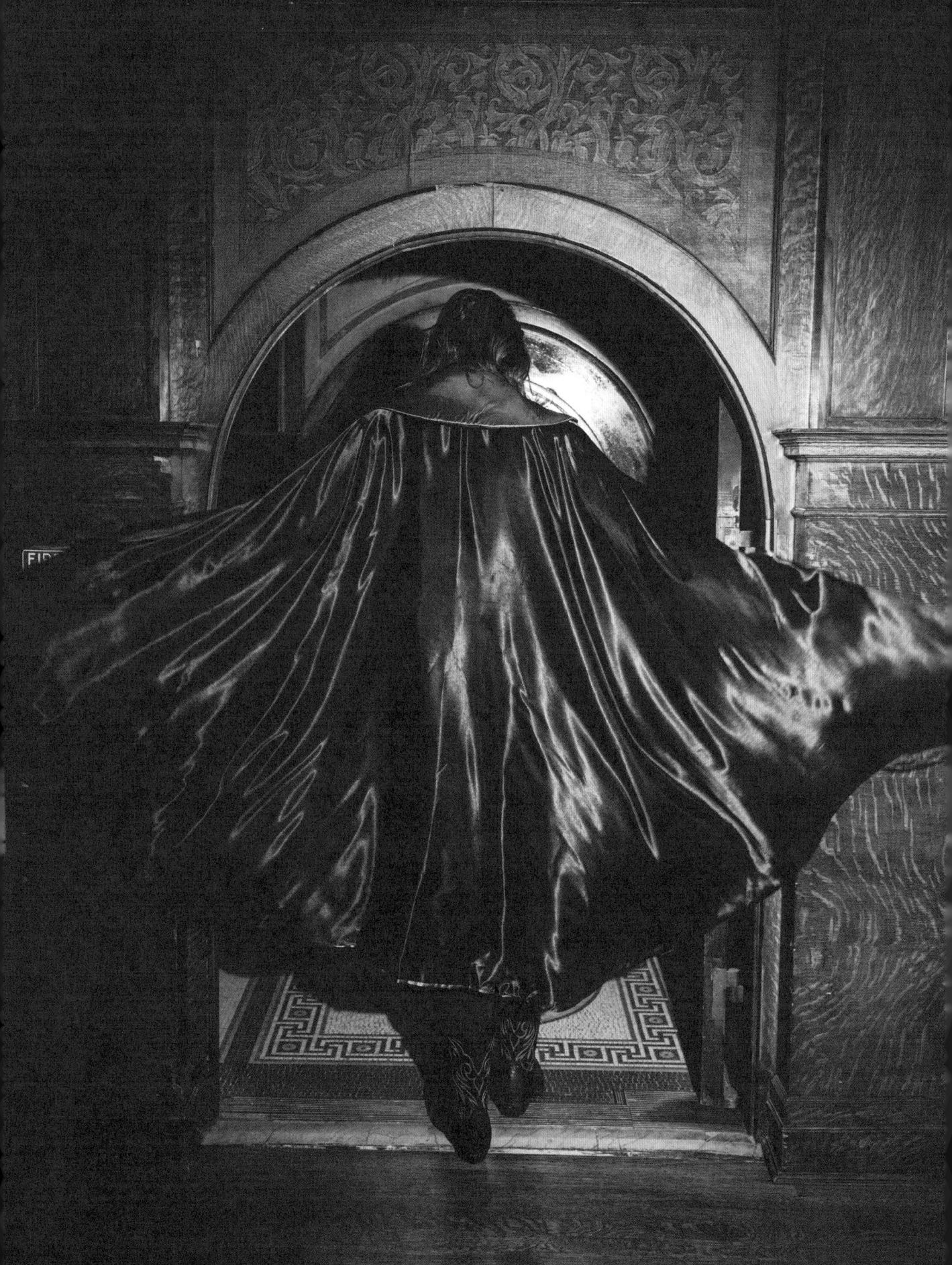

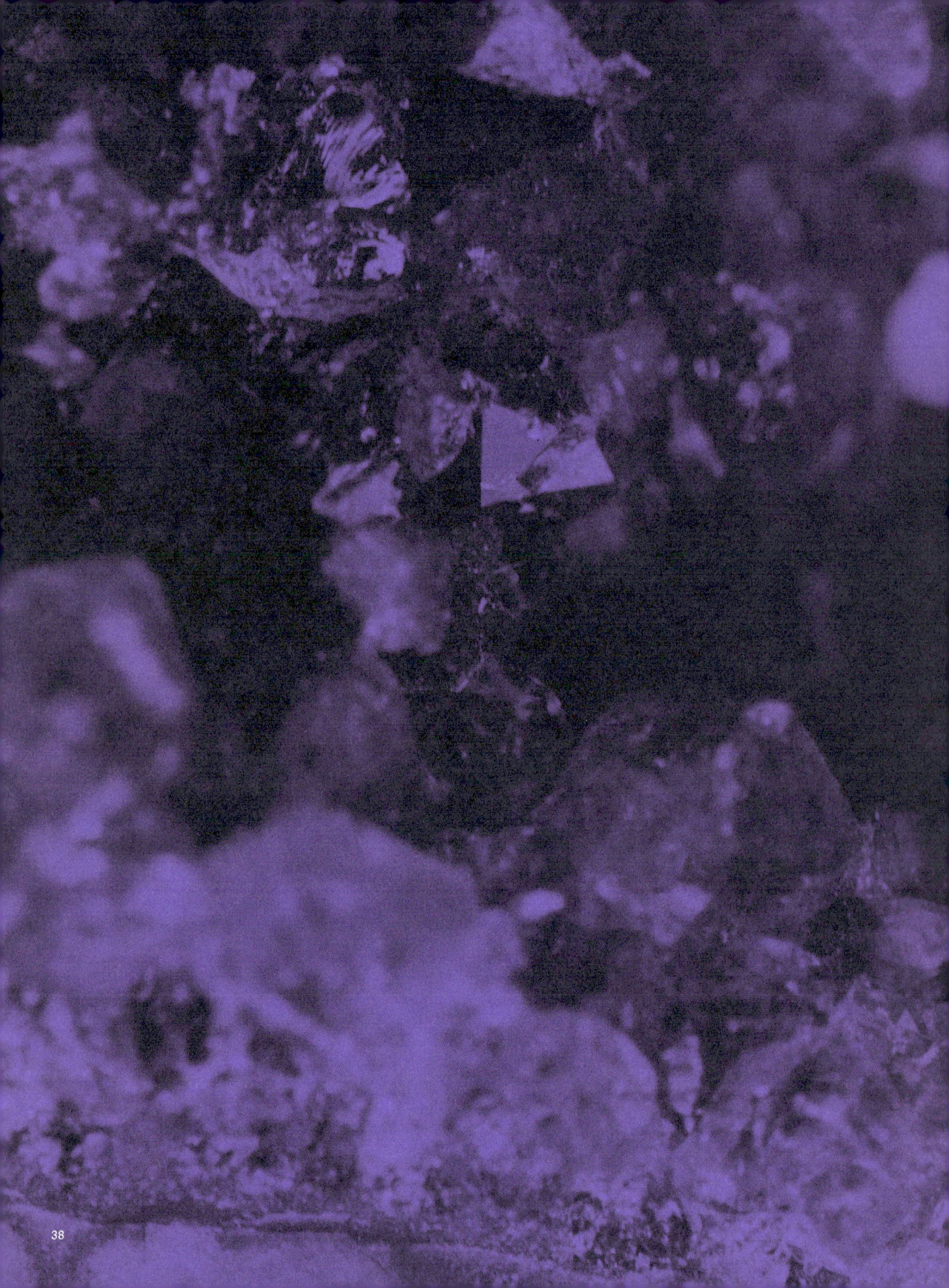

II

Behold a body of work wherein randomness reigns, and clarity is a stain on the real. / The devil, you say? I hear he's a sympathetic chap. / An unknown artist awakens from a coma, limns a final drawing, and enters the hereafter thereafter. / A t-shirt is perforated by buckshot; a fashion icon is born.

40 — 81

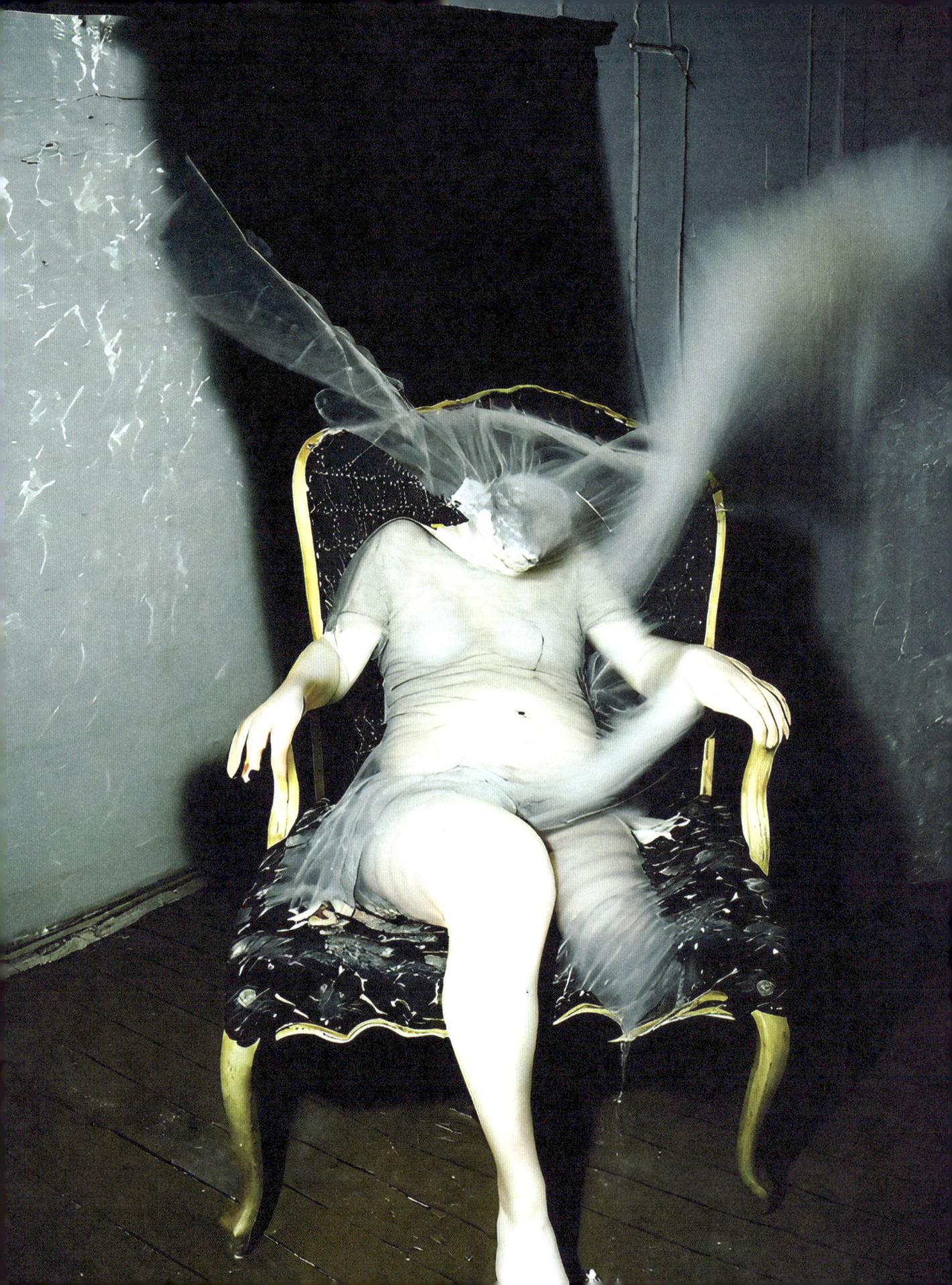

A colorblind former painter from the UK, Chris Friel picked up a camera in 2006 at the age of 46. His work quickly drew attention on Flickr with vibrant pastoral scenes, pastel-like landscapes, and layered portraits softened by camera movement. Shooting thousands of photos a day, his output was prolific and diverse. But after the death of his son in 2016, he lost interest in making "pretty pictures." His work grew starker, more stylized, and more haunting. Though widely exhibited and published, he gives few interviews. No matter—his photographs speak for themselves, revealing and concealing in equal measure, leaving viewers with silence and, perhaps, their own sense of loss.

Friel brings a painter's sensibility to photography, drawing on composition and texture from his years on canvas. He achieves many effects in-camera through tilt-shift lenses, long and multiple exposures, and intentional movement. The results are rich layers of color, blurred edges, and obscured forms that render subjects both familiar and foreign. He trusts intuition, pursuing each subject until it feels complete. His work, he admits, is "random," with no overarching theme.

Finding a unifying thread is like following the tortuous roads he has photographed in Scotland's Outer Hebrides—dark, misty, careening, yet transcendent of time and place. His "ghosts" resist easy definition, pulsing with a static energy that evokes restlessness. *Weddings and Funerals* captures faceless, frenetic figures at heightened moments, while his *Patagonia* landscapes embody stark beauty edged with menace.

What binds it all is transformation. Like his shifting career, his subjects hover on thresholds—apparitions coming or going, roads stretching toward horizons, landscapes transfigured by weather. His work reflects the human condition itself: restlessly shifting, unsettling, and beautiful.

CHRIS FRIEL
Transformative, Transcendent, Tragic

Words *Christopher Stella* / Artwork *Chris Friel*

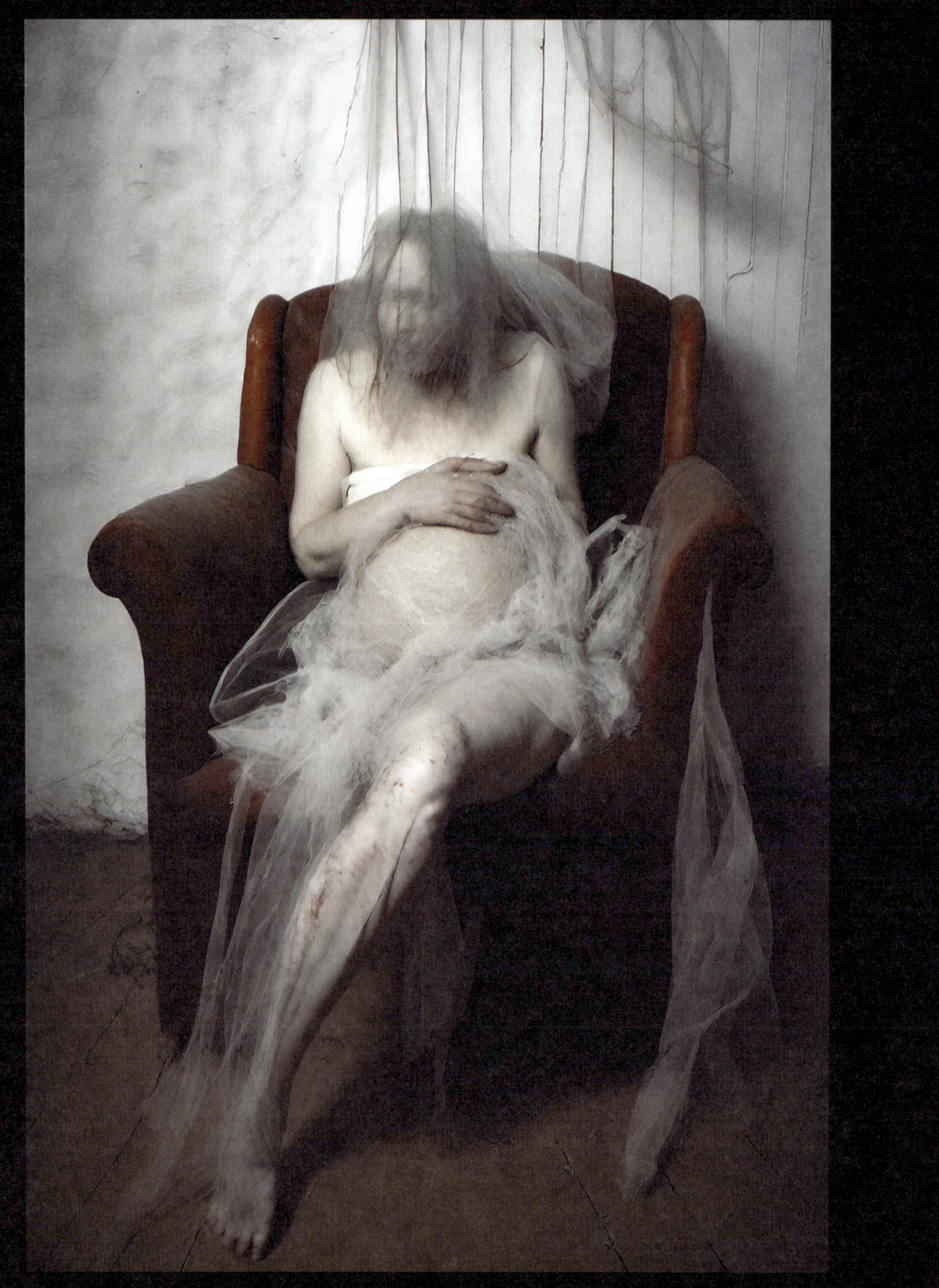

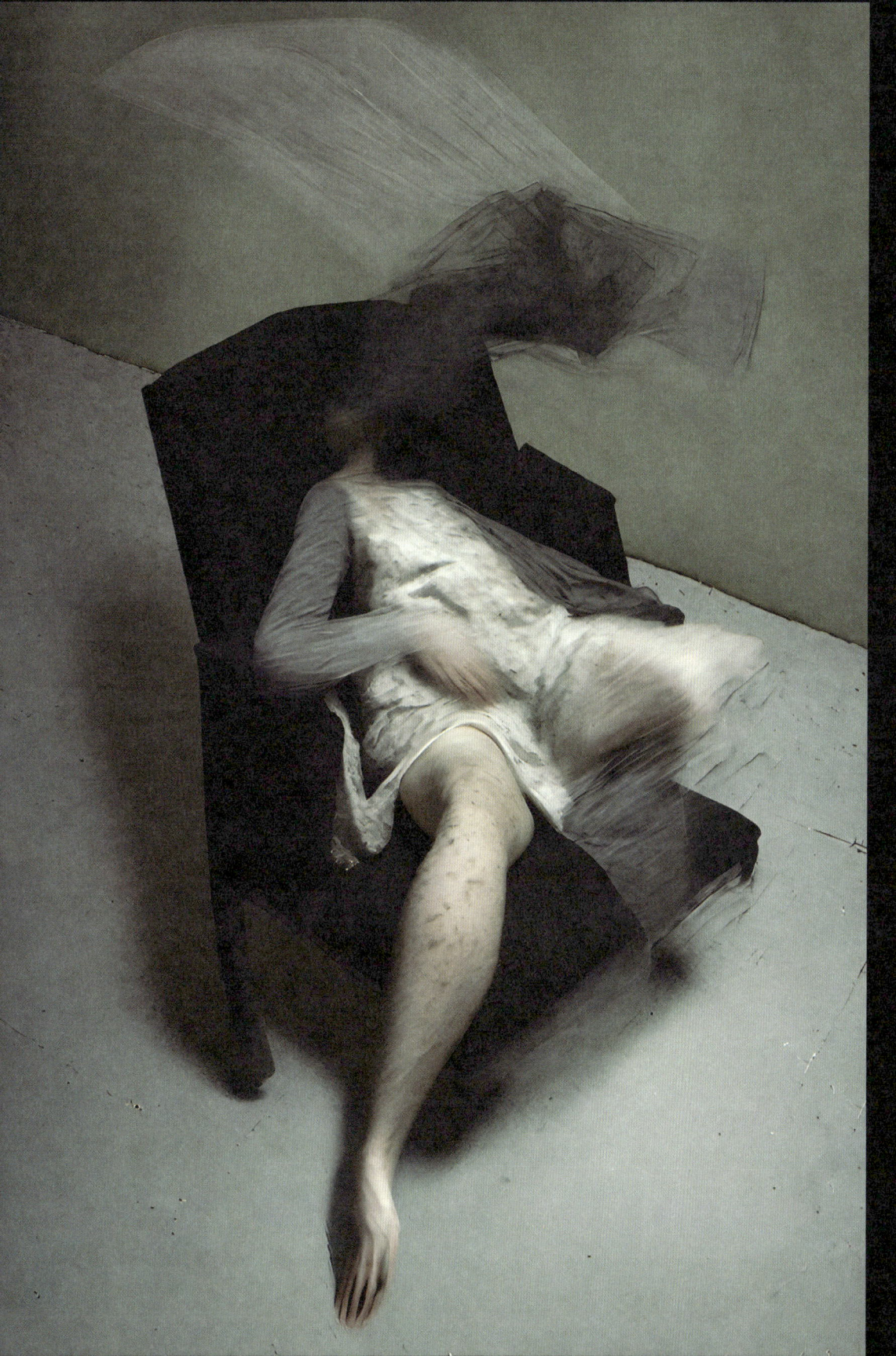

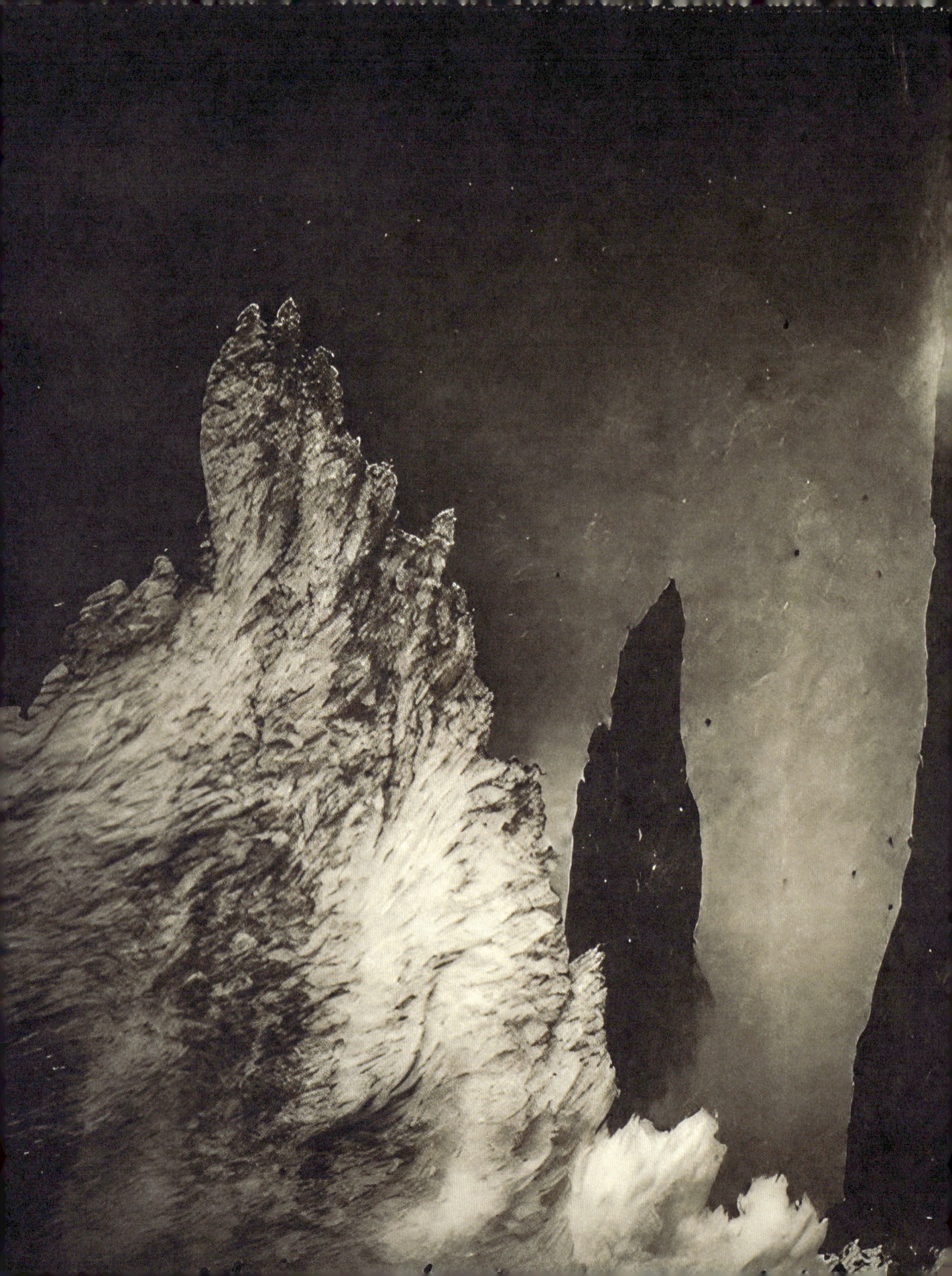

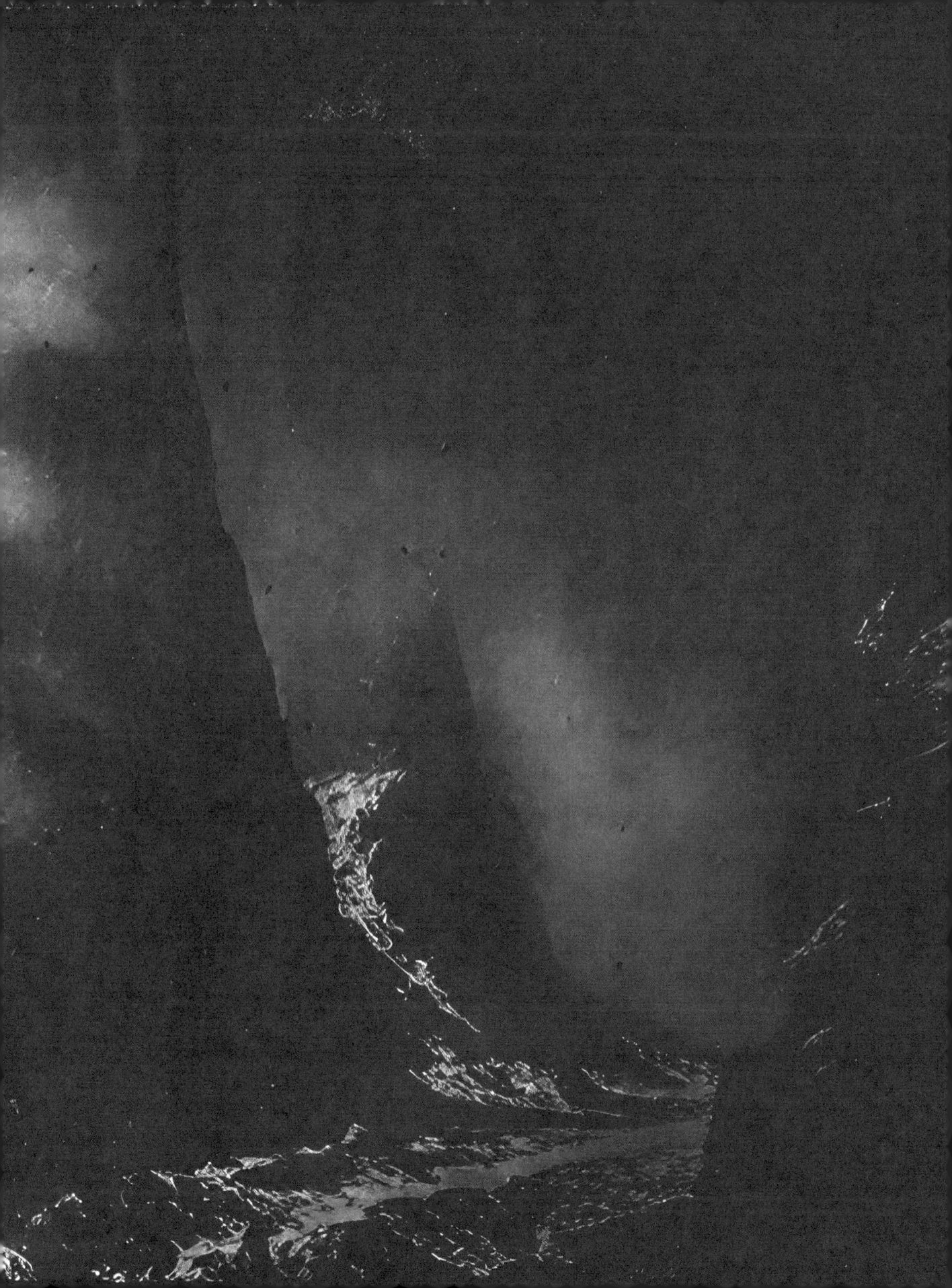

W You are a former painter turned photographer, and many of your series (e.g., *GHOSTS, WEDDINGS AND FUNERALS*) seem to have very painterly qualities—how does your background in painting influencing your current process?

C Hopefully years of looking at paintings have provided some sort of framework. Bringing that relationship between composition and texture from one medium to another.

W Your work is diverse in terms of subject matter, palette, and technique. Is there a common theme you strive to imbue across your work, or do you approach each series of photos as individual creations?

C Afraid I don't try to imbue any theme. I start each series organically and pursue it until I think it's run its course. Maybe the "common theme" is its very randomness?

W In a medium like photography that tends toward realism and clarity, you tend to obscure your subjects or alter their appearance through intentional camera movement. Why that choice—is there something you're trying to evoke in your subjects that simply can't be captured representationally?

C Not sure I agree with the premise that photography tends toward "realism and clarity." The people I admire most in the field all lean into intentional obfuscation/impressionistic imagery. I'm instinctively drawn to this approach over "realistic" representation.

W How do you select your subjects, be they people or places? Are there specific characteristics you look for or that appeal to you?

C I have a vast bank of images, accumulated over many years. It's often when I'm processing, experimenting with existing work that the places/people suggest themselves as "subjects" to further pursue.

W You've noted in prior interviews that you believe photographs in a series are more powerful than stand-alone images. What is your approach to conceiving a new series? Do you shoot with a specific outcome in mind, or does it emerge organically in your editorial process?

C It always emerges organically through the process.

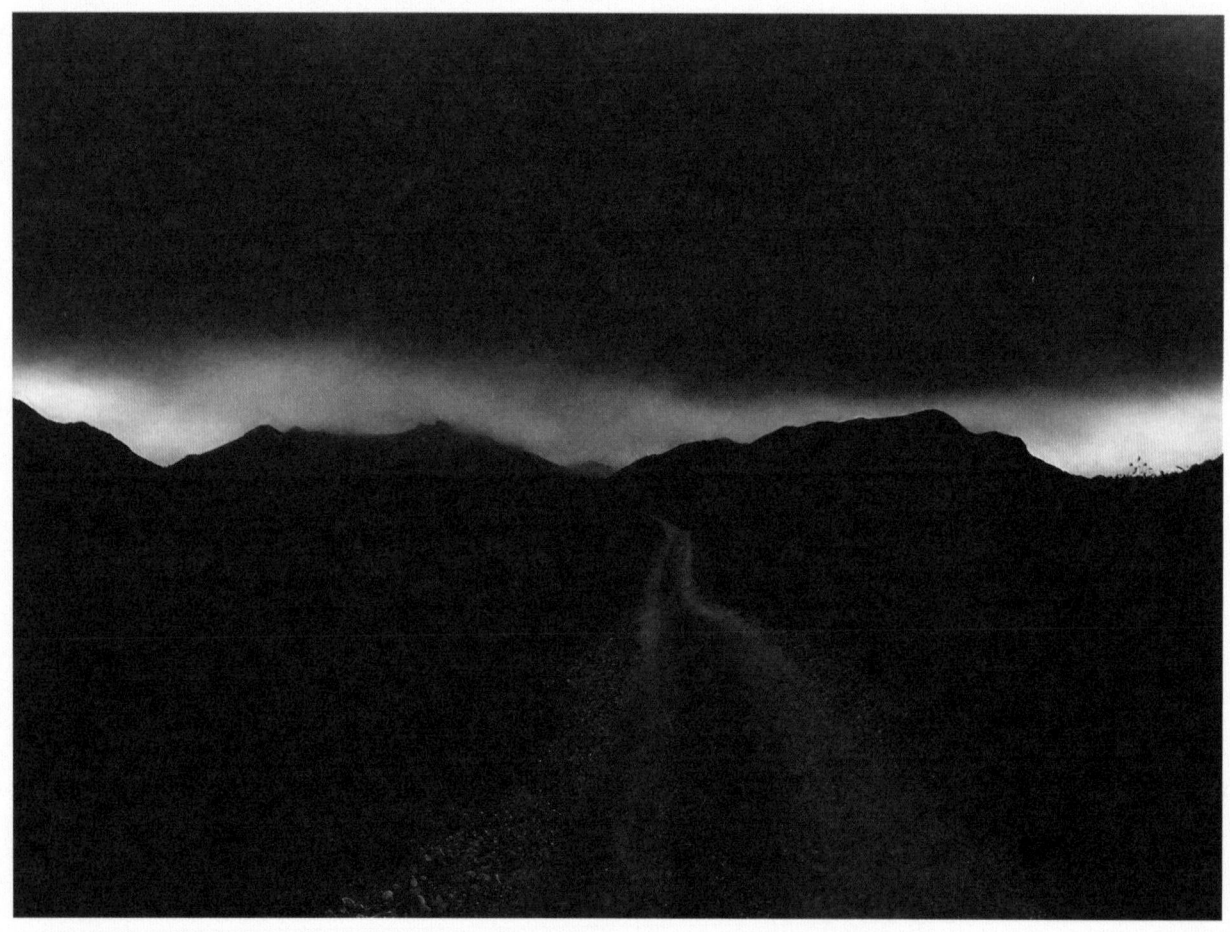

W In other publications, you've stated that grief has had a significant impact on your process and interests as a photographer. Has your relationship with grief changed with time, and how has that affected your work?

C Grief continues to inform my work. That's all I'm able to say about this.

W The images in your *ROAD* series seem to transcend time and place—what was the inspiration for this series? Was there a particular setting, or many, that inspired these photographs?

C These are remixes of old road images from the Outer Hebrides—a place I've returned to many times over the past forty years.

W The subjects in your *GHOSTS* series appear vibrant, present, and active—a contrast to a subject that typically evokes feelings of invisibility and elusiveness. How do you interpret ghosts—what do they represent to you?

C Not entirely sure how to answer this. All I can say is that despite the characteristic description of "ghosts" being elusive/ethereal, to me they are ever present and very close by.

W Regarding your *WEDDINGS AND FUNERALS* series, do the photos within it strive to create a commonality between these two seemingly different events?

C Yes, in the way that all "rites of passage" portray the vulnerability/fragility of the human condition.

W The landscapes in your *PATAGONIA* series are haunting—the mountain peaks seem to evoke shadowy figures, which are remarkably both vivid and shrouded. What about the landscape inspired this outcome for you?

C These are imagined landscapes after re-reading Bruce Chatwin's *In Patagonia*. Chatwin is renowned not only for his travel writing but his ability to create "internal landscapes." I haven't been to Patagonia, but this is what spoke to me when I revisited the book.

W You've worked all over the world—I believe nearly 150 countries. Where do you plan to travel next? Is there something specific you hope to find and capture there?

C I'm about to go to Dungeness in my home county of Kent. Does this count? ∎

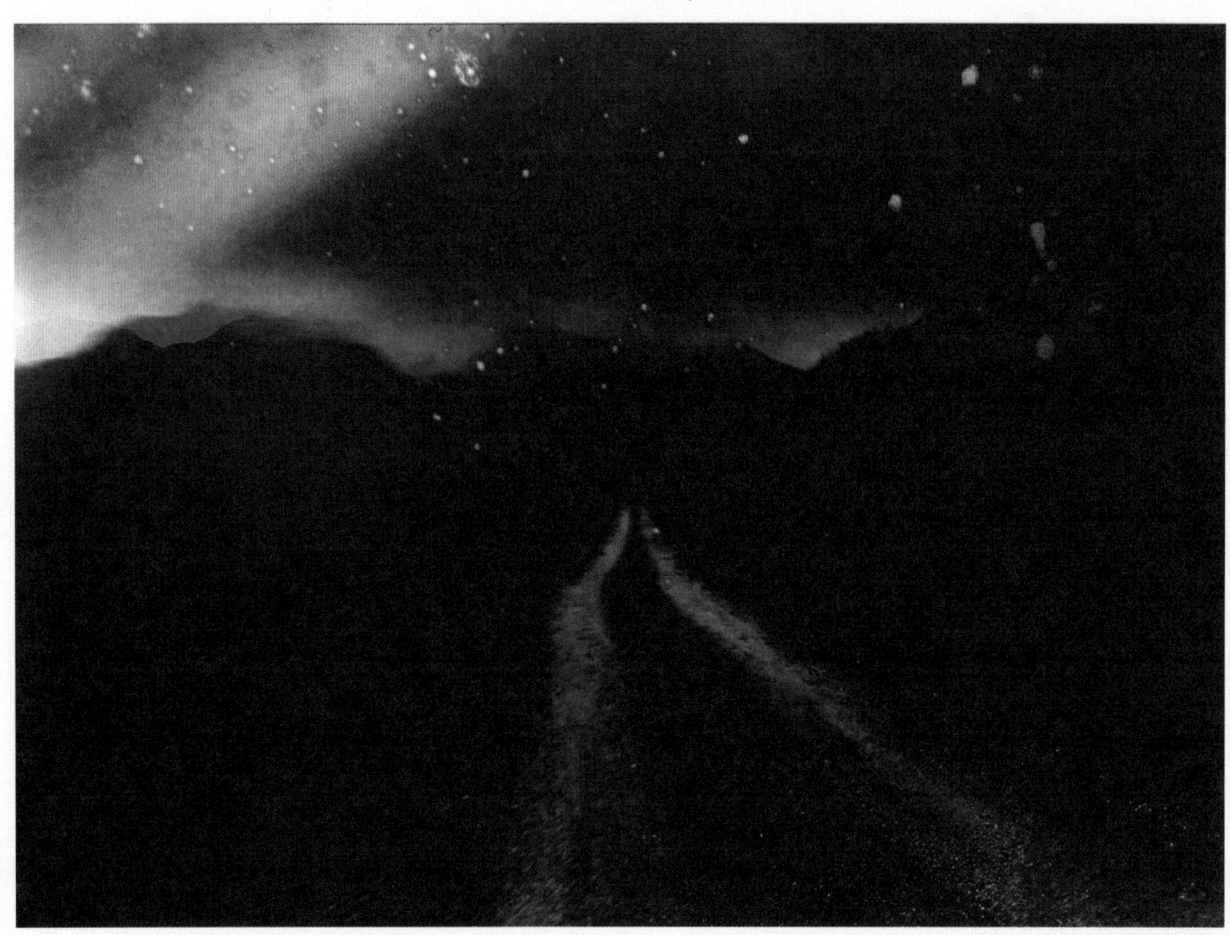

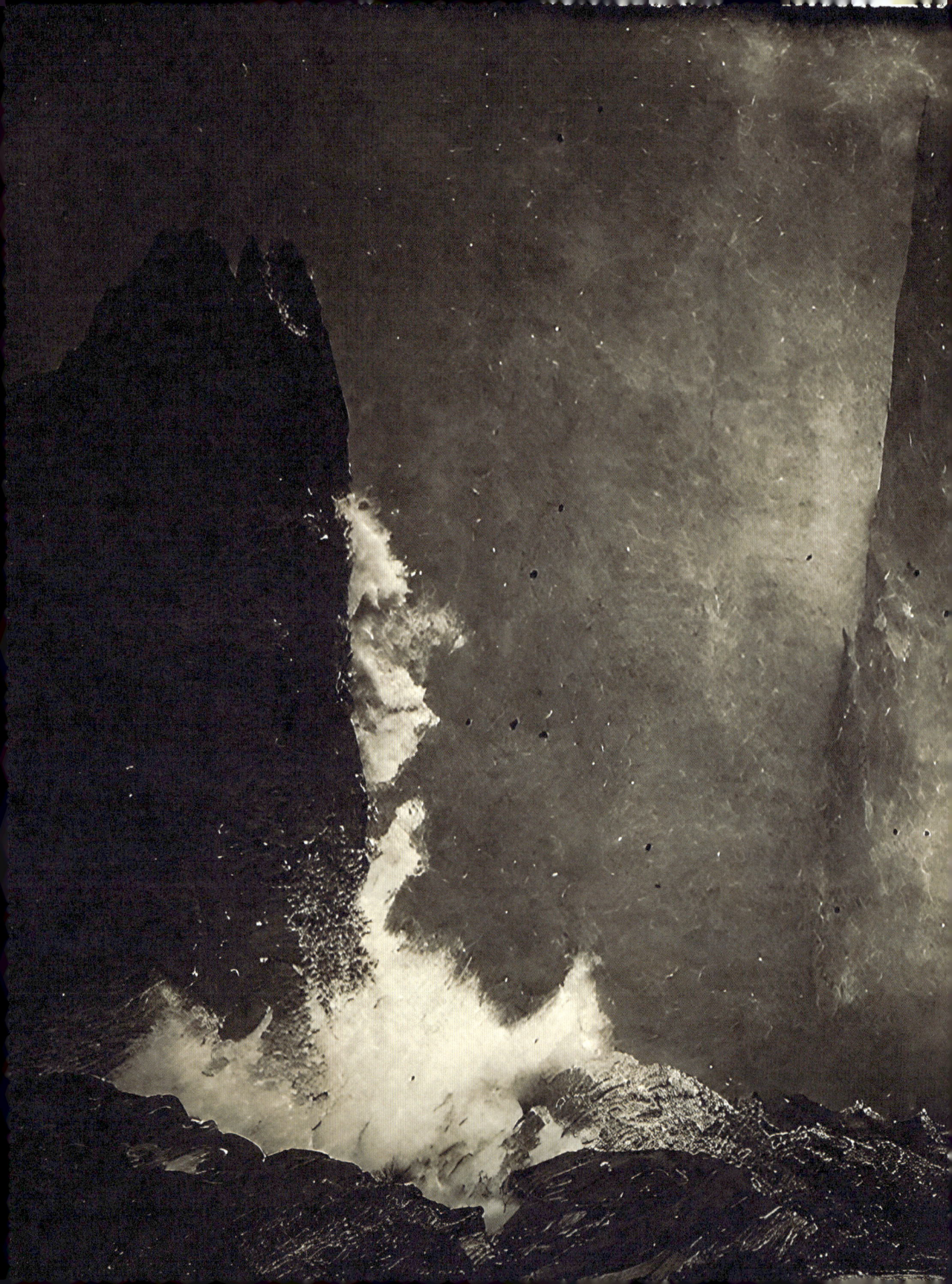

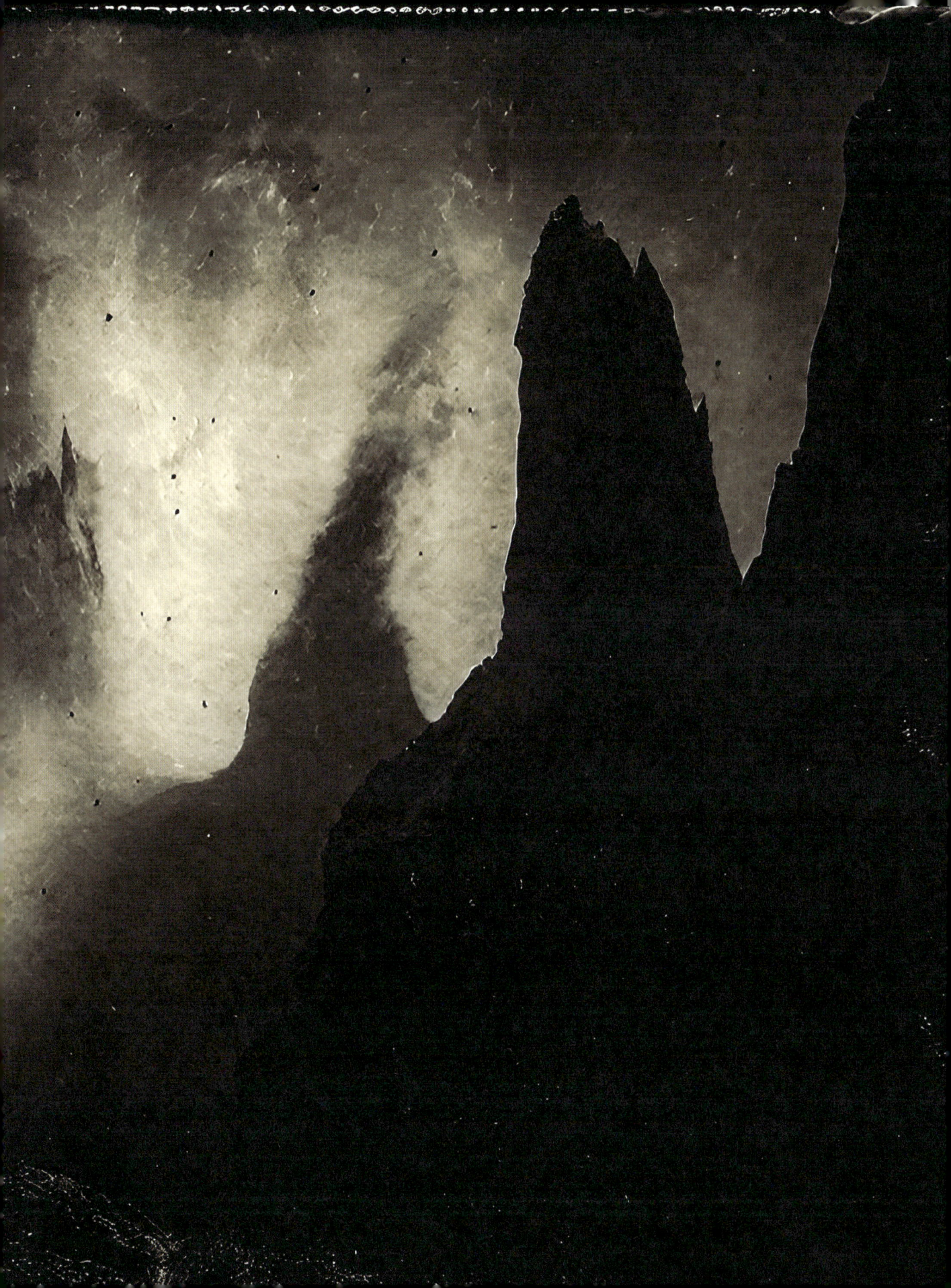

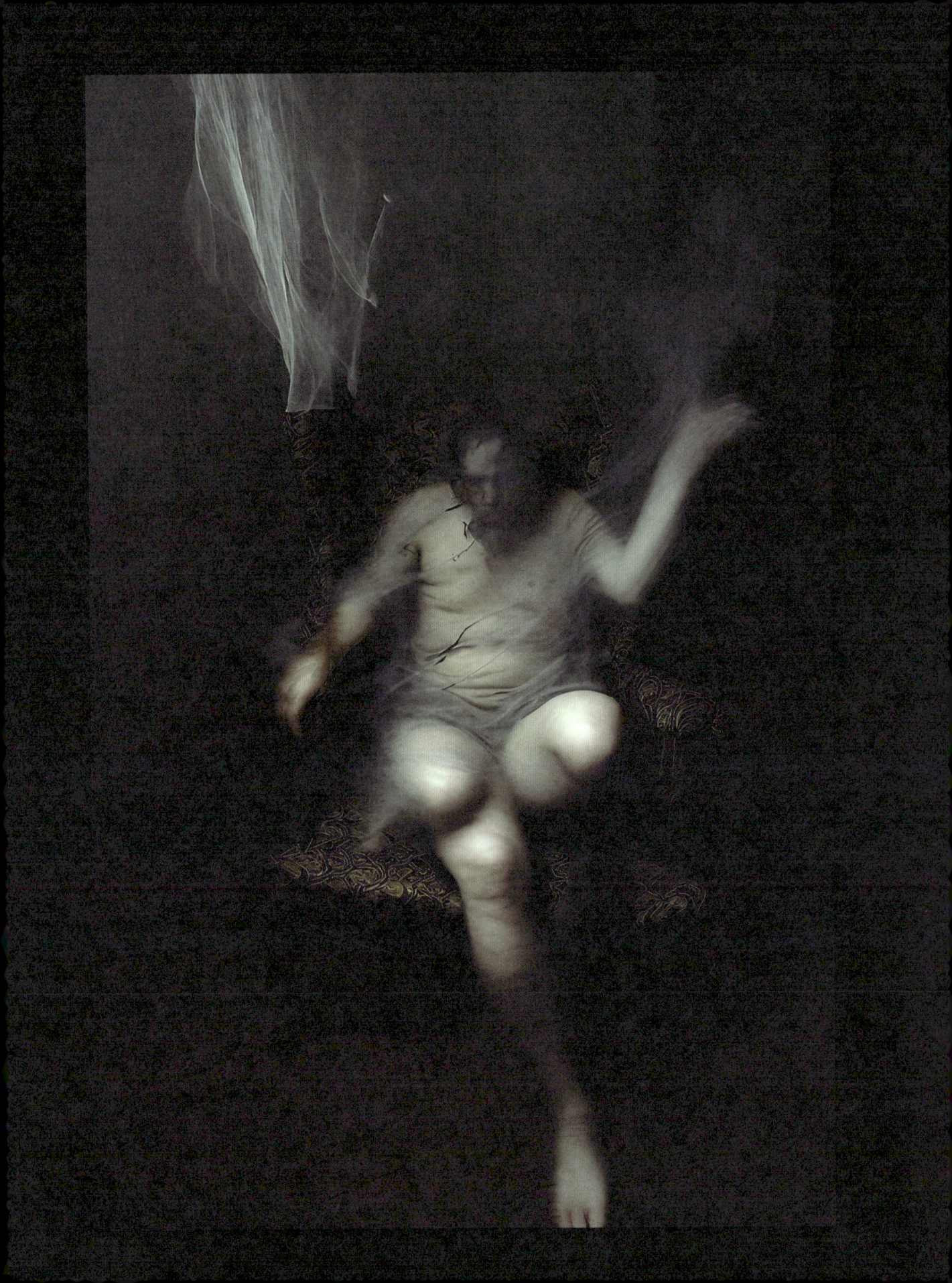

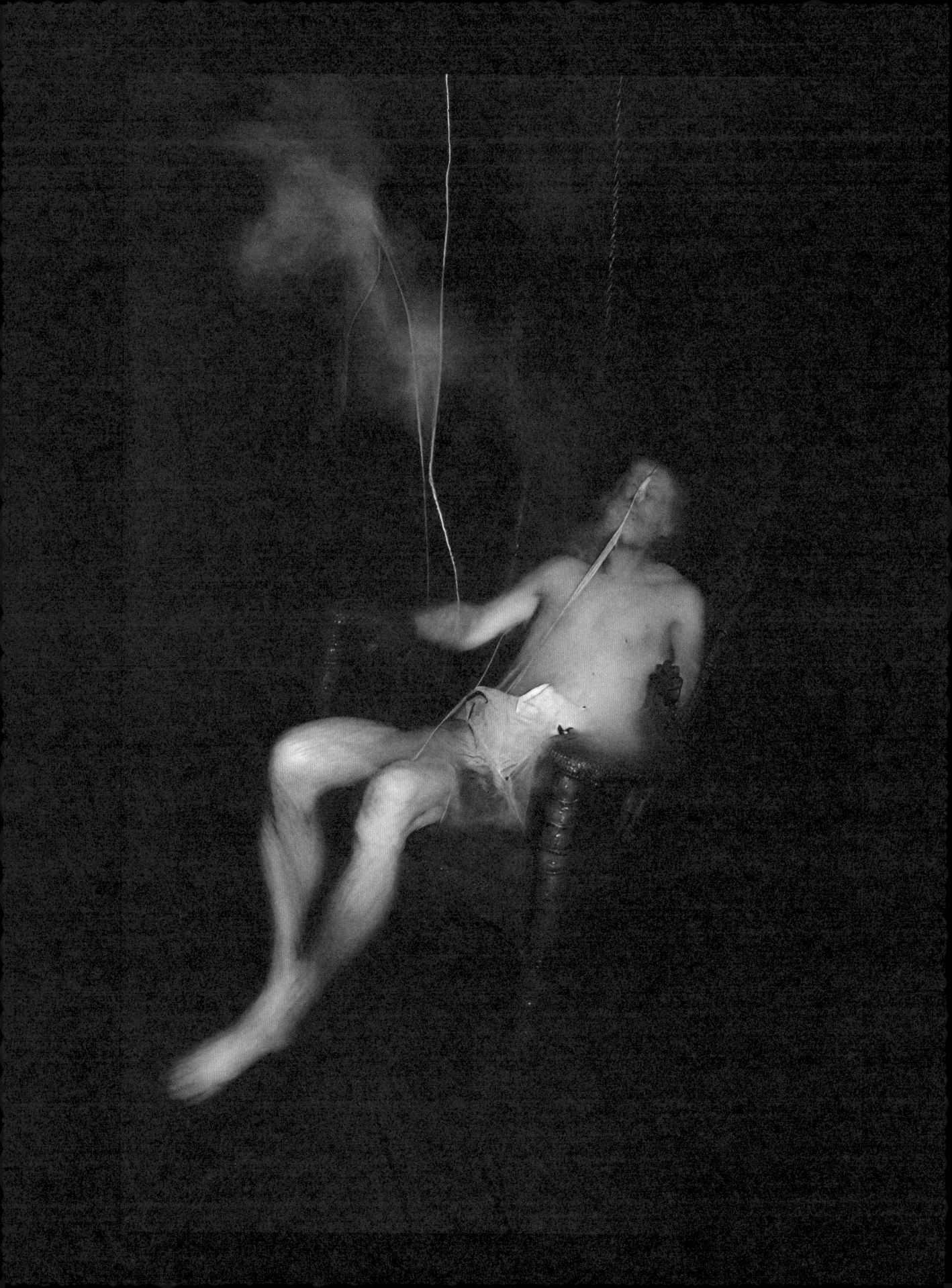

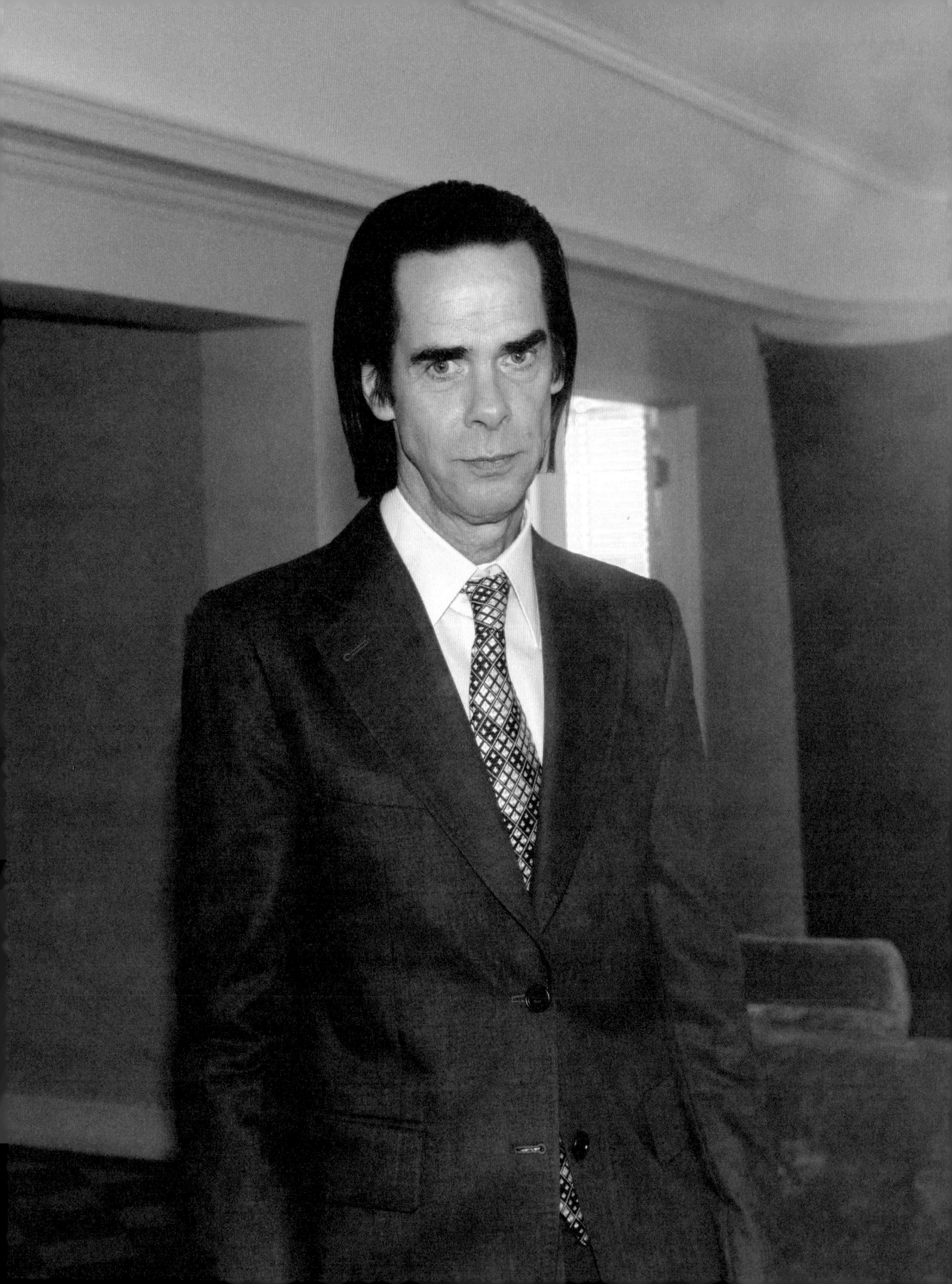

The devil has been around since the beginning. Whether you believe in him or not, his shadow casts across the globe as the ultimate antagonist, the intolerable antithesis. For many people, his machinations underlie everything they hate and fear on this earth. There are other people, fewer, who exalt him, and fewer still—mostly in movies—who would seek to summon him.

Despite his biblical debut, though, the devil was largely dormant in visual art until the eleventh century or so. What had been a benign physical form was newly endowed with the horns and cloven hooves of Greek satyrs and Roman fauns. After that, all hell broke loose.

The devil was soon envisioned as though a goat, a bat, a lizard, a bird, a cat, and a snake, often in chimerical combinations thereof. In the fourteenth century, Giotto painted a bearded, husky demon devouring one human torso while simultaneously excreting another.

In the sixteenth century, Vincenzo Foppa all but blasphemously depicted a possessed Madonna and child—complete with devil horns— to warn of the demon's guile and duplicity. Even Pablo Picasso, in 1952, included in his diptych *War and Peace* a smiling, round-headed figure with horns who brandishes a bloody butcher's knife and holds a dish filled with scorpions and centipedes.

Nick Cave is no stranger to the devil, who has appeared in lyrics throughout the musician's decades-long, multi-hyphenate creative peregrination. Still, *The Devil – A Life* is significant as Cave's first body of visual art: a series of seventeen glazed ceramic sculptures modeled after the Victorian-era decorative objects known as Staffordshire flat-back figurines.

NICK CAVE
Epiphany for the Devil

Words *David B. Olsen* / Portrait *Ian Allen* / Artwork Photographs *Thomas Merle*
All Artworks *Nick Cave, Courtesy of the Artist and Xavier Hufkens, Brussels*

Produced in the English county of Staffordshire during the eighteenth and nineteenth centuries, these figurative ceramics depicted everything under the sun. Children, dogs, naval valor, the royal family, Greek mythology, foreign dignitaries, a tiger eating a baby—there was almost no end to what counted as popular décor. Cave seizes upon the domesticity and ephemerality of these objects to depict an alternate history of heaven's terminally rebellious angel.

The series' story begins with the devil as a sleepy schoolboy who inherits the world and, in his later years, becomes a war hero (or criminal) before bleeding to death in gaunt, hoary agony. Along the way, the devil falls in love, poses for a portrait, and feels remorse—among other episodes in this tragic narrative—before he is forgiven by a rosy-cheeked, golden-haired boy in the series' last figurine.

Though his horns betray him *as* the devil, Cave's is not the devil we know. He's neither gnarly nor gruesome. There's nothing to suggest that he connives, maligns, or deceives. He elicits not terror but, dare I say it, sympathy? This devil's life might have higher highs and lower lows than our own, but it's one we can almost begin to imagine for ourselves, for better or worse.

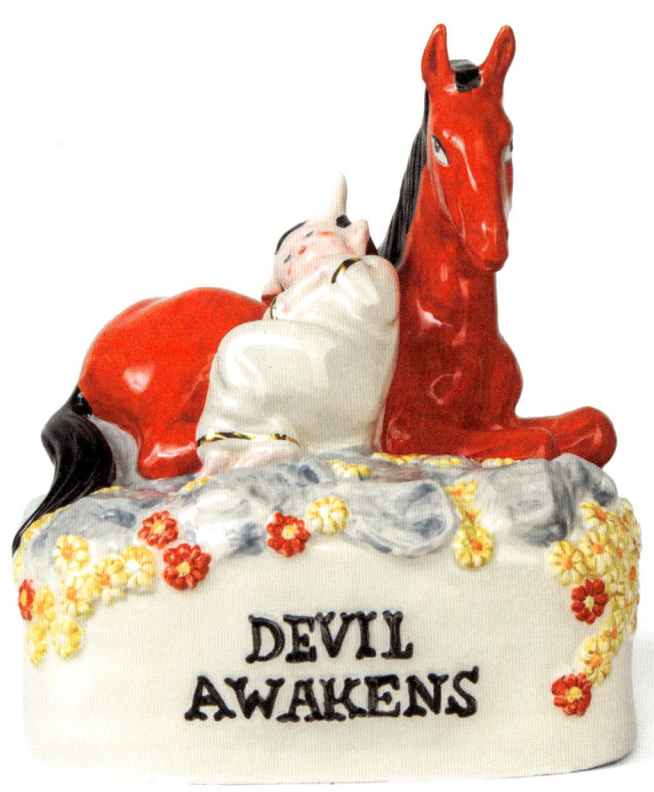

Devil Awakens, 2020-2024
Glazed ceramic, 6 1/8 × 5 1/2 × 4 3/4 in., Edition of 3

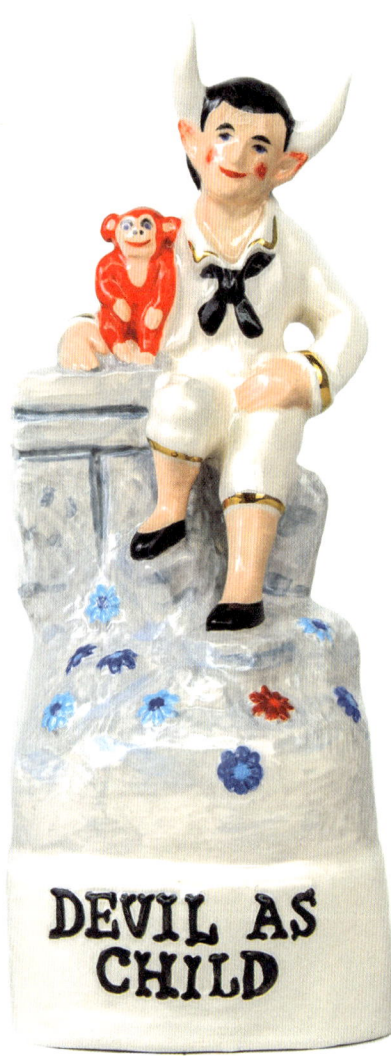

Devil as Child, 2020–2024
Glazed ceramic, 8 7/8 × 3 1/2 × 3 3/8 in., Edition of 3

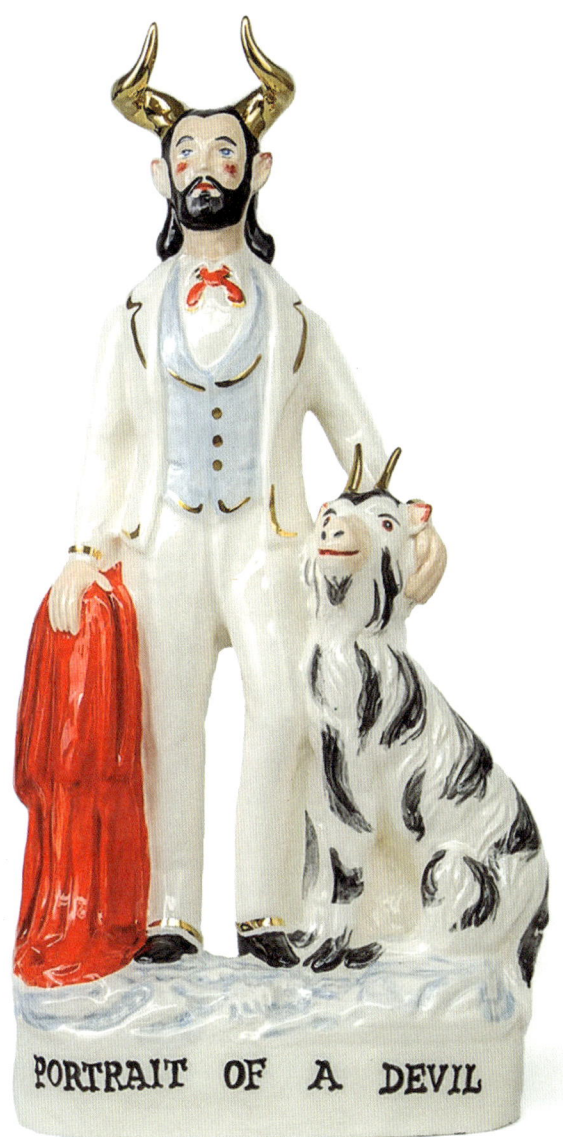

Portrait of a Devil, 2020-2024
Glazed ceramic, 15 1/8 × 7 5/8 × 4 1/8 in., Edition of 3

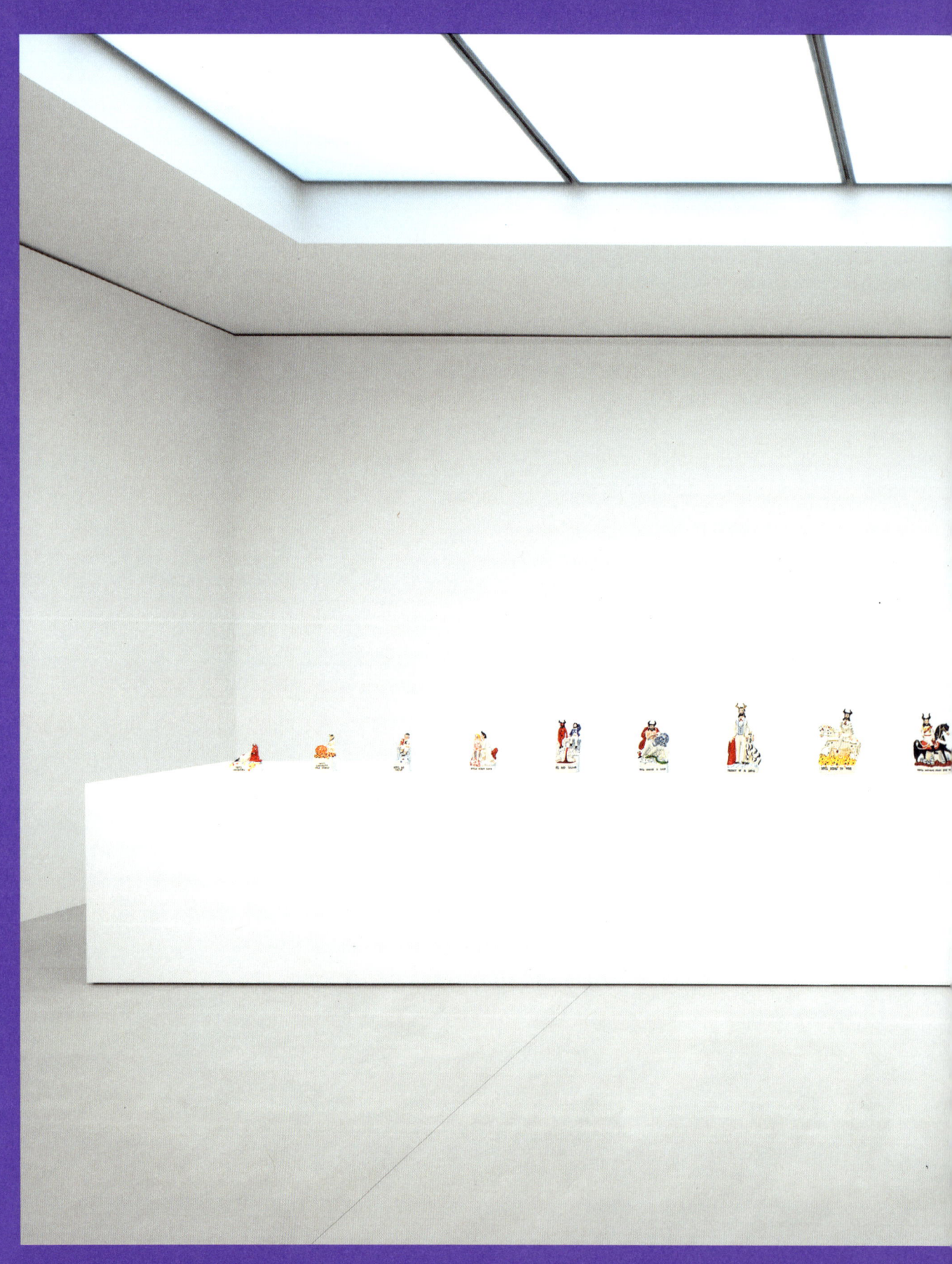

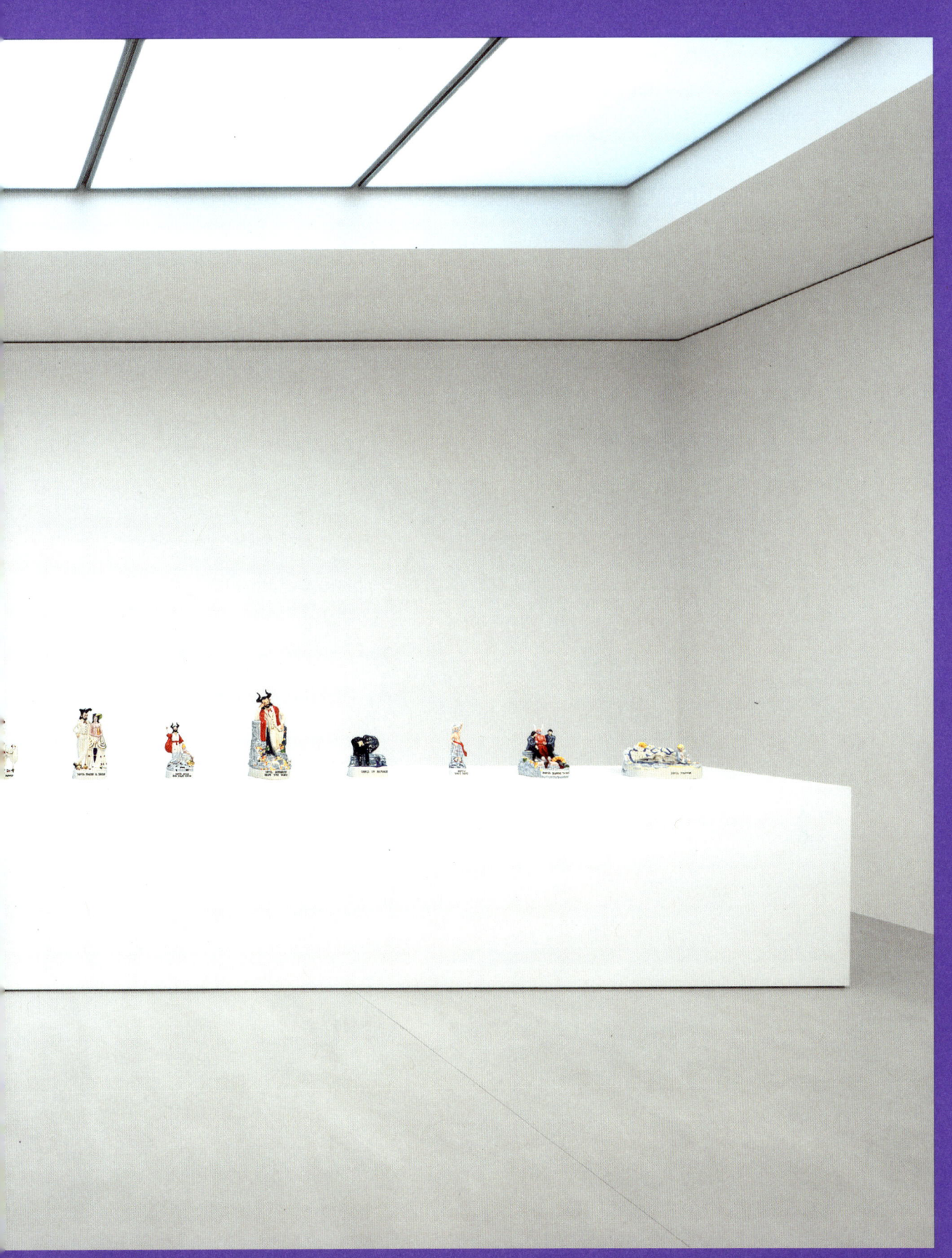

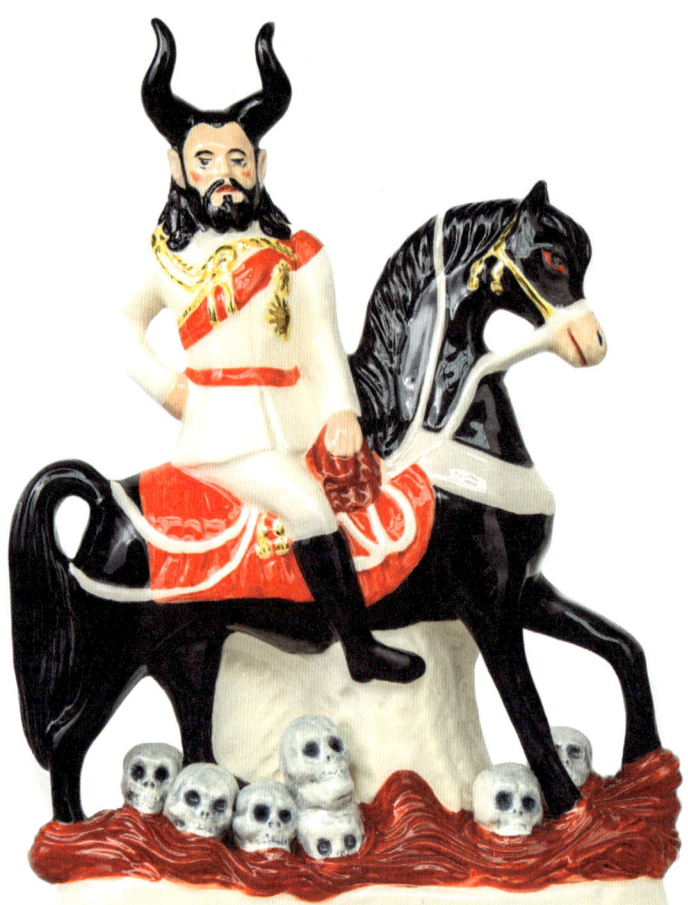

Devil Returns from the War, 2020-2024
Glazed ceramic, 13 1/4 × 9 × 3 1/8 in., Edition of 3

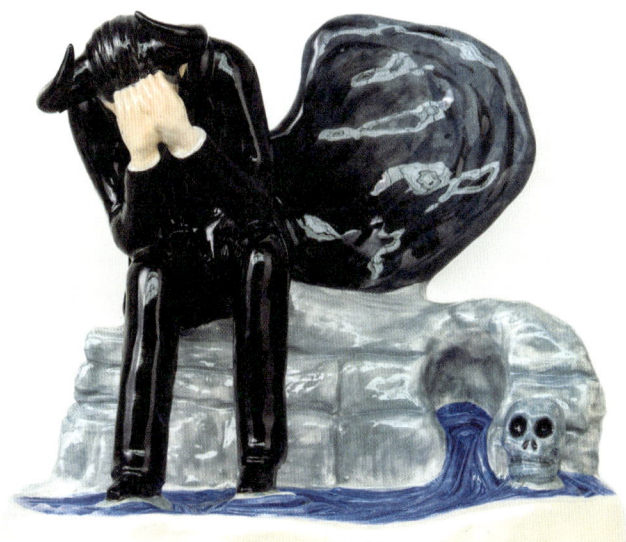

DEVIL IN REMORSE

Devil in Remorse, 2020-2024
Glazed ceramic, 8 7/8 × 8 1/4 × 5 1/2 in., Edition of 3

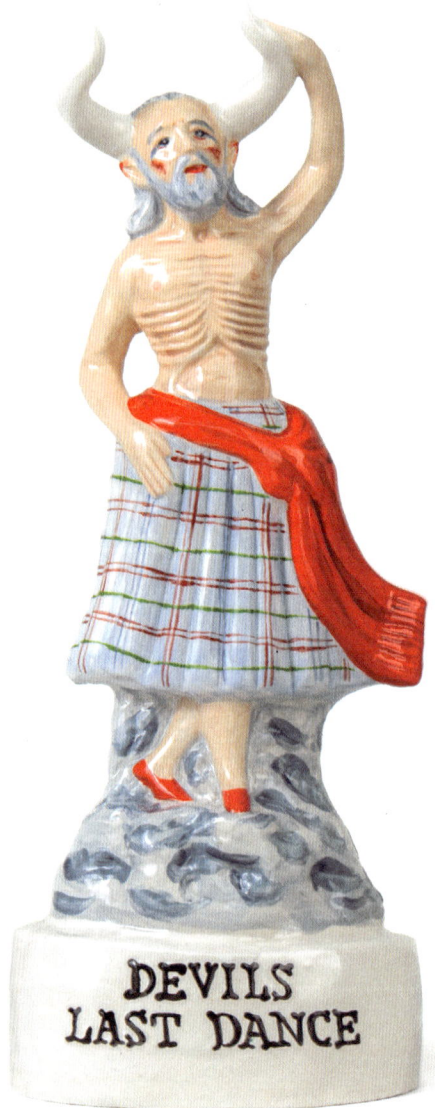

Devil's Last Dance, 2020–2024
Glazed ceramic, 12 × 4 3/8 × 3 1/8 in., Edition of 3

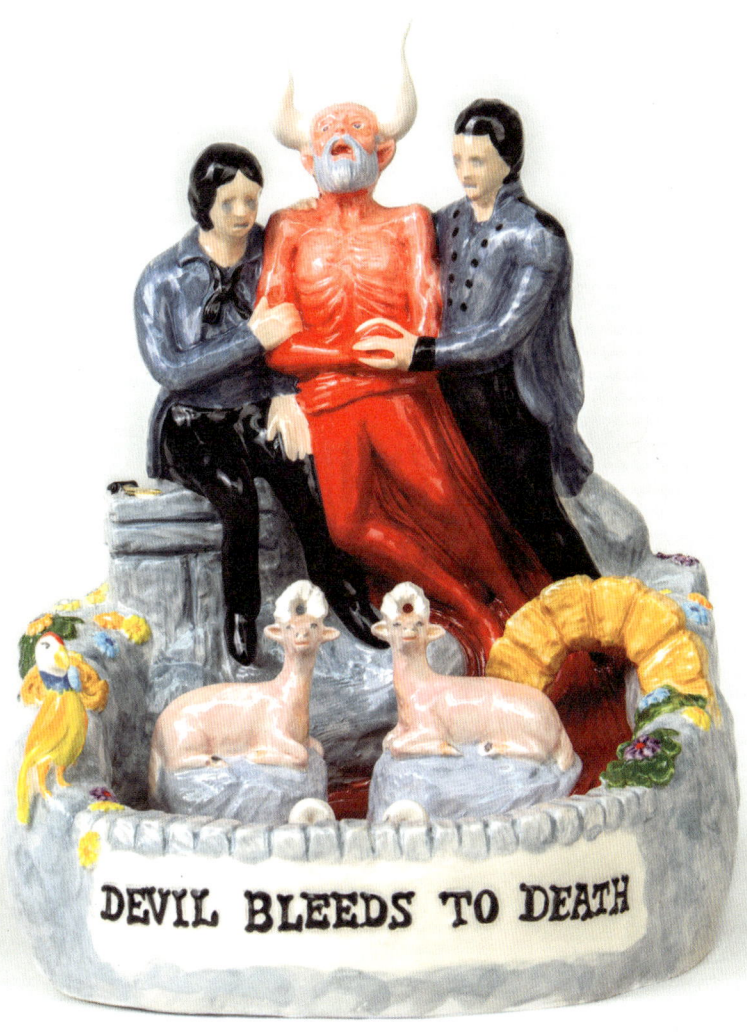

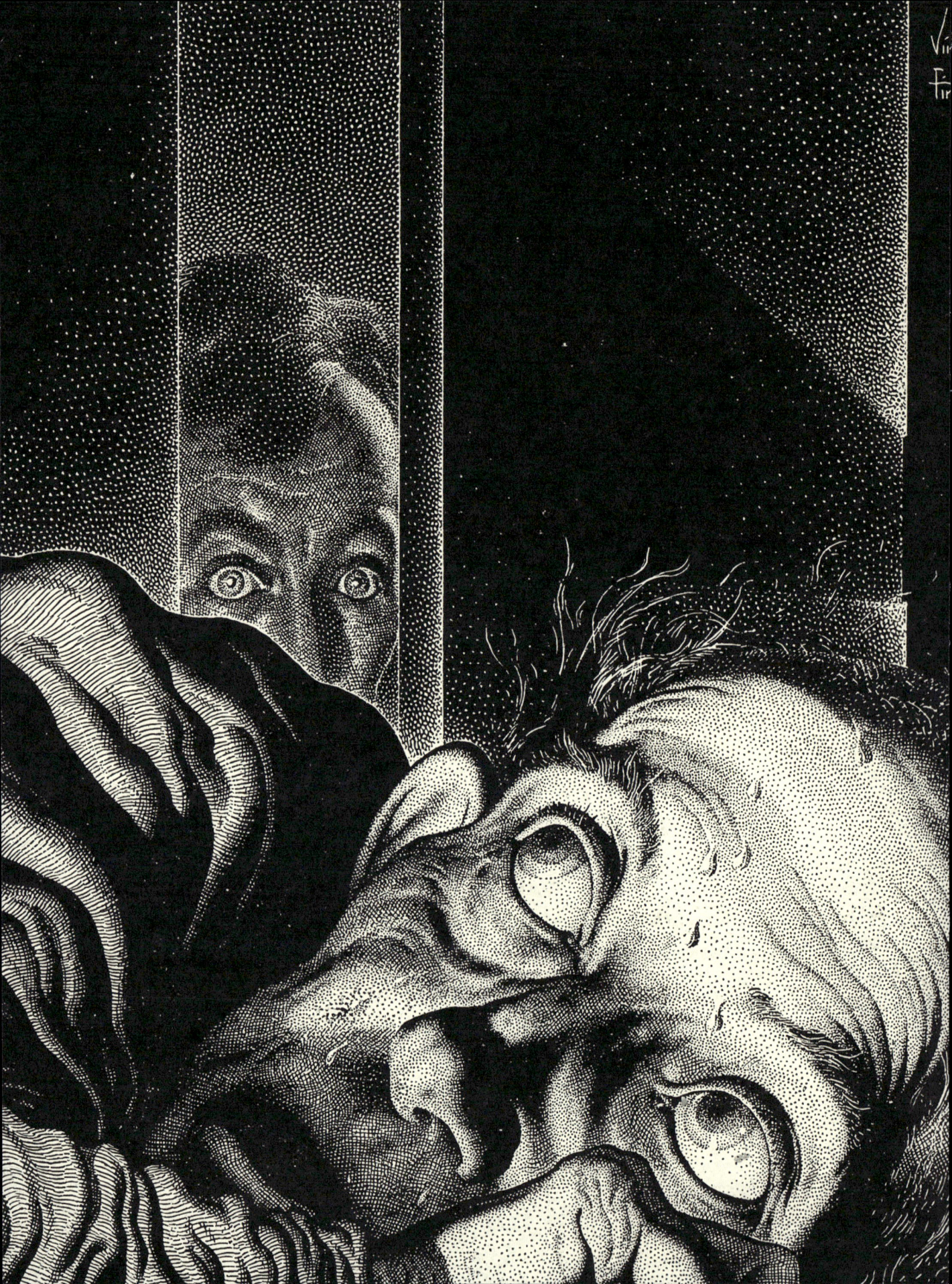

When *Wednesday* magazine asked, "Do you know who Virgil Finlay is?" my answer was to cheat and look him up on my phone. I've been working professionally in comic books for almost 30 years, so when I don't know who an artist is... it's a little bit surprising. Instead of saying "No," my answer became a strange trip into the arcane world of sci-fi and pulp art. Turns out I DID know who Virgil was; I just didn't know that I knew it yet.

Let me explain...

In 2001, I was working at Humanoids Publishing with frequent Alejandro Jodorowsky collaborator Fred Beltran on a new art book inspired by the original pulp novels and comics we'd seen only glimpses of as fans. Researching what became the hardcover album *Pin-Up Girls from Around the World* was an obsession for me. This era was still just the early days of a functioning internet, so I combed conventions, bookstores and thrift shops trying to consume as many of these volumes as I could.

While digging around, I often saw that the interior art of pulps often had an extremely different art style—a stark, dark, highly-detailed artist stood out among the gaudy, bright, and scandalous cover art I was looking for. I connected that this was also the case for many reprints of more famous fiction reprints I'd heard of. I took note of how amazing this mystery talent was.

Then in 2020, I was researching what was to be an epic history for an all-new comic book universe. These stories were to span literally from the beginning to the end of time. These days, researching at home has become a very easy way for me to get lost for hours and days. I'd found an online public archive containing high-quality scans of entire issues of sci-fi and pulp magazines from the 1950s, '60s, and '70s.

VIRGIL FINLAY
Into the Weird and Wild

Words *Ian Sattler* / Artwork *Virgil Finlay*

Reading these dense science fiction tales was like a real glimpse at being inside the Kurt Vonnegut novels I'd read where the protagonist is being driven mad from either reading or writing these exact publications. And now here they were... alive in the future on my phone screen.

I'd been collecting Finlay's art in my archives; a fan without realizing it. I was shocked to see how many hits searching his name delivered in my archives. Now enabled with clarity from *Wednesday's* request, I set out to once again research.

Virgil Finlay was a self-taught artist whose work was first published in the literally pulp pages of *Weird Tales* in 1935. His pen-and-ink works were largely used to flesh out the interior features. He worked tirelessly for decades, with an astounding 2,600 graphic images appearing in such varied publications as the mainstream *The American Weekly* and back to his gritty roots in *Amazing Stories* and *Famous Fantastic Mysteries*. He was a multiple-time Hugo Award winner and member of the Science Fiction Hall of Fame.

It's said that his lifelong obsession with art culminated with his wakening from a coma long enough to draw one final sketch before lying back down to die. I followed up on these Finlay revelations by asking several other creators across genres if they had ever heard of Virgil Finlay, and they were all stumped. Except one.

Artist Mark Chiarello, who has had a direct hand in scores of milestones in the comic book industry (and was my art director at DC Comics), responded to my text immediately. "Sure, I know who Virgil Finlay is," he wrote. "Super talented and way ahead of his time. Influenced a lot of people we know. I could go on and on. You should have asked me first."

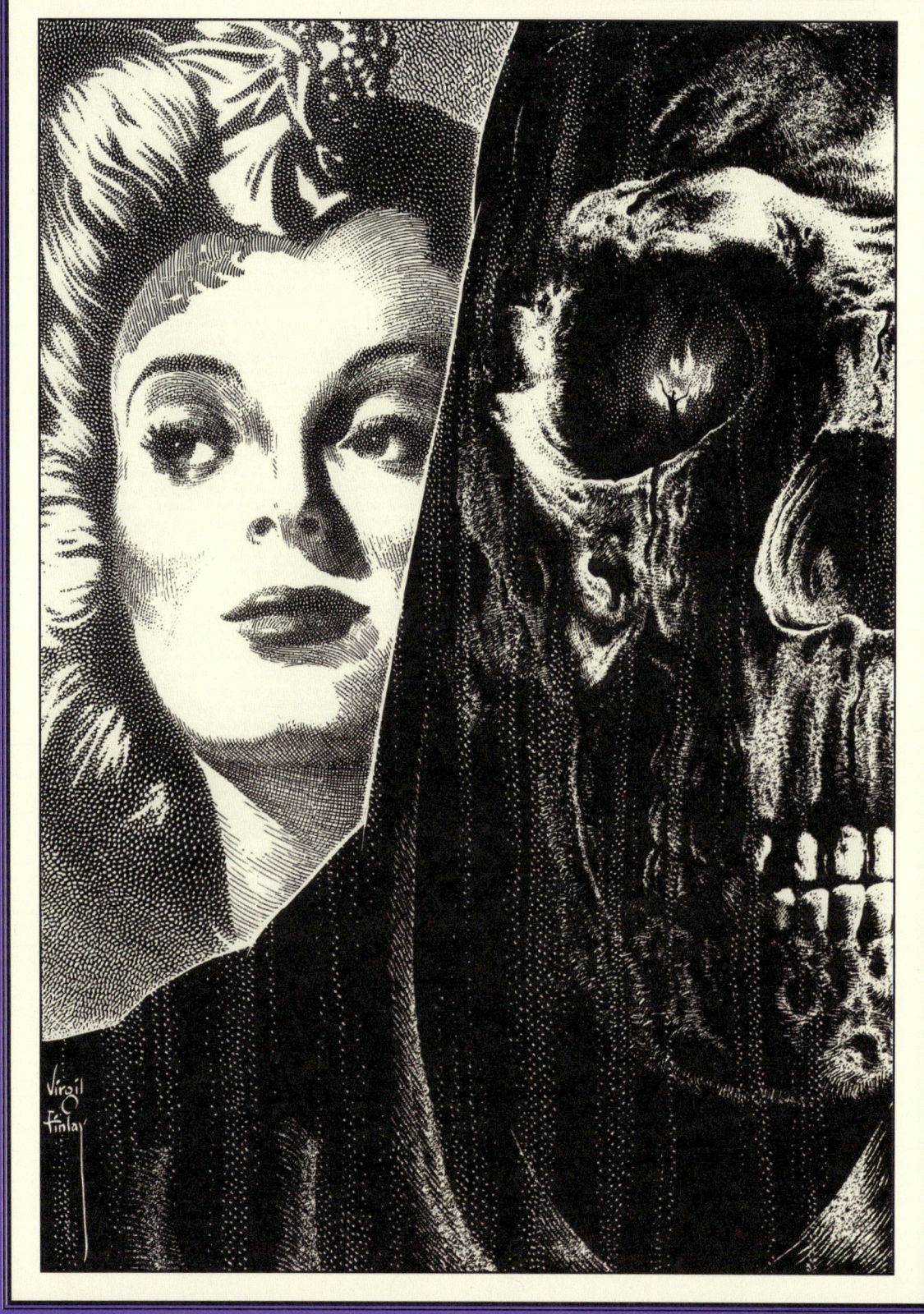

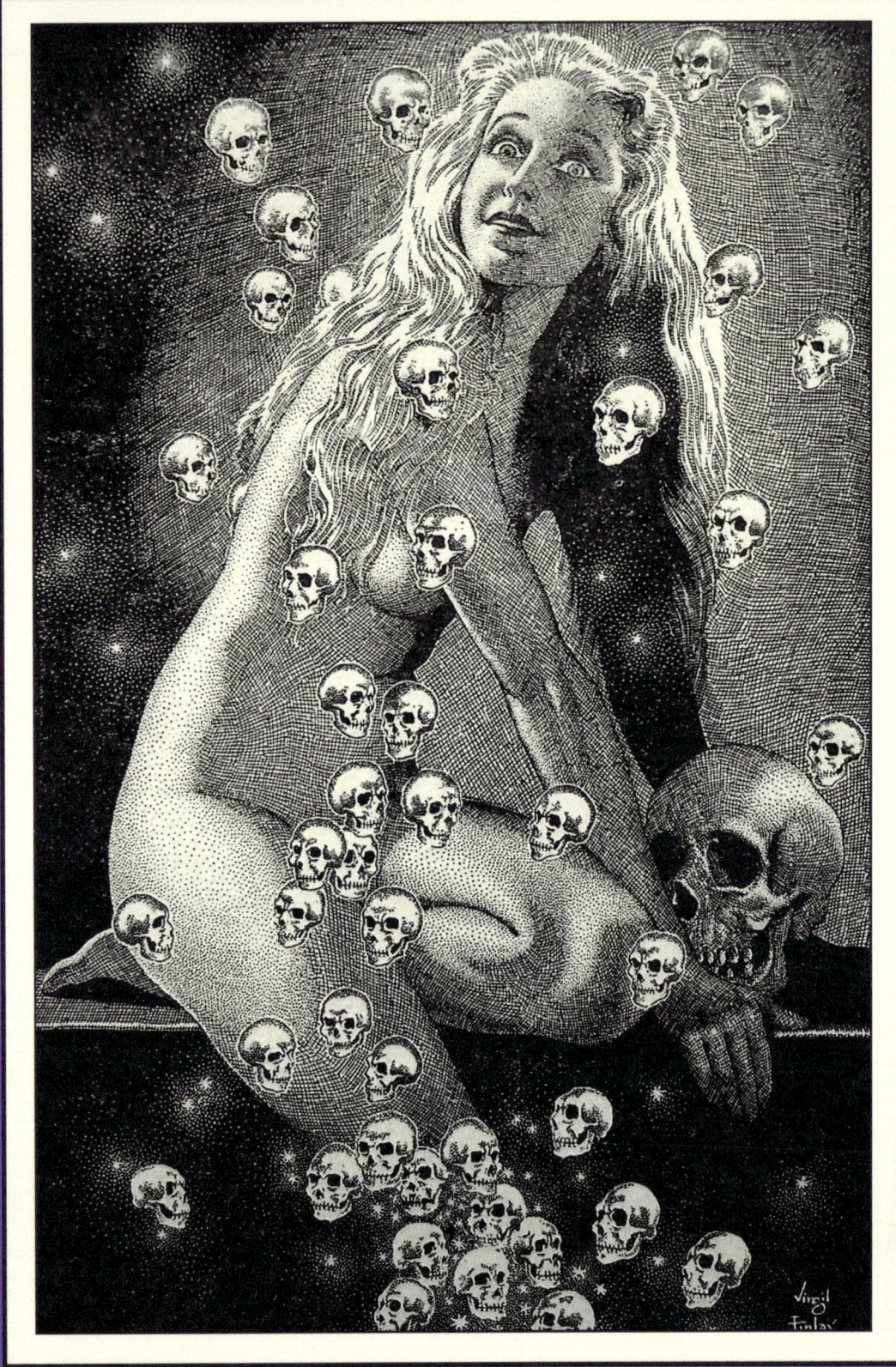

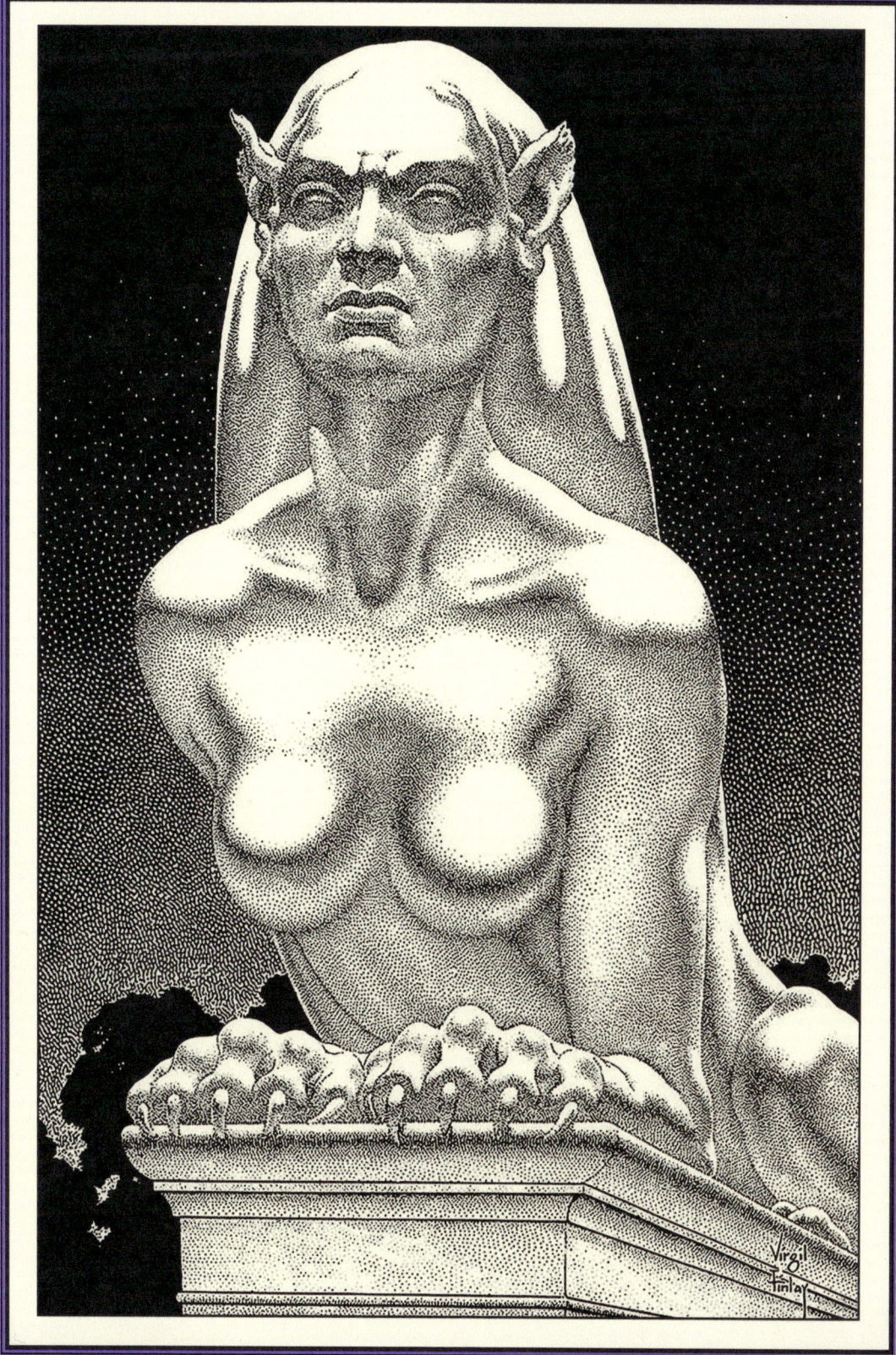

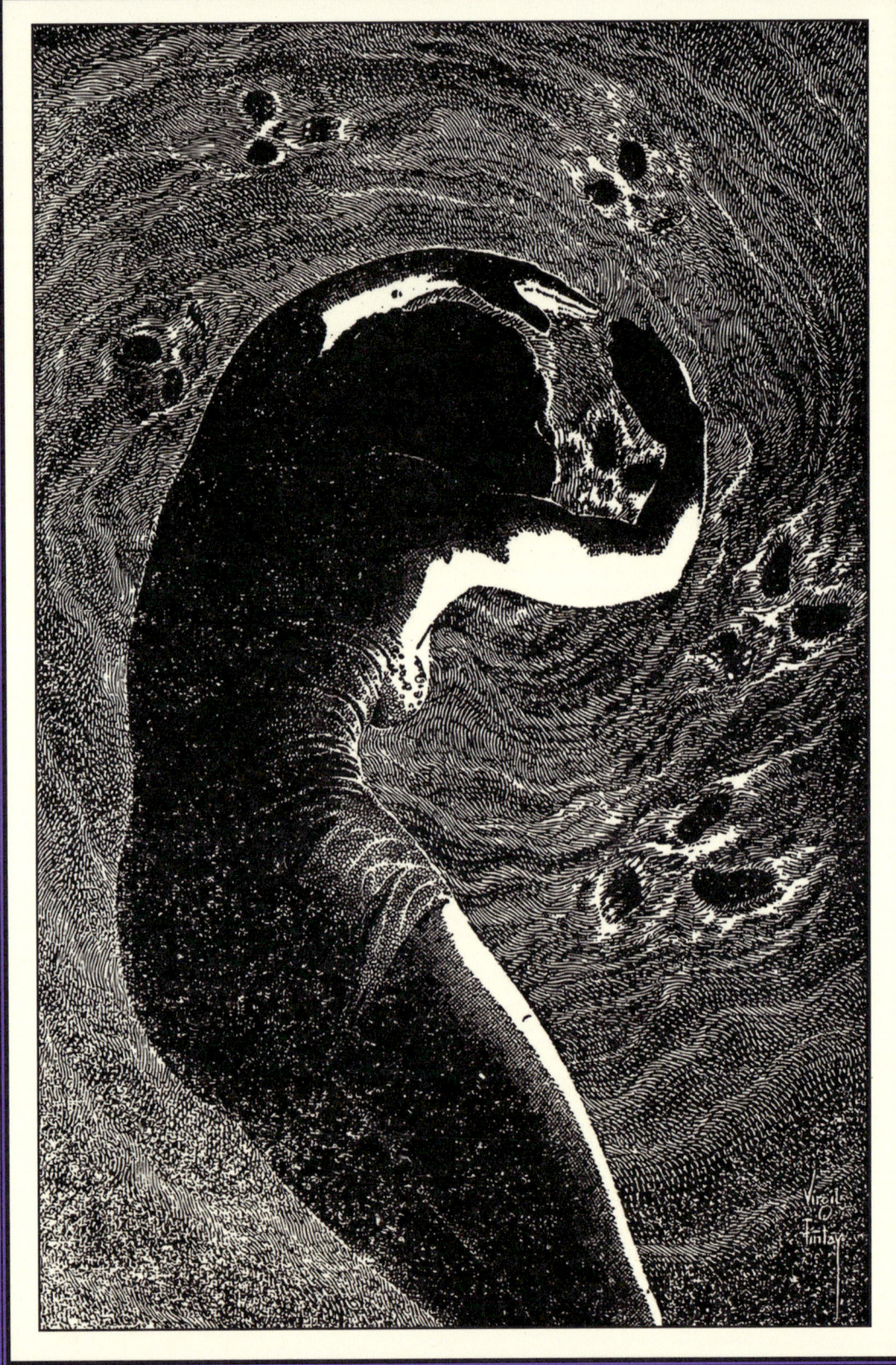

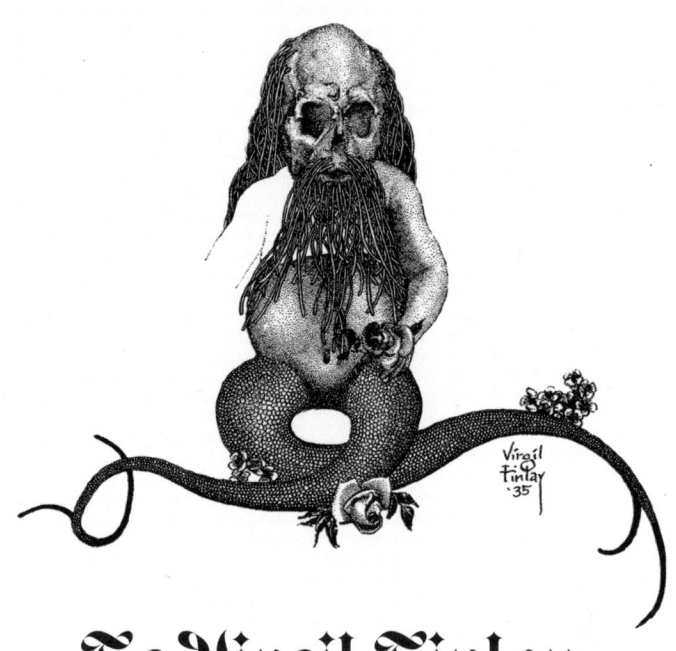

To Virgil Finlay

by H.P. Lovecraft

———

In dim abysses pulse the shapes of night,
Hungry and hideous, with strange miters crowned;
Black pinions beating in fantastic flight
From orb to orb through soulless voids profound.
None dares to name the cosmos whence they course,
Or guess the look on each amorphous face,
Or speak the words that with resistless force
Would draw them from the halls of outer space.
Yet here upon a page our frightened glance
Finds monstrous forms no human eye should see;
Hints of those blasphemies whose countenance
Spreads death and madness through infinity.
What limner he who braves black gulfs alone
And lives to wake their alien horrors known?

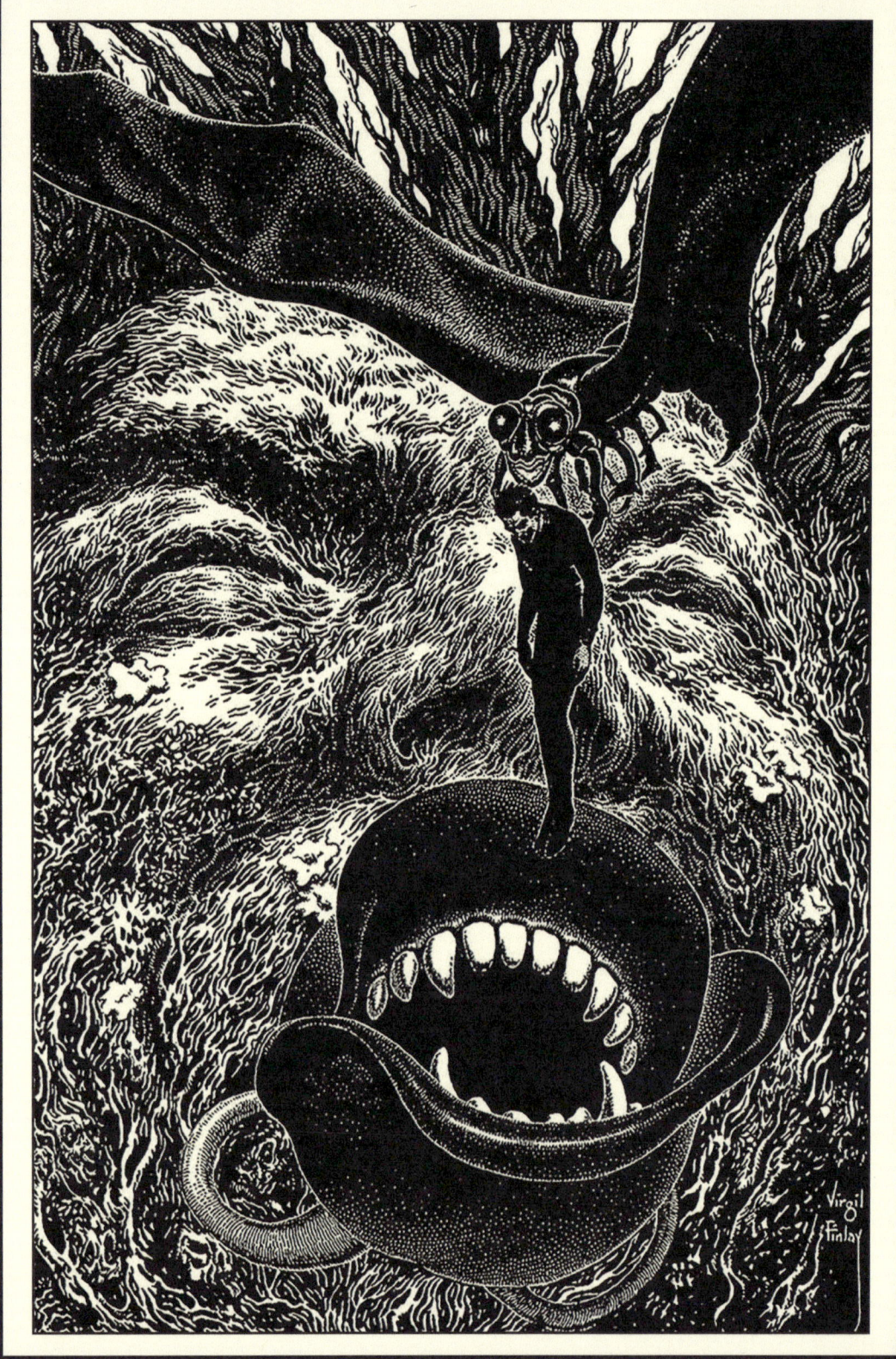

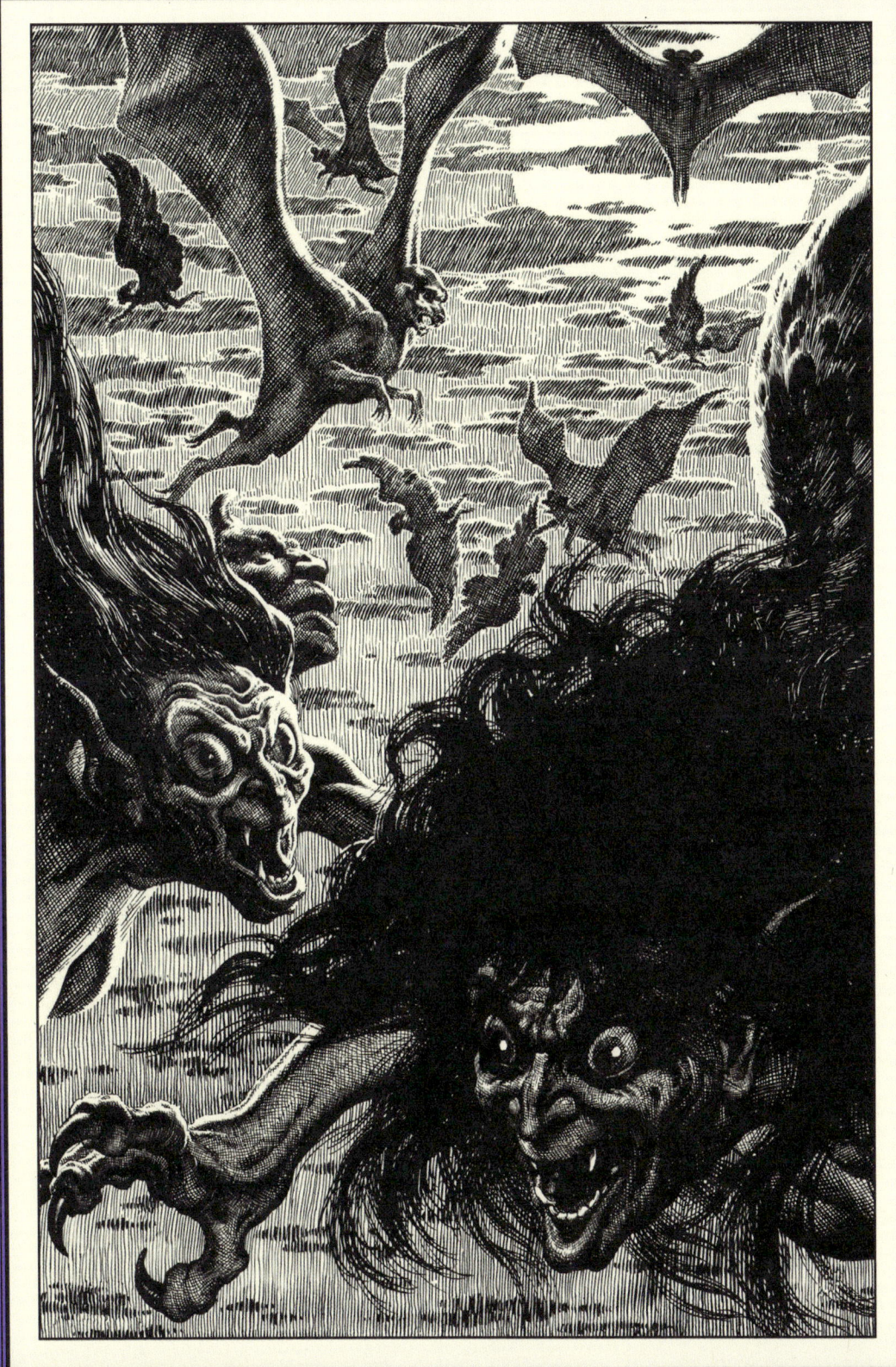

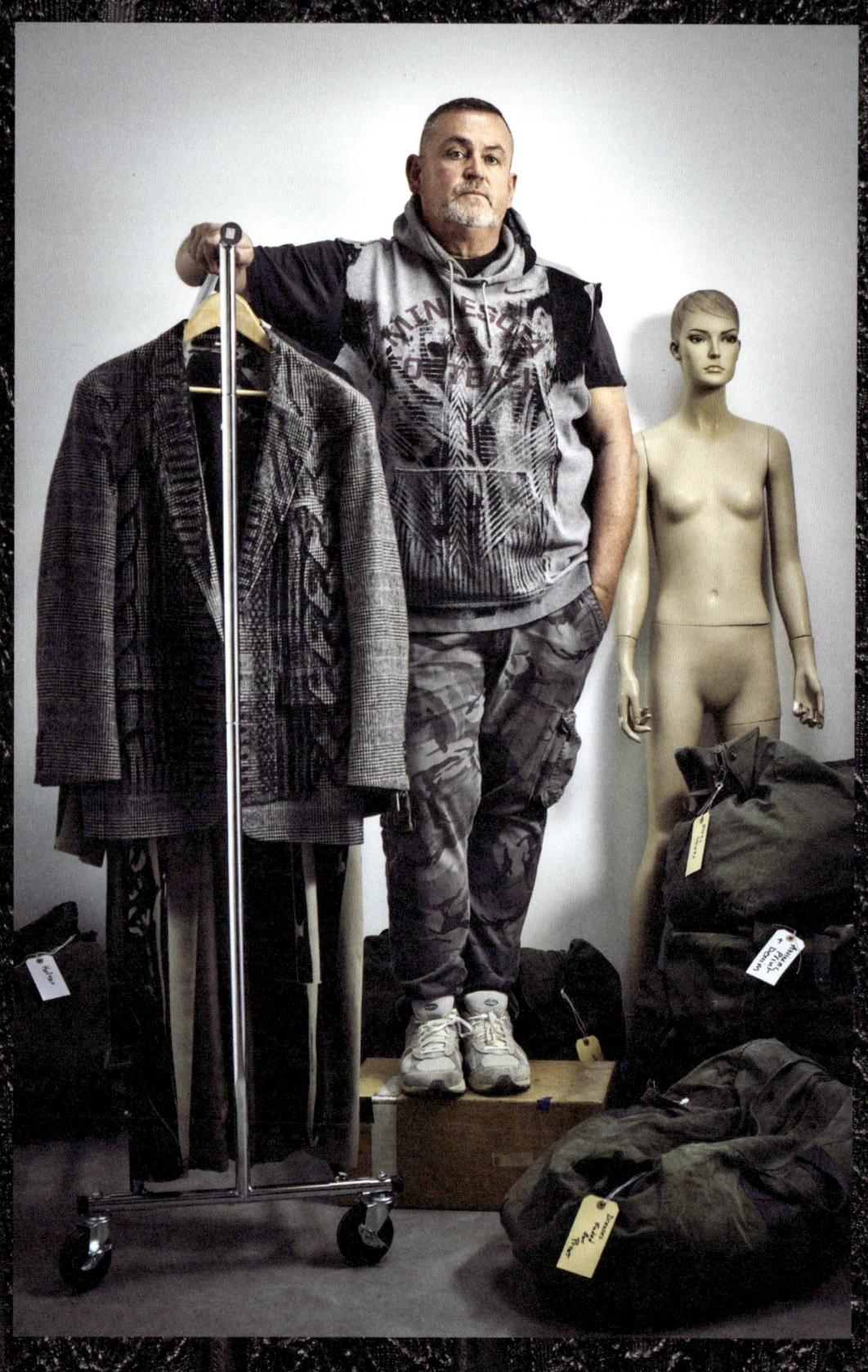

Simon Ungless has been shaping the fashion world since the early days of Alexander McQueen, long before his name became stitched into the legacy of 32 collections. As McQueen's flatmate and collaborator at Central Saint Martins, Ungless played an integral role in crafting the raw, defiant aesthetic that would become McQueen's signature. His influence never faded—years later, he returned to contribute to the brand after McQueen's passing, continuing to find beauty in the ordinary. Now, Ungless has shifted his focus toward a different kind of revolution. As the first designer in residence at Atelier Jolie, Angelina Jolie's sustainability-driven fashion boutique in New York, he's pushing boundaries in a way that feels both radical and familiar. Through his label When Simon Met Ralph, based in Sausalito, California, he transforms vintage and dead-stock garments into wearable works of art, layering prints, dyes, and unexpected embellishments. These "worn-wear" pieces retain the punk ethos of his '90s London roots but with a California-inflected, anti-waste philosophy that challenges fashion's relentless cycle of consumption. Working from his studio near the water's edge in Sausalito, Ungless continues to prove that true fashion subversion isn't about creating something new—it's about reimagining what already exists.

SIMON UNGLESS
Transubstantiation

Introduction *Kenzie Barrena* / Interview *Kevin Grady* / Photographs *Charlie Nucci*

W What inspirations led to your worn-wear pieces?

S Using existing garments goes back to when I first started playing with clothes and textiles, which was around 1977 and the punk rock scene. In the back of NME, they had t-shirts you could buy, and there was one with bullet holes in it. I grew up on a council estate about 60 miles west of London in Hungerford Park, and I couldn't afford it. My dad was a gamekeeper and had guns and stuff, so I went outside, put my t-shirt on a bale of straw, and I shot it. Then I painted it. I didn't know about print-making back then, but I knew how to use imagery and words to make a statement. I was fairly inspired by Jamie Reid and the stuff he was doing for the Sex Pistols. I loved it all, I wanted it all, but we were really poor. And also, 60 miles to London felt like it could be the other end of the earth. So, it was about making my own thing. It was about being resourceful, finding where people got their references from, and putting pieces together. I was always building looks based on what I could get, printing it, dyeing it. A lot of it was self-taught, and then I went to art school.

W What an exciting time.

S Yes. And I think I was always drawn to printmaking because of people like Marcel Duchamp, and his ready-mades, and he became a big hero for me. And Max Ernst and Man Ray were using found objects to create art, taking things from their environment that they already had. So, I think it was a natural thing for me—I've never consciously been like, oh, I'm making worn wear, I've always done that. So, when I was going out and looking for work or whatever, I'd have a pair of jeans on that I'd completely rhinestoned or something, and it would be that the company was interested in. And I started using the term "worn wear."

W Worn wear is fascinating because there's this sense of transubstantiation involved. You're taking something mundane, and because you've altered it, it's elevated into something new. The sweatshirt I have from you was made by Champion, and there's something that's so interesting about how it changes the garment from something that's just every day and transforms it into something quite special.

S That's kind of the ethos. Taking something quite ordinary, almost utilitarian in a way, such as a sweatshirt. And there's also the fact that I'm quite interested in picking on brands every now and again, because I really want people to consider the amount of stuff that they produce. So, the sweatshirts and things that I do are normally dead stock or second-hand vintage or something. But it's also something about the narrative that I can create regarding the person who is wearing the garment.

A few years ago, there was this big thing about Balenciaga putting Champion sweatshirts on the runway and people spending thousands of dollars on them, and I thought this is fucking ridiculous. I can get a Champion sweatshirt and print on it. I remember doing one for myself and wearing it to work, and people just thought, "Oh my god, is that one of the Balenciaga pieces?" Basically, it's a Champion sweatshirt I printed over the weekend. You can do this stuff yourself. You don't have to buy into the kind of bullshit of the brand or anything like that. So, there are lots of different elements that come together. But mainly, I'm very focused on trying to get people to stop shopping so much by looking into their own closet. Part of what I do is have clients send me stuff—I have it for a while so I can build a narrative, like get to know the garment and print it and send it back to them or dye it or something. I want people to just care a little bit more about what they have. It's not all disposable.

W That connects with what I read about you giving gifts to friends and family—you don't buy new things. And that's why I love going to antique stores. You find something that's been around, that you just know is still going to be around when you're gone. I bought this big, bronze panther at an antique place, and it'll be around long after I'm gone. It's heavy, you can't get rid of it, you know? There's something substantial about it. And I just appreciate it each time I see it. It has a new life.

S I love all that history. It's like, last year, my mum passed away. So, I went to the UK, and there were some pieces I wanted to keep. And this copper pot was my great-grandmother's. And she would boil the bed linens in it. She would make the stew, and she would wash her babies. Everything got done in that pot. And now I've got it on my kitchen table with some plants in it. It's so beautiful, and it's imbued with such history.

W My parents are in their 80s, and every time I visit, my dad tries to give me things. But he doesn't know which things are special to me, the things that carry with them some faint, warm memory from when I was three or something, you know? And that's the thing I'm going to want in my home, and it'll be in a completely different context. The things that I wanted were all things that have some kind of connection or memory, as opposed to anything of monetary value.

S There's a guy in Fairfax who has kind of a junk shop, and it's always one of the first places I'll go if I'm looking for a gift. Sometimes he's open, sometimes he's not. But he's probably got a real hoarding problem.

W That's great. I love going through places and finding treasure, you know?

S Yes, I do that. Every month or so, we do a road trip up the Russian River to Guerneville. It's amazing, just a whole great vibe up there. We go through Sebastopol because there are all these different antique arcades and antique houses. It's a nice day out.

W Wonderful. So, how did your connection with Angelina Jolie and Atelier Jolie in New York happen?

S My year-long stint at McQueen came to an end when Sarah Burton left the company, and I'd finished my projects and was kind of like, "Fuck, what am I going

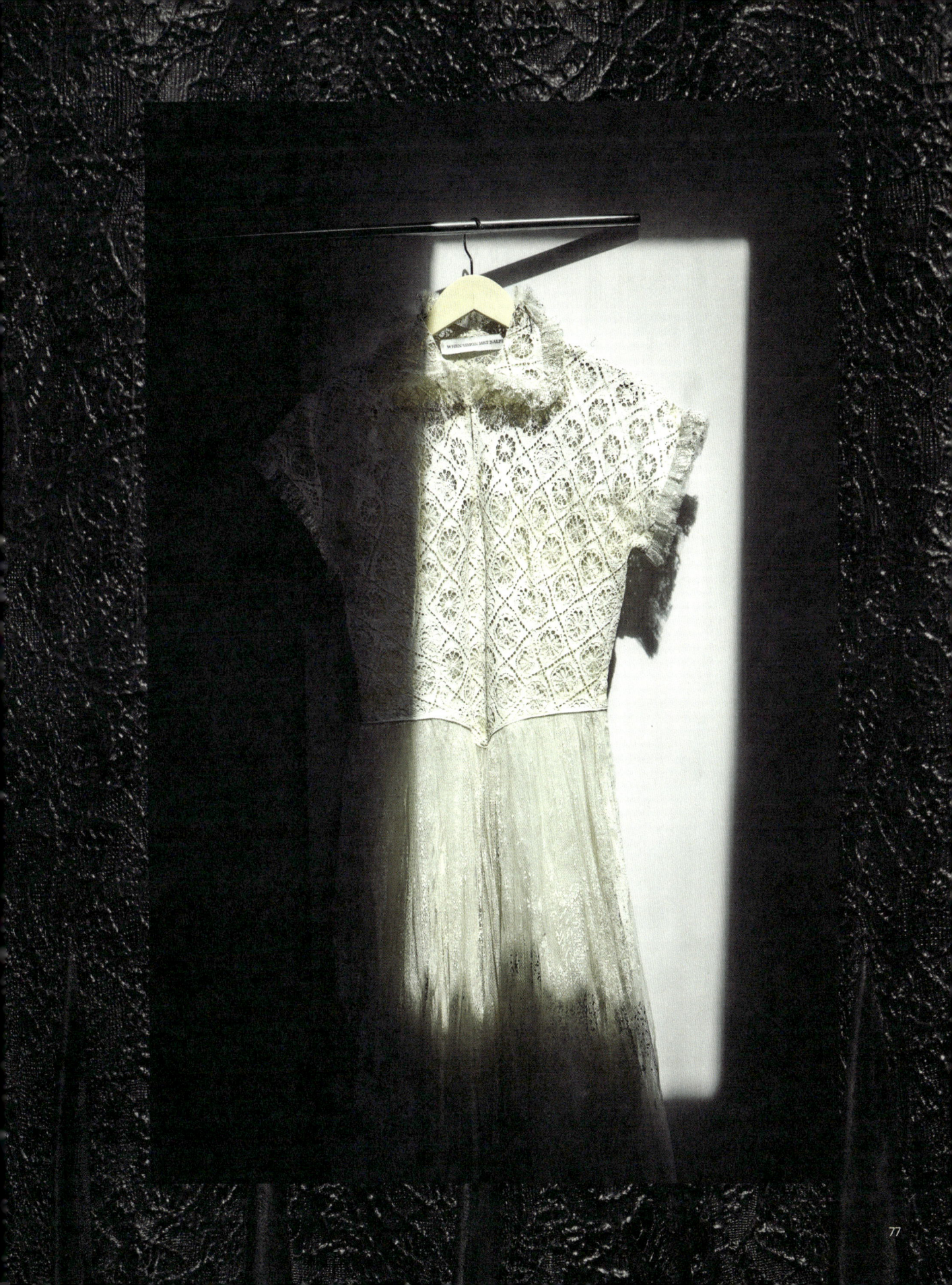

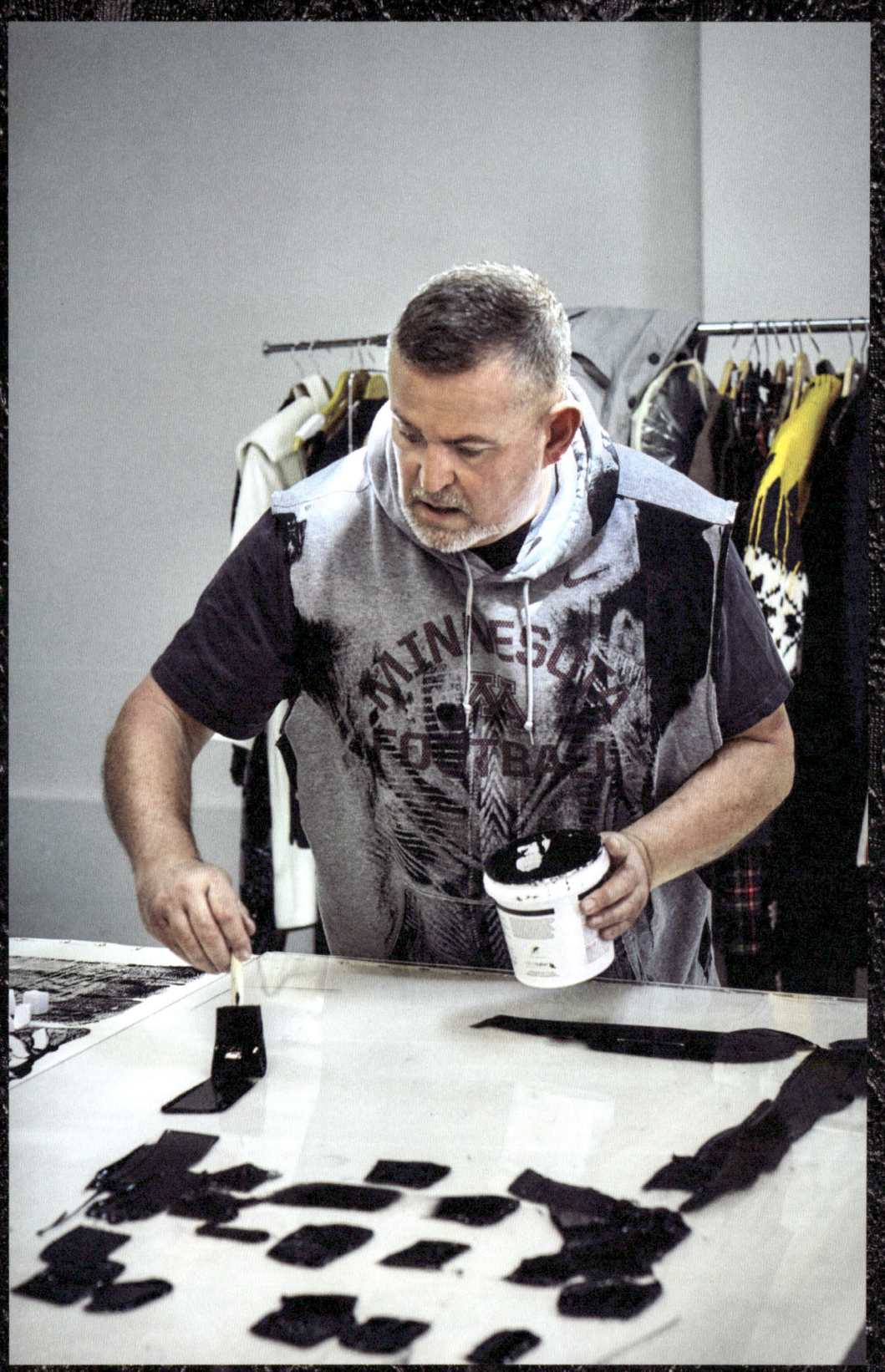

to do now?" And then within a couple of days, I got a message from a member of Angelina's team saying that she wanted to meet with me. I had no idea that she was doing this project—I don't spend a lot of time looking at publications and things, so I had no idea about it. And then I realized the person who messaged me was somebody I had heard of and highly respected in the industry. So, I agreed to meet. When we did, she said she'd been looking at my work through social media and knew my history with McQueen. And it just felt like a really good thing to do. It's kind of a community, a family of like-minded people who want to do things differently. It's not necessarily about building a fashion empire; it's about people learning, being generous with the skills and information that they have. I've got some of my collection in the store, and people can buy it, but it's more about me going to New York and spending time there working with people and teaching them how to do what I do. And encouraging them to make it their own.

W It's very counter to fast fashion.

S Absolutely. Everything is sustainable.

W Angelina has the one spot in New York, right?

S Yeah, in Warhol and Basquiat's old studio, down on Great Jones Street.

W Are there ghosts of the artists in residence? *(laughter)*

S Yeah, you can feel it! You really can. A couple of my friends were around back in the day, and they came down to visit, and it was spooky.

W That's always fascinating to me. I'm quite rational and agnostic, but I'm amazed by what people will tell you when you bring up that topic—almost everyone has a story or knows someone who does. Hard to make sense out of these things, but they seem to happen.

S I totally get that. I've had those kinds of experiences. When I was in London at McQueen, I had the most unbelievable experience of somebody working through me while I was in the studio making something, and it was kind of like, whoa! Part of our process back in the day was that Lee would drape these lace pieces on me—I was very skinny back then—and so he would drape, cut around me, and pin, and that would be a dress. And then I would finish it in latex. For the *Taxi Driver* collection for the *Rebel: 30 Years of London Fashion* exhibition in 2023, I wanted to re-create one of these dresses. So, they gave me fabric and a dress line, and I was just like, fuck—everyone knows I can't really drape. It's not my thing. So, I literally draped out of one piece of fabric, and I sensed that something else took over. I was pinning and folding and doing all of this, and then I did the latex, and I remember Sarah Burton came down, and she was just like, how the hell did you do that?

W That's fascinating! Clearly, we just don't understand everything yet.

How did it feel working on the re-creation of the *Taxi Driver* collection without Lee? Was it bittersweet to look back on some of that work?

S Yeah, it was. I mean, of course, I had a little apprehension about going into that. When they asked me to do it, I was a little like, should I? Because, we were at school together, we shared a house, and we started working together. It was just an organic thing. I don't know, I don't think he even thought at that time he was building a brand; it was just carrying on doing the work that we loved and then getting some opportunities. So that *Taxi Driver* collection was really just Lee and I working together on a small group of, I think it was 13 pieces. So, that's what we did. And it was hard times; it was a recession, and we didn't have work. We were signing on the dole. It was about going to market stores and haggling for fabric and going down to my parents' house and plucking a partridge and taking the feathers back and being resourceful, making something out of nothing. We could always make something. And so, we made this phenomenal 13-piece collection and showed it at the Ritz. There were only two or three pieces pulled for the press. So, there were documents of only two or three garments. And then right after that, we lost the collection. We went out to a club and put it in the black bag and put it behind a dumpster because we couldn't afford to pay for the covering. We didn't even remember it when we left. We remembered it the next morning, and of course, it was gone. So, Sarah wanted me to be involved because I knew the collection; I worked on the collection. Nobody else knew it, so it made sense.

W So, the rest of the collection wasn't photographed to help you reproduce them?

S Yeah, there were only pictures of around three of the original looks; the rest of it had to come out of what I did. So, I explained to them what the pieces were. And there was never a desire from anyone for me to re-create those looks; it was more to reimagine them, the spirit of them. The technique and what we started. It was emotional; there was a moment of grief within that.

W I can imagine there would be.

S Yeah. I was at the studio for just over a week. And the dress was hanging in the exhibition, and I did one with resin. My mum went off to where I originally got the partridge feathers from and got a lot of feathers; she sent them up to me, and I made this resin and feather piece. It came out really well. I had a little help from the other side on those.

W In terms of the names for the McQueen collections— *Nihilism*, *Banshee*, *The Birds*, *Dante*, *The Hunger*, all these dark names—where did the inspiration come from? I mean, beyond the obvious of knowing that Lee suffered from depression...

S I can't really speak for Lee on that, but what I think is that we instantly made a connection because we both leaned toward the darkness in a way. The kind of music we were listening to, the kind of photography we liked, and so on. We both read Marquis de Sade's *The 100 Days of Sodom*. We had that at the house; somebody gave it to me. The clubs that we went to, we weren't really into the glitzy West End gay club kind of thing. We'd go because our friends would, but we would be more interested in seeing what was going on at the back street in the East End. And I think also the kind of drugs that we took—what we would call "the vitamins"—were more the kind that would make you feel more submerged rather than ecstatic. So, it's just the whole combination of things. It was never going to be about a garden party and a floral dress. It wasn't that. It was more to do with a thumping house track or something.

W It was all concurrent with the pop culture at the time.

S Yeah. And it was also that reaction to what was out there—it was yet another really difficult time politically for people like us. There was the whole AIDS thing and everything. And for me, it was very often about pushing buttons. I knew right from an early age when I would go to the shed and take the dog collars out of the cabinet in the shed and put them on and go off, you know, my parents would be walking 20 feet behind me. And I would watch people move out of this 11-year-old's way, because I was this cool punk with these, you know, chains and dog collars. *(laughter)*

W You've been an educator for a long time. How do you characterize students today relative to back when you were a student?

S Education has always been about a two-way street. I can show you this, how to do this, but you've got to meet me halfway and then do your own thing. That kind of thing has mostly stopped. I don't want to be negative, but people seem more concerned about getting 27,000 likes on Instagram. I don't give a fuck if you've got 27,000 likes; it's still a piece of shit, not that I would ever say that to people. And recently, I've been a visiting professor, and it's just been unreal. I was just like, whoa. Everything must be about them.

On top of that, education is now just another toxic business. It's all about the money; it's all about numbers, so you have this whole group of people being conned into coming to college. When you've got an industry that's so fucked, with no jobs, why are we taking 700 students? It doesn't seem right. It's alarming.

W The Vampire's Wife recently closed. It seems that the environment for independent designers is really tough.

S Yeah. When you look at the industry, you know that pretty much everyone is owned by two or three great big, huge multi-brand companies. And everything's starting to look the same. I'm encouraged that there are some designers out there now who have no interest in participating in that kind of thing and are quite happy to work with what they have and sell a few things and have integrity in what they do. But it's a tough industry.

W And now with AI and everything, it feels like we're in a time where it's never been easier to do things, but it's so difficult to make any money doing them. It's so hard to develop a sustainable business situation on your own.

S It is. Young people come to fashion school knowing they don't have to sell anything, and they see Kanye West or whoever making $300 million in fashion and expect that kind of outcome. And I'm like, well, great. Are you independently wealthy? Are you a pop star? Do you have a sex tape? Which of those things do you currently have that's going to be your platform to then go and have a line?

I remember years ago, there was a young woman who came to the Academy, and her name was Heidi Montag. She came to see me one day, saying she valued my opinion. She said she met a producer, and he said he could turn her into a celebrity. And she asked me—should she become a celebrity, or should she stay at school? I said, "I think you should become a celebrity." *(laughter)* And she said, "Oh, okay." And she did.

W Wow.

S And I remember her leaving. I thought, oh, fuck. I bet he's a porn director or something. But the fact that she was asking about this told me everything. ∎

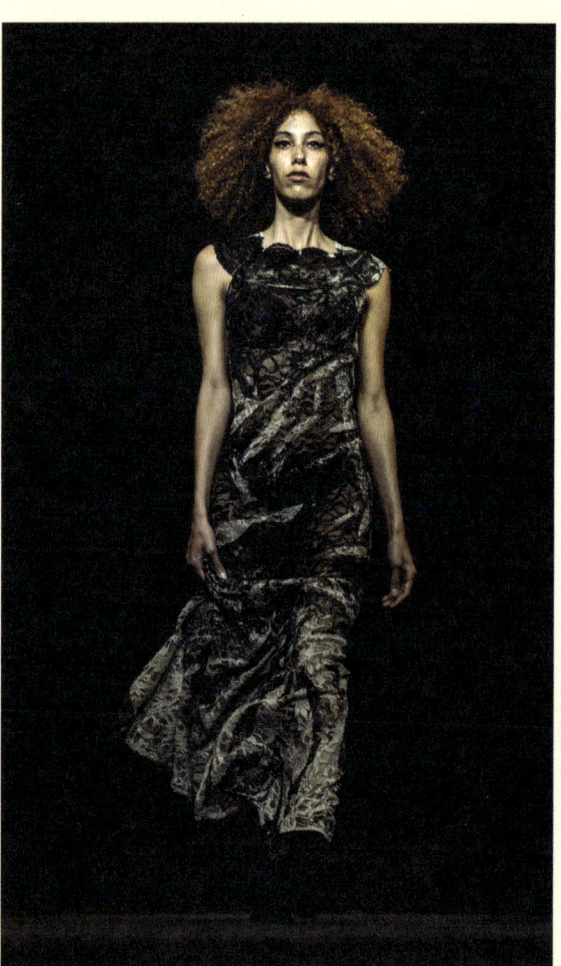

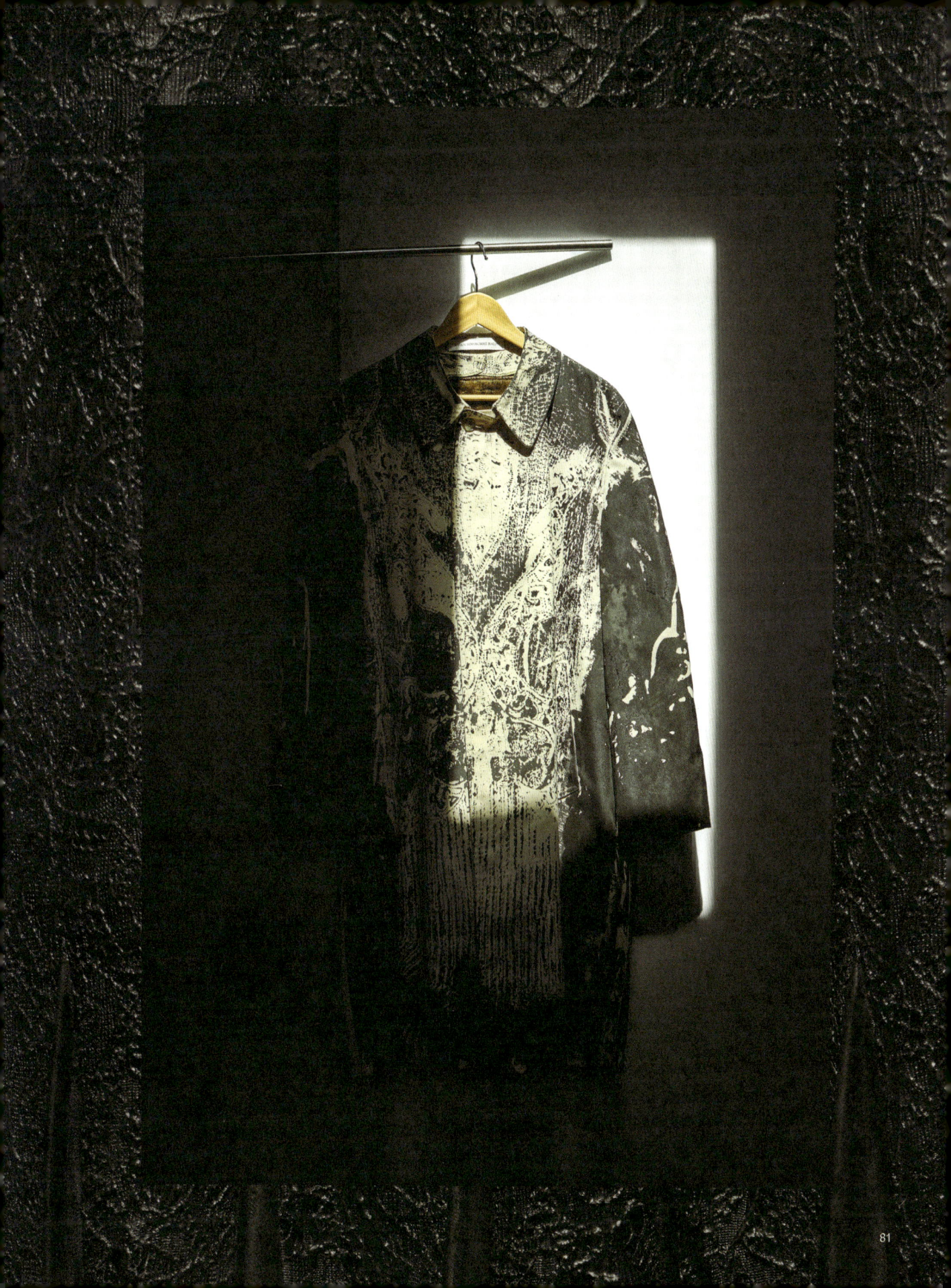

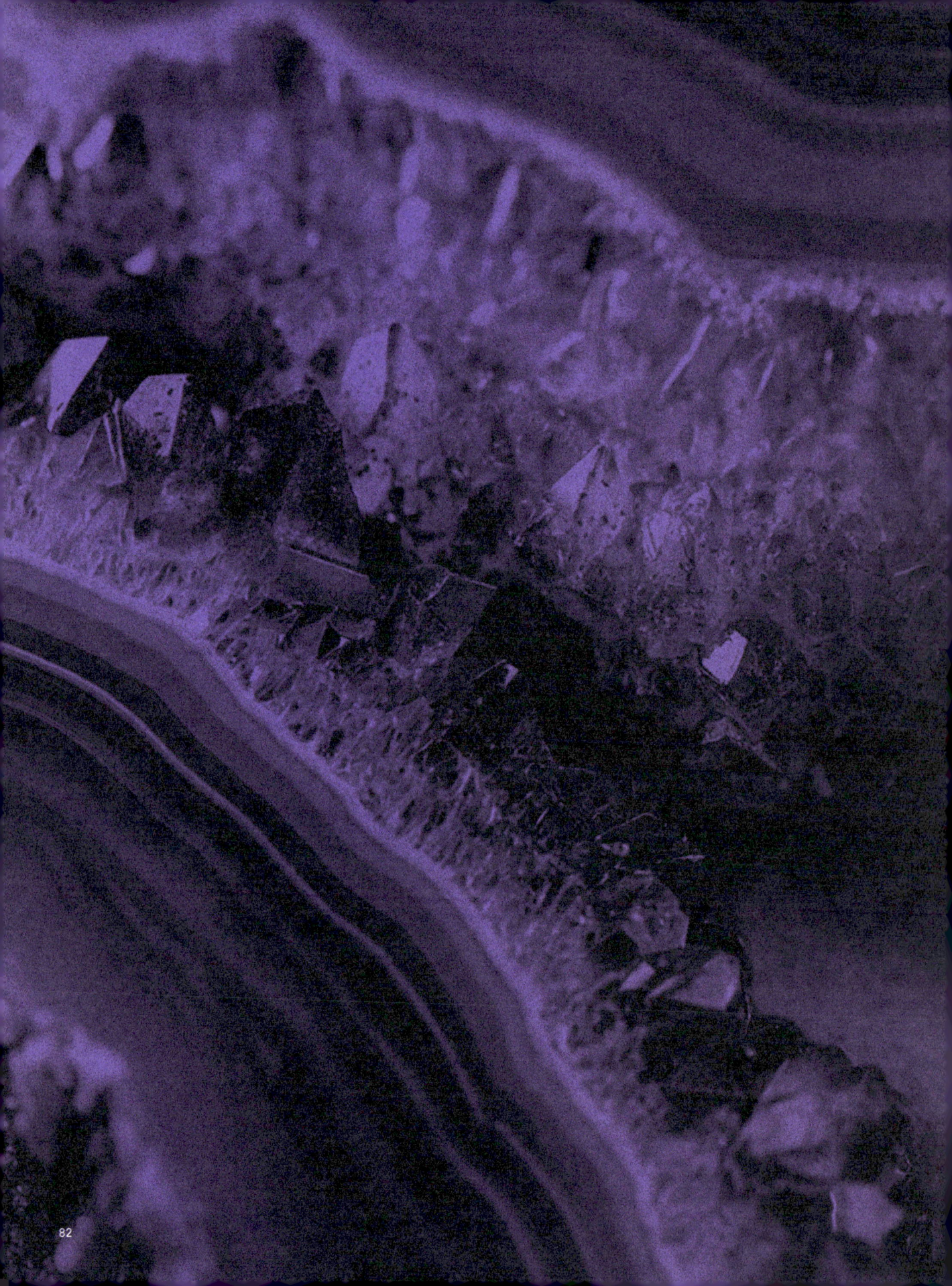

III

Pleasant conversation soon turns to tales of volcanic razor rock in Hawaii, an eyeball-evacuating accident in Berlin, catatonic art patrons in Beverly Hills, and, less interestingly, unreliable Wi-Fi in Budapest. / A pair of auteurs write albums as films, although they still write films as films. / The morning of an interview for the annual gazette in your hands, dear reader, is described, aptly, as "aptly dark."

84 — 141

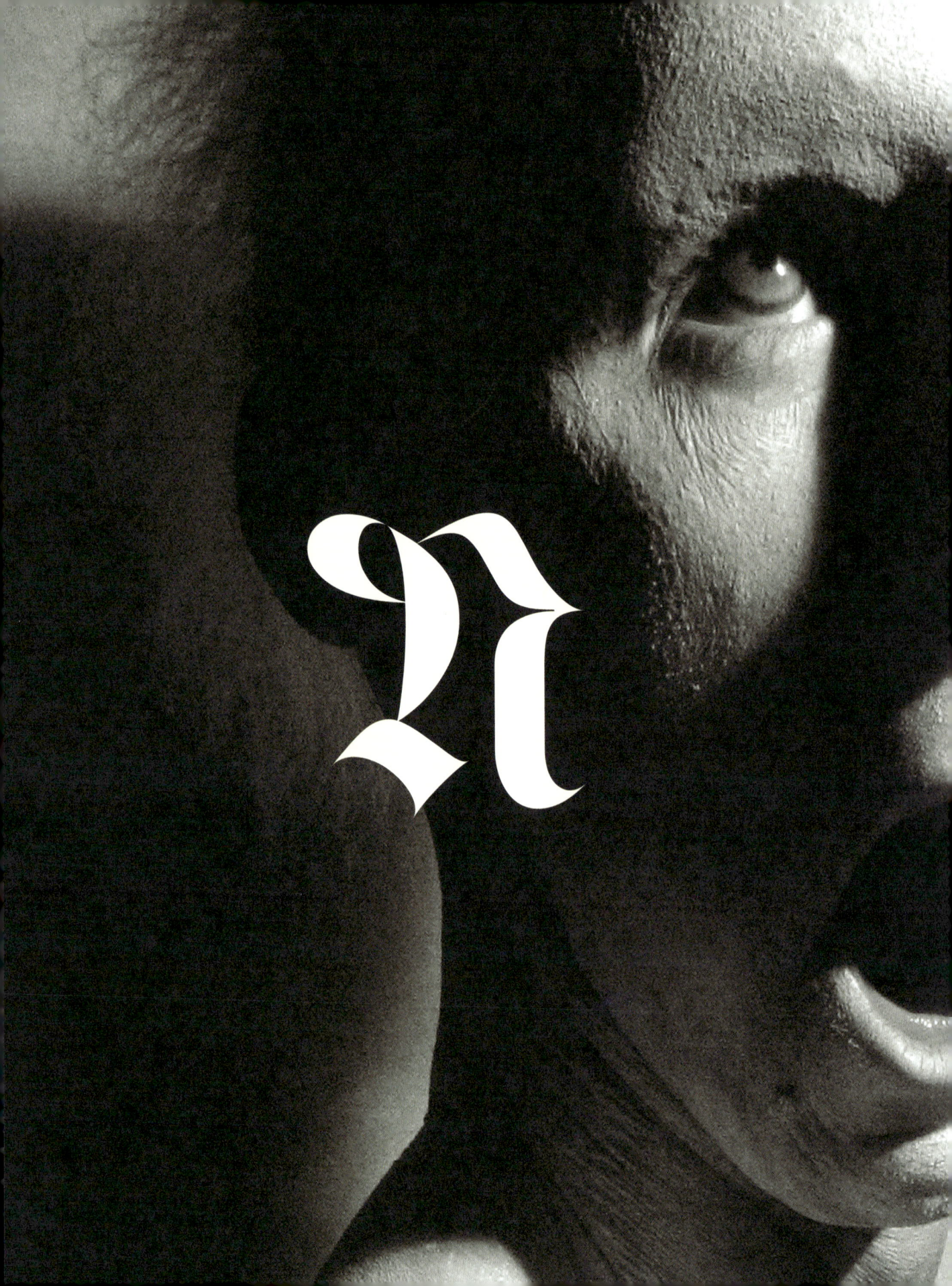

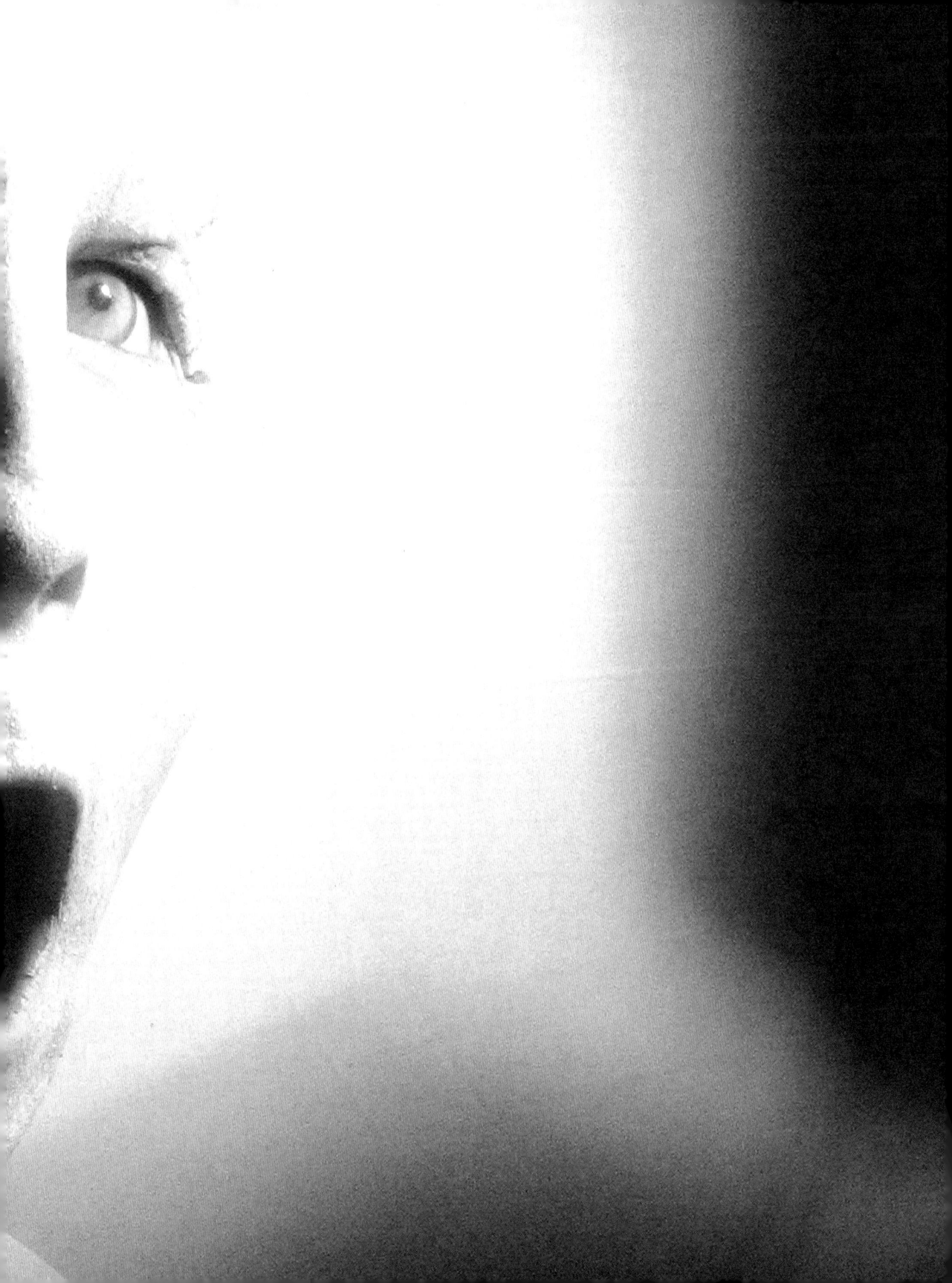

NORMAN
REEDUS

Words *Kevin Grady* / Photographs *Corinne Schiavone* / Wardrobe provided by *Simon Ungless*
Grooming *Laila Hayani* / Production assistance *Sébastien Biache, Sadie Liebo*

Sun's Coming Up

Norman Reedus doesn't just step into the shadows—he lives there. With a career forged in the fire of cult classics and post-apocalyptic sagas, he's become an icon of grit, intensity, and haunted charisma. Whether he's stalking the undead as the crossbow-wielding Daryl Dixon on *The Walking Dead* franchise or diving into dreamlike nightmares in Hideo Kojima's *Death Stranding,* Reedus gravitates toward characters who exist on the fringes—hardened, hunted, and often misunderstood. But for him, darkness isn't just a mood—it's a map of the human psyche.

Offscreen, Reedus is no less layered. He's a painter, photographer, and motorcycle obsessive—creative outlets that mirror the raw, visceral energy of his acting. His art is messy, intimate, and often laced with the macabre. He doesn't shy away from the grim; he charges into it, wide-eyed and unapologetic. That tension—between brutality and vulnerability, shadow and soul—is what makes him so magnetic.

Wednesday sat down with Reedus to explore the contours of his singular world, from his scrappy beginnings in Hollywood to his recent roles in genre-bending films like Darren Aronofsky's *Pendulum.* The stories he shared were as unfiltered and captivating as the man himself. Which is just another way of saying what everyone already knows: Norman Reedus is a badass.

W Hello, Norman. How's it going?

N Good, man. I'm good. I'm in Budapest right now with some bad Wi-Fi, so hopefully this works.

W Oh, okay. Well, I'm just about to do a cross-country trip with my cat, from SF to New Hampshire to see my folks. Going to be an epic journey. *(laughter)*

N Fun. Yeah, I did that once. I had this little Persian cat, and I drove from New York to California in a Karmann Ghia, and I was like 19 with a Persian cat through the snow in the mountains of Colorado. Cat was freaking out.

W Wow, I'll bet. Mine's a Maine Coon, and I was trying to think of a name, and he knocked over and broke this vase that I loved, and he walked casually away as if to say, "My work is done here." That night I had seen *The Bikeriders,* and I found his name: Vandal.

N Oh, that's great! That's super cool. I love Maine Coons, too. Those are such cool cats. My friend had one, and I loved it. It was huge.

W Yeah, they keep growing for like three to five years. It's crazy. Well, *The Bikeriders* was a wonderful movie, as is the book it was based on. Motorcycles seem to have played an important role in your life. You once worked at a motorcycle shop in Venice, California, and you have your *Ride with Norman Reedus* series. If you could keep only one motorcycle for the rest of your life, what would it be?

N My favorite is a 1987 Harley FXR. It's root beer brown, has gold trim. It was made by a friend of mine, Yaniv Evan, at a company called Powerplant out in Los Angeles. That's my favorite. So, probably that one.

W Does your son Mingus ride? I know he's been on your show, but is he interested, or is it not his thing?

N No, he lives in Manhattan. He doesn't even have a driver's license. Yeah. Kids in Manhattan don't have driver's licenses for some reason. I mean, he keeps talking about how he wants to ride. Sometimes when we're at a little house upstate, he'll get on one, but he's not a real rider yet, you know?

W Do you have any fear when you're riding? I know you had a pretty horrific car accident back around 2005—what's been your scariest experience on a motorcycle? Have you had any particularly challenging rides?

N I was riding in Los Angeles once, and an old couple pulled into my lane as I was coming toward them to turn and get on a freeway. I hit the front of the car and kind of flew up over the car. And I could see them watching me fly over the car. I had warrants out for my arrest at the time. So I hit the ground and sort of slid. Then I was lying on the ground convulsing, and people were driving by going, "Sue him, sue him," because it's Los Angeles. But nobody stopped to help me. They were just yelling, "Sue him."

W Jesus. Gotta love people.

N And then I had to get up and take the bike and push it into the bushes. And then I went to a friend of mine's house that was nearby—he was also an actor—and I laid on his sofa all day, twitching. And then years later, like 15 years later, I read an interview with that actor, and he told my story as if it happened to him.

W Oh, really? There's a quote about when it comes to telling the truth or creating a legend, go with the legend. Guess he did that! *(laughter)*

N Yeah, he told the whole story, and I read it, and I was like "That was me, not you." It was familiar.

W One of the memorable parts in *The Bikeriders* was when the character Brucie died; the build-up was that it was going to be some dramatic motorcycle gang-related thing. And he's just going down a quiet neighborhood street, and then that car pulls out. Boom! And that's it. That's how it happens.

N Yeah, exactly. I had another scary moment. I was in Hawaii shooting an episode of *Ride,* and we were coming down a mountain. There was volcanic razor rock all the way down the mountain to our right, and the wind was so heavy and blowing so hard that our bikes were leaning. I was on a Triumph Tiger 1200 Rally Pro, which is a giant tall motorcycle, and the wind was catching me, and I was coming down at an angle. I kept screaming at the camera van not to move because it was blocking the wind. Then they would speed up to catch us to get a shot, and I'd speed up trying to catch them. And we were screaming, me and Patrick Hoelck, a photographer friend of mine who was on that episode with me. Finally, our safety guy comes up and he's like, "Stop it, this is way too dangerous." We were coming in at like a 45-degree angle. That was terrifying.

   And I've been in a couple of crashes. Sometimes, if I'm coming around a turn, I'll imagine how I'm gonna lay the bike down just in case. So I don't know. I think eventually you will crash.

W Hopefully you have luck on your side. But they have these new airbag suits, at least for racing, that pop up like a balloon...

N They gave me one of those suits, and I tried to get on the airplane with it, and they made me take it apart, and I couldn't get on the airplane because it was combustible, or something like that. So, I ended up coming back home with just the jacket and no balloon.

   Do you ride?

W I'm just learning, and I have an electric café racer made by some obscure company called Denzel. It's the one I showed you. So, at this point, it's just easy rides along scenic routes while I get used to the basics. But it's been so much fun. At one point, I was surrounded by a group on Harleys in a parking lot, and they were a bit perplexed at my bike. But it's better than being that middle-aged guy who goes out and buys the biggest Harley he can find and crashes it within a week.

N I have one of those electric bikes in Paris, a Zero FX. It looks like a dirt bike, and I stripped it all out, and it looks like a Mad Max electric dirt bike. I zip around Paris on that thing. And up where you live, I rode with the East

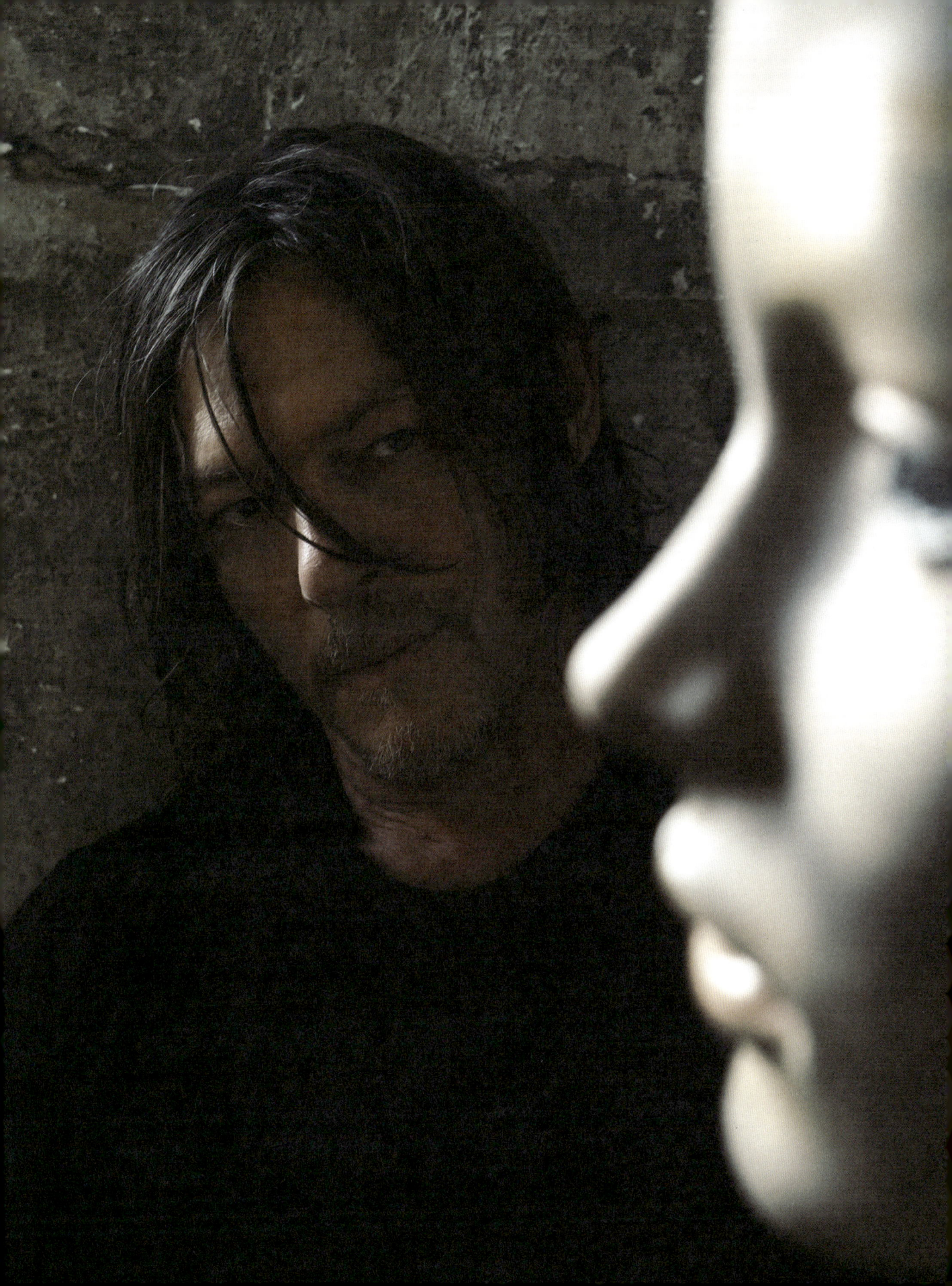

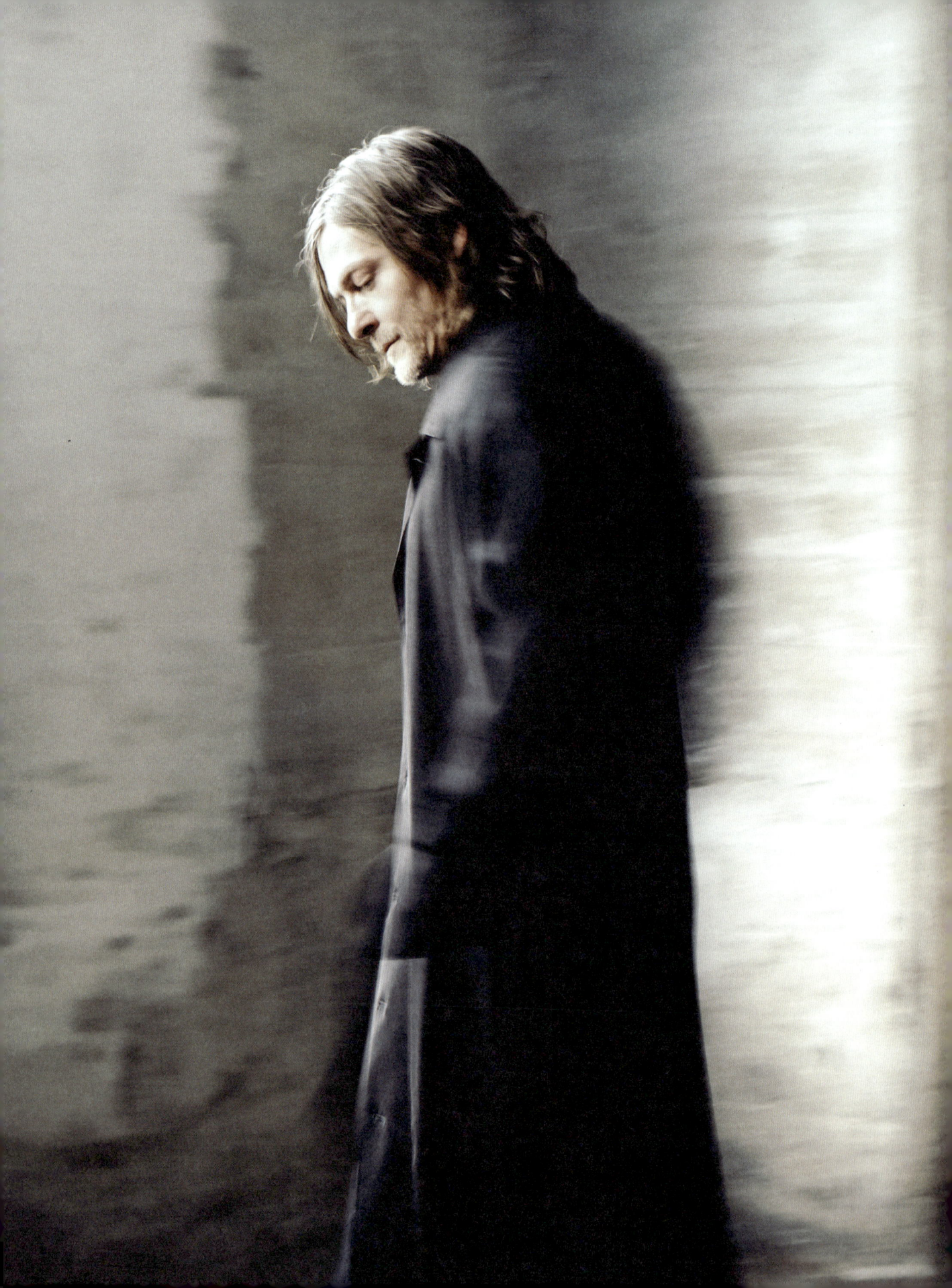

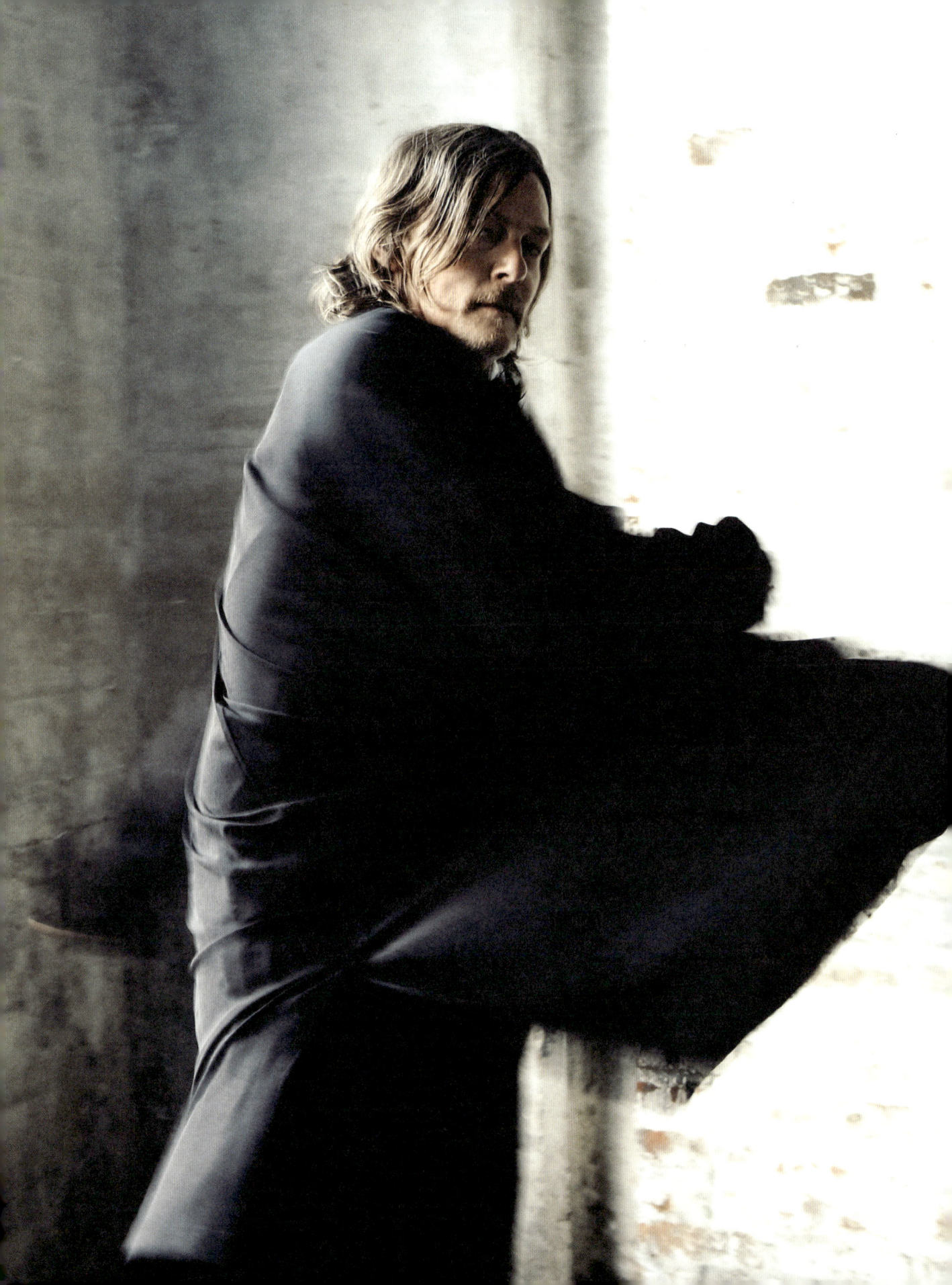

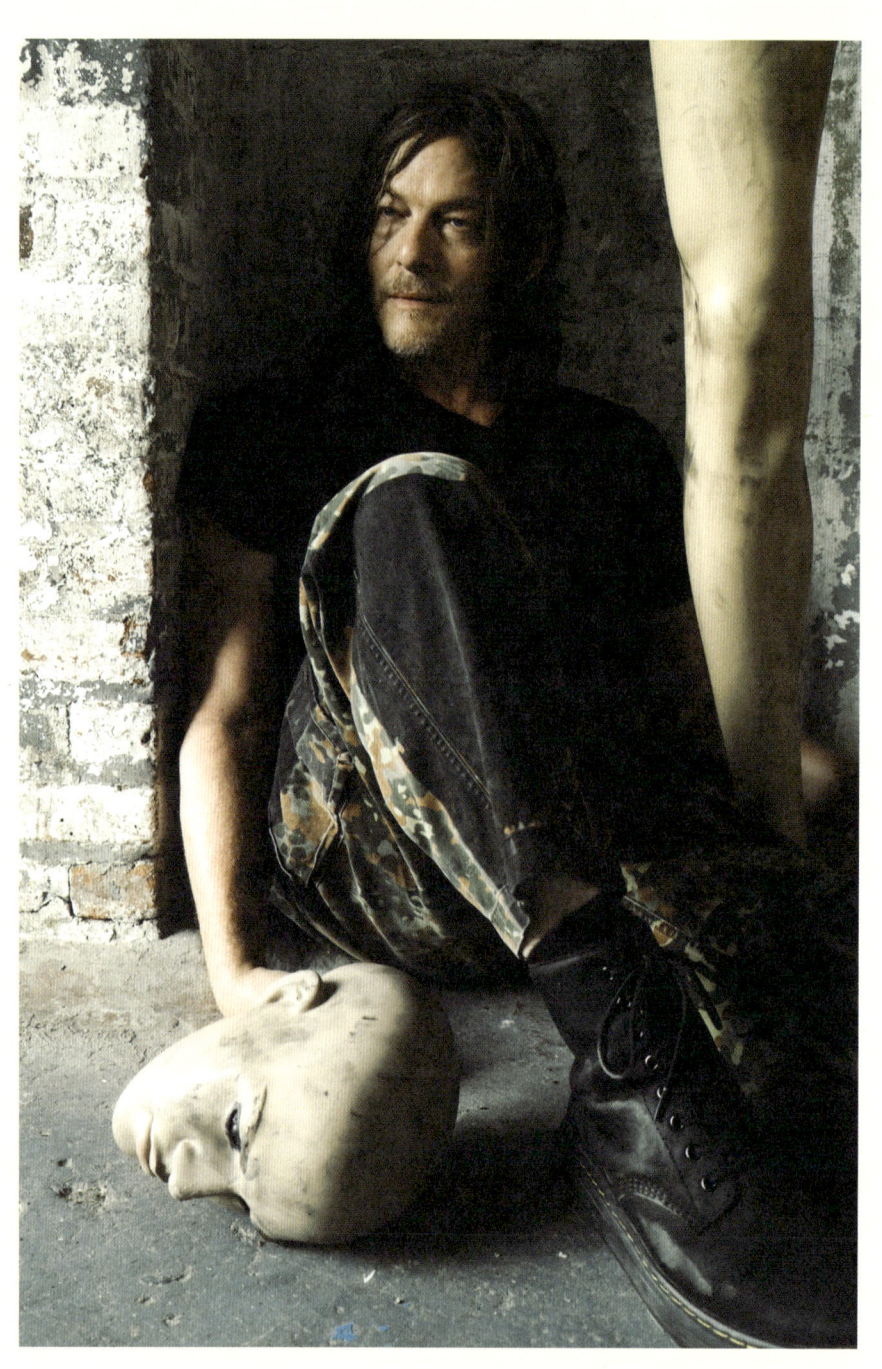

Bay Dragons through Oakland and San Francisco. You know the East Bay Dragons?

W Yeah, they're the all-black Harley riding club, right?

N Yeah. So, I rode with probably like 200 motorcycles in a row going through Oakland and San Francisco, and it was really cool. Went to their clubhouse and everything.

W Very cool. Oh, and speaking of crashes, you had a horrific car crash in Berlin. What happened?

N I went to the Berlin Film Festival to get a Shooting Star award or something, and a friend of mine who sings in this band texted me and invited me to one of his shows. So, I went to the show, and after I was gonna get a cab, and he's like, "No, take my driver." So, I took his driver, and the guy pulled in front of an 18-wheeler. It hit me from the side, and I flew through the front window with my eyeball hanging out. And then I woke up in a German hospital. Wait, where was I going with this story?

W Through the windshield, apparently! *(laughter)*

N Yeah, it was a bad crash. My eyeball popped out!

W Sounds horrific.

N So, that's what I was going to do from there on out, make these short little films or do art shows to pay the rent, because I had this hamburger face. But then John Carpenter offered me my first acting job after that, for a movie called *Cigarette Burns*. And I was like, dude, look at me, I'm purple, right? I'm never gonna be able to do this. And John talked me into it. I was so nervous, so self-conscious, because my face was so swollen. But John managed to convince me to do it.

W He got you back on the horse again.

N Yeah, and then when *The Walking Dead* happened, Frank Darabont and Greg Nicotero called Carpenter to ask what I was like to work with. So, in the end, it all worked out.

W How did your involvement in *The Bikeriders* come about, and how did you prepare for your role as Funny Sonny?

N I met a guy in Cannes, and he said, "Hey, I've got a movie, you want to play a part in it?" I said, "Yeah. Who are you?" He was Jeff Nichols. And I was like, "Did you direct *Modern?* And he said he did. And I was like, "Why didn't you tell me you were that guy?" And then he sent me the script for *The Bikeriders,* based on the Danny Lyon photography book. I have a signed copy of the book, and also some prints. I have the shot of Austin Butler, you know, looking over his shoulder, riding over the bridge, in my office in New York. Such a great shot.

W It's iconic.

N Yeah, it is. So anyway, he sent me the script, and I said, "Jeff, you got a lot of good-looking guys in this movie. Can I go in a different direction? Can I try something else?" And he said, yeah. So, I had (*The Walking Dead* prosthetic makeup artist) Greg Nicotero make the teeth for my Funny Sonny character, and then I would sit on the plane and try to talk to the stewardesses with them in my mouth and see if they could understand me. I kept bouncing back and forth from Paris to Ohio while

shooting Daryl Dixon. I'd ask the stewardess, "Can I get a giant Coke?" You know, see if they could understand me. And then I was going to stores and stuff in Ohio before we filmed, walking around town, talking to people with the teeth in.

In the book, the character has a certain energy to him, and I just had a short amount of time to get that energy out, to work out the character. In my mind, Funny Sonny was sent from California to Ohio to beat a guy up because he didn't turn in his colors, his jacket, before he joined another biker club, right? To ride your bike all the way from California to Ohio, especially on that bike would take a while, and it would hurt your butt and your back—it's not a job you volunteer for. So, I think this was Hell's Angels saying, "Fuck you. You've been trouble and you're going to do it." It's like having to go clean out the toilet or something. So, I didn't want to come in and be like a killer, a macho guy. I was more like, "Okay, I'm in trouble with my tail between my legs. I got to go to another club full of guys and somehow do this." So when we had the campfire scene, Sonny realizes these guys are fuckups just like him, you know? These guys are a good time. And Jeff let me be less bravado and more like, yo, I'm one of you. So that's kind of how that went.

W It was an indelible character. He just felt so well realized

N Yeah, he was a fun character to play, and I had only a little time to play it. There's a picture of the real Funny Sonny making out with this guy in the book. So, I wasn't sure what that was about. But then I talked to Danny and he said with those guys, if a cop showed up, they would like kiss in front of the cops just to fuck with them. You know, they did what they wanted to do. It was cool to talk to Danny about the real stuff. He tried to scare me by telling me that the Angels were going to kick my ass because I played one of them in a movie. He was like, "You're fucked!" I later heard from a friend of mine that a guy named George Christie—a former Hell's Angels president for the Ventura chapter—said that he was friends with Sonny and that I nailed it. That made me super happy. It made my whole day.

W That's amazing. Great validation. I'm curious about your creative process, because your output is so broad. Is it the same energy, applied to different mediums?

N Everything's a little bit different. You can sculpt, or you can do photography, and you do it by yourself. So, it's a little more internal, and it's more about yourself. And then, you put the work in a show situation, you put it up on the wall, and you sit back and see what happens. That's how I used to do it. But then, as *The Walking Dead* got bigger, I had more opportunities to do more photography shows and books. I did two photography shows in Paris recently, and then one in Japan. And you know, it becomes all about social media, which is a fucking nightmare. They all want me to post about the shows—that's really what it's about for them. In Paris so many people showed up that the police had to shut

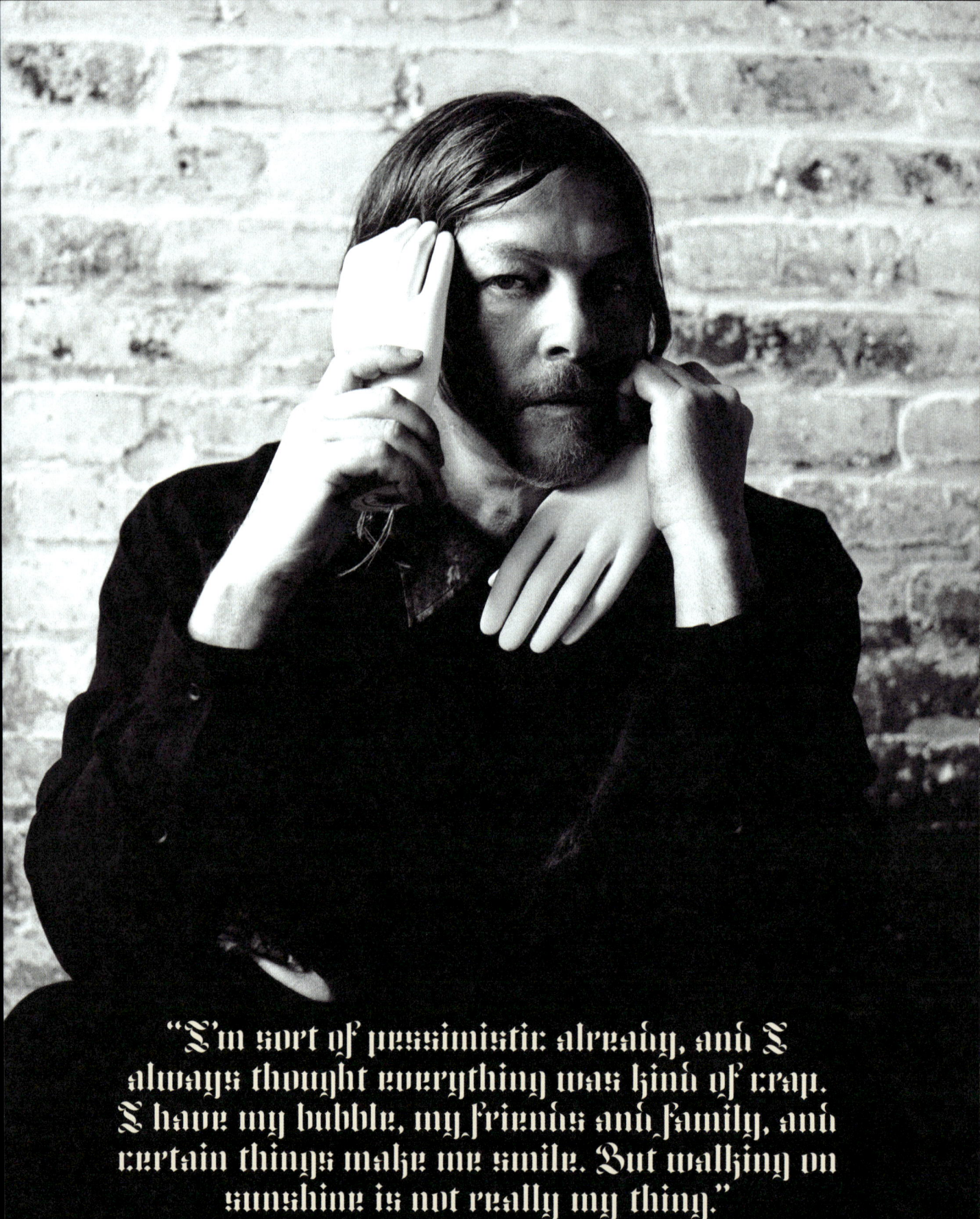

"I'm sort of pessimistic already, and I always thought everything was kind of crap. I have my bubble, my friends and family, and certain things make me smile. But walking on sunshine is not really my thing."

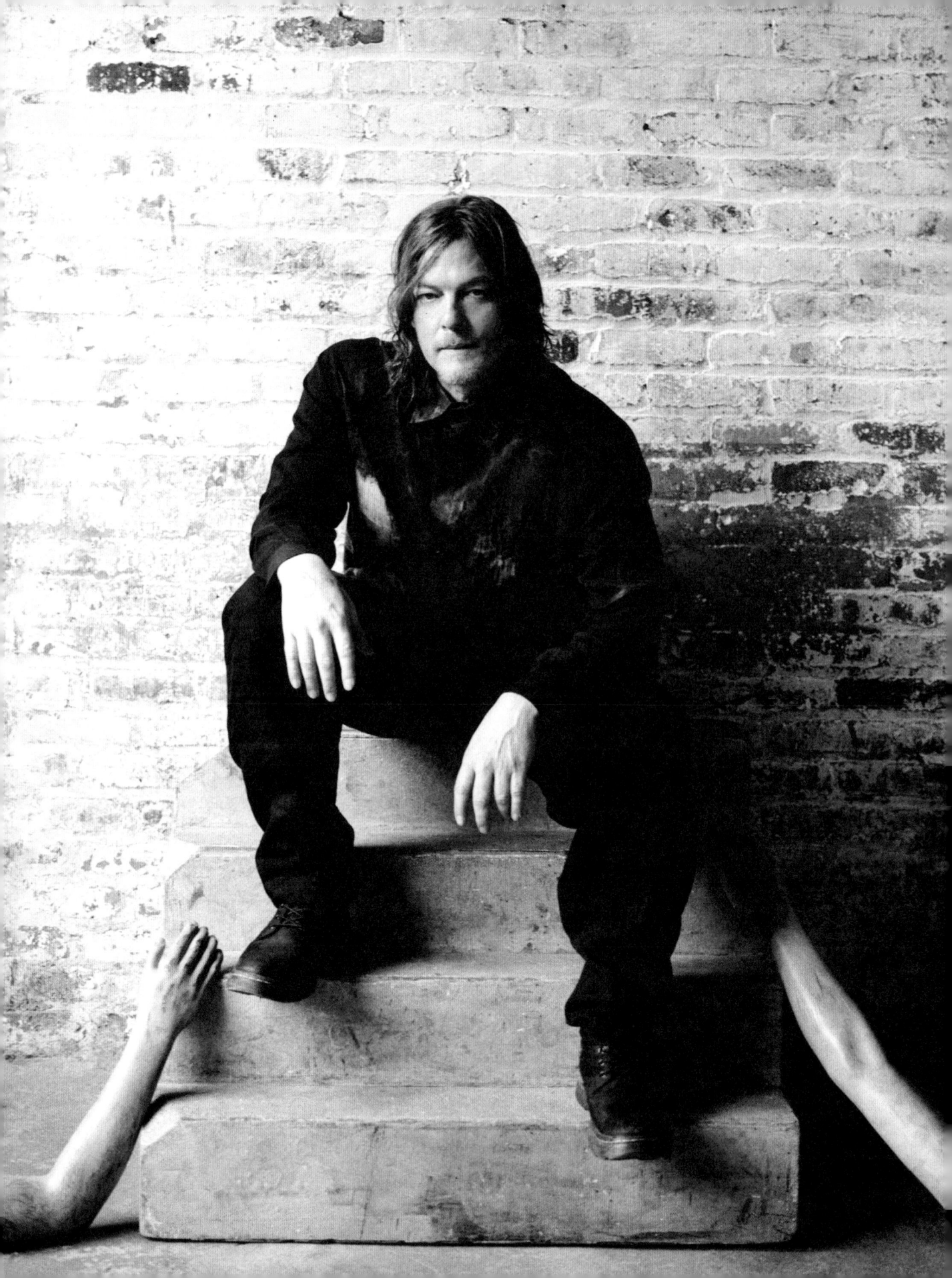

down the street, all because of social media. I miss the days when I could just go to a show, when I was like 25 or something, and I was invisible. It was just about the art, you know, not about celebrity or social media. I loved those days. You'd just bring your work, and if you sold anything, that was your rent for a couple of months, or whatever. My goal when I was a teenager was to live in a big, dark house with a bunch of cats and make artwork. That was what I wanted.

So, it's different processes for different stuff. If you do stuff like that, and you can be a fly on the wall and watch people, you get a truer response to the work. I take a picture of something, and it's my point of view; it's very individual. If I'm playing a character or a movie, I squeeze me in there, but it's a whole bunch of people. It's a different thing.

W Yeah, that makes sense. On the acting side, from your debut in Guillermo del Toro's *Mimic* through to your role as Daryl Dixon, you've depicted characters in apocalyptic situations. Today, we're living in dark times—COVID, climate change, war, political unrest, and everything else. The homeless situation in so many American cities recalls these dark, apocalyptic scenes. Is fiction becoming reality? How do you deal with the darkness?

N I don't know. I mean, I take really grotesque images and make them pretty. And I never really thought about it until people kept telling me that. I started with photography in junior high school, shooting in graveyards at night, and I always liked that type of music, Bauhaus and stuff like that, when I started making art. So, I don't know, I guess I'm sort of pessimistic already, and I always thought everything was kind of crap. I have my bubble and my friends and family, and certain things make me smile. But walking on sunshine is not really my thing. *(Vandal, Wednesday's resident Maine Coon, walks by and captures Norman's attention.)* Oh, wow, there he is. Look at that! He's like a werewolf. They look like a lynx or something, with those ear tufts.

Anyway, we artistically oriented people create our own worlds, and that becomes our reality. There's darkness around it, but I'm always trying to learn and try things. I'm never bored.

W Yeah, I think that's the important thing. When you're learning new things, it's inherently a positive process.

N Yeah, it is.

W And it seems like Big Bald Head and Big Bald Gallery (Norman's production company and forum for his art, respectively) give you plenty of opportunities on that front. Where'd that name come from?

N Yeah, for sure. The name came from a Laurie Anderson concert my mom took me to when I was little. She had a song ("Sharkey's Song") with the lyrics "Sun's coming up, like a big bald head." Years later, I started doing everything under the name Big Bald Head. I think it started after an earthquake in Japan—I have a soft spot for Japan, and I was making these little DVDs of movies and

trying to sell them to contribute to the Japanese people because they had this disaster. And then my photography books started happening, and then the art shows and then everything just sort of became Big Bald Head. Once I was with Debbie Harry at a movie, and we ran into Lou Reed and Laurie Anderson, who were a couple. I was elbowing Debbie, I'm like, "Oh my God, I'm trying to put together this book of photography, and I want to call it *The Sun's Coming Up Like a Big Bald Head*." And she tells Laurie, and Laurie says to send her the photographs, and if she likes them, she'll say yes to me using her title. So, I sent her the photographs, and she liked them, and I got the green light.

W You were at the right place at the right time.

N Yeah, it was crazy. I mean, I'd already started using Big Bald Head, but the name of the book of photography was *The Sun's Coming Up Like a Big Bald Head*, which is a line from her song directly. So, now, everything is Big Bald Head, you know? I recently released my *In Transit* photography book, I have a whiskey coming out, and my production company has a bunch of projects that are happening, including an Edward Gorey thing "Neglected Murderesses."

W I'm excited about your upcoming horror/mystery film *Pendulum,* in which you play a friend who introduces the central couple to a mysterious retreat. This film marks Mark Heyman's directorial debut, with Darren Aronofsky producing—both known for intense psychological stories. What was it like collaborating on set under that creative tone?

N It's still a little too early to be talking about the film—but I can say that I'm looking forward to folks seeing it. New Mexico was great to film in.

W Plus, *The Boondock Saints 3* is coming next year, right?

N Yeah, it is. *(Norman's daughter, Nova, suddenly bursts into the room.)* Hey, Nova, how was camp?

N My favorite was the pool time.

N Did you kiss anybody?

N No.

W How old are you? I distinctly remember being four and how much fun it was, but I can't remember too much before then.

N I'm six. Four was horrible. That was drama queen.

W Really? *(laughter)* What do you like to do?

N I do calculations now.

N Yeah, she's big on the calculator. She does calculations.

W Do you have your own calculator?

N Yeah!

W That's good; that will come in handy. Just don't drop it in the pool!

N She's gonna drop me in the pool. *(laughter)*

W Sounds like a perfect day. Enjoy the big, bald sun. ∎

Between Darkness and Desire

—

*Norman Reedus's photography lives in the shadows,
where beauty and menace overlap.*

Photographs *Norman Reedus*

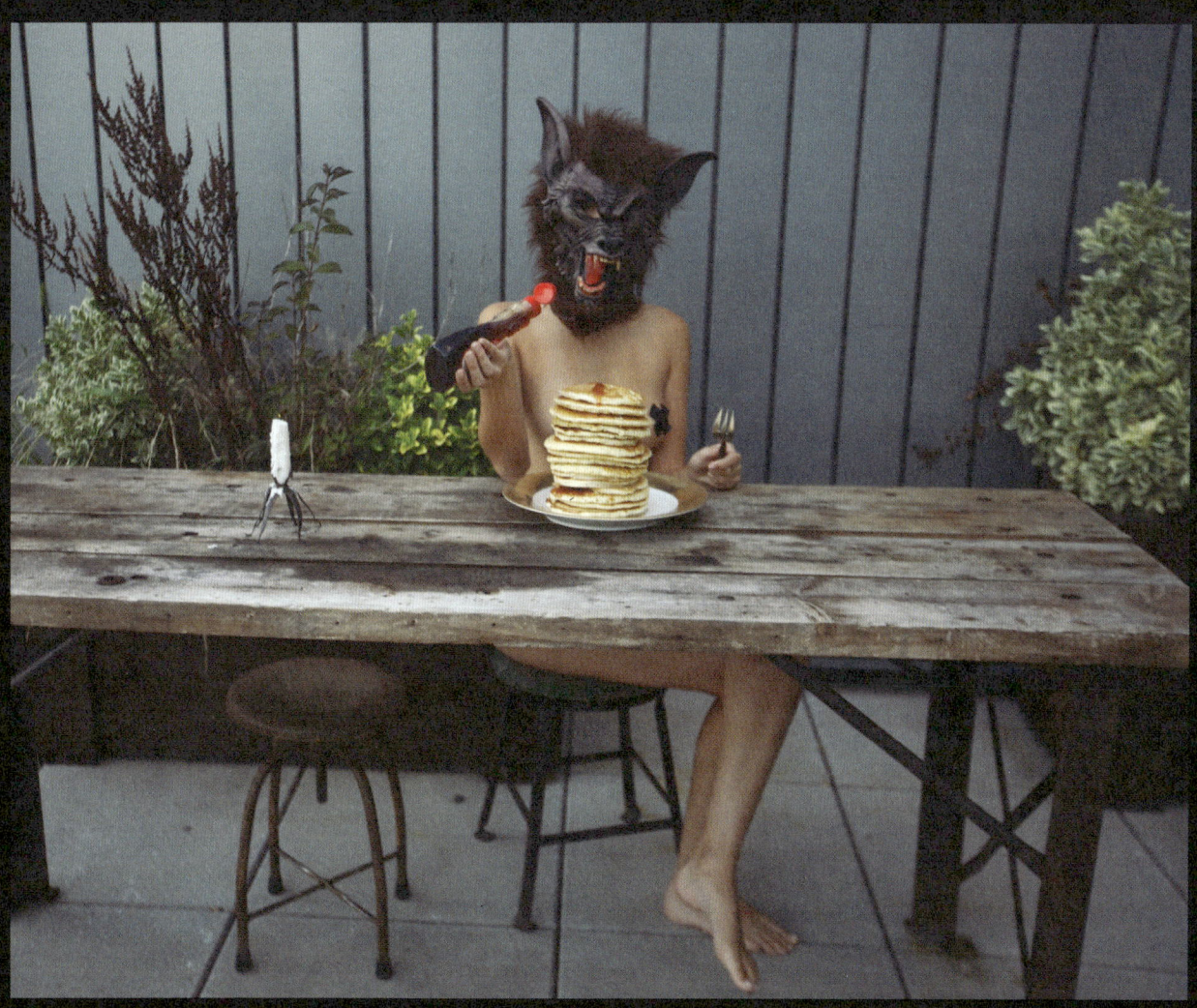

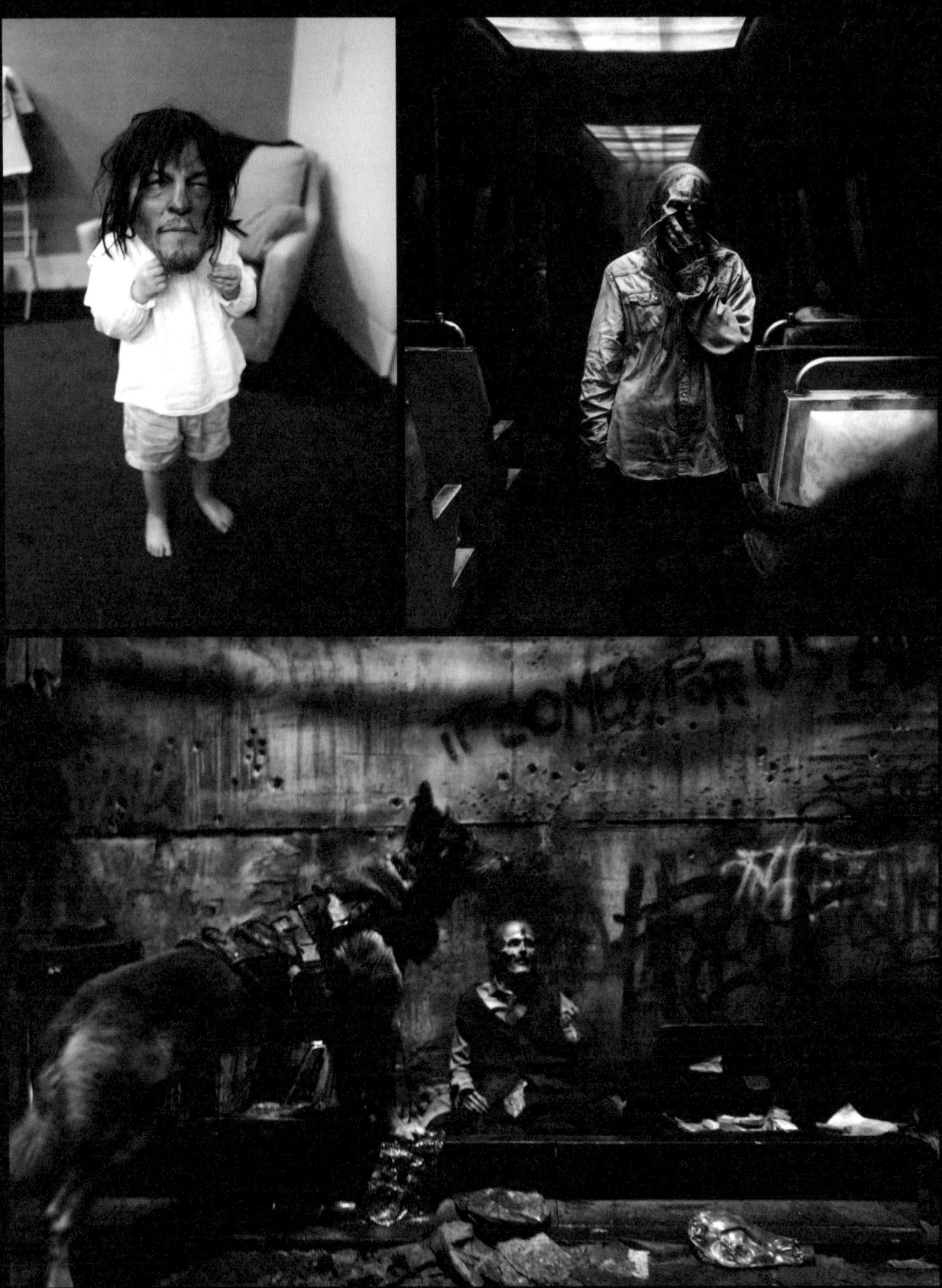

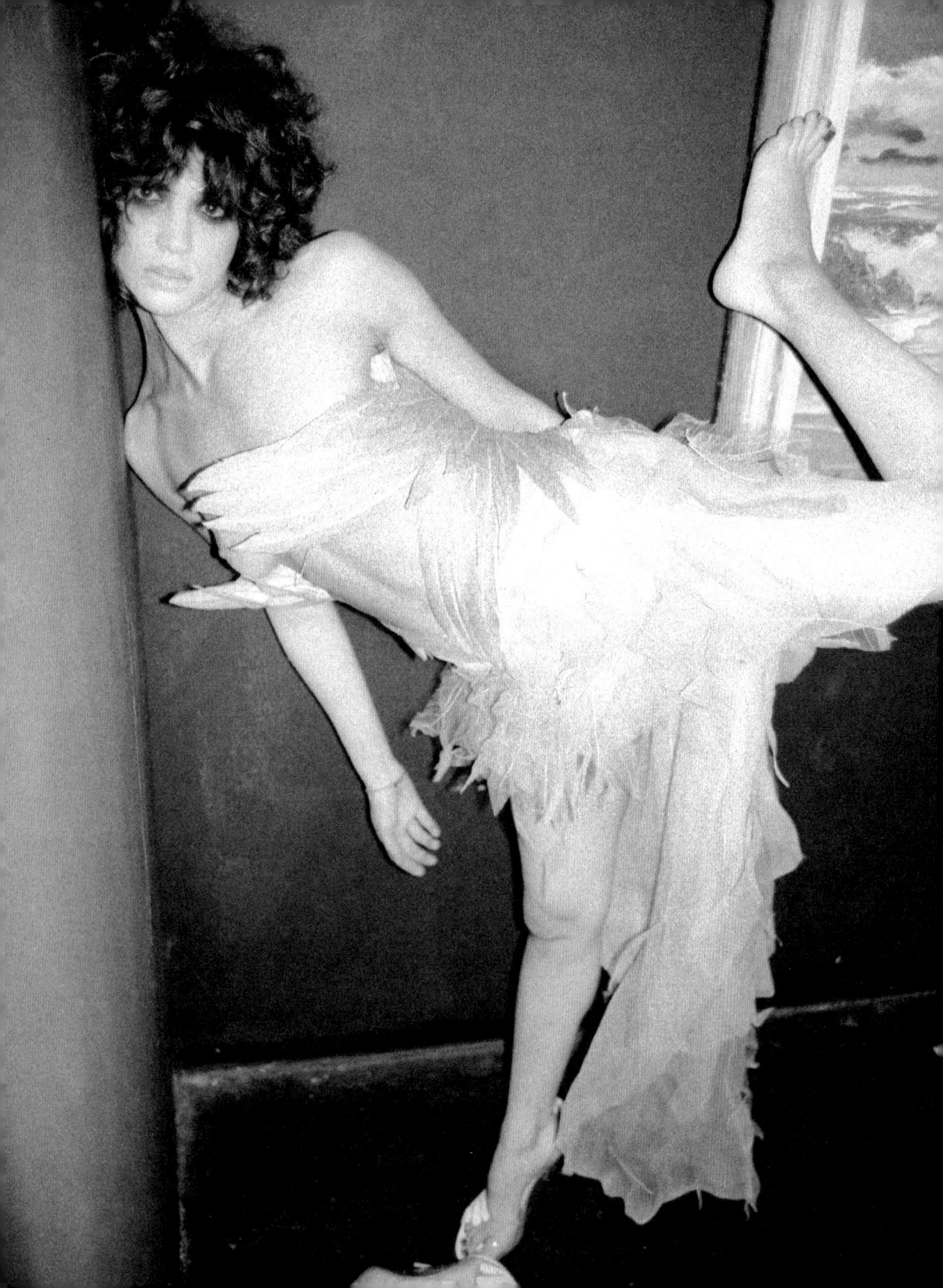

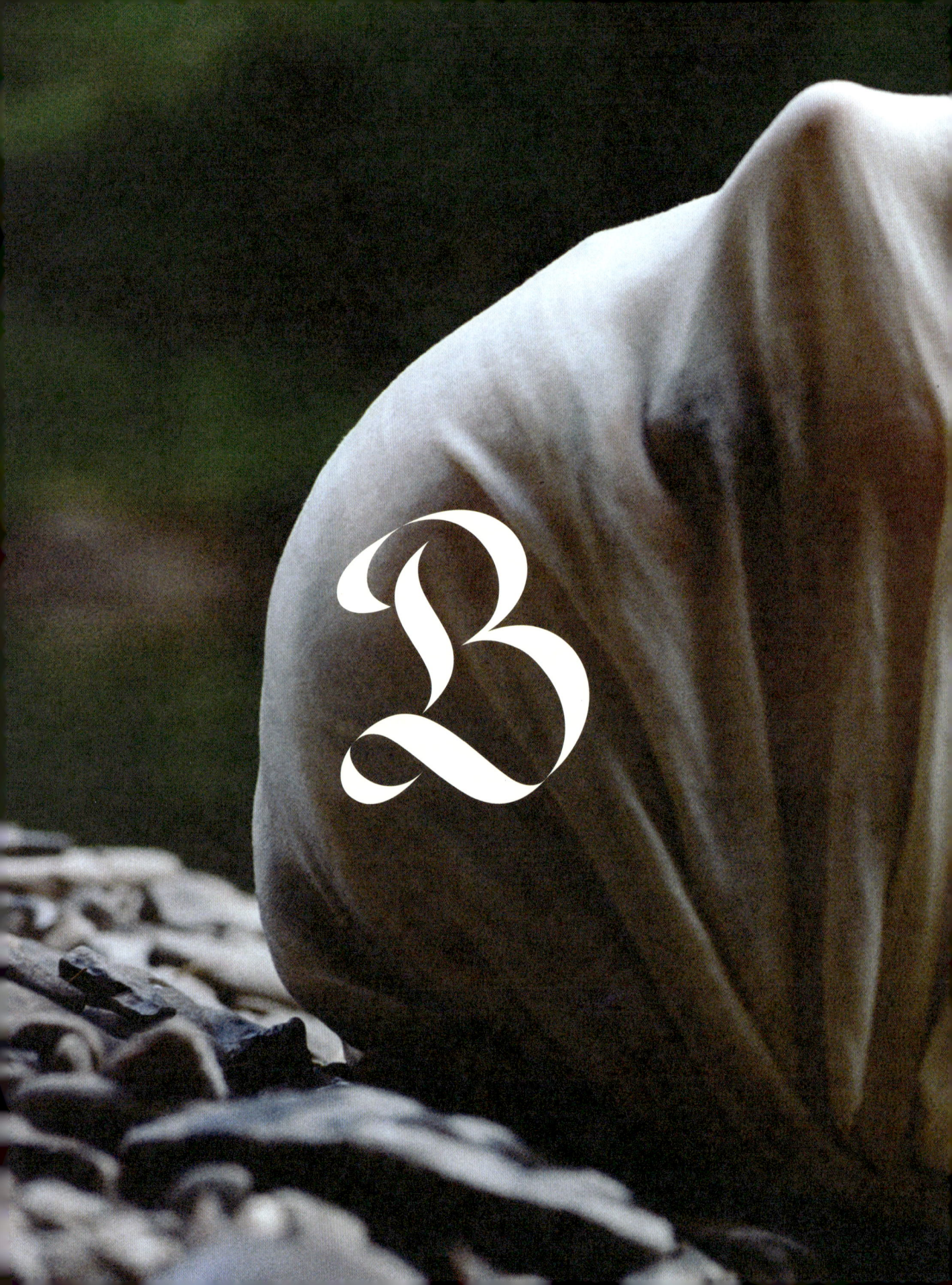

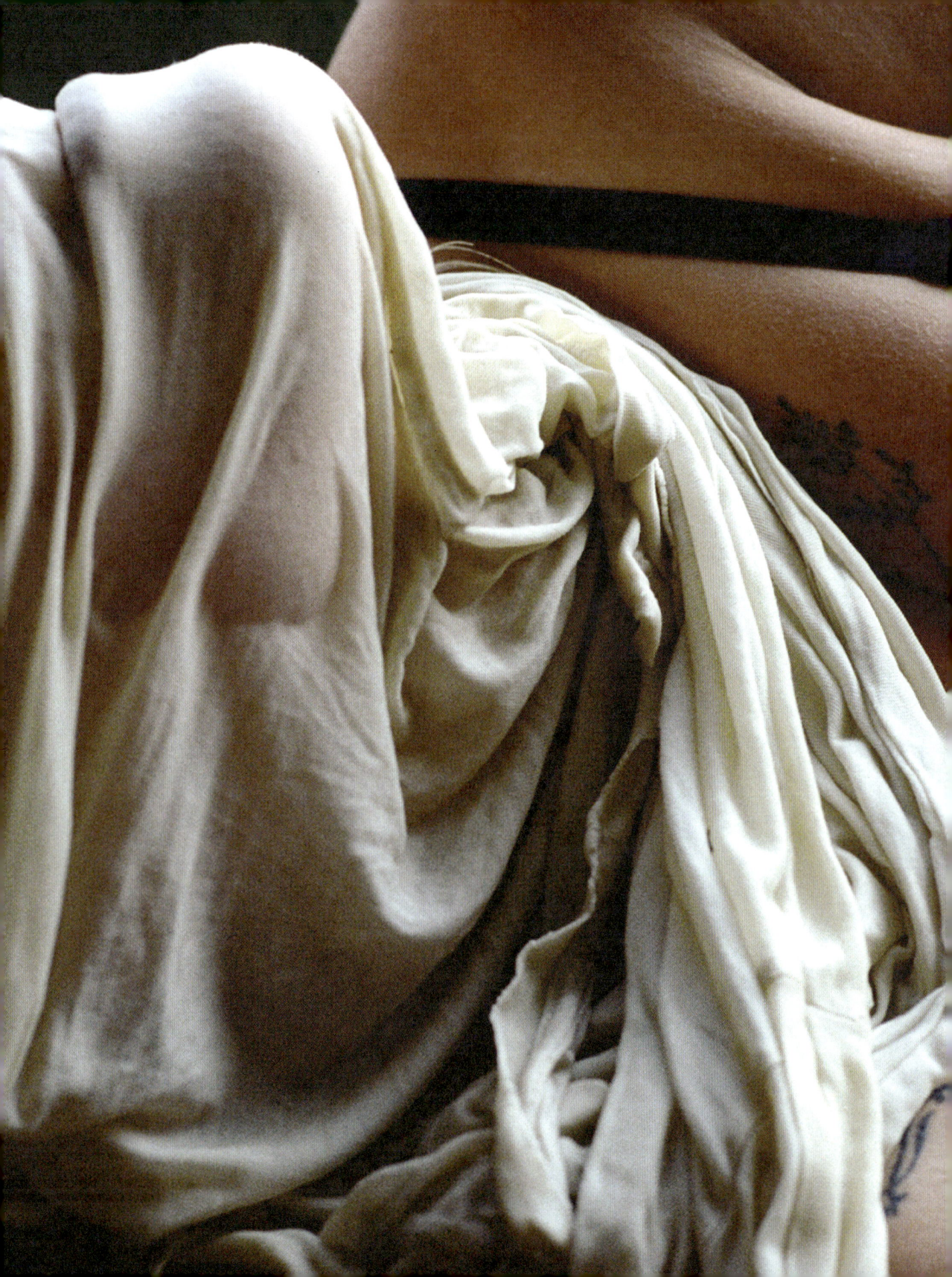

BOY HARSHER

Words *André Obin* / **Photographs** *Rebekah Campbell*

Falling Through Water

Fresh off a summer DJ gig in Montreal, Jae Matthews and Augustus Muller, of the incredible Massachusetts band Boy Harsher, arrive at the *Wednesday* interview, having just narrowly escaped death.

"We had just gotten home, and it was raining intensely. The moment we shut the door, lightning struck. It was massive. The actual lighting moved the ground around us." The duo makes music that feels electri-fied and dangerous on every listen, so it makes perfect sense that our beloved EBM heroes barely outpace a lightning strike to share their tale.

Matthews and Muller met in Savannah, Georgia, while both studying film. Matthews would write screenplays, and Muller would compose scores for the nonexistent films. They'd exchange marked scripts for cassette tapes filled with sparse melodies. Gradually and steadily, the duo grew into an artistic force, amassing five albums of evocative, cinematic, master-level electronic music under the moniker Boy Harsher. Over their 10-year career, Jae and Gus have gone from playing basement DIY shows to performing at Coachella earlier this year.

Despite their most recent brush with death, both Jae and Gus show up to our interview looking incredibly vibrant, relaxed, and youthful, especially for a band that's been touring for the past decade. Gus is wearing a fitted white tee that shows off his svelte figure, wielding a charming Southern drawl. Jae is wearing a stunning black blouse—her blue eyes piercing, her skin radiant. They both seem acutely aware of the moment, articulate and tempered, careful not to talk over one another. They take turns fielding questions related to their specific role in the band, telepathically triaging one by one.

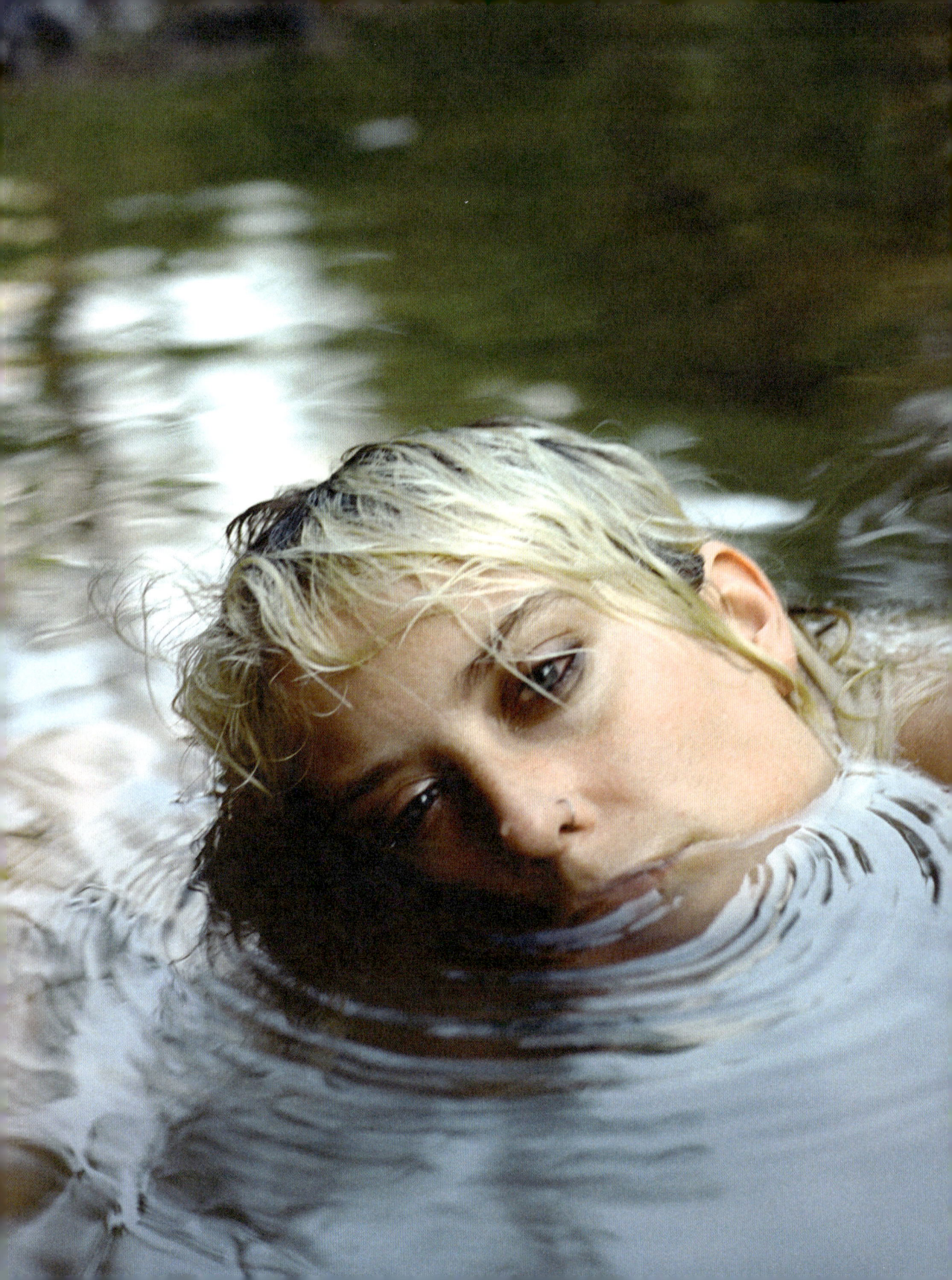

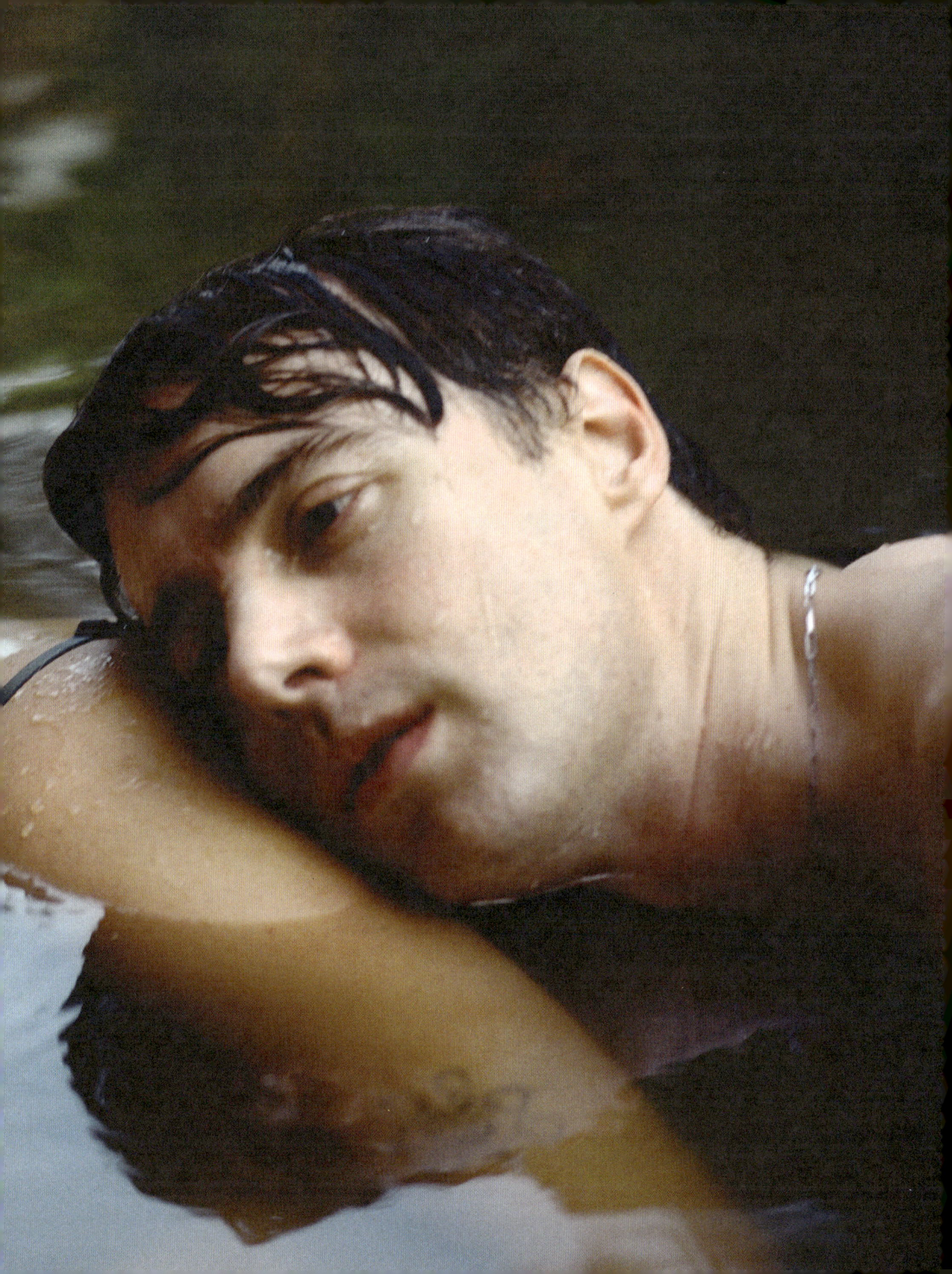

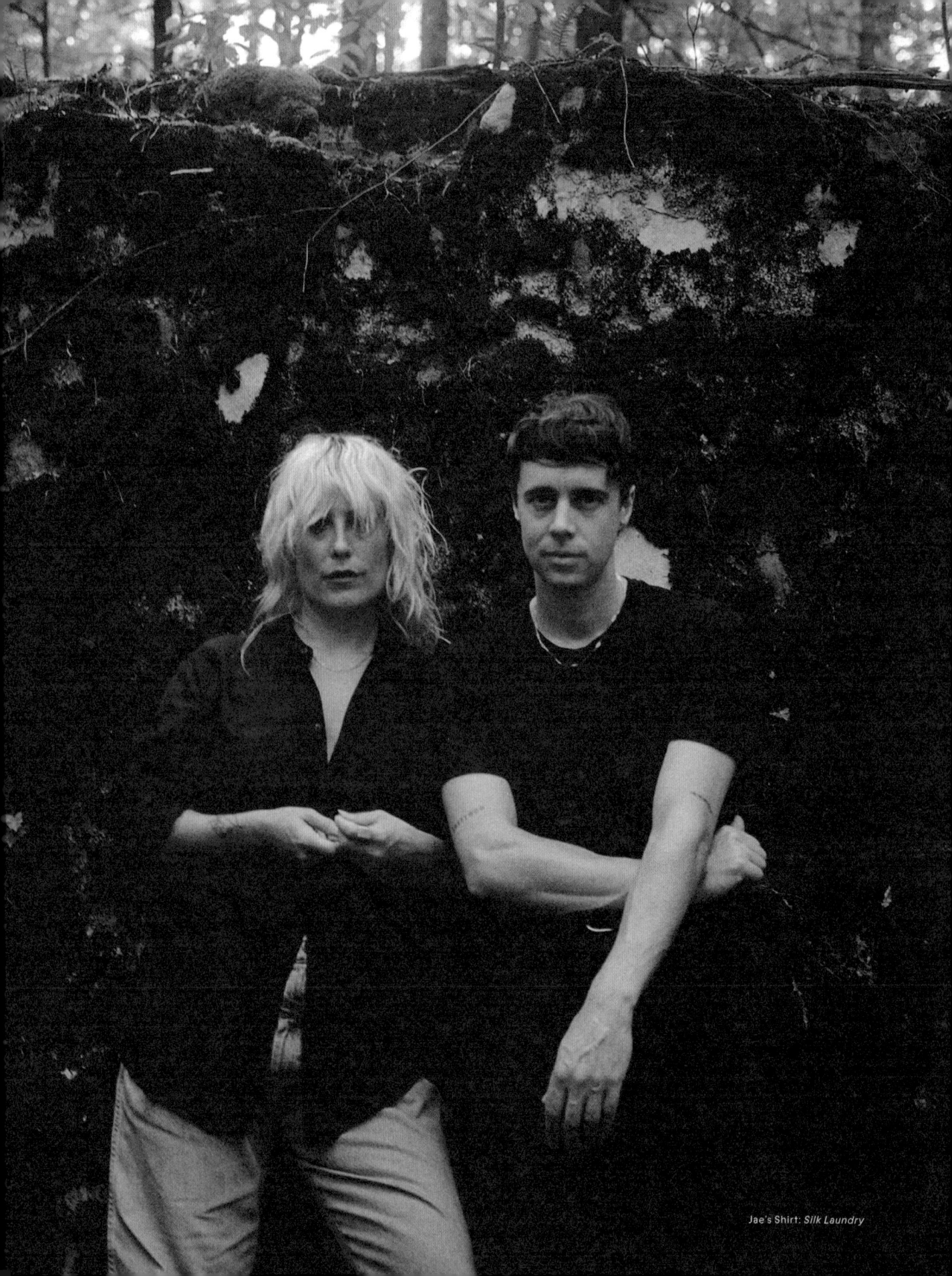

Jae's Shirt: *Silk Laundry*

W So, curious how your photoshoot for *Wednesday* went?

G Great. Rebekah Campbell is the photographer. We always wanted to work with her since college. With photos, we've become more trusting. If I like a photographer's work like Rebekah's, I just go with it.

W You were at the peak of touring when the pandemic struck. I imagine that was very tough given the success you were riding. Can you tell me about the band during that period?

J There wasn't intentional decision-making at that time. We had to slow down from constant touring. I thought, "Now I finally get to spend summers in western Mass." It illuminated the fact that what we were doing was very delicate, and perhaps we were taking our career for granted a little bit. The biggest thing that came from that moment was that Gus and I had always had an interest in making films together, and that's when we decided to make *The Runner.* Most of the pandemic I spent writing and developing *The Runner.*

W *The Runner* is incredibly impressive and a true work of art. Is it true that you wrote the music after you had written the script and shot the footage?

G Half and half. We had some songs that we had initially written the screenplay for, and when it came time to edit, we wrote some more songs to match the picture.

W It seems the band is working within very specific parameters, perhaps based on limitations. Is it intentionally stripped back? The timbre of the group sounds very crisp and inviting. Do you think that some of that has to do with limitations around gear or a writing discipline?

G We developed our sound based around limitations. When we first started, we didn't have a lot of gear, and we developed our sound that way. It's something that really resonated with me and a style that I wanted to continue with. Ten years later, I have too many synths and too many options sometimes. We designed our sound when we had limitations, and we have carried that aesthetic forward. Also, you've got to come up with some techniques if you are going to make something in a timely manner. I've certainly learned this again with my soundtrack work. You should just pick a few synths to use, or you'll just spend forever cycling through new sounds.

W I get the sense that the gear is not the important part. Your music sounds dangerous, and perhaps that's part of the sex appeal. I have a DJ residency at the club ManRay in Cambridge every first Friday. I play "Come Closer" every time I'm there. It works every single spin. Can you speak about making that track and putting together the album *Careful?*

G "Come Closer" was about two and half years old before it appeared on *Careful,* and some of those songs on *Careful* were written in the studio almost right before the album was finished, so it spans a long time. I've always said that we've been trying to make one song, forever. I've got an idea for a song in my head, and I still haven't made it yet. For *Careful,* I was in that cycle where I was trying to make that singular song, and all the songs on that record are like renditions of this one song in my head.

W Very cool. And Jae, you write all the lyrics for the band?

J Yes, I write all the lyrics except, famously, the chorus for "Pain."

W Ah yes, the underground smash.

J Gus approached me in 2013. We were not friends at the time. We were, I think..., we had been kind of lovers and then we got into some big fight, and he approached me trying to record this song because he had the best chorus. He said "Try saying, 'pain breaks the rhythm.'" And that's where that song came from.

W Damn.

G I do most of the instrumentals. I have helped with lyrics in the studio. There's some finessing going on.

W Gus, when you're making music, do you know quickly whether something is going to be for Boy Harsher or a soundtrack?

G Well, with work on a soundtrack, I'm working on a tight deadline, and I'm writing to picture, and it's like, yeah, I have to make soundtrack music. I'm never in the studio just writing and putting things aside for soundtrack work.

W I know you are partners and that you've had some intense things happen with your family. Is that why you were in Northampton, MA?

J My twin sister lives in Kingston, NY, so that's why we visit there a lot. I really love Kingston. We moved to western MA to be closer to both families. Gus is from western Massachusetts. It was an attempt to get closer to my mom, who was in upstate New York at the time.

W From what I can see as an outsider, Boy Harsher has been very resilient. I'm wondering, are you taking a break now, or do you have new projects in the works?

J My mom died last year after five or six years of decline. During that time, to help with her care, I was attempting to remain as present as possible and visit weekly. It really took a toll on the band and my relationship. It's so nice to hear that we were projecting resilience. I don't know if I've ever really felt that. You know, when you slip, and you just keep falling down? The grief cycle is like that, like falling through water. After she died last year, I think I needed to do some introspection. It's hard to say. I've given 10 years of my life, every moment of my life, primarily to Boy Harsher and secondarily to my mother. I've reached a funny position where I need to reevaluate what life is about, and maybe that's where I am now. I've been trying to do a lot of projects that sit outside of the band. Don't get me wrong, I love Boy Harsher, and I want to have an album right now, but it's just so hard to write.

W Write for music, or just write in general?

J I'm having writer's block, and I think it's just part of it all. I do screenwriting. It's a process that I find incredibly rewarding and challenging. However, at this point, I'm not sure how I feel about anything.

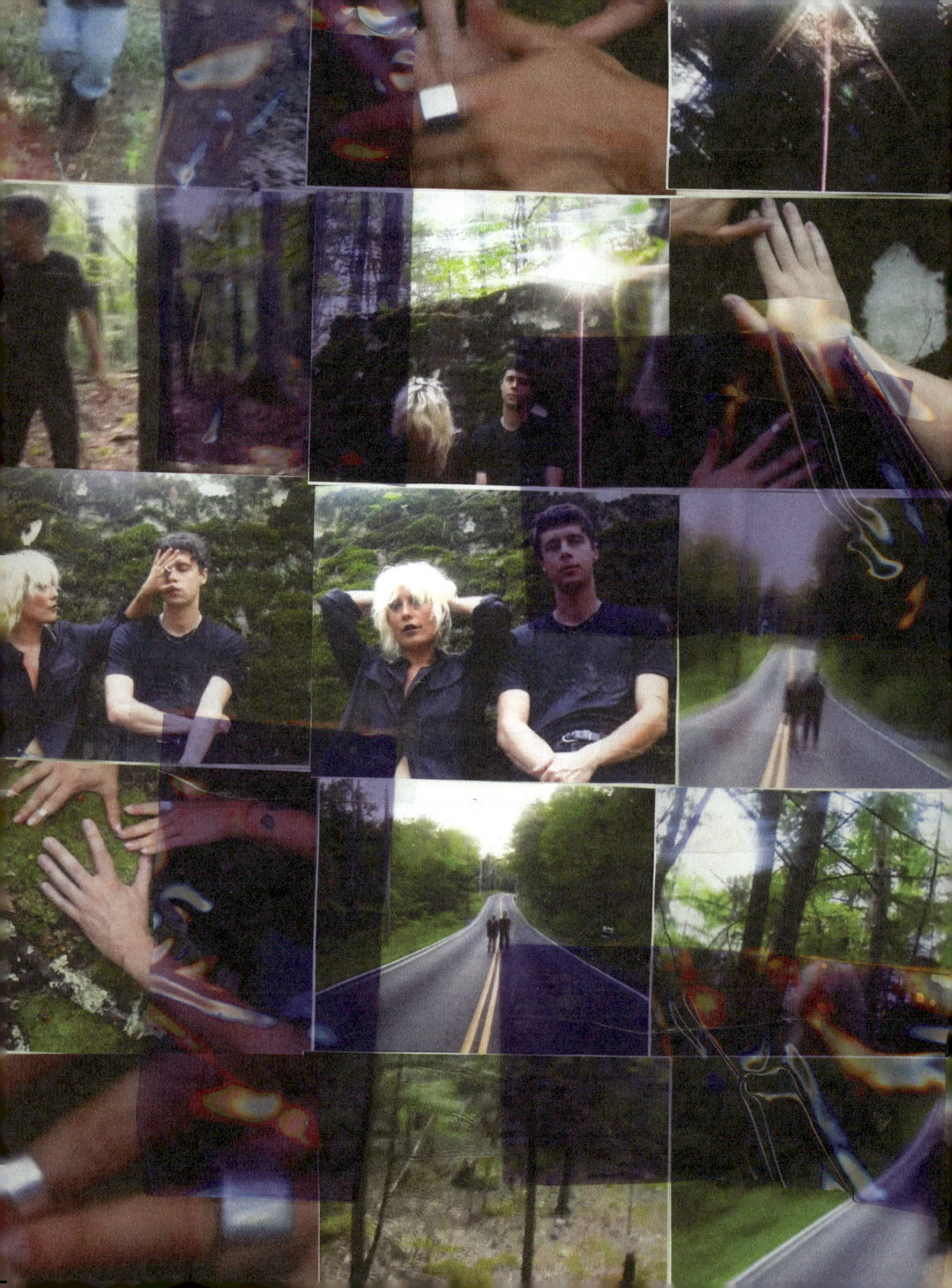

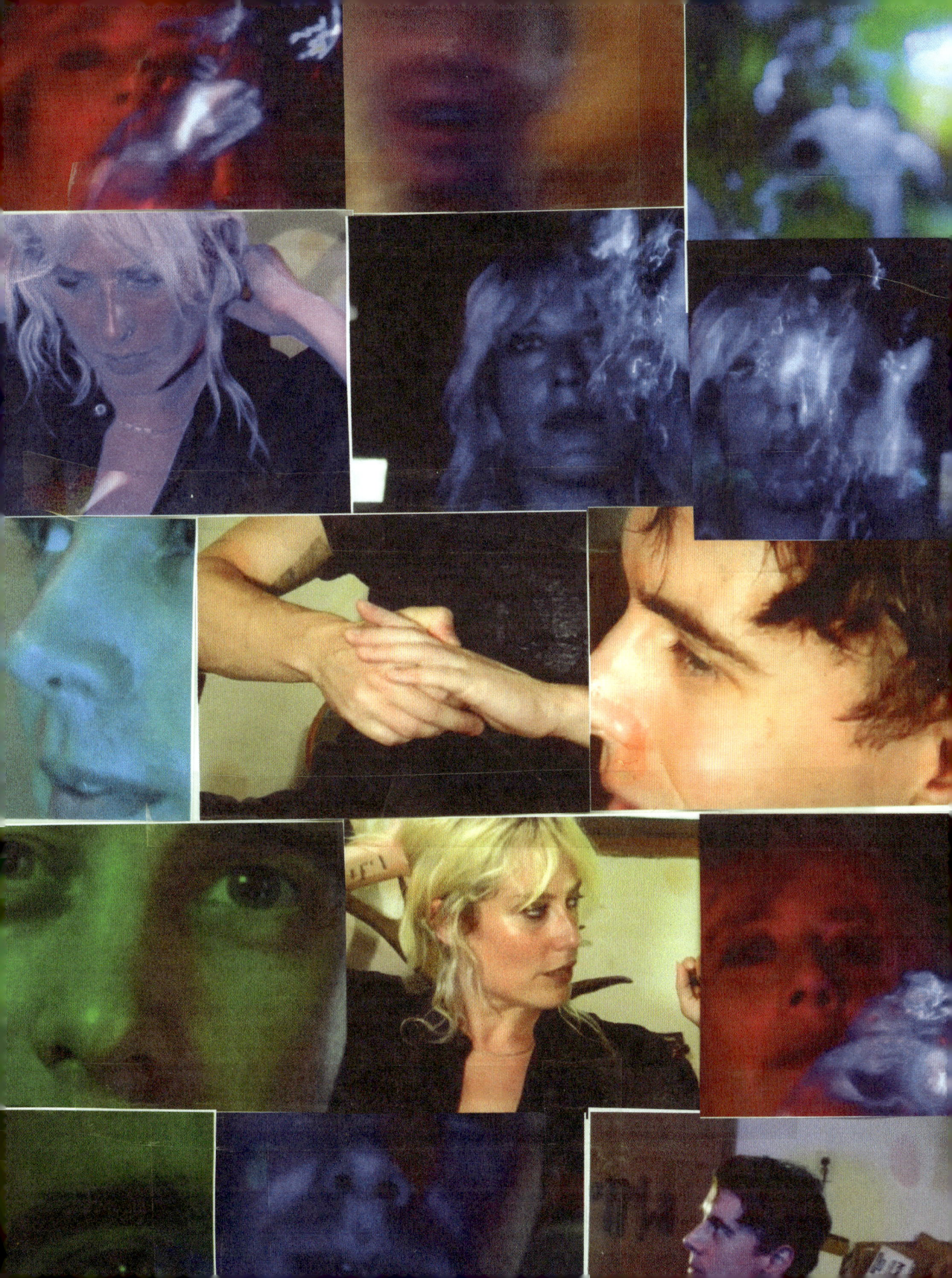

> ## "I've made some horrible decisions in my life for no good reason other than to embody a fleeting feeling."

—*Jae Matthews*

I hate that my identity is so wrapped up in my personal pain and grief, but then, here I am, and it's like the only thing I can talk about. So, I understand where Gus is coming from, too. It's important to acknowledge all the amazing opportunities that we have and all our amazing projects.

It's an interesting time for an interview as we're in between projects right now. Usually, we're promoting a record or something like that. But right now, we're sort of in the writing phase.

We're trying to write Boy Harsher slower this time, too. It's a very determined attempt to not rush an album.

We're five albums in at this point. So, I was just trying to find something to get excited about. We were touring for so long after *The Runner* came out. I don't think any of us anticipated that we'd have so much touring after *The Runner* because it was kind of like a soundtrack; it's not quite a full album, but we hit the road for like two years straight nonstop. It sucks up a lot of time. You get to the end of that, and you've been playing the songs for so long, and you have been immersed in the band for so long, you need to just follow what excites you. At least for me, I need to follow what excites me. Hitting the studio, writing an LP, and touring it for two to three years is not exactly what I want to be doing. We found some success with *The Runner* that was very exciting. We made a low budget indie long form short film. It was really... redeeming, and for me, it was something I wanted to keep exploring. So, Jae and I, since that came out, we've been writing screenplays. The last couple of years, we've been fundraising for a screenplay that we're trying to get off the ground. And now we've started another screenplay. We've been surrounding ourselves with the film industry and trying to break into that. We're finding that it is a little bit colder than the music industry. We've decided that the next Boy Harsher project is going to be a feature-length film with an album to go along with it. A similar approach to *The*

Runner. We learned a lot with that last endeavor, and we'll know how to do it differently. I think the big thing is that we needed to write a feature film.

W My Animal is a feature film, but that's not your film?

J I wrote the screenplay, and Gus did the soundtrack, but ultimately, it's Jacqueline Castel's film.

W They had a bit of a budget. Is it a different game when you collaborate in that setting?

J It's interesting. They did have a budget, but we weren't included in production. We weren't on set or anything. Being physically there wasn't possible. I wasn't around.

G It seemed like a fun film to be on set though.

J They shot in the northern region of Ontario in the winter.

G It definitely taught us a lot. It took us to the next step.

J It taught me a lot about writing and collaborating with someone that I did not know. Jacqueline came to the script after it was optioned. It was all so foreign to me. Filmmaking is a constant lesson in letting go.

W You've talked a lot about the capacity for evil. Is this something that you are grappling with during creativity? Is it something you are facing or fighting?

J I fear that deep down, ultimately, I'm a bad person. I have tendencies that are incredibly self-destructive, and when facing that behavior, it's proof that I'm a bad person, and it's why you lose everything that you love. It's this classic abandonment fear; it's not necessarily based in reality, but I am very interested. Is the capacity for evil just selfish behavior? What's the difference between selfish behavior and righteous behavior? Ultimately, I serve myself, and that makes me righteous. With a lot of my written work, I explore self-destruction and transformation because those are processes that really appeal to me. They are me. I've made some horrible decisions in my life for no good reason other than to embody a fleeting feeling.

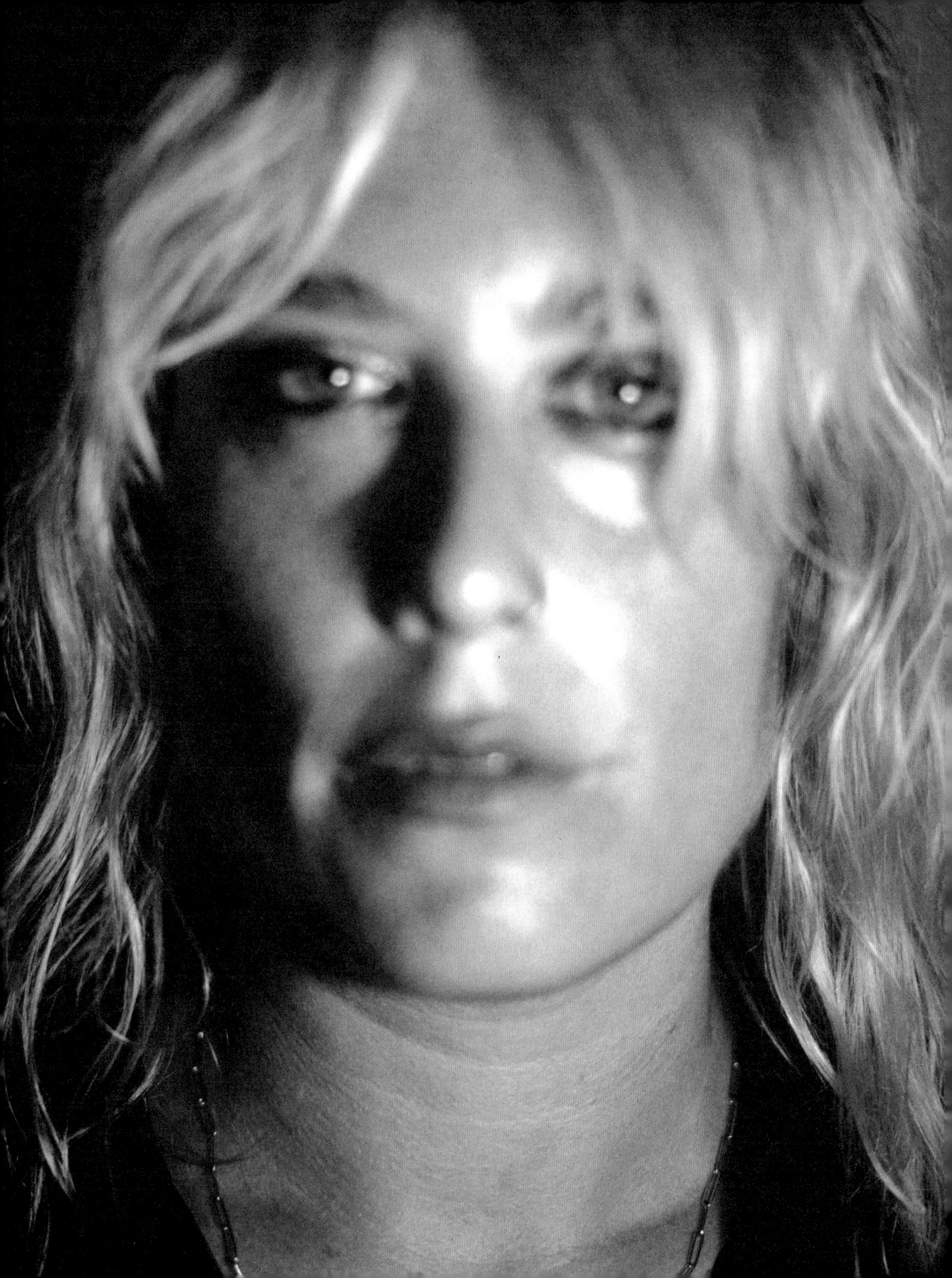

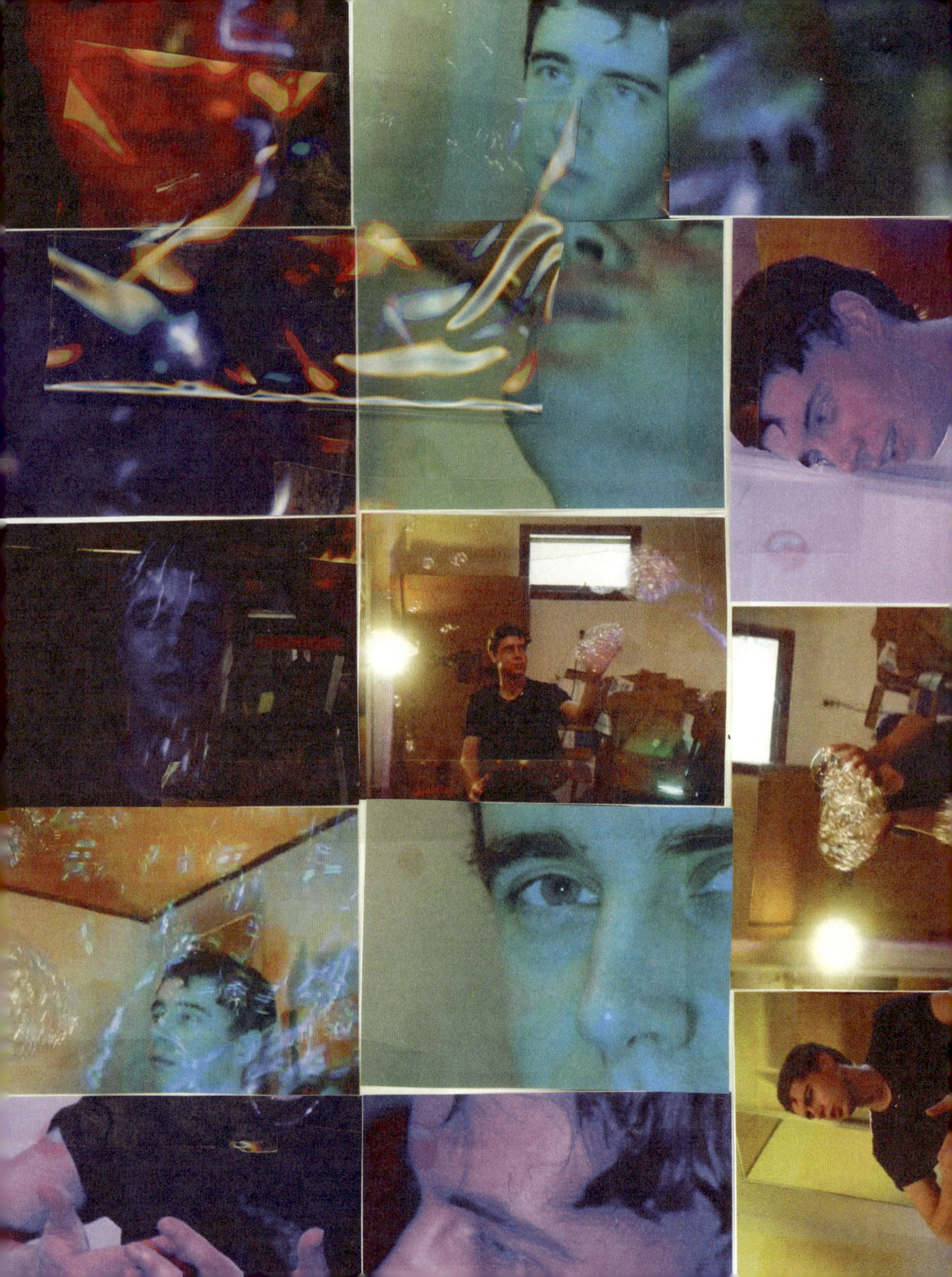

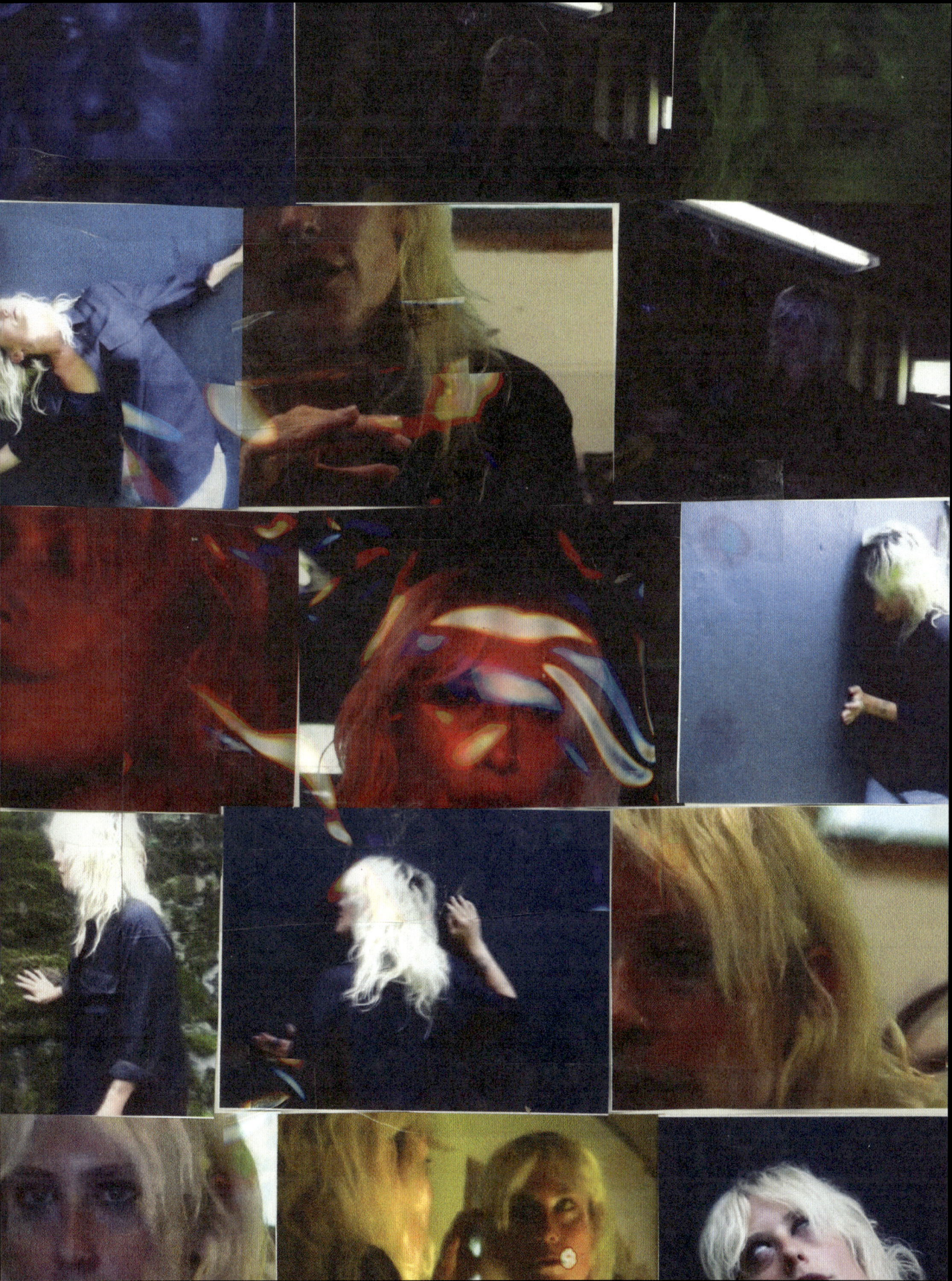

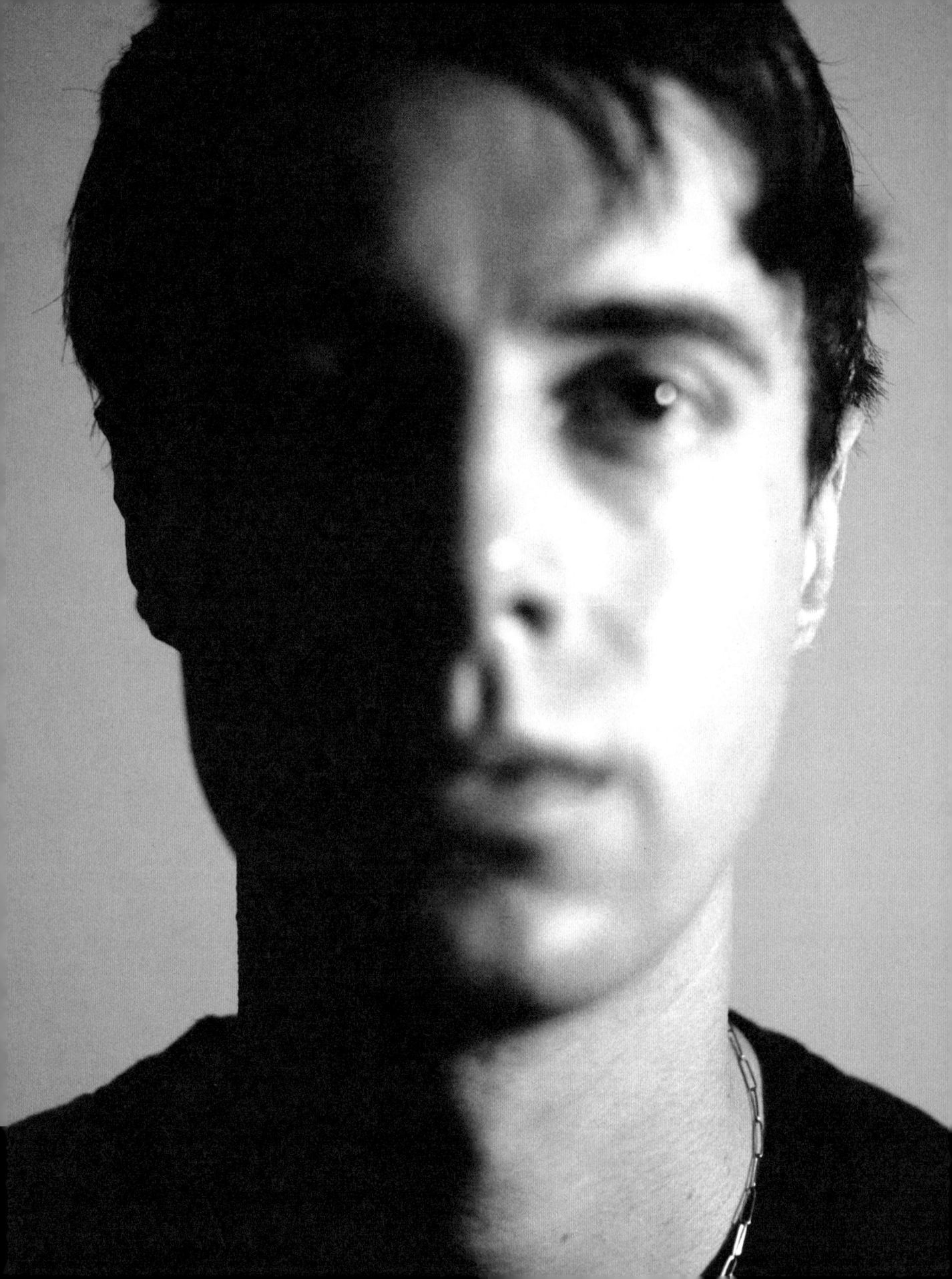

Wednesday asks about the recurring image of strong female collaborators and characters in the group's themes, such as Nedda Afsari (Muted Fawn), Kristina Esfandiari (King Woman), Sara Cummings, and Mariana Saldaña (Ms. BOAN). Gus points out that they also have many male collaborators, including Maurizio Baggio, who tours with the band and acts as a Swiss-army-knife-like third member who helps with mixing, mastering, and running front of house sound for the band whilst traversing the globe. There's also "Autonomy," the stand-out tune from *The Runner* soundtrack featuring Cooper B. Handy (LUCY), the male voice one would imagine Boy Harsher naturally gravitating toward. These collaborations alone prove that the band consistently places their collective art before their individual egos. They are willing to share the spotlight with their amazing group of friends and, in many cases, shine the light directly upon them.

W It seems that there is a great deal of excellent darkwave music right now; there is a strong community, and you are the leaders of the scene. Would you agree?

J If we had to select a genre, I think we would go with electronic body music.

G The few times that I have told people that we're a dark-wave band, my eyes have immediately rolled back in my head, and I've thought, why did I just fucking say that? We don't have guitars, so we can't be a darkwave band.

J I don't think we're the leaders of anything. Do we like the other darkwave people? Yeah. Everyone is super nice.

W It seems like these like-minded artists like TR/ST, they don't have inflated egos.

G These people in modern industrial bands are coming from really DIY backgrounds. None of us are on major labels. We're all just digging through the mud together. I can say for sure that the more you help another person, it just helps everybody and lifts everyone up.

J There's no use in gatekeeping or trying to be posses-sive of some opportunity. Life doesn't work that way. I feel so much more fulfillment in helping others, and I would love to have other people feel that way about me. So many of our contemporaries and peers have this DIY ethos. We were all isolated and lonesome teenagers, and now it's very exciting to have community and have incredible buds.

W Hell yeah!

J I have a weekly phone call with Kontravoid, my best friend. We'll talk for two hours straight about the desert.

W Can you speak about your record label, Nude Club? Was it always your intention to go it alone with a label and retain complete control? You must get a ton of attention from other record labels.

G We started Nude Club in 2018 to release *Careful* and re-release some stuff.

J We had an issue where we were constantly out of print.

G We were looking for a label, and there was interest, but it's just like, it was more complicated. Our manager,

Marco, had this idea that we can do a lot of this ourselves: we don't need to rely on a label. And it ended up being a pretty good decision. I mean, we worked with this label City Slang as sort of the back end of Nude Club. And on *The Runner* and *Careful*, they were big partners. They were released using the name Nude Club, so you don't get the name recognition of signing with a bigger label. We felt that we didn't need that. People were fans of the band.

J And it awarded us the opportunity to have more control over the release schedule, which obviously, currently, is helpful. And then also, be in print.

G It's hard to say what would have happened had we gone a different route.

W Going it alone has its challenges, too.

J You don't think about everything. It's impossible for a singular person or a singular entity like the band to consider every element of something as big as a release and something as minor as an Instagram post. It's almost psychotic. The number of details that you need to have organized and understand. And plan. Oftentimes we've found ourselves really frustrated because we are the ones responsible for these logistics and these details. The frustrating element of, man, I wish we could have planned better. It falls on us, 100%.

W From an outsider looking in, I can't imagine either of you doing anything else other than taking care of your art day in and day out, 24/7. Can you tell us what the rest of the year looks like? Is Mexico City the only show you are playing for the rest of the year?

G We're going to announce some more dates around that. We're going to play Guatemala and South America, too.

J It will be really fun. We love Mexico City. I pushed for this show initially because we have a friend that is starting a residency in the mountains outside of Mexico City. I thought, we could do the show, and then I could go live at this residency. Now I don't even know if that is a possibility. That was my big incentive. I love the fans. I don't want to say the best Boy Harsher fans in the world, but they are excellent people, and I kind of wanted to go live in the mountains in Mexico for an indefinite amount of time, but that's very cheeky.

W Do you guys take off time from each other, or are you always together?

J We take off a lot of time.

W Why are you together right now? I know you were just in Montreal, which is one of your other favorite cities. Gus had a DJ gig. How'd that go?

G Great! Montreal. Great town. I enjoyed it. DJed on the roof. There were fireworks. It was Bastille Day.

W And Jae, you go to the gigs and chill, dance, vibe?

J Some of them. I go to the ones that feel appealing, and I love Montreal, so I was thinking it would be fun to go up there. I'll probably go to Bushwick as well in September.

W Let's talk about the correlation between your recorded work and live performance. You do not wear a mask. You present on stage as who you really are. Is that fair to say?

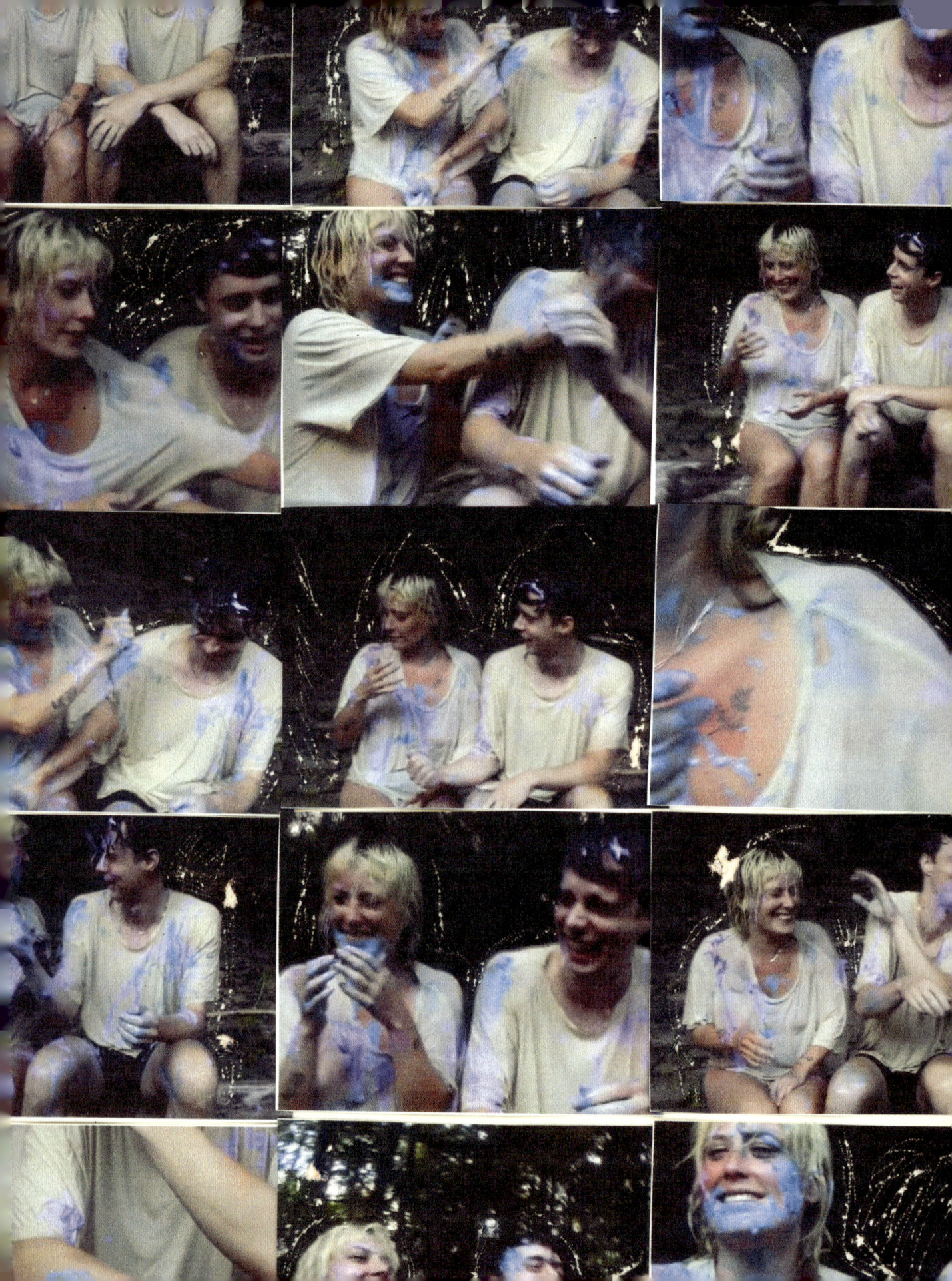

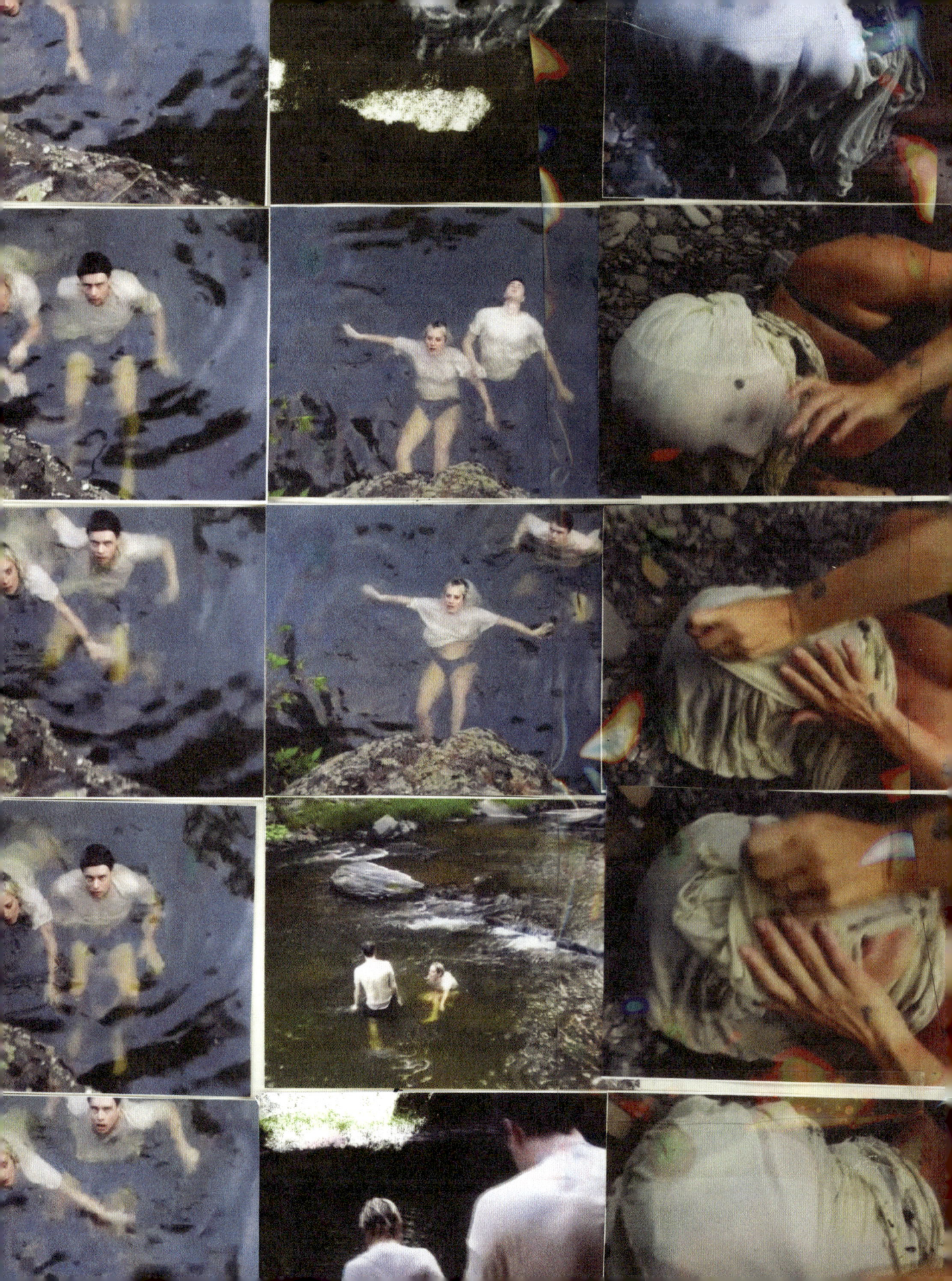

G I'm not sure I agree with that. I think when we play live, I'm myself, but with the albums, we are trying to be filmmakers.

J That's interesting because live is the time I feel least like myself. It's this persona; it's out of body. To get there, I kind of have to embody someone else.

G When I'm playing live, I'm trying to be sincere. The albums are fiction.

J The persona, for me, is someone who is strong and ferocious, and maybe someone who can utilize their pain and grief in a way that's pretty aggressive. My writing is authentic to me. These are letters, repetitive mantras that I say to myself to help me overcome the sad space.

G The album and the live show are not connected. You design a live show, and it's a logistical thing. Boy Harsher, the albums, that's the persona.

W Can you speak about the recurring characters in your imagery, such as the Desperate Man who appears in *Careful* and *The Runner*?

J Narratives are important to us; they connect our themes across releases. *The Desperate Man* represents just that, desperation, and transformation through darkness.

W Have Chris and Cosey inspired you?

G They're a big influence for me. I listened to Throbbing Gristle in high school but didn't understand the whole context, with like Psychic TV and Chris and Cosey. I sort of forgot about it. And then we were on tour in 2014. We

were in South Carolina, and I bought Chris and Cosey's *Songs of Love and Lust* on vinyl and got into it from there. They've definitely been a major influence for us. When we're writing a song, there are sounds in there that reflect our love for them.

J I love Cosey so much, too.

W I love her, too. I read her book *Art, Sex, Music* last summer. What an amazing story of resilience.

J Anytime we're in the UK, I attempt to reach out and invite them to a show. They haven't attended yet, but we'll see.

W Before we wrap, can we quickly talk horror films? Are there are any films that have done if for you recently?

J I loved *It Follows*. We got to watch it in Detroit where it was filmed. It was very special to watch it in a theater there.

G I got really into *The Ring* this year.

J I just spent two months in Chicago. I love *Candyman*. The remake was admirable, but the original is just so stunning. It was a movie about gentrification that became a self-fulfilling prophecy. It's a strange and unsettling thing.

G We love David Cronenberg. Boy Harsher follows the same approach of using a genre to convey a narrative.

W I think Gus will get asked to do more scores. I was listening to the *My Animal* soundtrack, and it reminded me of Jóhann Jóhannsson's score for *Mandy*.

G Thanks. It's definitely something I want to get more into. ▪

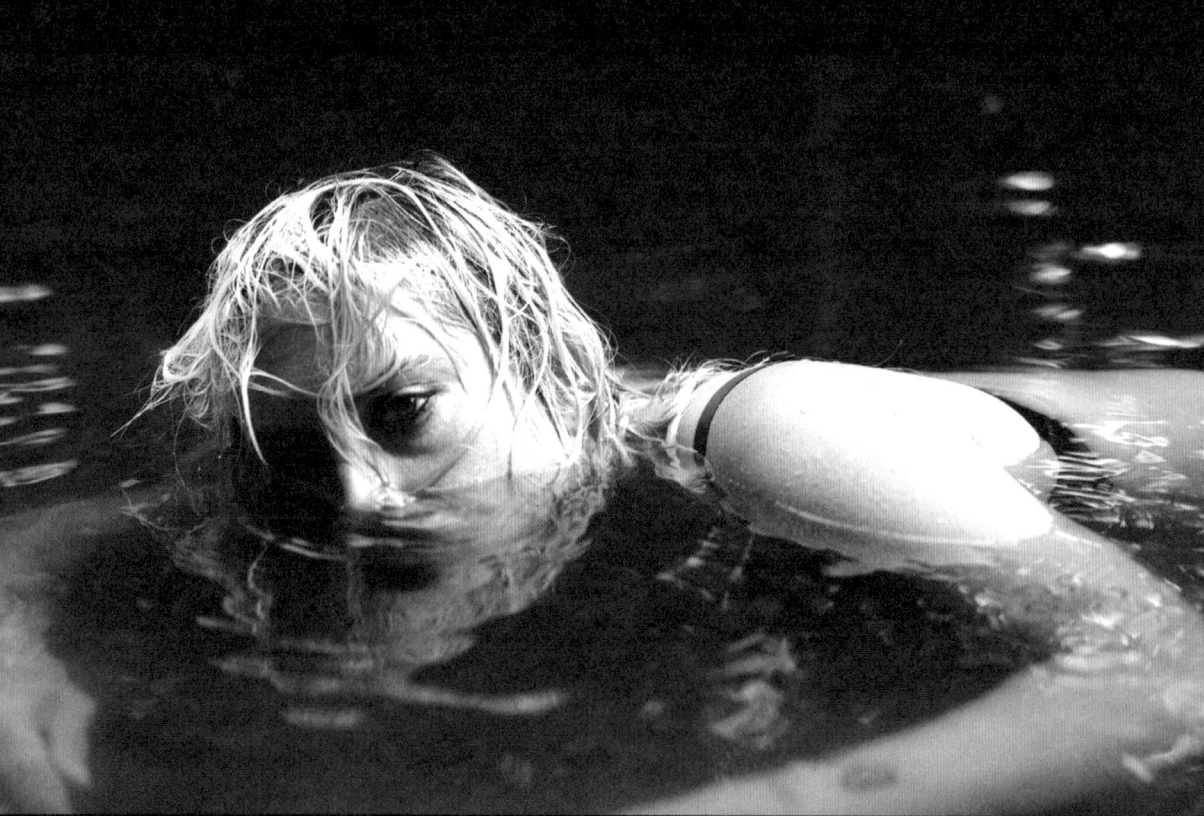

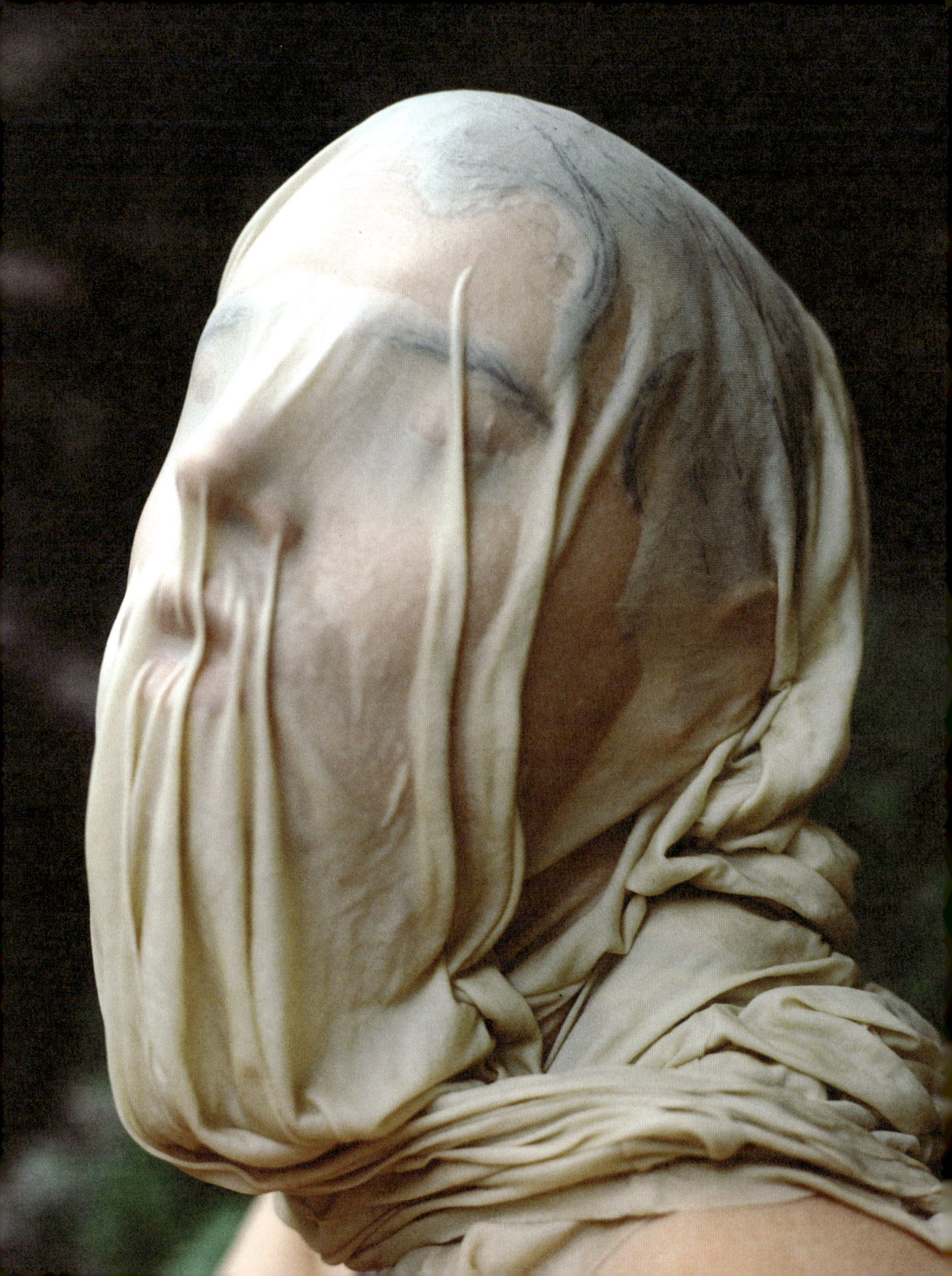

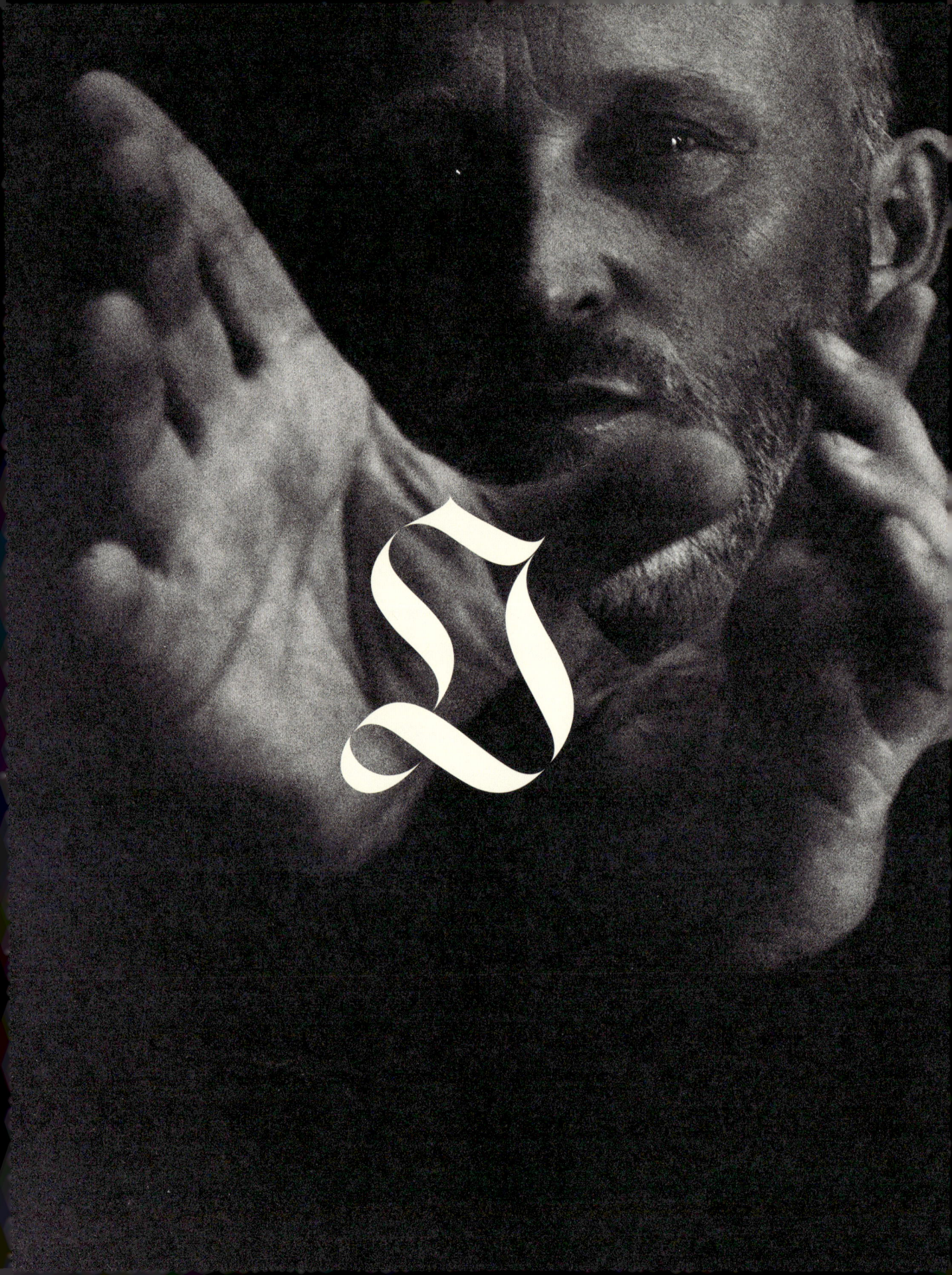

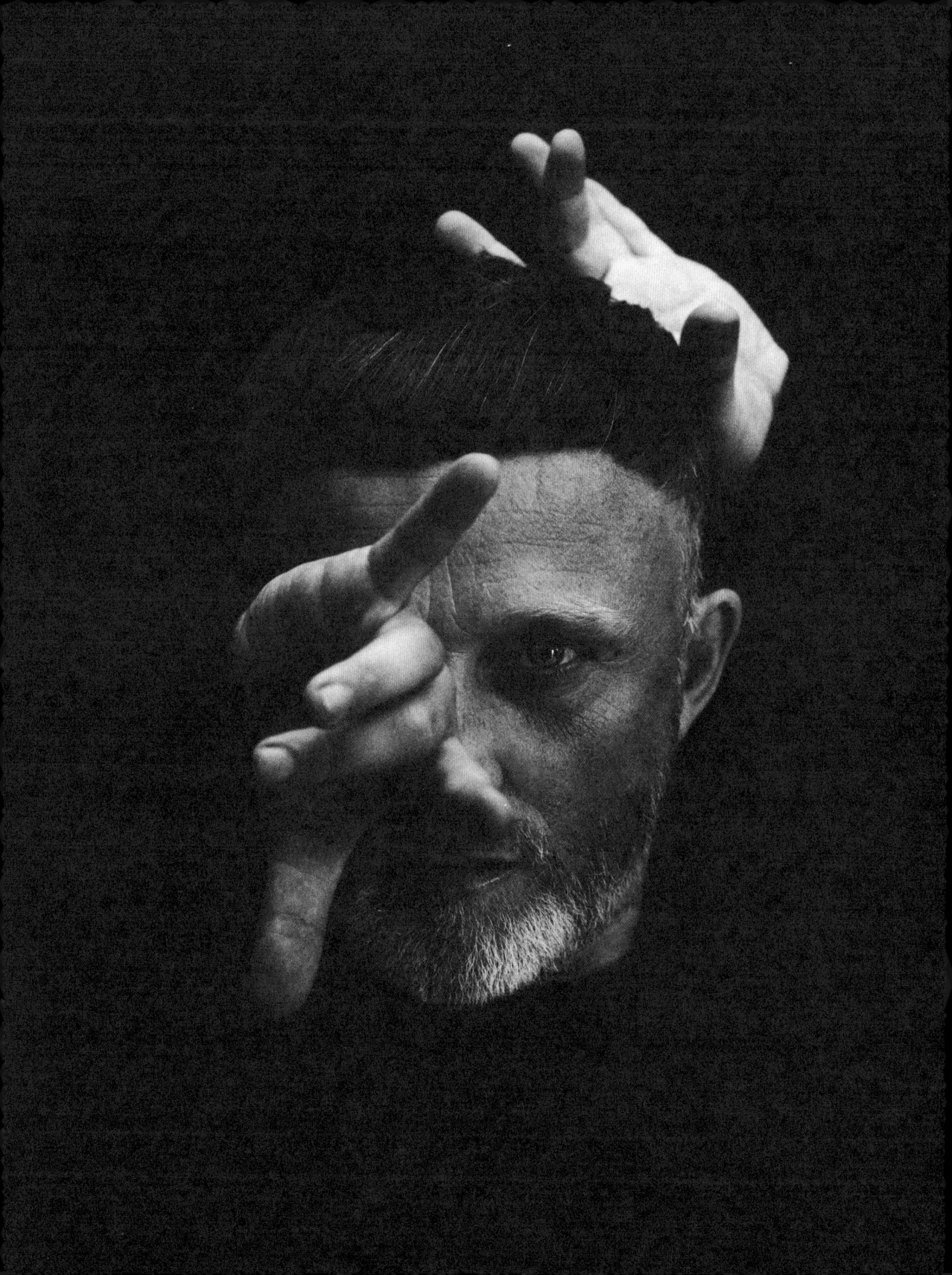

DAMIEN JALET

Words *Adam Larson* / Photographs *Tarek Mohamed Mawad*

Life and Limb

I was first introduced to the work of Damien Jalet after seeing a recording of his piece titled *Skid*. Choreographed for 17 dancers, *Skid* presents a contemporary metaphor for the human condition as the performers commit to a cyclical engagement with the laws of gravity, repeatedly ascending and descending a 10-square-meter stage set at a 34-degree incline. The work is epic in its conception yet minimal in its presentation, remaining a perfect example of why Jalet is considered one of the most innovative choreographers working today.

Nature, ritual, restraint, tension, myth, and duality—perpetual forces in life that we all experience, yet rarely focus on—serve as generous sources of inspiration for Jalet's unique brand of dynamic existentialism. He creates beauty out of darkness, conflict, and turmoil and brings forth newness in each work with timely precision.

His approach to dance and choreography is ever-evolving, pushing the boundaries of the art form by embracing more than just movement in a piece. Damien works across multiple mediums from the stage to film, incorporating architecture, music, the visual arts, and fashion through his collaborations with prominent artists such as Kohei Nawa, Marina Abromovic, Antony Gormley, Madonna, Jim Hodges, Luca Guadagnino, Thom Yorke, Iris Van Herpen, Ryuichi Sakamoto, and JR, to name a few.

On an aptly dark morning in June, days before jetting off for his next project in Japan, I caught up with Damien to discuss the differences between creating for the stage vs. film, the importance of legacy, personal rituals, and the ephemeral nature of dance.

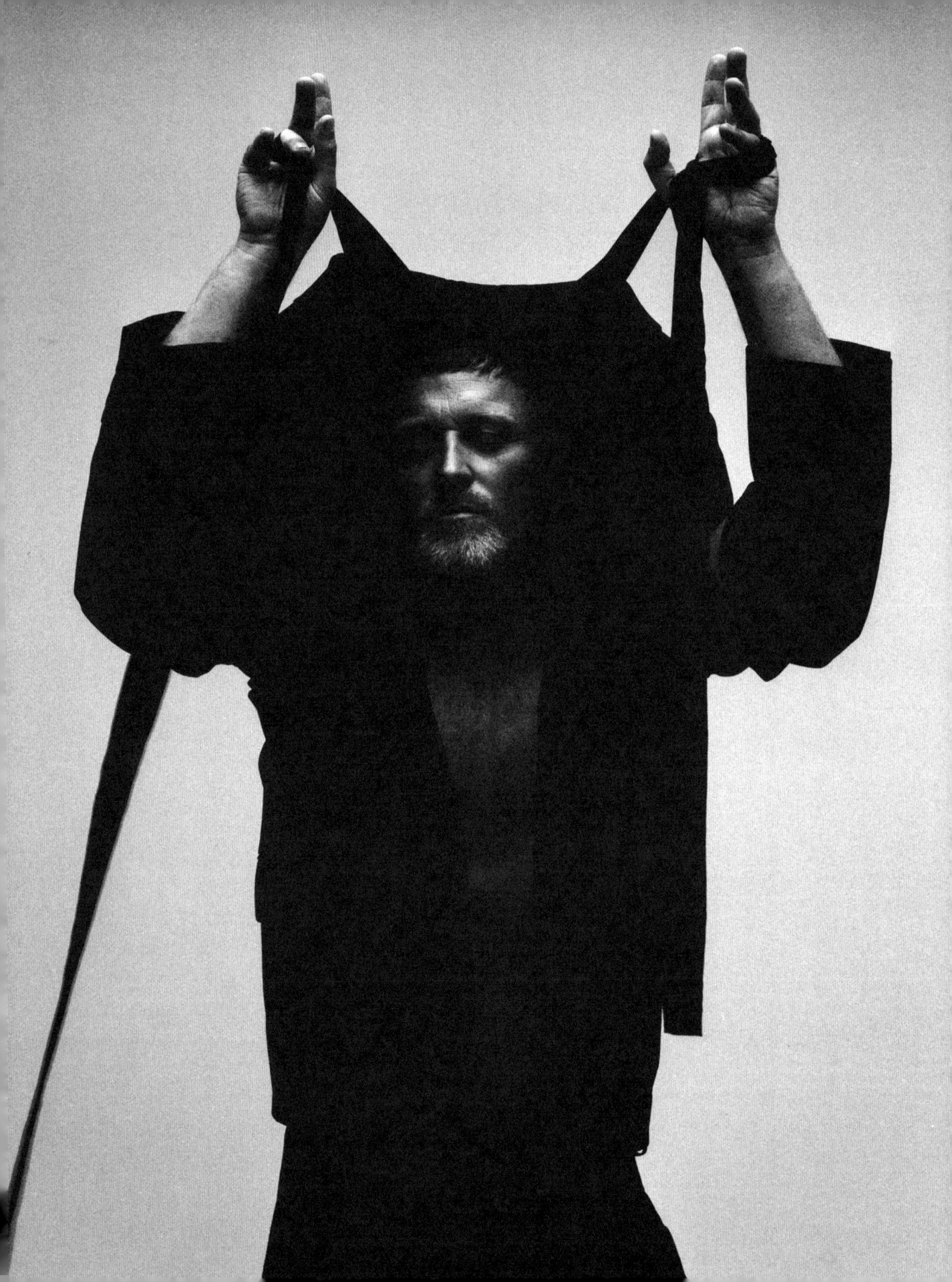

W Thank you for taking the time to speak with me. I imagine you're a very busy man. Where are you located currently?

D I'm in Brussels. Talk about darkness, the weather has been shitty here for the last, I don't even know. But, I'm traveling a lot. I was recently in Brazil, Mexico, and Japan for work, and recently just in Cannes. My work has always brought me to different places. Lately, it's been a little bit crazy because it's a lot of different projects in different worlds, so I'm constantly moving, but Brussels is my base. That's where I was born. I'm half French, half Belgian, but I grew up here. It's an interesting place. Have you been to Brussels?

W I have been once, years ago, but I'm sure it's changed a lot since. It is an amazing city.

D It's a very contrasty city. Very chaotic and constantly reshaping but, at the same time, always remaining the same. It's very cosmopolitan, with a lot of different cultures. The identity of this country is a bit blurred. It's a crossroads between so many different cultures, which makes it an interesting place to grow up because you never identify with just one culture or resist against it.

W You work with people from all over the world. I'm curious how working across cultures and in different places around the globe has influenced how your work has evolved.

D We all have mirror neurons, and we pick stuff up from whatever surrounds us; we are very permeable in that sense. When you travel, even just a little, it changes your perspective from where you're from. You have your own cultural departure point, and when you get into a completely different environment, you find commonalities, but most of the time, you notice what's different. When you collaborate with people in new places, you push this even further. You get into the zone and explore the unknown, which can be a very vulnerable place. If you're making a creation in Japan, you'll understand what hyper precision is and how when you say something, it very quickly becomes part of reality. In Mexico, there is a very different relationship to time. Things happen in very different ways, depending on the economic situation of the country, the culture, the habits, and the ways of communicating. All of this is incredibly enriching. A part of me is also a researcher. Performance is a tool to get into my subconscious but also the collective subconscious. Mythology exists in every culture and can be extremely specific, yet you encounter similar archetypes. Rituals and mythologies are very much an inspiration in my work. I consider them to be a little bit like the backbone of humanity. I'm always very curious to understand how those fundamental stories shape the identity of a culture and the way people organize themselves. It's interesting for me to be in places where rituals and mythology are very vivid and very different from where I come from.

　　Japan has had a much deeper effect on me. I've been going there for more than 20 years. Collectively,

it's at least two and a half years in total. It's a culture that really impregnated me and completely changed my point of view. Other places did, too. Mexico is one and Iceland. I do think we change the world, and the world changes us. I have a hunger to constantly place myself where I'm not necessarily comfortable. You learn by being there, by collaborating, and by developing a language. I think that's the most exciting part and probably why I keep doing what I do. It's very exhausting to have this kind of life, to be constantly traveling, constantly readjusting. There's the excitement you get from the discovery of a place but also the fear of the unknown. So, to answer your question, it changes me tremendously.

W It requires a strong sense of self and personal constitution as you are regularly being displaced in a new place. Different versions of yourself are being exposed to people and cultures, as you said, that challenge who you are and where you come from. Earlier, you mentioned that you've worked in film. Can you tell us about that experience and how it differs from the worlds of dance and theater?

D Yeah. I mean, even before becoming a dancer and a choreographer, I was much more into acting and theater. That was actually my first love because it was the most immediate tool of transformation. When I started working, I did some theater director study at the National School for two years. I worked a lot with dramaturgy, with light, basically all of the things that surround performance. The school was connected to the National School of Belgium, so I had a lot of contact with directors and moviemakers.

　　I actually fell in love with contemporary dance when I saw some contemporary dance films at that school. That's when I discovered the work of the Belgian fellows, like Anne Teresa de Keersmaeker. They had a way of working with dance that was not just ethereal. I guess I always felt that ballet was connected to something slightly aristocratic, with a sense of elevating oneself, pretending to be something that you're not.

　　When you look at the fundamentals of dance, it's often used as catharsis. What I felt when I discovered some of those works was the roughness and the violence that dance could express. I saw that dance could have the potential to actually explore darkness. It's like passing through the fire, so you clean yourself of something. You go into your fear; you go into your dark spot in order to get out of it and to ultimately exorcise it. Which I think is very fundamental. Dance allows you to explore all of these very intense emotions so you don't have to live with them.

　　I did a show at the Louvre in 2013 called *Les Medusés*, where nine performances happened over two hours. One of them featured a female trio. We had actually watched the original *Suspiria* when we created it. For me, *Suspiria* was always a classic and a film that

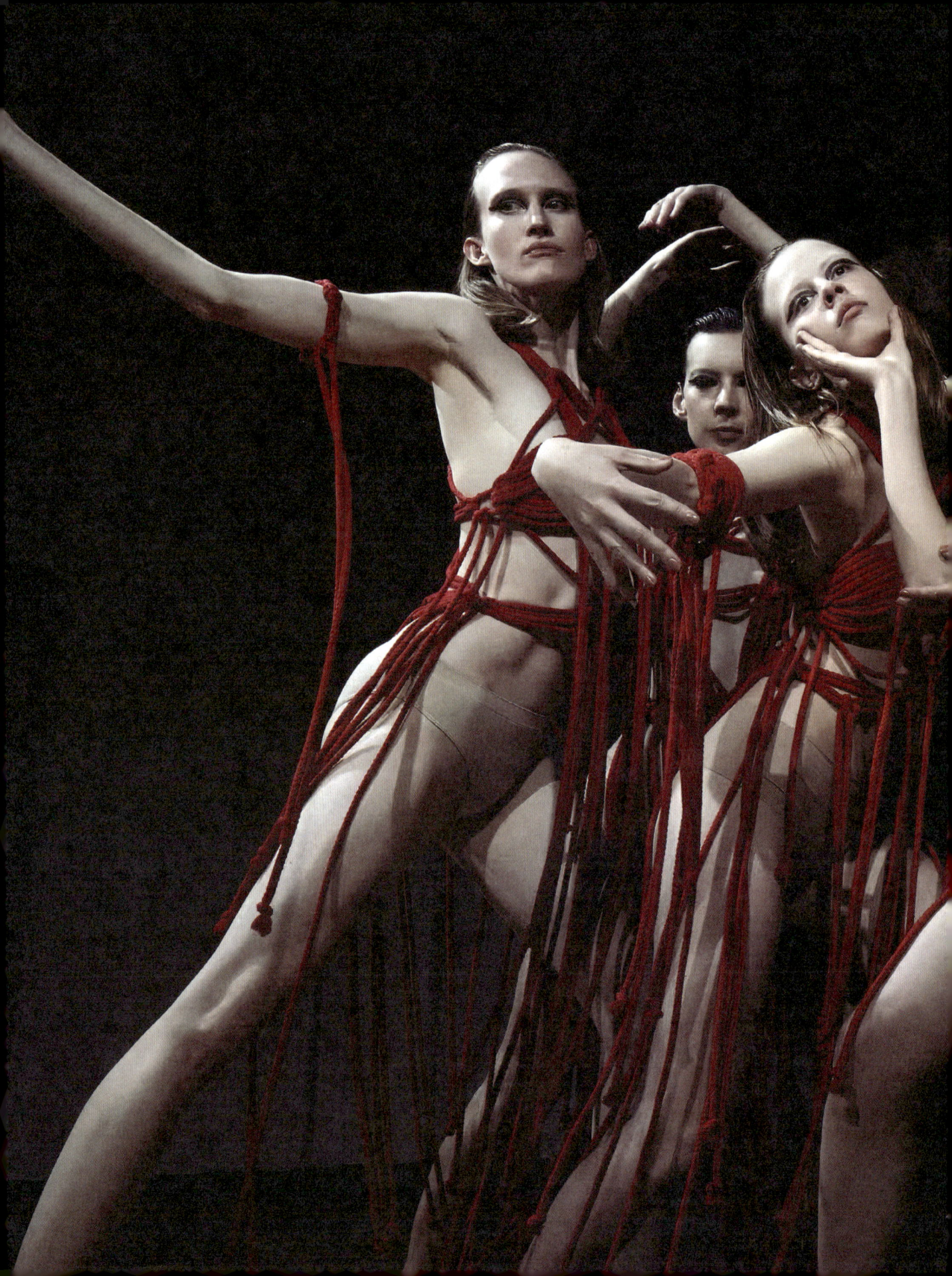

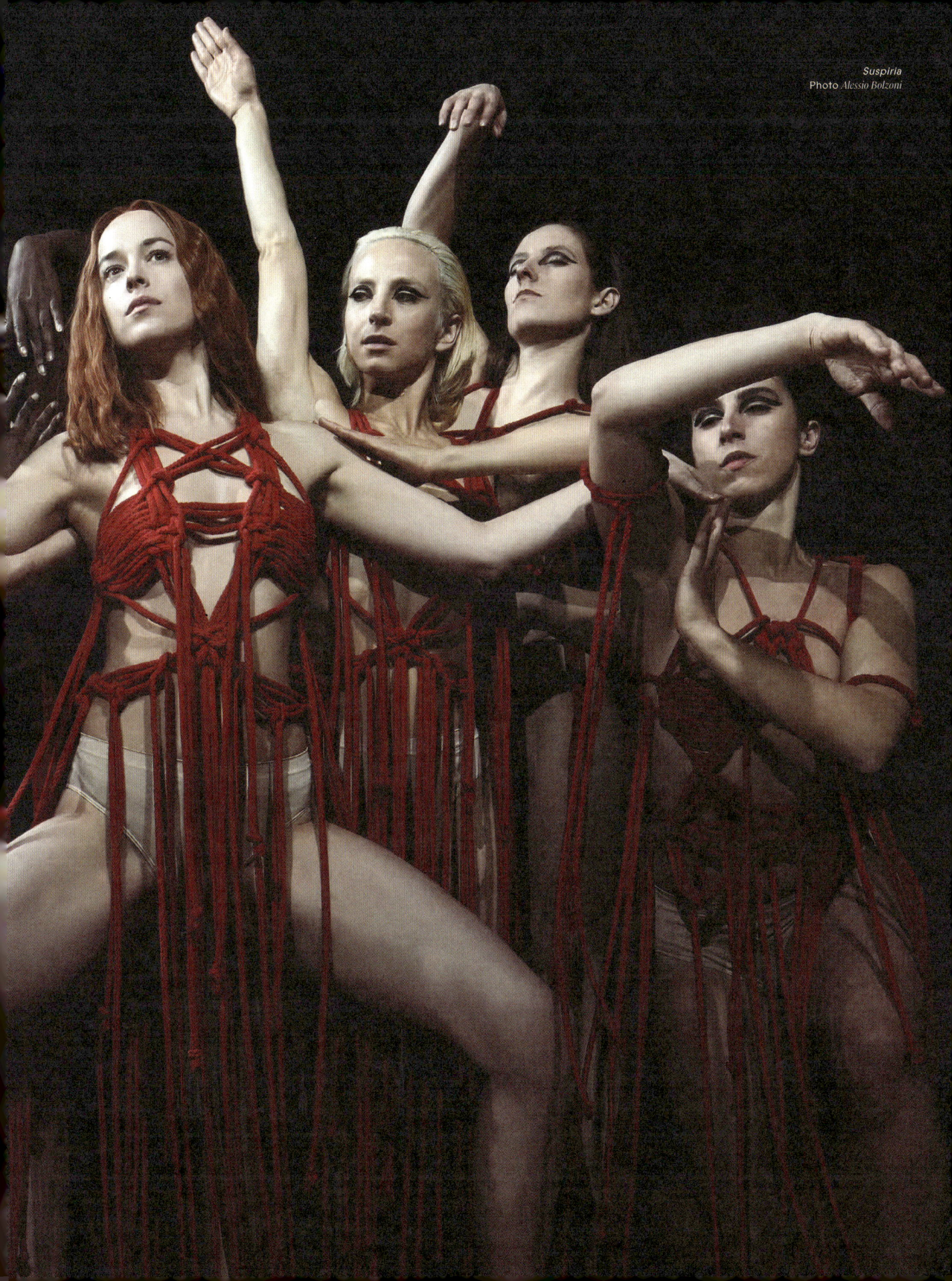

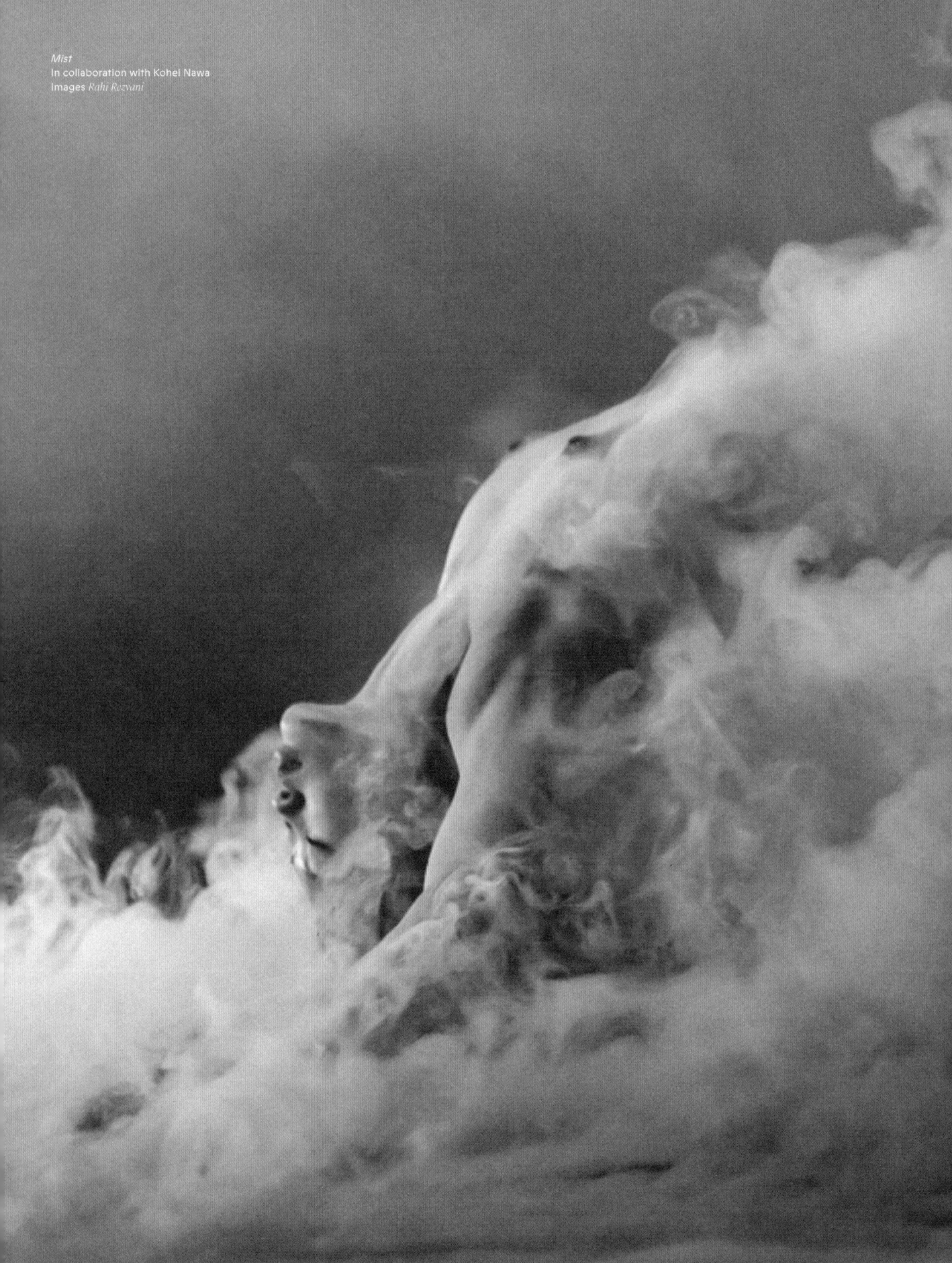

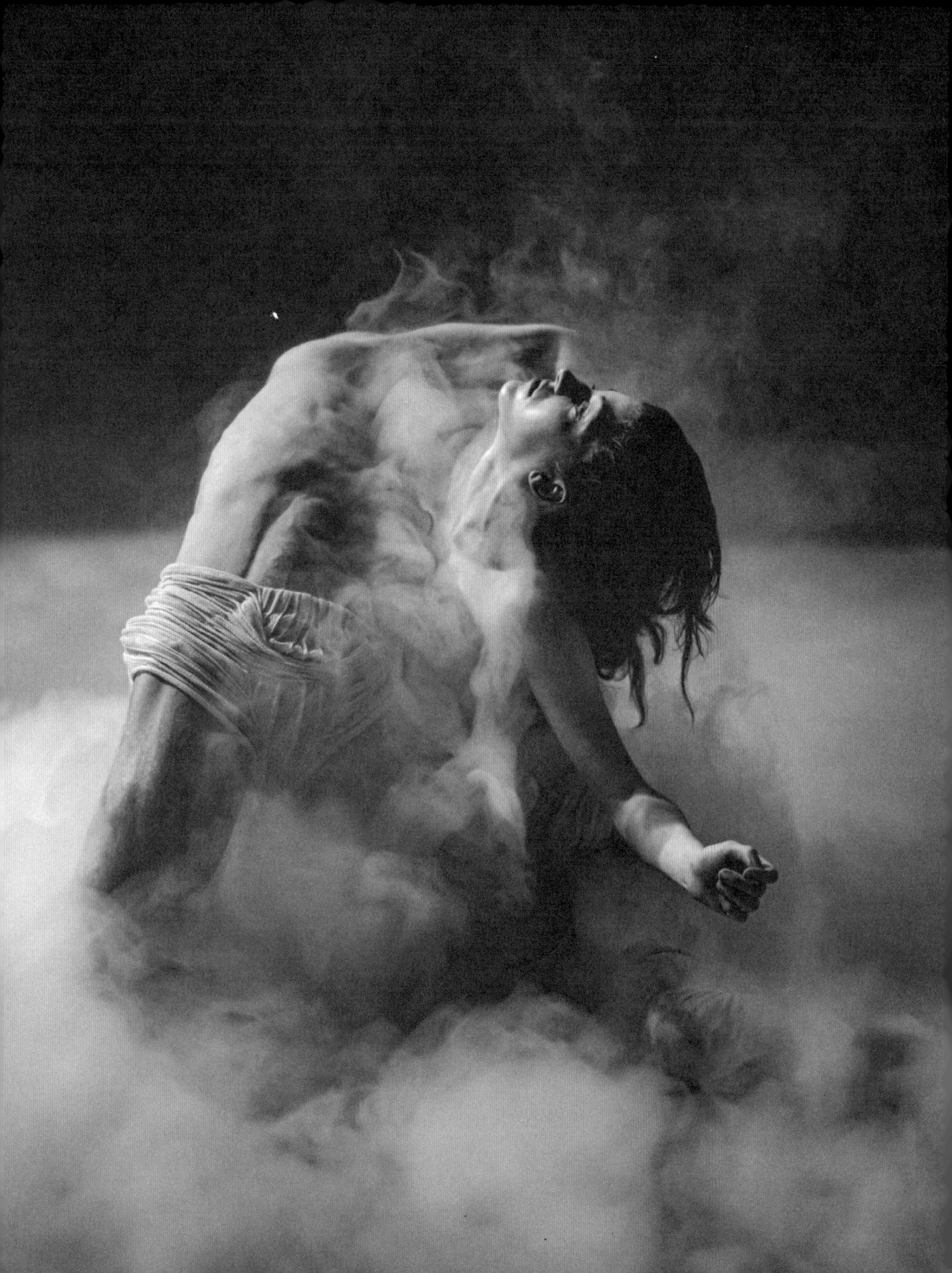

I loved for its aesthetic but also its music. Three years later, Luca Guadagnino saw that video and then invited me to help create *Suspiria.*

Luca was like, "I really need you; it needs to be you that does this." What I really enjoyed about his take on the film was the fact that he was not considering dance, unlike the original, as something in the backdrop. He really wanted it to be the magic in the film that brings all the distortion and the horror. The fact that he would use dance as the basis for the most hardcore scene of the film was a very interesting challenge.

Being able to show the raw, visceral, dangerous, untamable aspects of dance was something quite unique. He didn't know that I had inspired this trio from the original *Suspiria,* it was just a coincidence. So, it was too much of a sign. I used that choreography and multiplied and transformed it. (And then Thom York spent six months recomposing the music.)

A lot of people had no idea that this kind of dance even existed. I got a lot of demand from people wanting to learn the choreography, which is the most complex choreography to learn because each dancer has a different rhythm score. To actually dance it is a really demanding and mental exercise. And that's what I love about dance. How you can combine something that is emotional, mental, really spiritual, and sensual.

W It's really unique in that way. It's always fascinated me how it needs to be witnessed for it to actually exist.

D When COVID came, I realized how vulnerable dance is. How difficult it is each time you make a dance show. It's like Sisyphus: Each day, you have to start again from scratch; each time you go to a place, a dancer could be sick, or there could be some technical problem. You need to constantly reconcile so much effort.

To make one performance happen itself is exhausting. I've been dancing for 20 years, and each time, I would not do anything that day because I knew the energy I would have to deliver each night. It gives you a lot of structure because you need to eat in a certain way, you need to manage your energy, and you need to stay healthy. It teaches you that nothing can be taken for granted, and that every day, you have to start again from scratch.

There's something really beautiful about it but also very dooming. At one point, I thought to myself, okay, what's left from all of the things I did 10, 15 years ago. All of the energy I deliver on stage. Maybe it becomes a memory for the few people who have seen the show. Beyond that, what's left is just a few pictures or videos that nobody really watches firsthand because it's a secondhand experience to see a film.

When you do theater, the text survives, so the piece still exists. But when you do dance, it's very temporary. I think that's probably why it's not the most popular medium, because you can't really own it. You can't really grasp it. You can't really hold it.

When Luca arrived with *Suspiria,* I realized suddenly, "Oh, wow, finally, I can break the spell of the ephemeral aspect of dance." So, having dance infiltrating the narrative of a film that will be experienced as a firsthand experience is a beautiful thing, especially if you work with great directors. Paul Thomas Anderson, Jacques Audiard, and Luca Guadagnino are masters, all of them. I've been really lucky to work with them.

And to have a very deep and meaningful collaboration, when you feel that dance is going to be used in the right way and not just as something that gives a cool color to a project, but that it becomes a necessary element of the film. That's why I feel blessed to have this foot in cinema and feel that also the work is appreciated in the sense that there's a recognition for the contribution it gives to the film. And I hope for more.

W So, is the idea of legacy an important part of your work? It sounds like it's something that pushes you to reinvent or continue to evolve.

D I think every artist creates with a desire to leave something behind. You know, we are all human, so it's a way to deal with death and with the fact that we're not always going to be here. As an artist, you try to create something that would leave a trace behind. But I guess being an artist is also about being incredibly in the present, trying to capture something of the time you're living through, the Zeitgeist. Having worked on films and some books, making works that remain is a way for me to deal with the very scary side of dance, which is how ephemeral it is in its true essence.

W It's funny because in the contemporary art world,

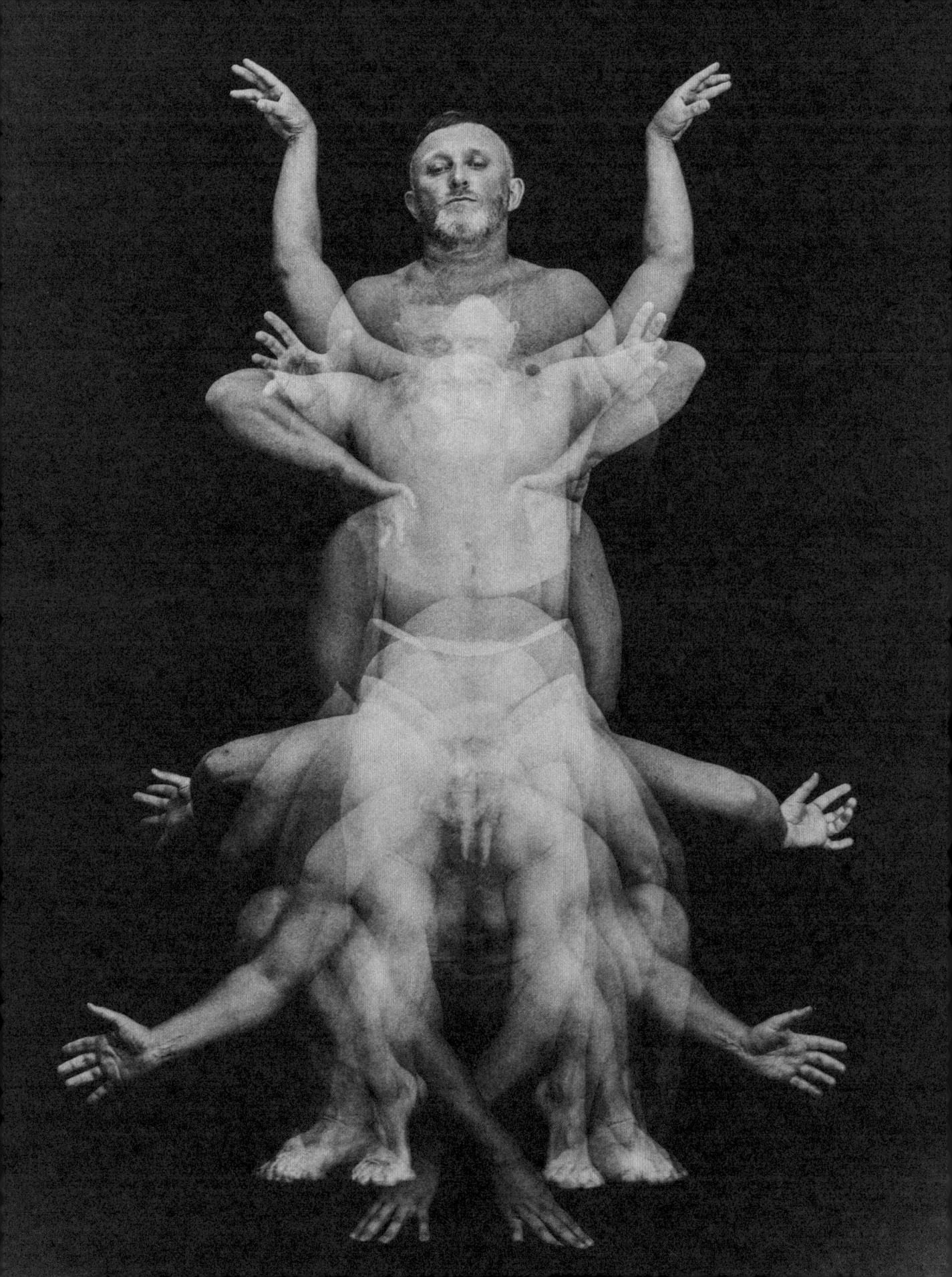

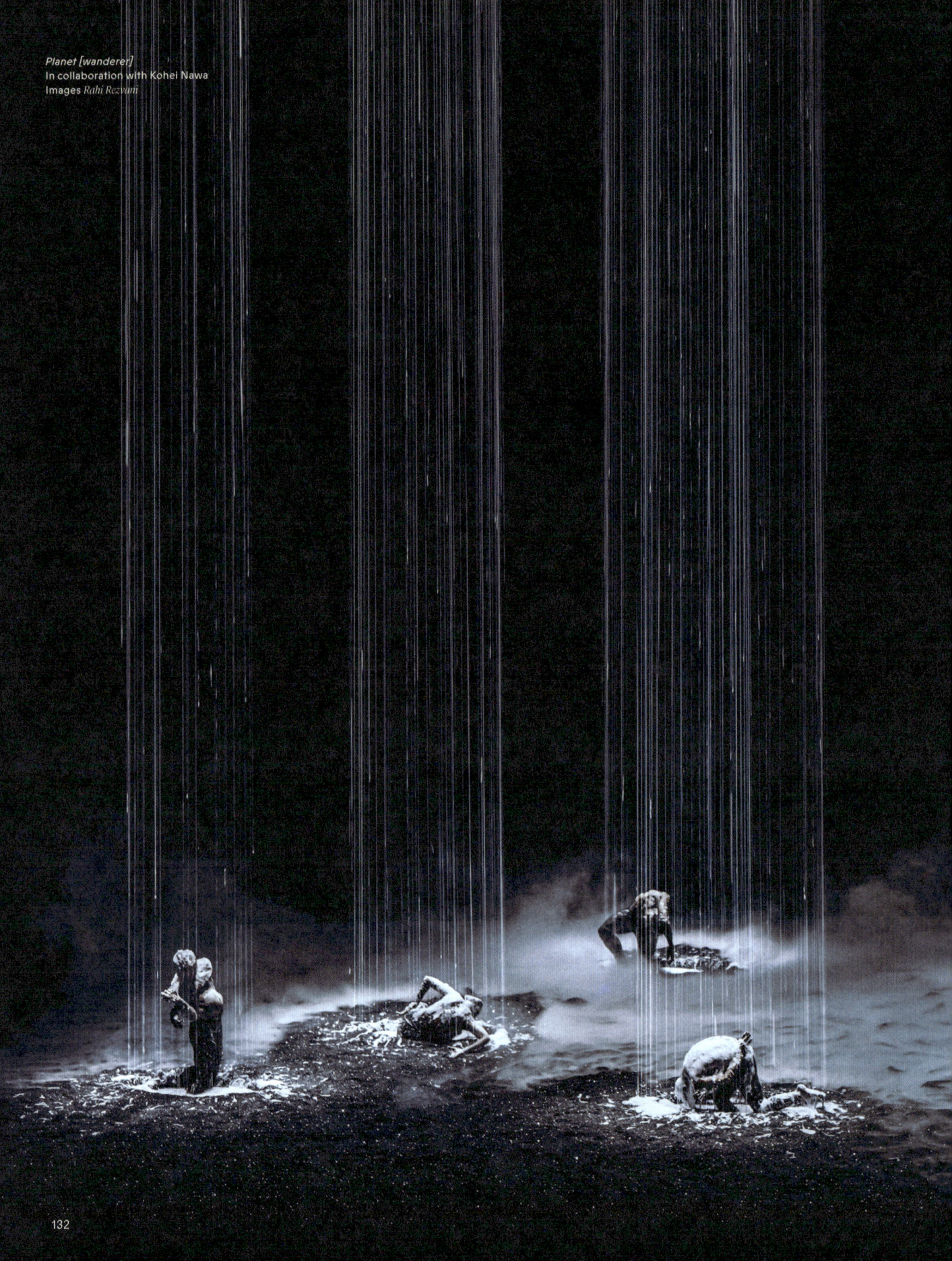

Planet [wanderer]
In collaboration with Kohei Nawa
Images *Rahi Rezvani*

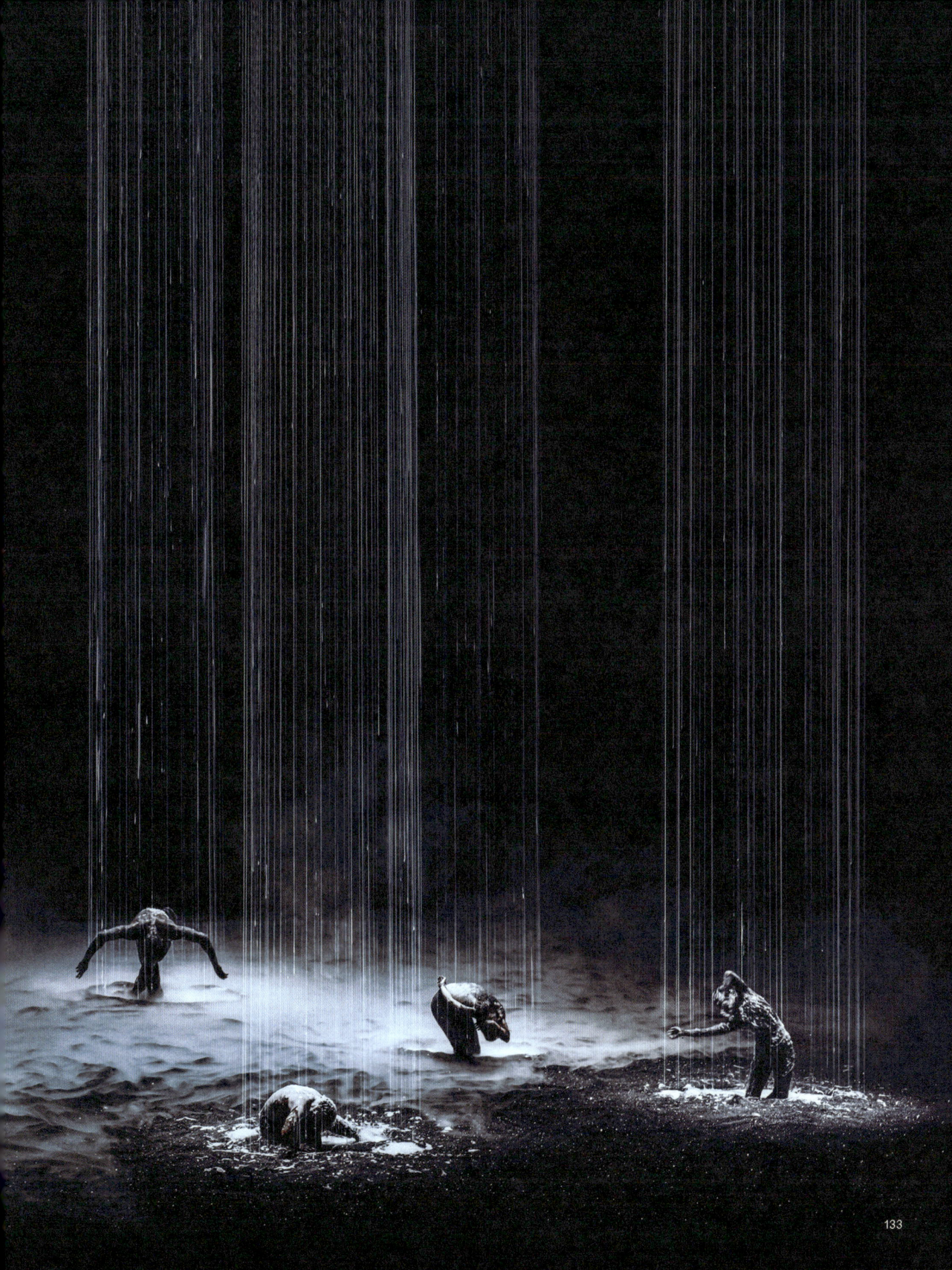

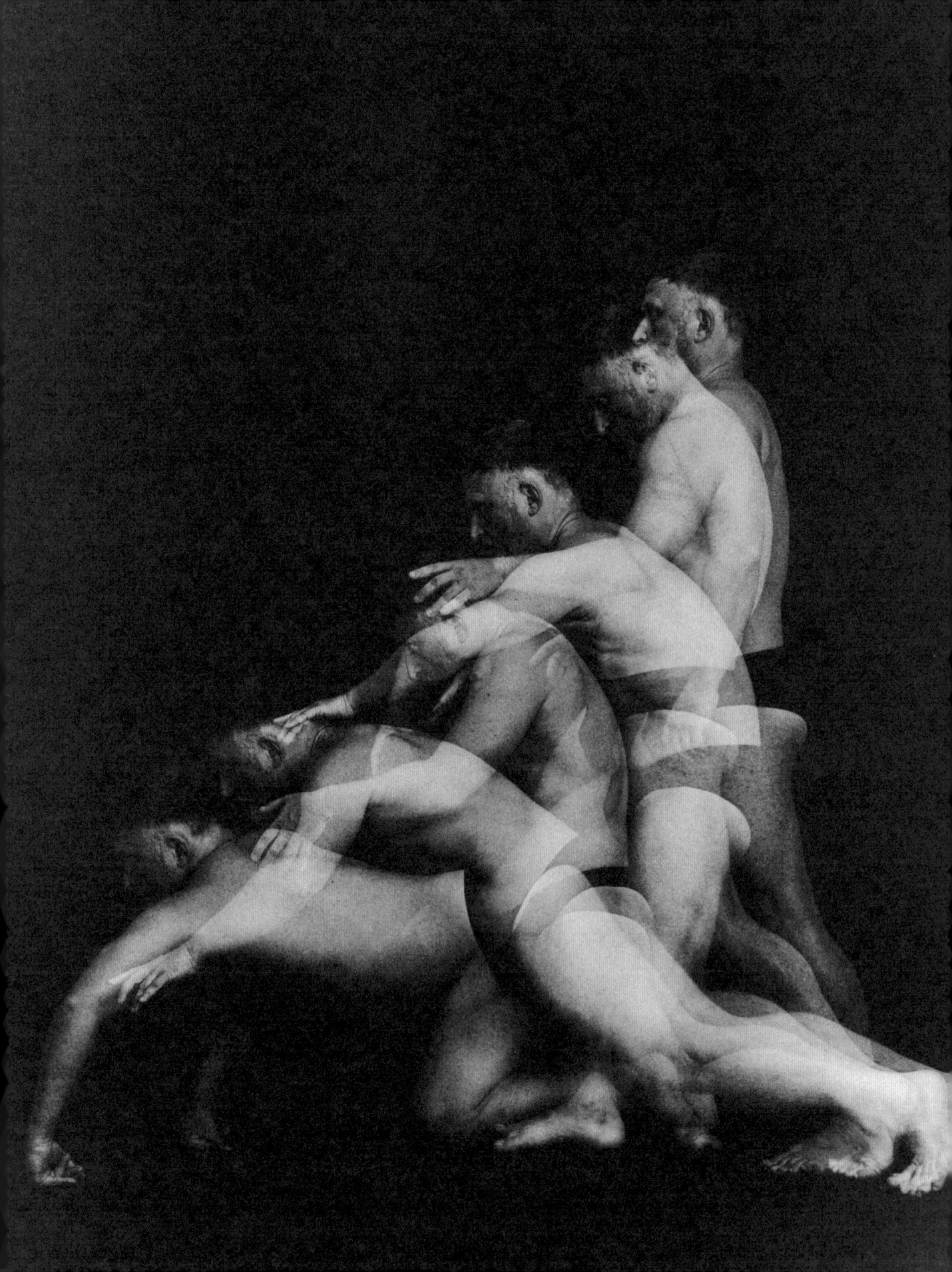

seems people want you to do the same thing repeatedly. They fall in love with that thing that you did and want that from you again and again. I find that would be difficult in dance because, like you said, it's so ephemeral.

D   I won't give any names, but I know some choreographers that always just do the same piece. They just change the music and change the costumes. There is that in dance as well. It's pushed by certain repertory companies that definitely want a certain kind of brand and certain kind of product. And that's also why I'm starting to distance myself from that kind of world. Production requires you to always think in a very planned kind of way. You need to deliver your costume and your set a year in advance. So, all of your choices become mentally deliberate. There's very little room for experimentation and asking, "What if we do this?" It's something that I'm very afraid of. If you look at my body of work, you realize that things take extremely different shapes, different aesthetics. Even choreographically there are extremely different choices. Some pieces are nearly static and very slow, while some pieces are extremely fast and fluid. I'm trying to create contexts like where the dancers are stuck with their feet in the ground. I'm always trying to introduce certain limitations that will push me out of what I've done before. You try to figure it out as you are in it. The world is changing so much. Since I started dancing, the means of production, of building a set and traveling have become incredibly reduced. COVID also had a massive impact on the reduction of budgets for performing arts and the possibilities of touring work. I remember a time when you could tour constantly. You'd do one show, and it would be performed hundreds of times. That time is gone. It's a very different world. But the question of legacy, of course, like any artist, I'm thinking of it. I don't want to be stuck in it, which prevents me from enjoying the moment and the sense of experimentation. I have to say that working with films helps my work to be seen and understood by way more people than the little circuits of dance that I've evolved into. Recently, I did this project with JR. He invited me to create this massive work on the front of the Paris Opera which dealt with the concept of light and dark. Performers stood on scaffolding in costumes that were white on one side and black on the other. As they turned, they acted as pixels, creating large scale words and phrases.

W   Yes! I saw this online. So wildly beautiful and impressive.

D   One phrase was "darkness holds the grace of the light." It was only two or three weeks after the Hamas attacks in October 2023 and the start of intense bombing by Israel on Gaza. Paris suddenly became very tense, with threats of terrorist attacks and police trying to reduce public events with large gatherings of people. It became a question for artists: What do you do? Do you let fear paralyze you and make you shrink, or do you try the opposite? Try to keep on delivering a message of

hope but not by erasing darkness or pretending it is not there, but rather acknowledge it. The darkness around that's maybe the best place to understand what light is and what we carry. Another quote, by Maya Angelou definitely inspired the work, that we have two sides: we have a dark one and a bright one, and it's our choice to decide which side we want to show most. We have this duality within each of us, and sometimes it's very important to go through anger and through refusal to find light again. It's a way to defend obscurity, to distinguish you. There is something very true about dance. It's why I left the theater, because I realized that words could be so corrupted, so floating, and so disconnected from reality. Words are the vehicles of lies, and actors keep the lie because it is their job.

W   Right.

D   And I guess with dance, I felt there was something different because you really need to walk the walk. You need to work really hard to go through pain every day. It's truly transformative. And it gets you into a third state of consciousness. When you have a good show, it's not just mental. The human body carries so much information from even before the moment we were considered humans. It comes from millions of years of evolution, and it's still within all of our physical memory. I'm quite fascinated by that heritage and how civilization and contemporary culture tries to push those things down or to erase them. Dance is a tool where you can let things emerge again and create around it.

W   We've talked a lot about rituals. I'm curious if you have any personal rituals that you practice outside of choreography and dance?

D   My own rituals? Yeah, this is one… I'm drinking green tea like matcha, every single day. Ritual implies a certain kind of regularity, and my life is very irregular. I'm here this week; next week, I'm going to be in Paris; the week after, I'm going to be in Japan. My life will always adjust to the time zone I'm in but also to what I'm supposed to do in each of those places. Since I don't really have regularity in this, there are certain things I'm trying to hold on to. For example, in Japan, I did some practice with monks called Shugendo, which is kind of an animist Buddhist kind of combo. Japanese are very good at syncretism, combining different spiritual movements and creating something new out of them. The monks were the first to connect the land of the man to the land of the gods. They consider the mountain as both a mother and a grave, the place that gives to you and that takes. I did this ritual twice there, or like a practice, which is ascetic. You hardly eat anything. You are walking 18 hours in white funeral clothes. You walk in silence, even if with your partner. It is something like a rebirth. Like extracting yourself from the world while being in the world and developing your senses. It has deeply influenced my way of thinking.

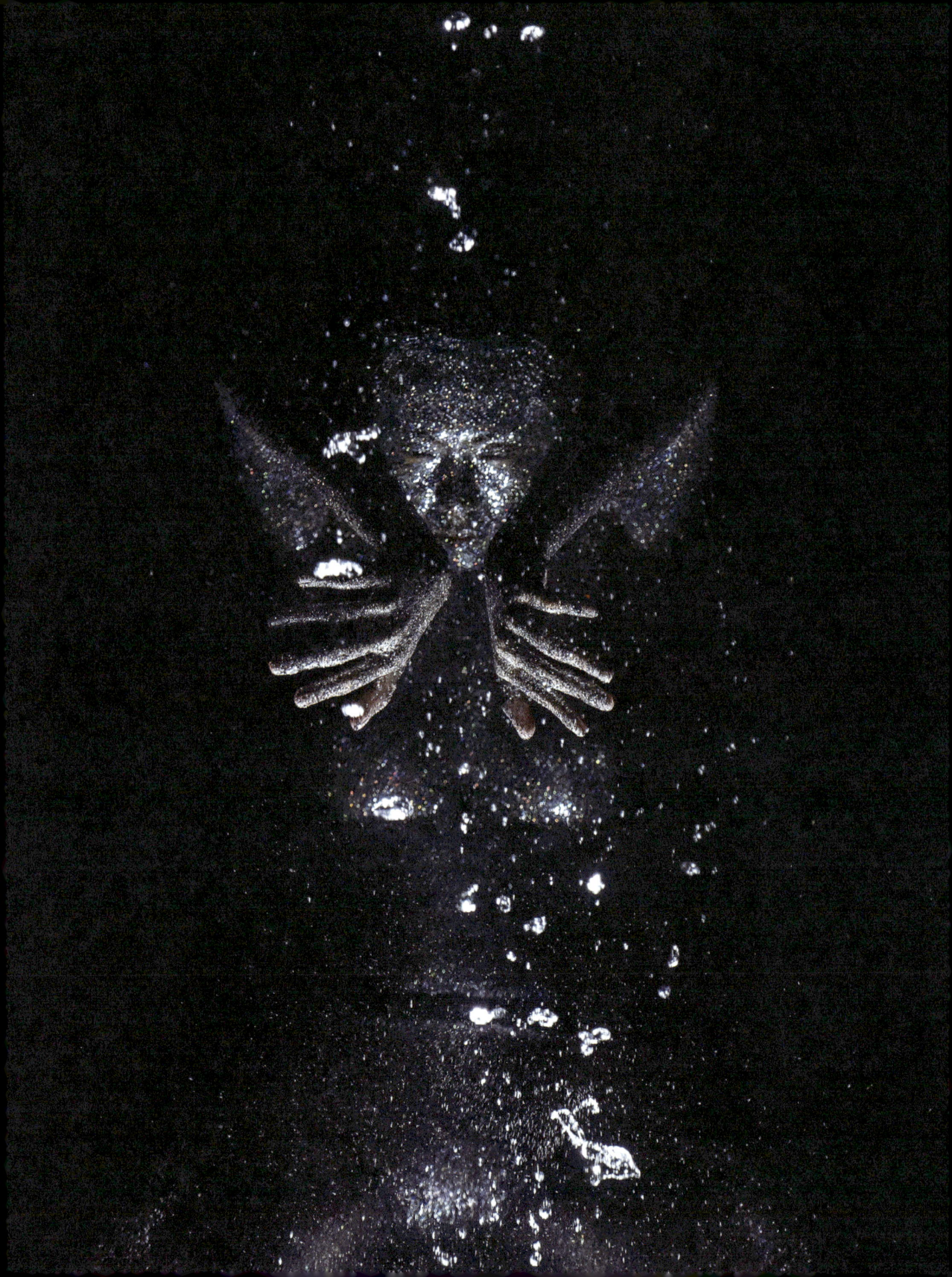

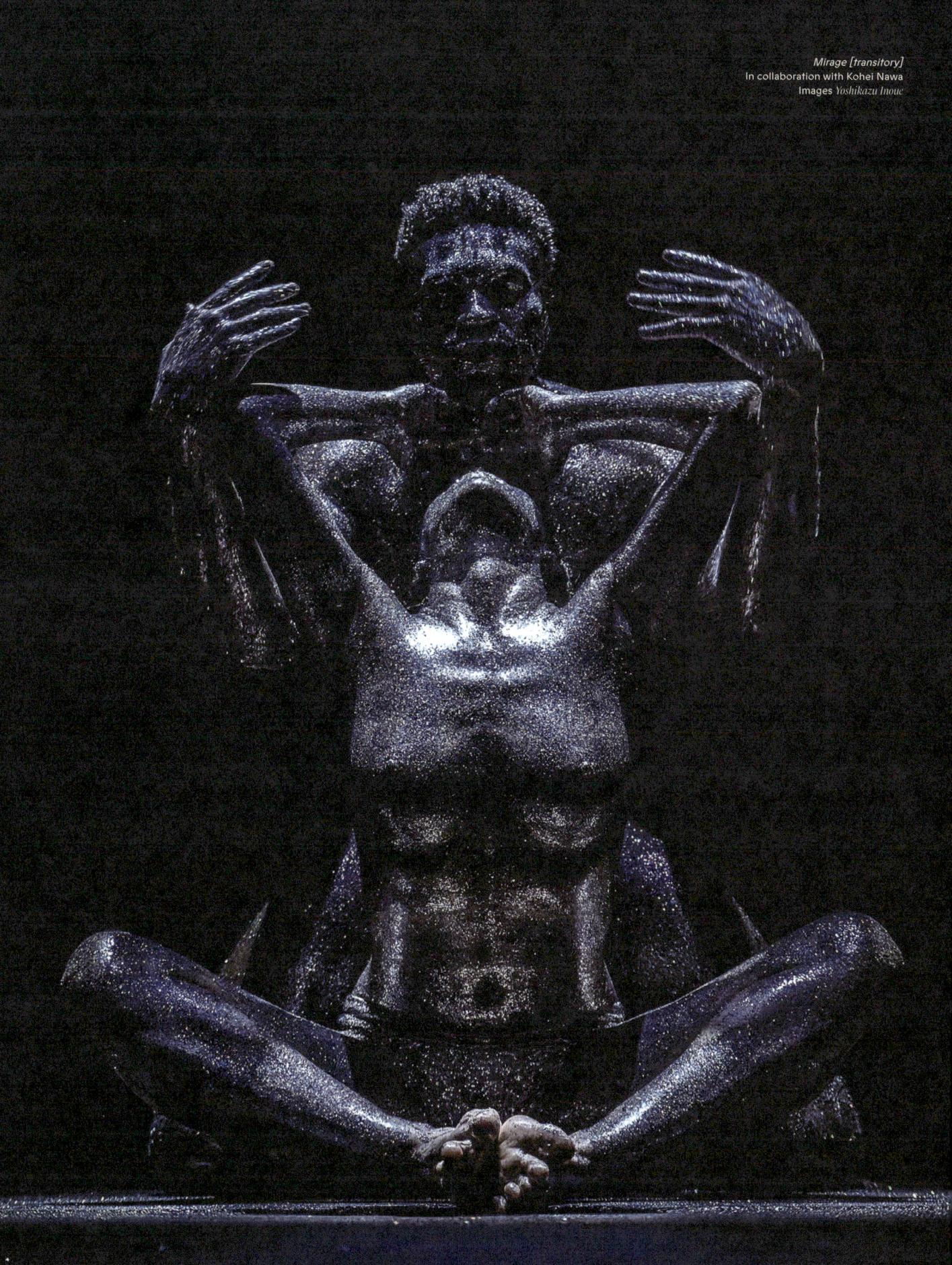

Mirage [transitory]
In collaboration with Kohei Nawa
Images *Yoshikazu Inoue*

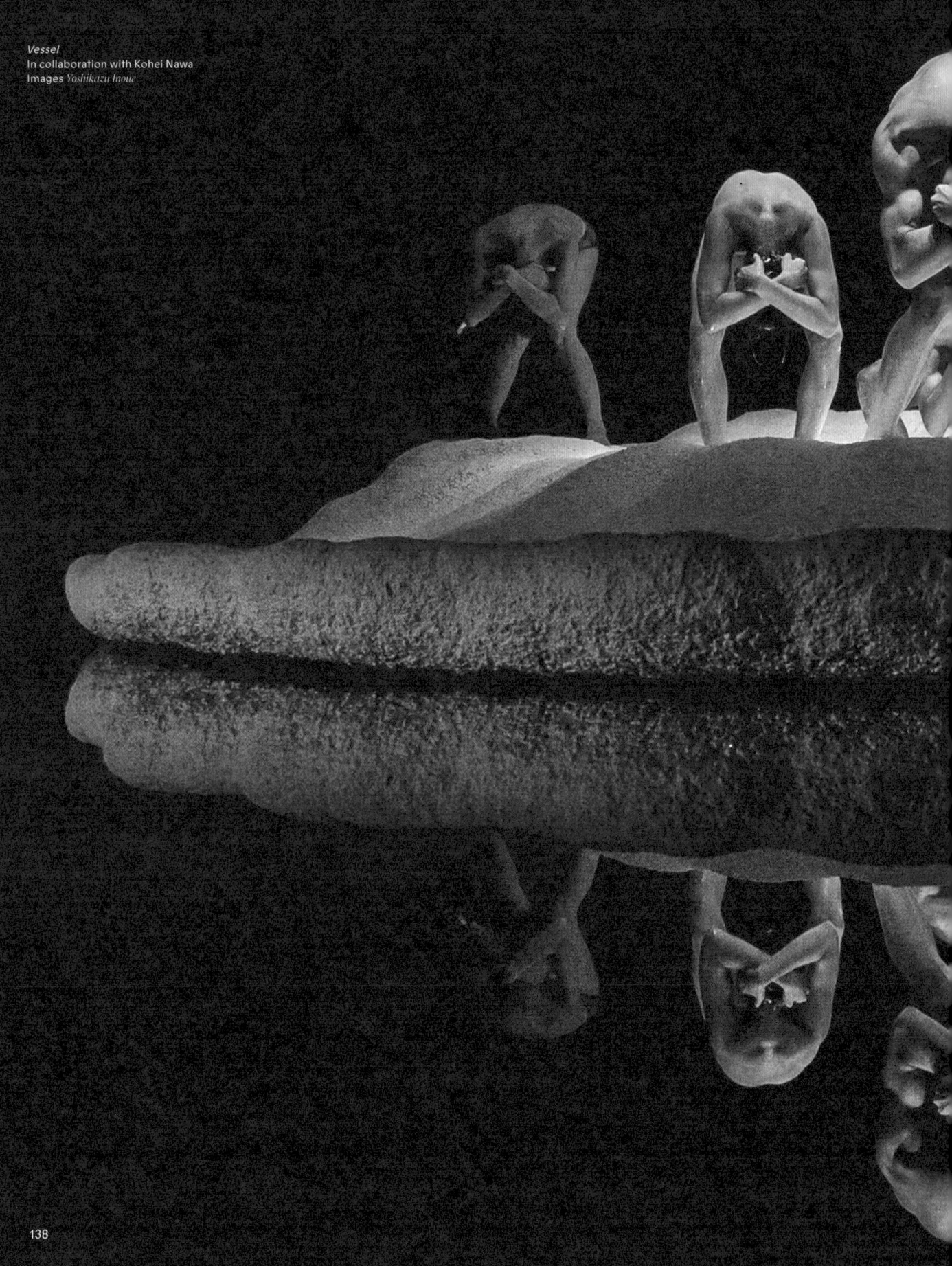

Vessel
In collaboration with Kohei Nawa
Images *Yoshikazu Inoue*

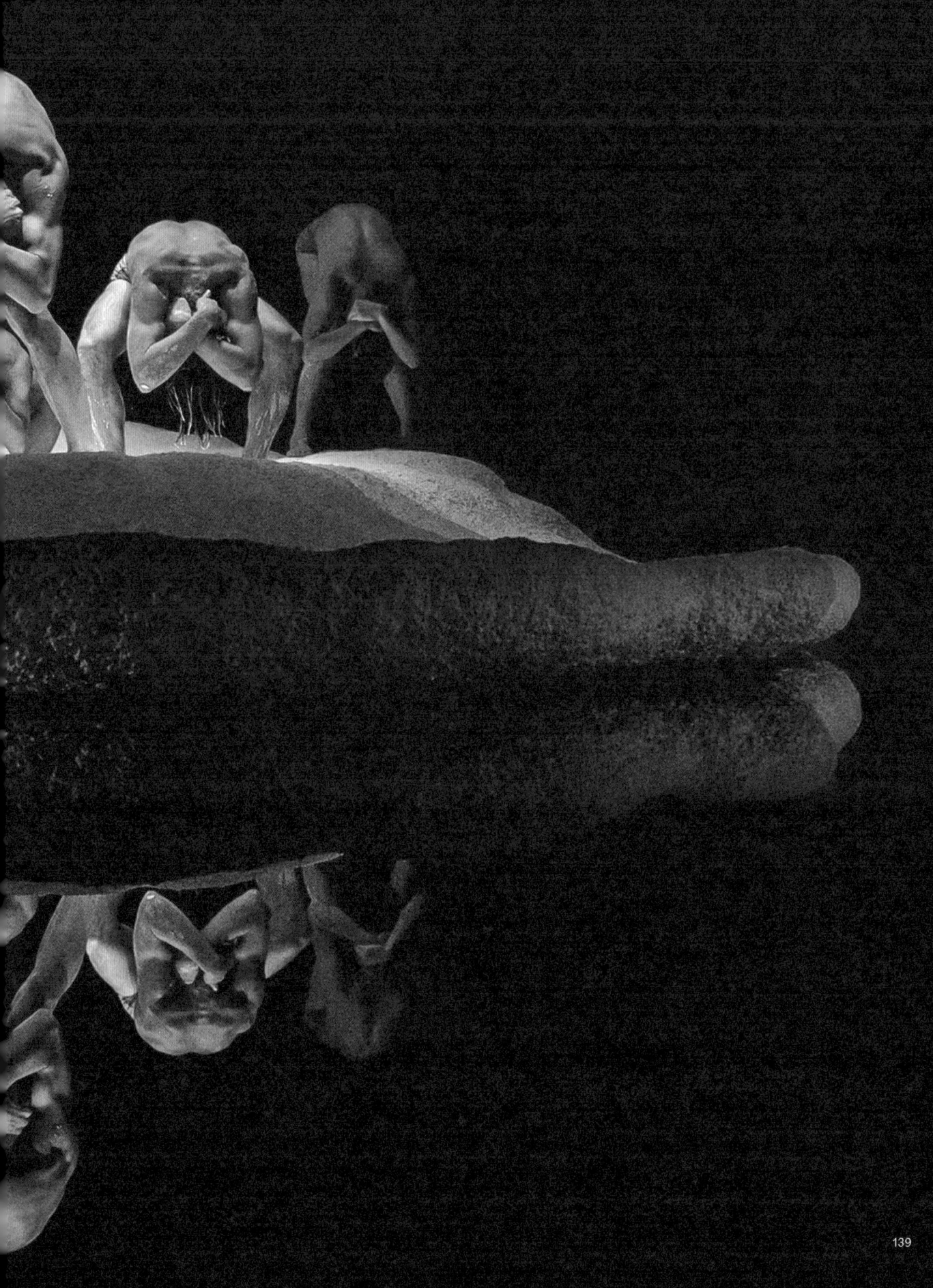

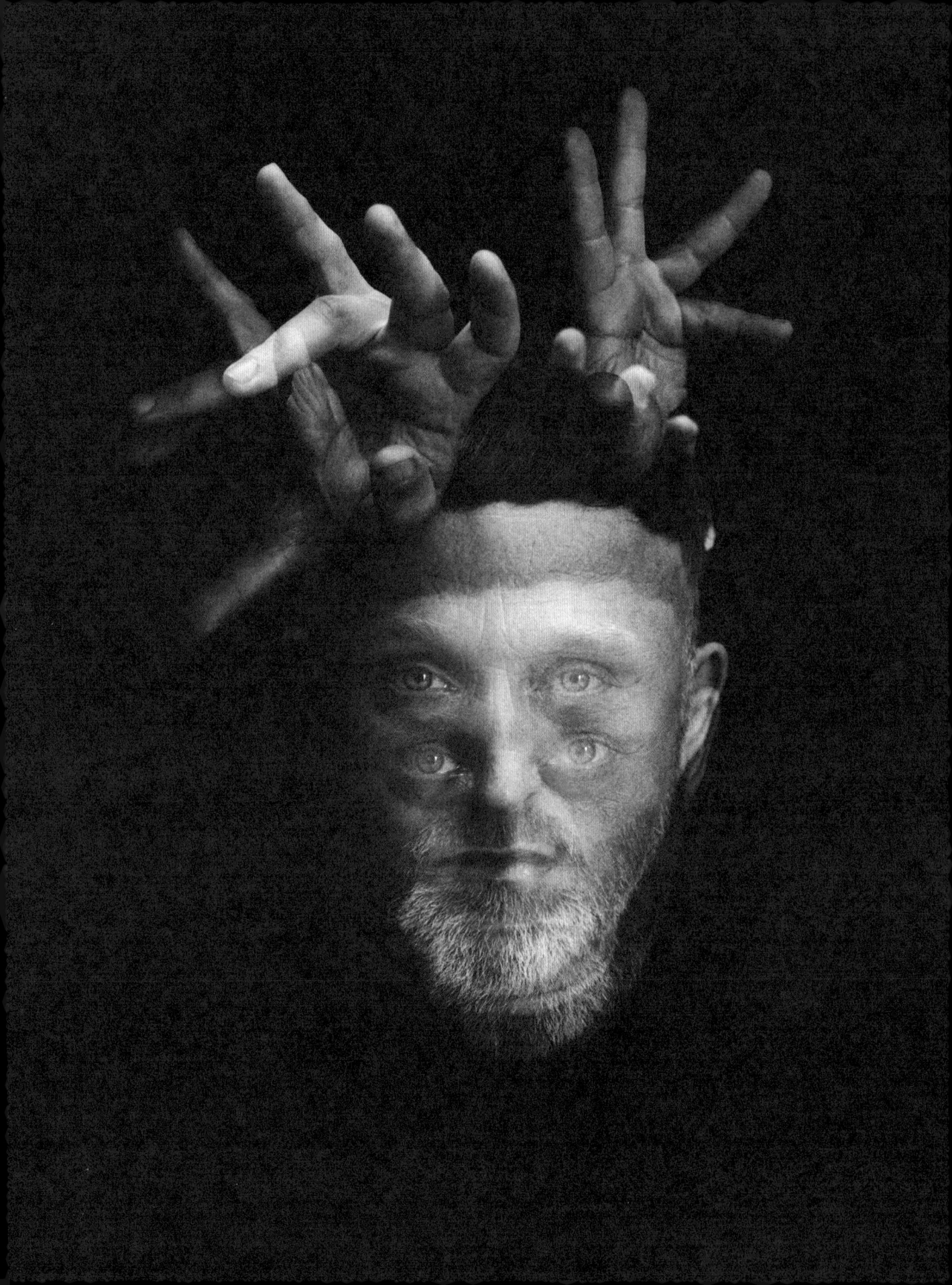

"I'm always trying to find a new language that feels very true to not just me but the people I'm working with. It's a transformative process."

W I'm now curious if you are familiar with the dance troupe Sankai Juku? I saw them perform when I was younger, and it's always stuck with me. It was so beautiful and moving. Our conversation brought them to mind...

D Of course. The choreographer died two months ago. Like really recently. I had met him and worked with two dancers that worked with the company. Yeah, it's an amazing group. Butoh is more known in Europe, but you have to know that butoh in Japan is not a popular art at all. Butoh dancers would also be strip dancers to get money, a lot of money, to be able to practice, because in Japan, there's hardly any funding for the arts. So you need to find an alternative way. Many people think that butoh is a very ancient, traditional thing, but it was created after World War II as a reaction to the atomic bomb, basically. It was a dance of darkness, a dance where you are aiming to go into the nonacademic, the organic, trying to make the invisible become visible. I completely connect to this. Sometimes, people think my work is butoh, but it's not. it doesn't affiliate with it in structure or the aim. There are a lot of similarities in some of my work, but I don't pretend to have any affiliation to it. I'm always trying to find a new language that feels very true to not just me but the people I'm working with. It's a transformative process. ▮

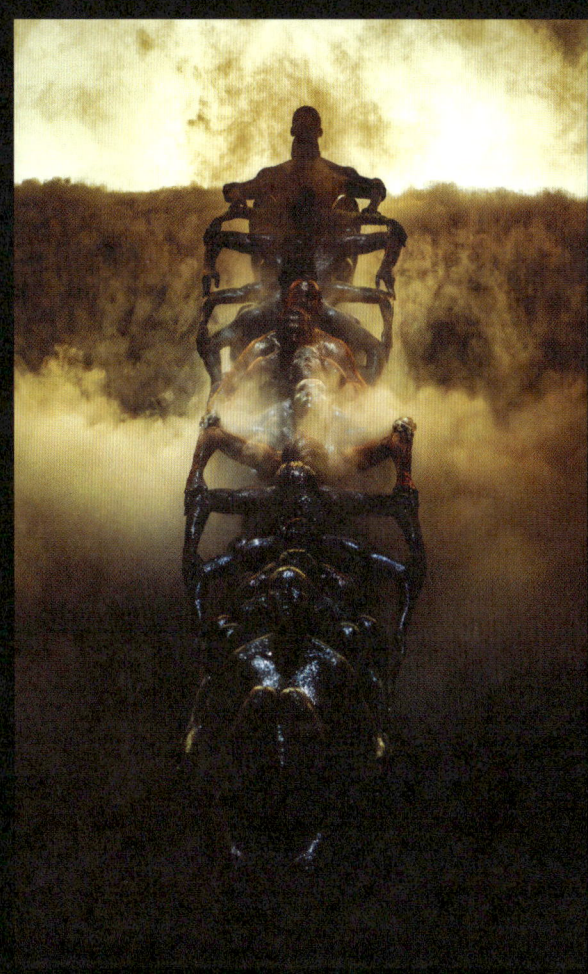

Mirage
Image *Rahi Rezvani*

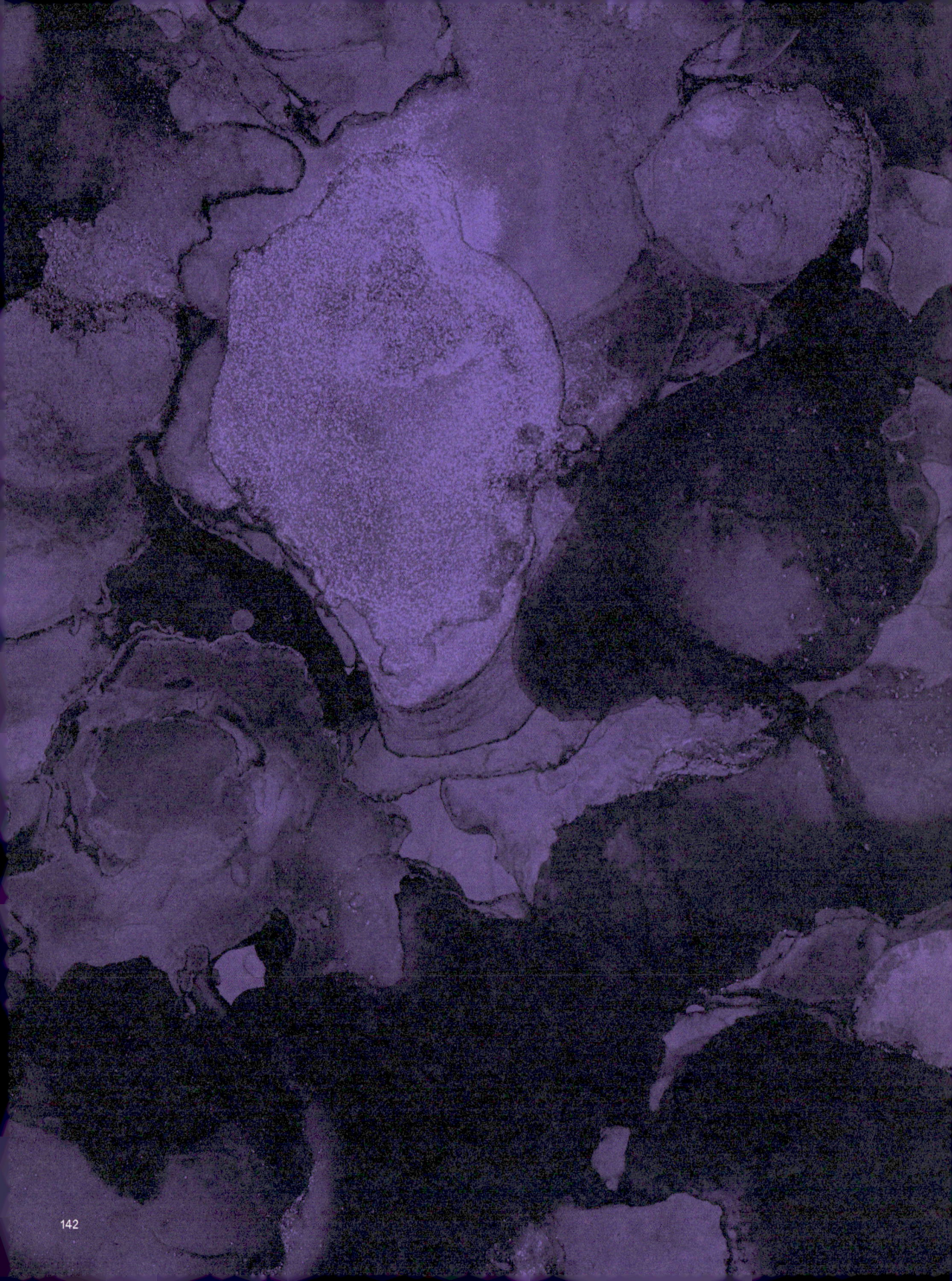

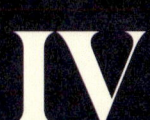

IV

For one auteur at least, things are not overthought. / Mr. Hansel meets a doomscrolling demon, and all things bacchanalian and aberrant are unleashed unto the world. / Buttresses fly, as they are wont to do. / A palanquin is pictured. / A masked musician synthesizes melodies at once uncanny and unholy. / Naughty names are bandied about among the disreputable, while Bela Lugosi remains dead. / The vastness of space is pondered on the dancefloor; a photograph of Prince's cat is taken.

144 — 235

EVERY DAY IS HALLOWEEN

*Filmmaker and composer John Carpenter
on things that go bump in the night*

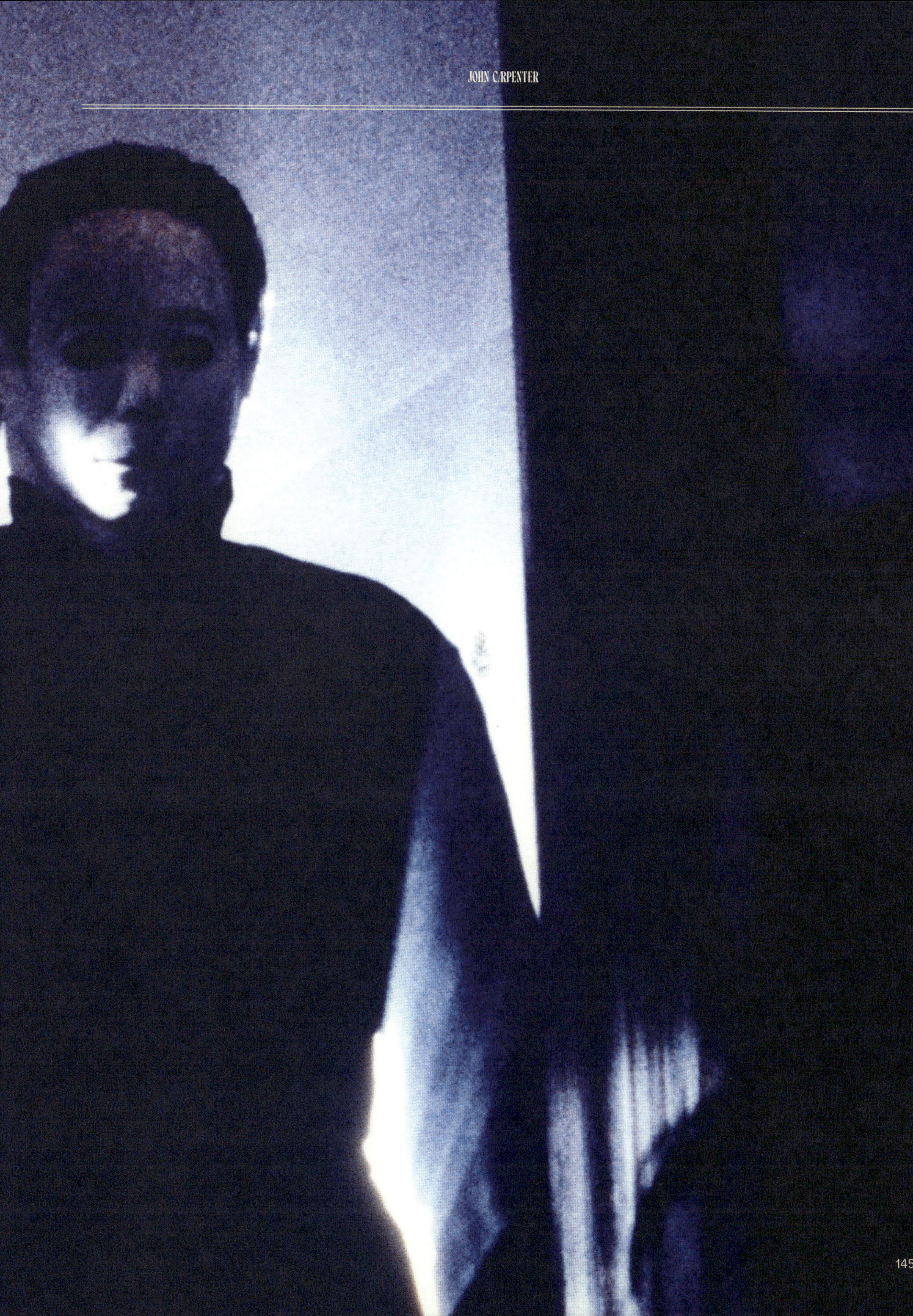

Serial slashers. Evil aliens. Ancient Chinese demons. These are the kind of characters that inhabit John Carpenter's movies. From the mute, knife-wielding Michael Myers in *Halloween* (1978) and the shape-shifting extraterrestrial in *The Thing* (1982) to the supernatural kung-fu killers of *Big Trouble in Little China* (1986) and rotting maritime ghosts of *The Fog* (1980), Carpenter's films seized the collective imagination of a generation raised on heavy metal, MTV, and horror flicks.

In 1981, he introduced the world to Snake Plissken, the unshaven, eye patch-rocking convict (played by Kurt Russell) sent into the future open-air prison of Manhattan to rescue the president from the ruthless clutches of Isaac Hayes in *Escape From New York.* In 1983, he famously adapted Stephen King's killer car thriller *Christine.* In 1987, he cast shock rocker Alice Cooper as the leader of a homeless gang possessed by Satan in *Prince of Darkness.* The following year, Carpenter made one of the most politically salient films of our time in *They Live,* an anti-capitalist sci-fi masterpiece starring pro wrestler Rowdy Roddy Piper.

A perennial multitasker, Carpenter also scored many of his own films. The pulsing synthesizer themes he created for *Halloween, The Fog, Escape From New York,* and his 1976 crime thriller *Assault on Precinct 13* are as indelible as the films themselves. And music is where Carpenter is most prolific these days. Along with his son Cody and stepson Daniel Davies (son of Kinks guitarist Dave Davies), Carpenter has released a series of four excellent *Lost Themes* albums over the last decade and written scores for the last wave of *Halloween* flicks. We recently caught up with him for a glimpse behind the scenes.

Words *J. Bennett* / Portrait *Corinne Schiavone* / Film Stills *ScreenProd, Photononstop, Alamy Stock Photo*

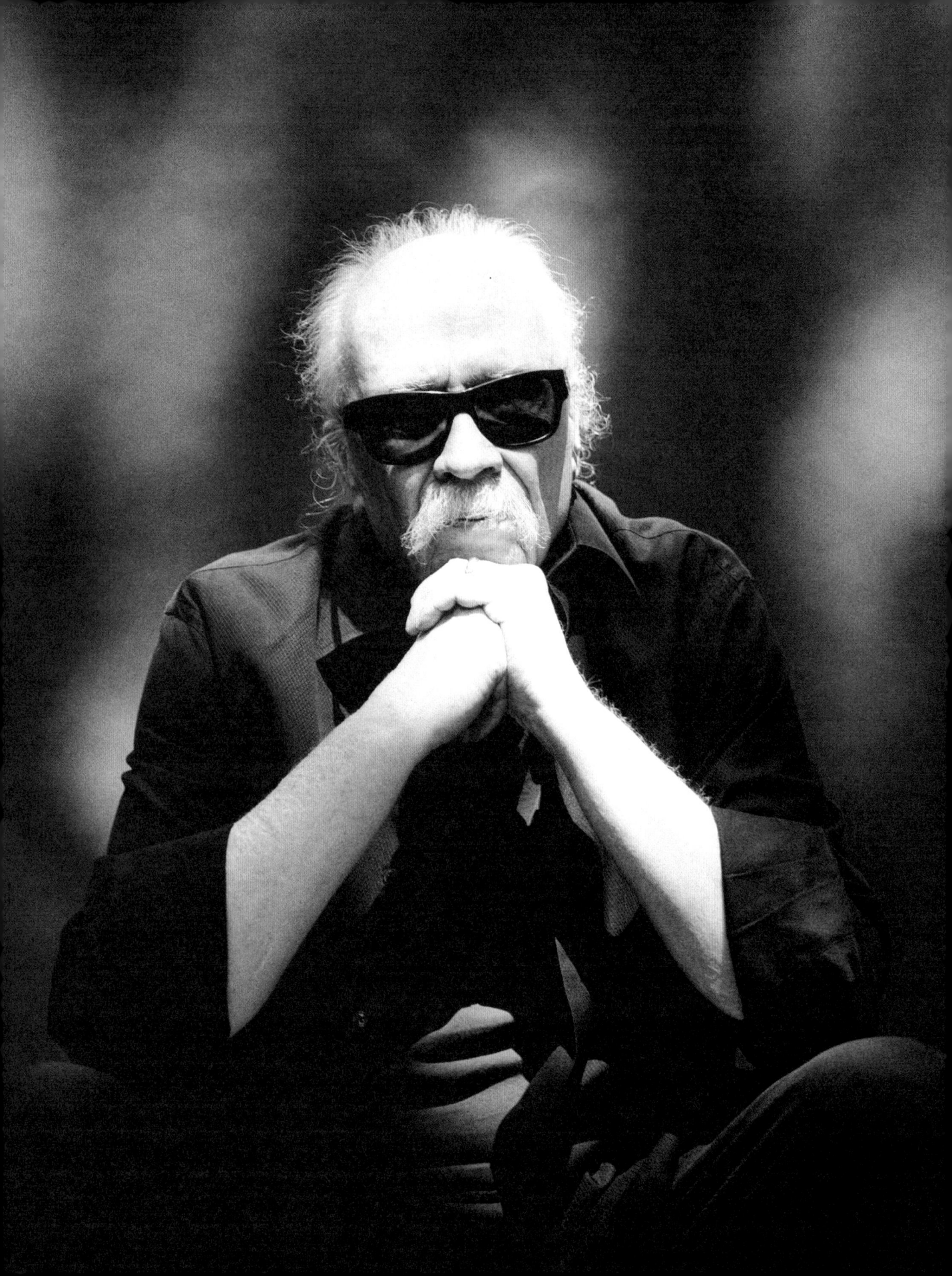

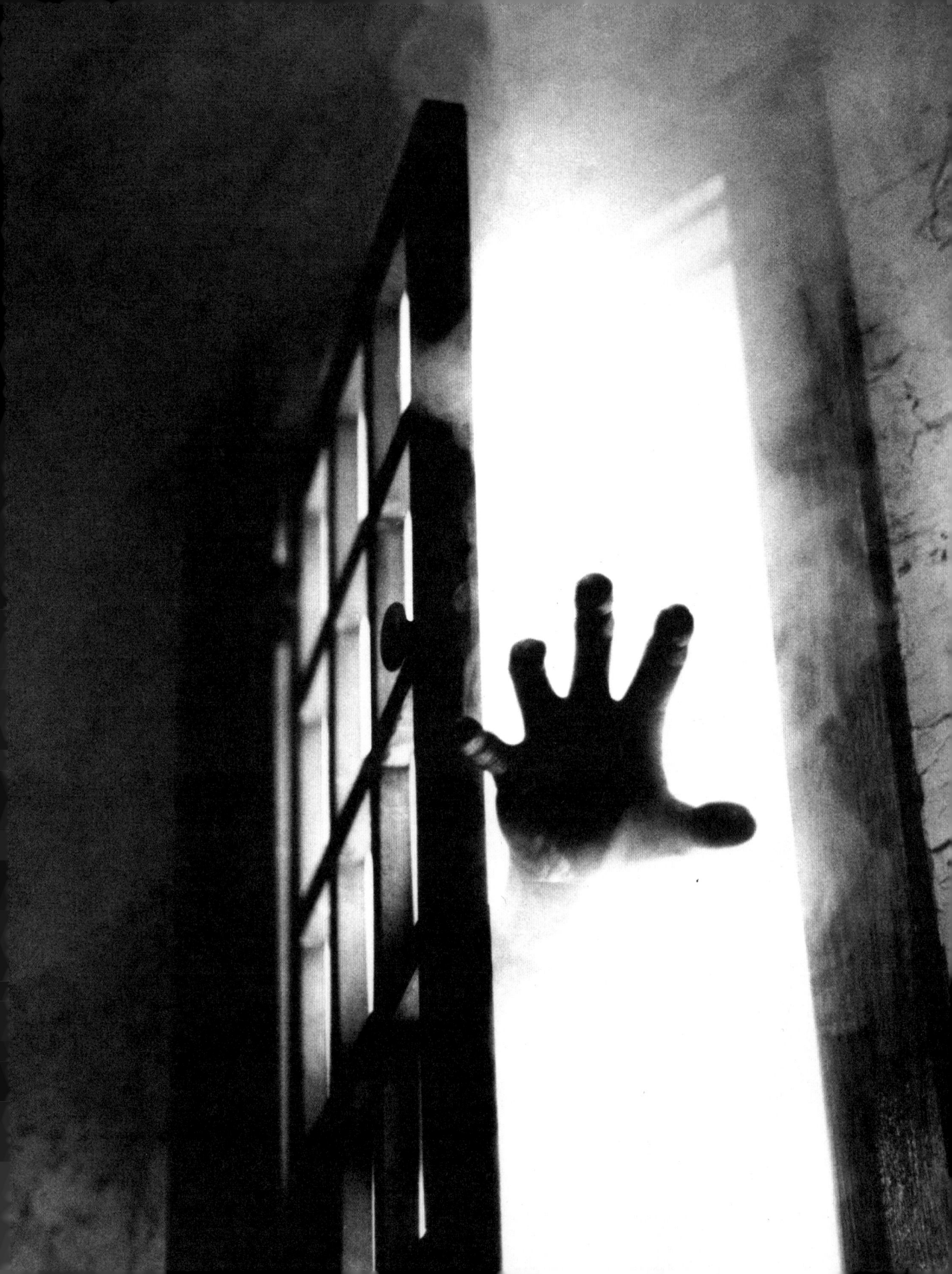

W *Wednesday* focuses on dark themes in the arts, and of course your films and music have plenty. What draws you to these types of subjects?

J Well, it's really a combination of things. I grew up loving science fiction and horror movies when I was a kid. They were my favorites—those and Westerns. When I was an adult trying to get into the movie business, the genre found me. I made a movie called *Halloween,* and it was successful. And then the assumption became, "Well, he does horror movies." And that's how it happened.

W Before this interview, there were only two of your movies I hadn't seen: *Someone's Watching Me!* and *Elvis*—both made for TV. I watched them earlier this week and realized that they happen to be the movies you made on either side of *Halloween.* What was it like moving between those three films?

J With TV movies, you have to move fast. You only have a few days to do it in, so you have to plan everything out. You have in your head as a director that you need to just execute it quickly. That's what I learned from *Someone's Watching Me!,* and that helped me in *Halloween.*

Elvis was a different story. It was a huge under-taking. It had 188 speaking parts and so many different locations. Oh, lord—I have never been so tired in my life. The climax of all this was the final scene, where Elvis was singing. Kurt Russell was in his jumpsuit singing away, I was watching the dailies, and I fell asleep. I didn't watch it; I was just so tired. But you learn how to shoot quick and make decisions fast. It worked out okay.

W You've said that *Elvis* was the most difficult movie you've made. It's over three hours long. Was it simply that you had to shoot so much material?

J I have to qualify that now. I did one a few years later called *The Thing.* And that was physically difficult because of the snow. It was so hard. But yes, *Elvis* was hard because we had to shoot so much, and we just didn't have any time. I think we had 30 days on that. That's unrealistic, really. But we did it.

W *Elvis* was the first time you worked with Kurt Russell, so there's a silver lining there, at least. You went on to cast him in *Escape From New York, The Thing,* and *Big Trouble in Little China.*

J Oh, big time. He's a brilliant actor. People don't realize it. He's really underappreciated by Hollywood. He can play anything you ask, and he comes up with these ideas for his character that are genius. I just love working with him. We did some great characters together, and he became a friend.

W You mentioned *The Thing,* which is now considered one of your best. But it wasn't very well received at the time it came out. Why do you think popular and critical opinion shifted so dramatically over time?

J I can't understand it, but wow. Jesus, I was excoriated for that movie. I was hated by the fans, and I lost a job because of it. It was a miserable time. Then, somehow, in some way, it was all reevaluated. I think it happened

when it hit home video. I think that's when people saw it and they began to like it. But I don't know. I don't question it. I just accept it and say, "Thank you very much." A little late, but thank you. My career would've been very different had that been a success.

W When it started to catch on, did you feel validated? Like "Yeah, that's right. I made a good movie!"

J Well, no, not exactly that. It's a great test when something you really care about fails, and I hung on to the movie. A lot of people said it wasn't any good, but I held it as my best work, and I still feel that. But what the hell? What can I do? It's stuff that's beyond your control.

W What was your impression of the practical special effects that were done for that movie? Even watching today, some of that stuff is amazing.

J There won't be another movie like that again, with those practical effects and that many of them. It was mainly the work of Rob Botin, who's kind of genius. He was a flawed human being, but that's all right—we all are. Rob Botin came up with the idea that the Thing can look like anything. It can imitate anything in the universe. And I thought, "Oh, wow—that's great. We can just go nuts here." And that's what we did.

W Stephen King doesn't like Stanley Kubrick's adaptation of *The Shining,* and he doesn't like your adaptation of *Christine.* Do you care if the author of the source material is happy with your work?

J Well, I'd prefer it. But he didn't like the movie. I have no idea why. But what can I do about it? As far as *The Shining,* I don't blame him. I don't like that movie, either. It's not scary. The two sisters standing in the hallway? Please—they could be delivering food. He's not the right guy to do a scary movie. He doesn't understand it. Blood coming out of an elevator? It has nothing to do with anything. It's completely detached from the story.

W I know you don't like to watch your own films because they make you relive all the work involved, but what was the first movie you made in which you accomplished the goal you had when you started?

J I've never felt that. Never. It's always just: Get 'em done. And you're happy that they're finished. And that you didn't get fired off them. That's the triumph. Finishing a movie, you never know what people are going to think of it. You just don't know.

W Okay, let me rephrase it: Which one came the closest to accomplishing your goal?

J I don't know. I'm the wrong person to ask. I can't watch my own movies because I start critiquing everything. "Why did I do that?" I say to myself, "What the fuck was on my mind? Why is that so slow?" I do all sorts of crazy things. I can't watch them objectively.

W You obviously have a much better relationship with the scores you've created for your films. You re-recorded them for an anthology a few years ago, and you started playing them live about 10 years ago. How are you able to separate the two?

"I don't like The Shining. It's not scary. The two sisters standing in the hallway? Please—they could be delivering food."

J Well, music is... how do I put this? It's the ultimate art form that man has created. It's better than any other. It doesn't require language. It doesn't require explanation. It doesn't require talking. It bypasses all of that. It bypasses intellect, and it is profound. Music is the closest we are to God.

My dad was a music teacher, so he taught me the respect for it. And it's astonishing how much fun it is. And there's no pressure. The pressure of movies is extreme. They make you carry about 150,000 bucks a day on your shoulders. If you get behind, you're spending somebody else's money, and that's not good. And the pressure, the constant pressure to succeed. At the end of the day, there's a long hallway, and standing there with the film cans is the director. People come and say, "This was shit," or "This is okay," or whatever. It didn't go that way with music. So, I discovered a second career for myself with music in 2015, and I love it.

W You once told me a story about seeing footage of yourself working on one of the last movies you made, *Ghosts of Mars.* You knew it was the beginning of the end for you.

J Oh, yeah. I thought, "Look at that pathetic old man. He's dying. He needs to stop."

W You did one more movie after that, and then you did stop. That must've been such a huge, profound moment in your life.

J I had to, but it's okay. I'm not excluding directing. I would direct something if conditions are correct for me. But it's harder now. Look, I'm 77. Come on. It's tough to get out of bed when you're 77. I'd need a good budget and enough time. I don't want to get up early. And I don't wanna do it on a glacier in British Columbia like *The Thing.* No, no, no.

W Nearly a decade before *Ghosts of Mars,* you made *Memoirs of an Invisible Man* starring Chevy Chase. You've said that movie made you want to quit. Why?

J Chevy Chase. That's what happened. He's a horrible, horrible human being. And he was a producer on it, so that made it worse. He had too much power. It's too bad, but it doesn't matter now. I survived.

W You're unique as filmmakers go in that your scores are often as beloved as your films. And you did so many

of your scores out of necessity—there was no time or money to hire someone else. But some part of you must've wanted to do it, right? People don't write scores as memorable as yours by not caring.

J Well, I fell into it. After I did a number of them, I felt I needed to do all of them. They became another creative voice in the movie. But it didn't start that way. As you said, there was no time and no money.

W You've said that some of your most famous scores, like the *Halloween* theme, are successful because of their simplicity. Do you generally take a less-is-more approach to writing music?

J I take the approach that I can't do more than that. I have limited chops. My son, on the other hand, is a virtuoso musically. He's unbelievable. He has far surpassed me. He and I work together still, but I can't play like that. I never was able to. I have limited ability, so that's what I stick with.

W Beyond working with your son and godson, how is making music different for you now than it was back in the '70s and '80s when you were writing these scores by yourself?

J It's joyous now, because I never thought I'd work with my own family, and that's just the greatest. But I just love making music. There's no thought involved in it. It bypasses all that. It just comes out, and you can't explain it. There's a line in an old song about trying to tell a stranger about rock n roll: You can't explain to people what it's like. But when music just pours out of you, it's unreal.

W Much of the music you write is improvisational. Why do you like to work that way?

J It's the only way I can work. It's the opposite of making a movie. It's much more spontaneous, and that's why I love it so much. In filmmaking, you have a scene to shoot, and it depends on what's in the scene, but you have to have a lot of angles, and you have to figure out ahead of time which ones you need, where you're going to put your camera, and so forth. There's a lot to think about.

W Your godson and collaborator Daniel Davies told me that your philosophy for making music is "Don't overthink it."

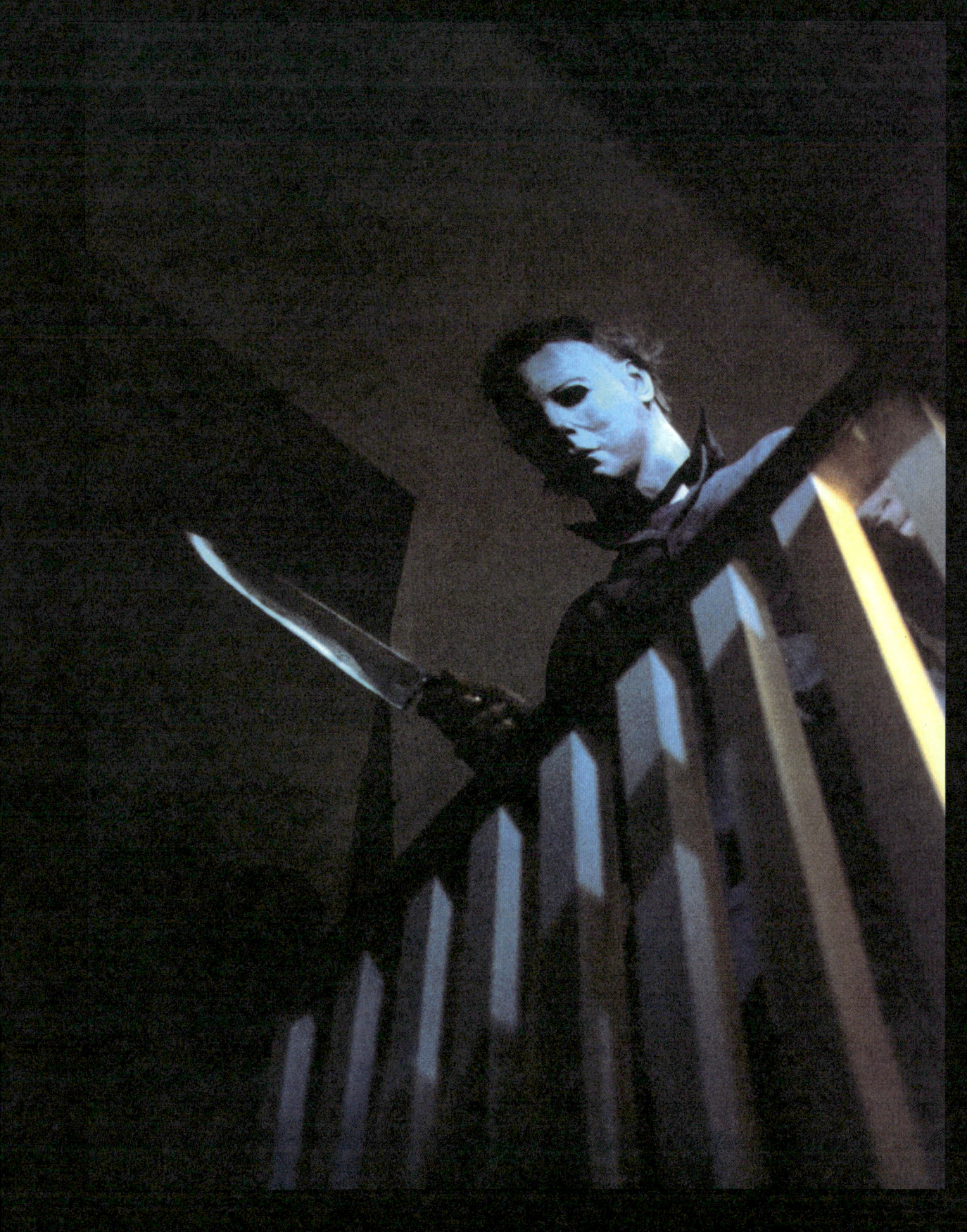

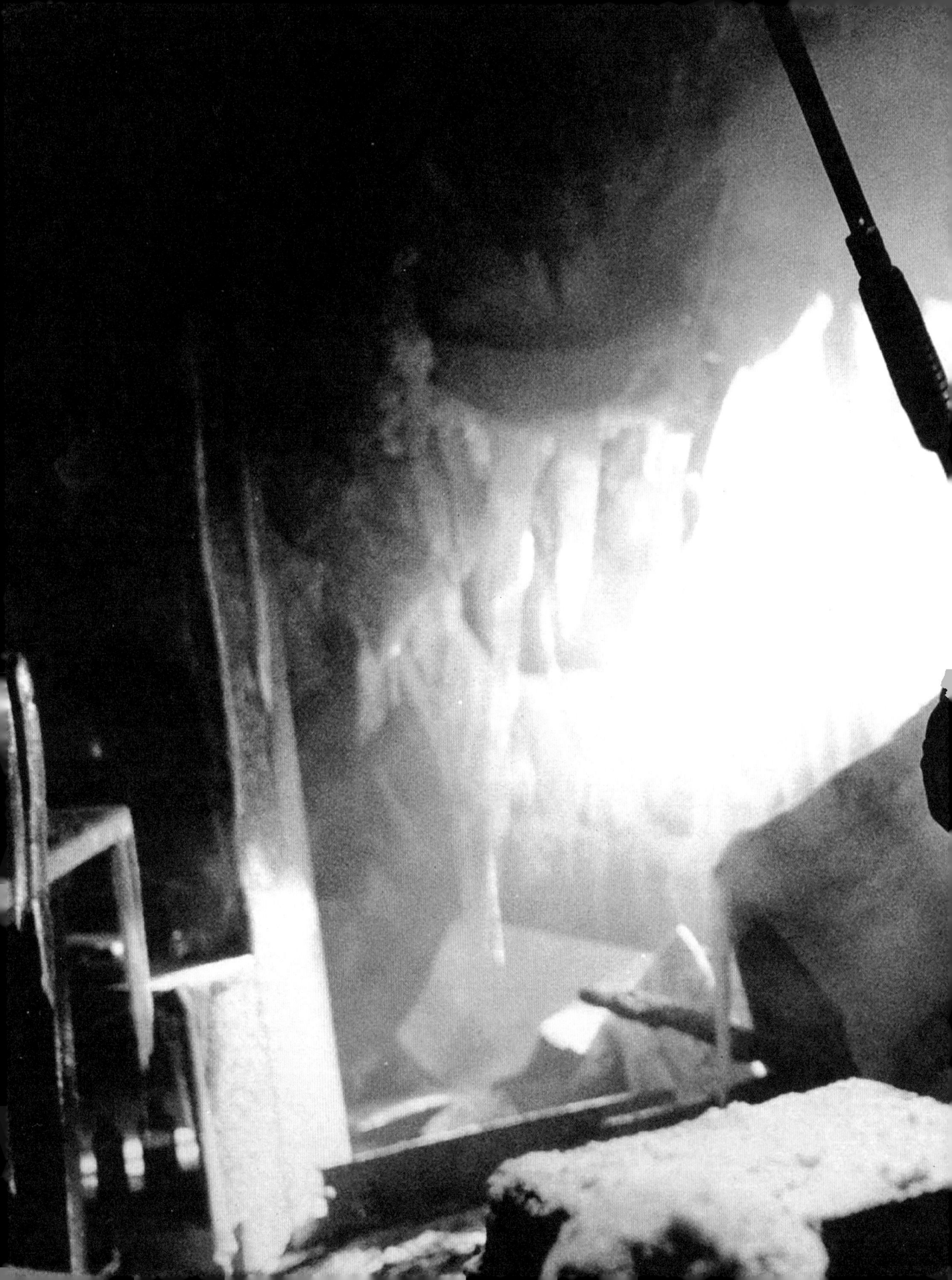

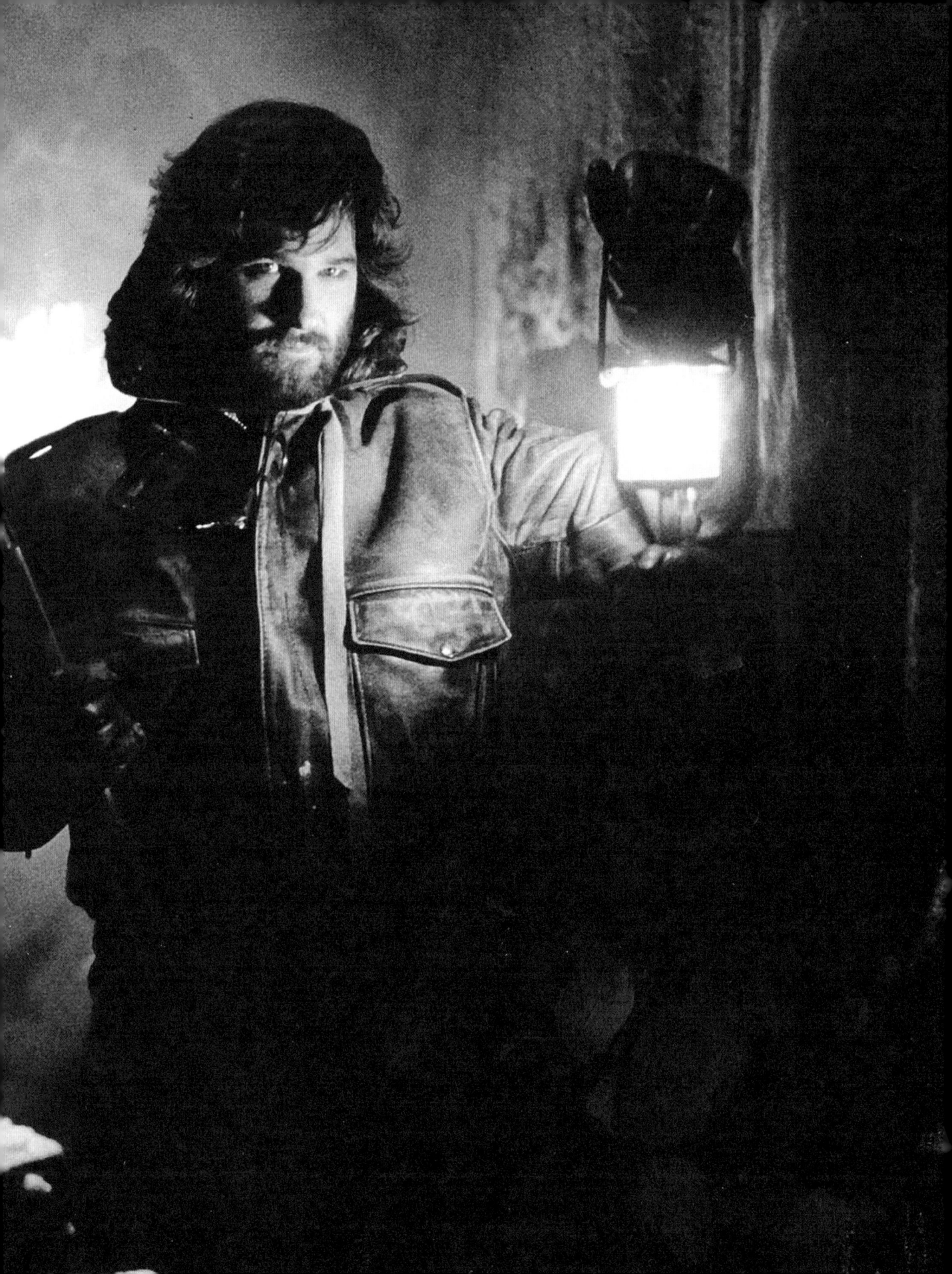

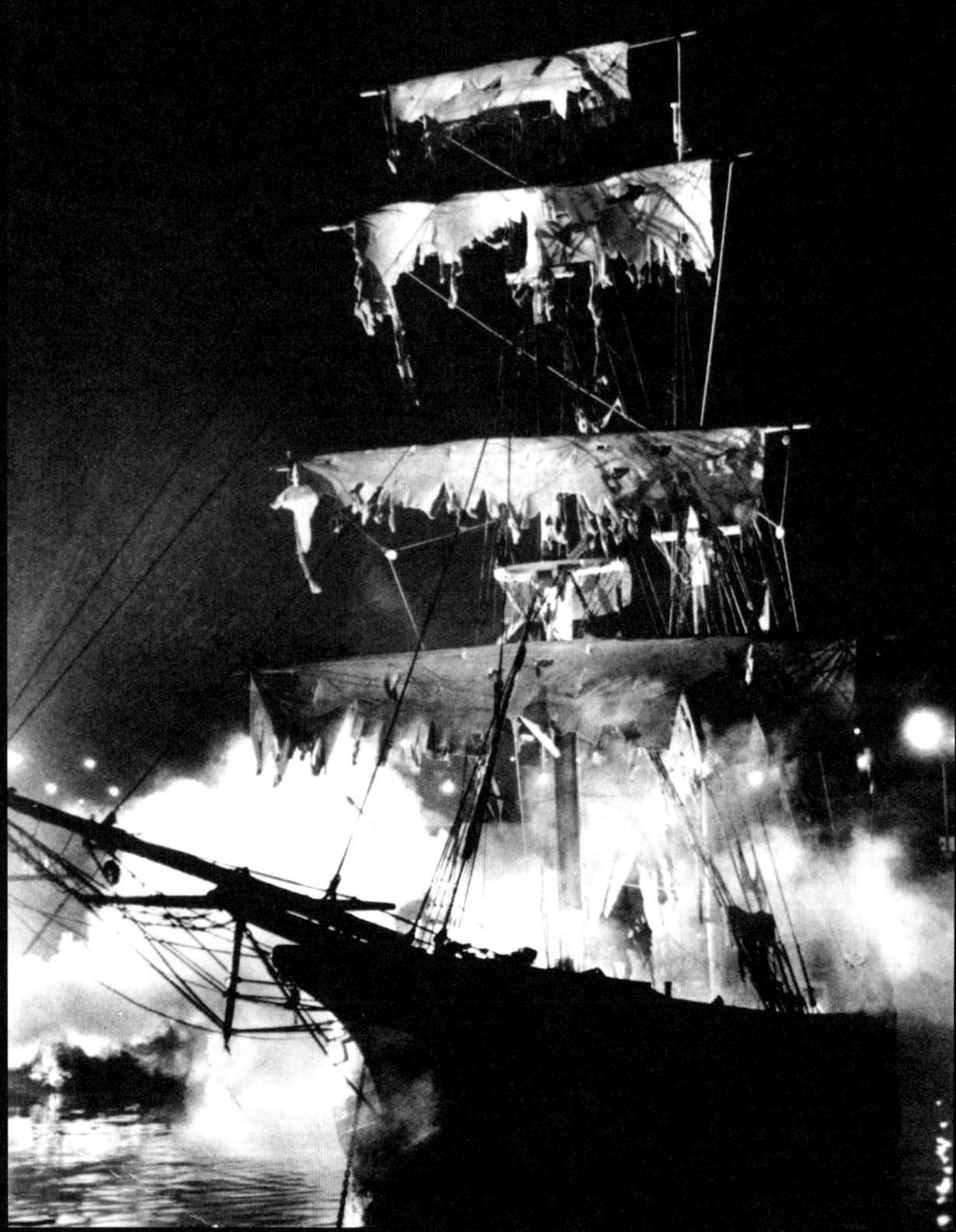

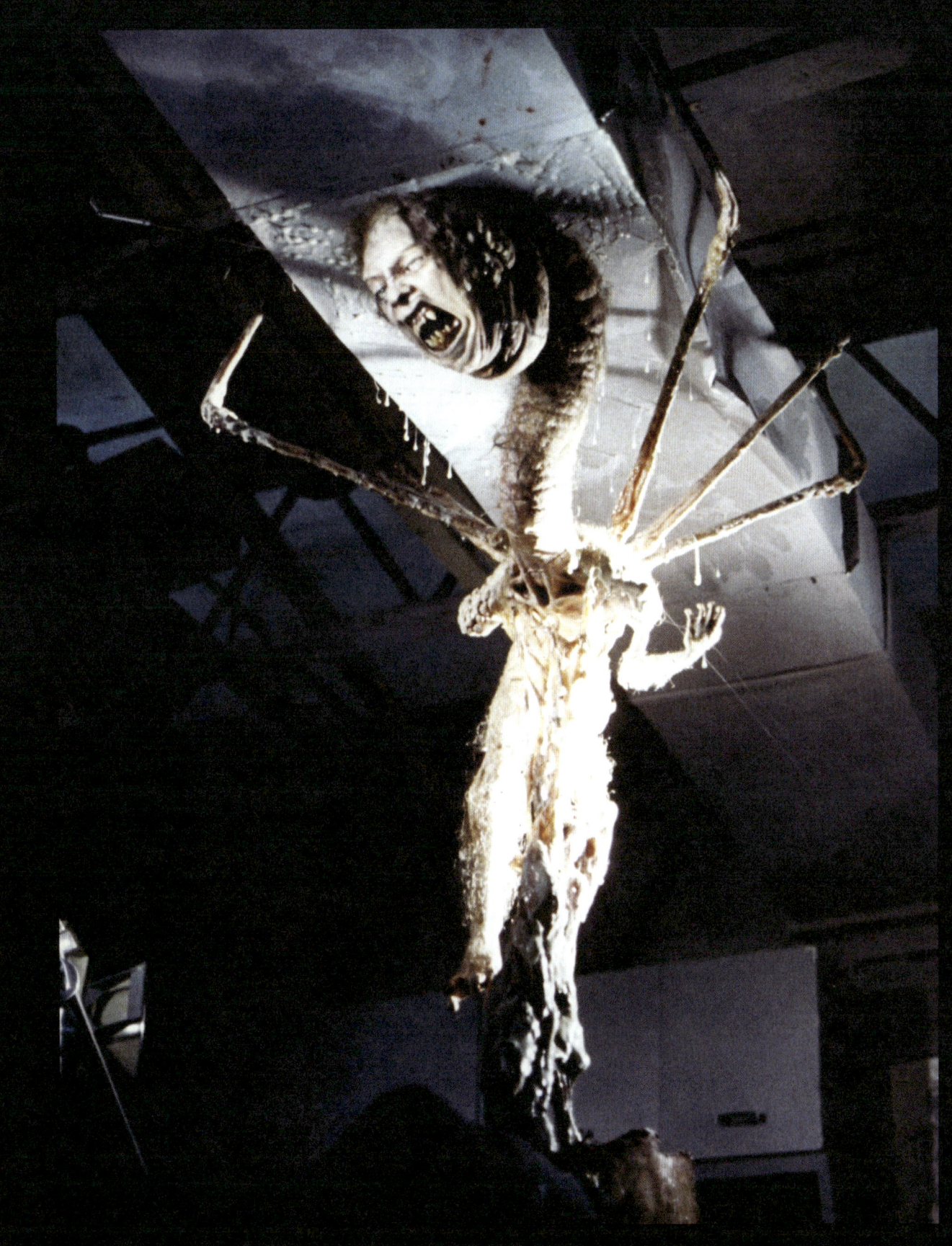

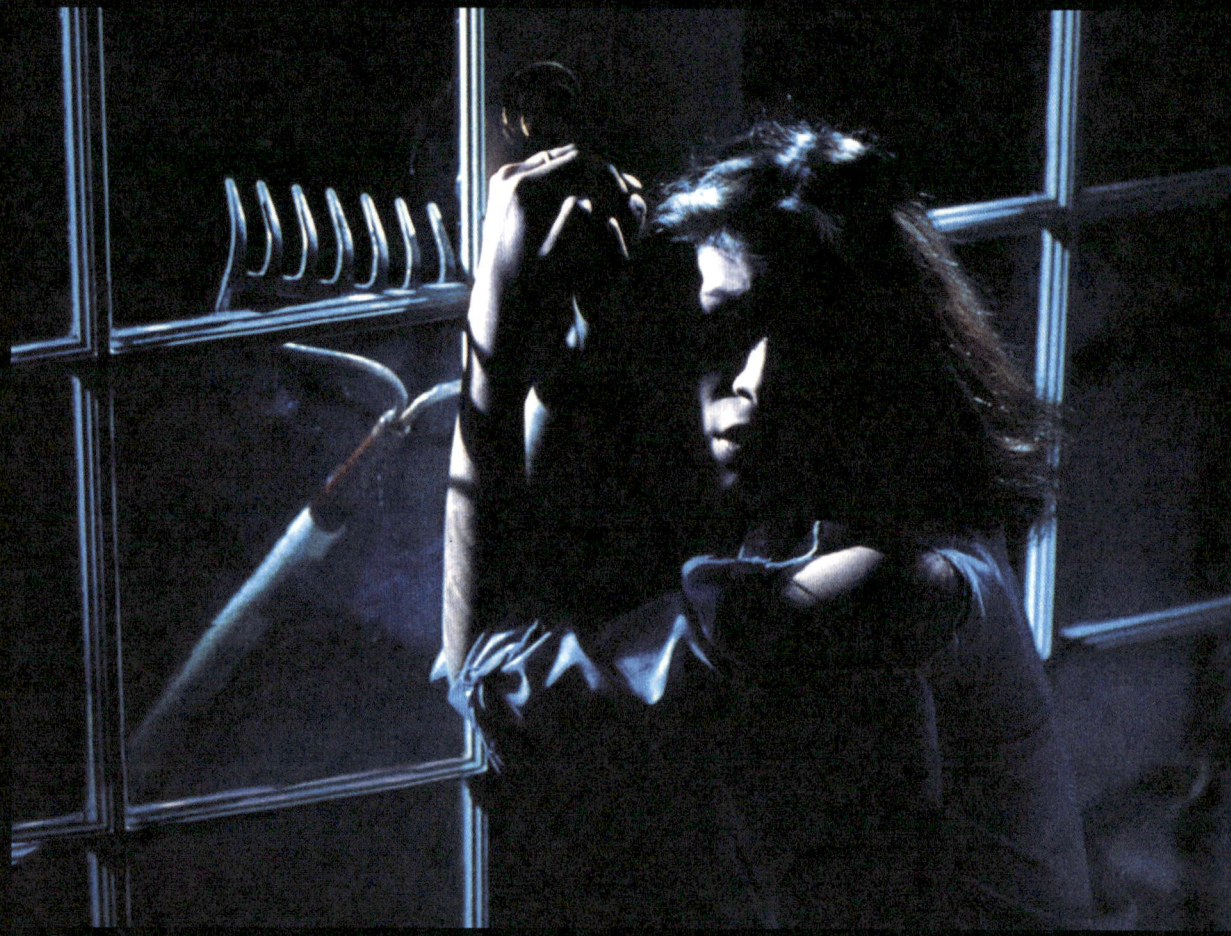

J   Yeah, that's right. Don't think about it at all. That's the way I started: Just sit down at the piano and sketch out a song. I've seen other people write out sheet music for something. Ennio Morricone did that when he scored *The Thing*. It's brilliant. But I just can't do it that way.

W   Over the past several years, you and Cody and Daniel have scored other people's movies, like David Gordon Green's *Halloween* trilogy and the *Firestarter* remake. How is that process different than scoring your own films? Is there less stress because it's not your movie?

J   It's just different because other directors have other needs. They have their own ideas. But it's great. I love it. I'm detached from it in a sense, but it's all the same process. You do what's necessary to enhance the movie. It's fun.

W   The last time we spoke, you were working on a score for *Death of a Unicorn*. But now I see someone else ended up doing the music. What happened?

J   They fired us. They suddenly sold the company to somebody who decided that what the movie needed was an orchestral score. So, they said bye-bye to us. And it

didn't do very well, so we kind of escaped the blame. But check out the movie and see what you think. It's got a great cast, and it's not too bad.

W   You've often talked about the score of *Forbidden Planet* as an influence. What are some other film scores that influenced or impressed you?

J   Growing up, I was very impressed by some of the master composers, and two of them especially. One was Dimitri Tiomkin, who was really well known in the old days. He was unbelievable. I can tell a Dimitri Tiomkin movie without knowing he scored it. I could just listen: "Oh, that's him." I love his stuff. He did *Rio Bravo, High Noon, The High and the Mighty* and *The Thing from Another World*. He won Academy Awards for some of those. The other one is Bernard Hermann. All you have to do is listen to an old Hitchcock movie. He did a lot of science fiction and horror films, too.

W   Speaking of Hitchcock, I noticed quite a few references to his work in *Someone's Watching Me!* Not just the score—which wasn't yours—but the shots, the camera angles—even the story was similar to *Rear Window*.

J That's correct. I was a young filmmaker, and the influence just came through. That movie comes from a true story, too—apparently, I got it from the newspaper. And I really loved working with Lauren Hutton. She's not really an actress—she was a model—but she gave a great performance.

W At this point, there have been 13 *Halloween* movies. What has it been like to see your original creation go through all these permutations, many of them without your involvement?

J Yeah, 13 movies—and many of them pieces of shit. But they're not mine, you know? Mine ended with the first one. See, I thought there was no more story. I may have told you that before. Boy, was I stupid. But I share financially when they make one of these things, and I thought David Gordon Green's movies were really good. I enjoyed those, especially *Halloween Kills.* He's a terrific director and a nice man. He really worked with us on the score, too.

W In the last one, *Halloween Ends,* they put Michael Myers' body in an industrial shredder. It's got a genuine air of finality to it, but do you really think it's over? Do you even care?

J Hell no. It's not over until there's no more money in it. That's what motivates it—you know that. We all know that. They're already talking about another one, so it's never going to end. The character keeps coming back. He can't die. But they see success in it because it's cheap to make. We get some idiot in a mask and we've got a movie.

W When you finished cutting the original *Halloween,* you got a note from the studio saying it wasn't scary. What did you do?

J I didn't know what to do with that. I just try to forget them as quickly as possible. I've got some notes from studios that were just unbelievable. Some of them are nonsensical. On *Starman,* somebody said, "Why does the military have to be evil?" That was the story in the movie. I didn't write that story—someone else did. You green-lit it. Fucking idiots. But you can't say that.

W You've said that the modern film industry doesn't know much about film history. Why do you feel that way?

J They just don't know old movies. They don't know where they come from. I don't get it. It's a mystery to me. Most directors know what they're doing—or at least they're working with someone who knows how to direct. There's a certain basic deal to directing. It's like being a traffic cop. You have to know certain things. A lot of it is personality—how to get people to work for you. That's an unknown deal to a lot of folks in the movie business these days.

   Look, I watch many of the big movies that come out. Some are good, and some are shit. But the business has changed so much since I got in. Movies are made by committees. In the old days, it used to the be the head of the studio that green-lit the movies. It would be him or her putting themselves behind the film and believing in it. Not anymore. It's a division of a corporation.

W Who do you like as far as directors working today?

J David Fincher. *Fight Club, Panic Room.* Terrific director. He's probably my favorite. I like Jordan Peele, too.

W What recent films have you enjoyed?

J *Mad Max: Furiosa* was great. Tony Scott's *Unstoppable* was fabulous—I love that movie. Ridley Scott's *The Martian.* I'll watch that over and over.

W Are you working on music for any other films?

J Oh, hell yes. We have new stuff planned. I'm not going to tell you what it is, but it'll be out next year. We're constantly working on new stuff. There'll be more *Lost Themes,* too.

W When you scored your own films in the '70s and '80s, did you ever dream of becoming the full-time composer you are today?

J No, I was never dreaming about it. Never. My first love is cinema and directing movies. I can't leave it. ∎

FOLLOW CONSUME STAY ASLEEP OBEY NO THOUGHT DOUBT HUMANITY WATCH TV

MATT HANSEL
Morbid Delectacio

The fantastically demon-obsessed world of artist Matt Hansel

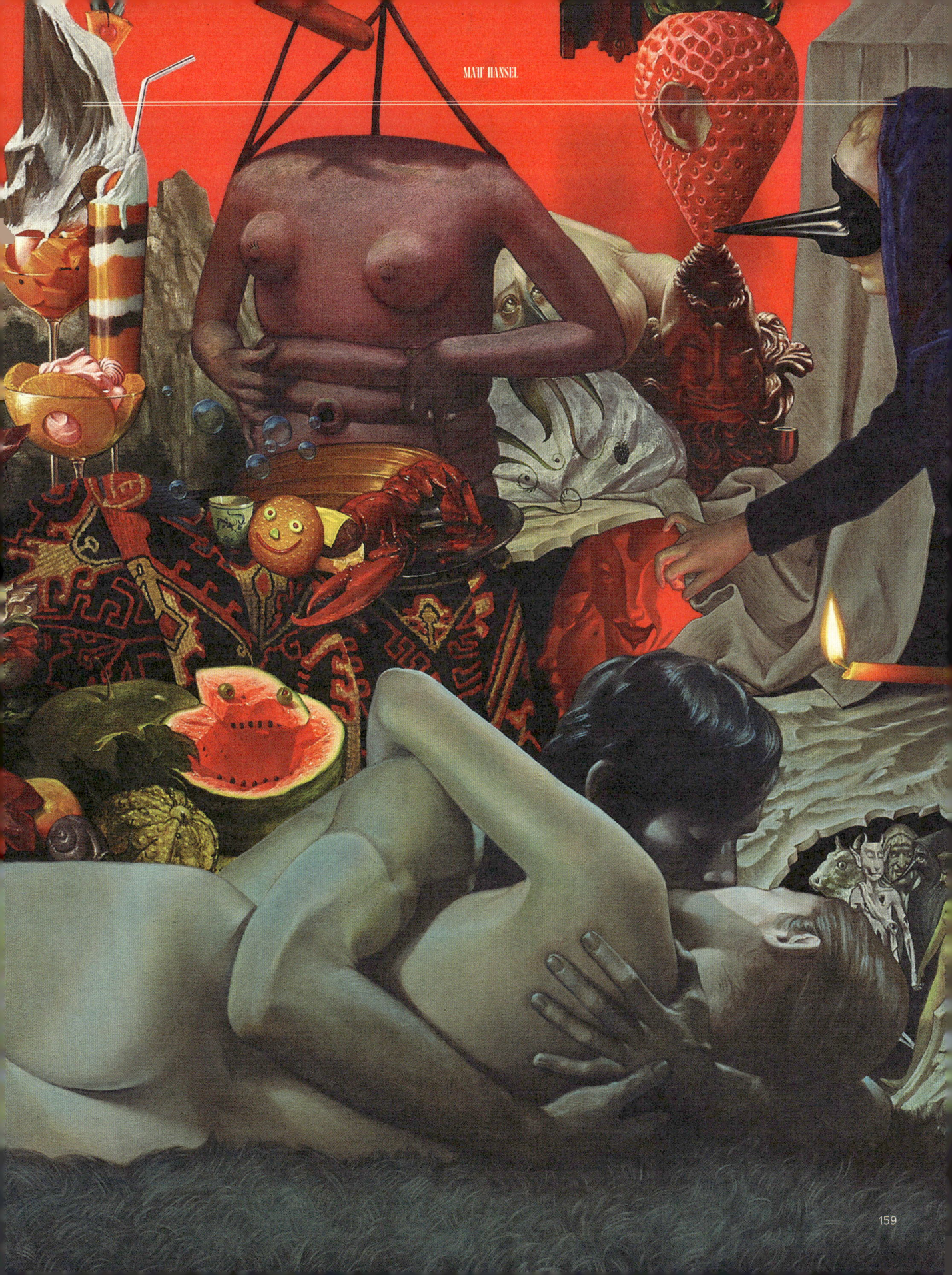

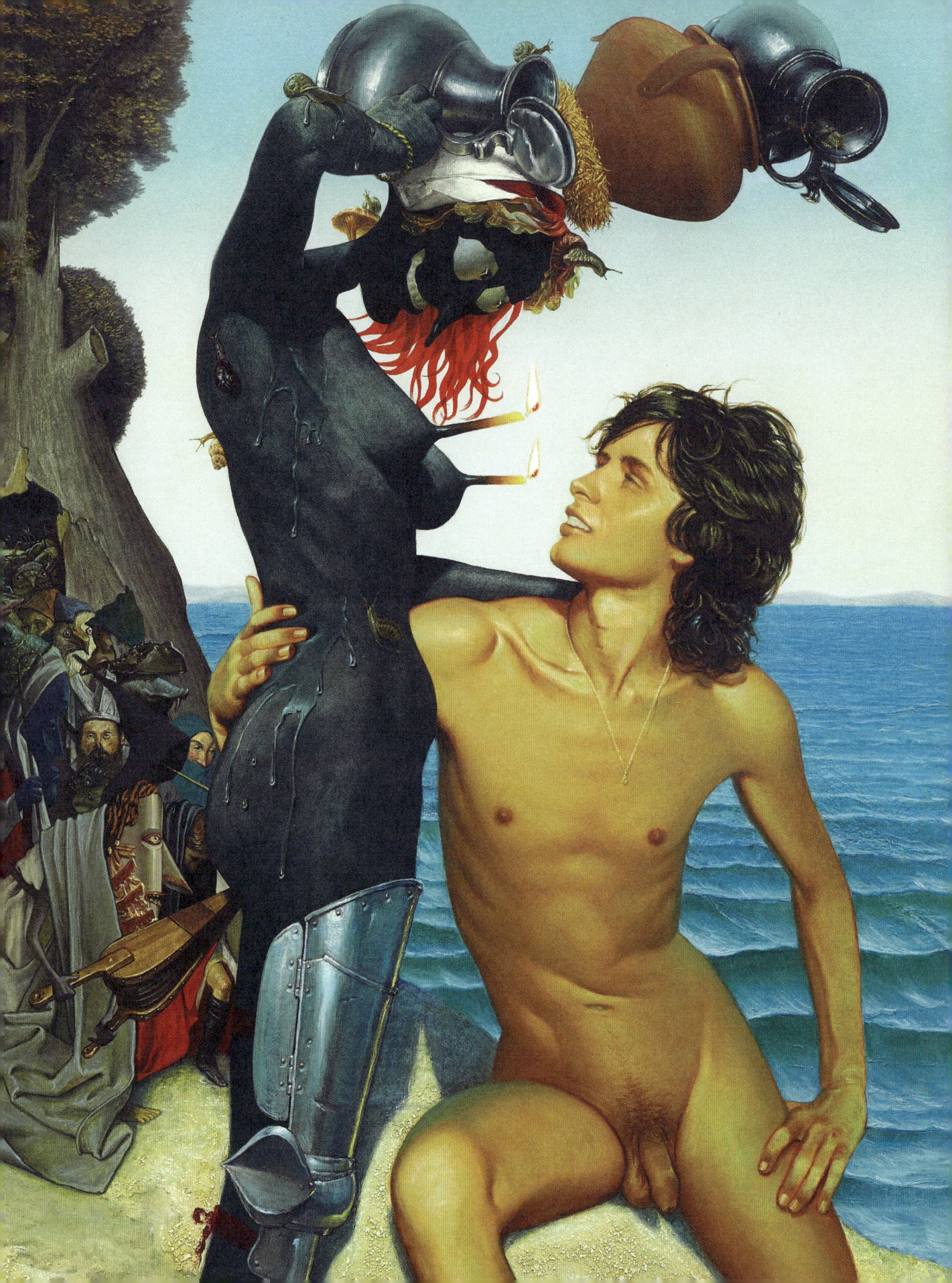

It's the end of the world as we know it, and judging by the expressions of ecstasy found on the faces of Matt Hansel's blithe subjects, everyone is doing just fine. Rendered in a notably Boschian aesthetic, Hansel's paintings present voyeuristic scenes from a global bacchanalian party hosted by the denizens of our collective unconscious. All are welcome; clothing is optional. Bringing new meaning to the term "wrestling with your demons," Hansel meticulously depicts seemingly jovial humans engaged in a wide variety of acts with surreal, imp-like characters—the patron saints of indulgence. But these shepherds lack malevolence. Instead of presenting moral conflicts and entangled truths, they bring forth unabashed pleasures, catering to the freedoms their mortals find in "letting go." The images read like states of mind, exploring the delights and vulnerabilities of human desire. They possess a peculiar sense of familiarity, inviting viewers to engage with their lived experiences by challenging their own personal demons. What *we* see is a delicious, consequence-free utopia. If this is what the brink of the apocalypse looks like, we'll bring the popcorn. See you there.

Previous Spread:
*And the Lovers Lie Abed with all
Their Griefs in Their Arms*, 2021
Oil on canvas, 70 × 92 in.

Opposite Page:
*We Are But Souls Who Dwell
Within Our Dust*, 2021
Oil on canvas, 52 × 42 in.

Interview *Adam Larson* / Artwork *Matt Hansel*

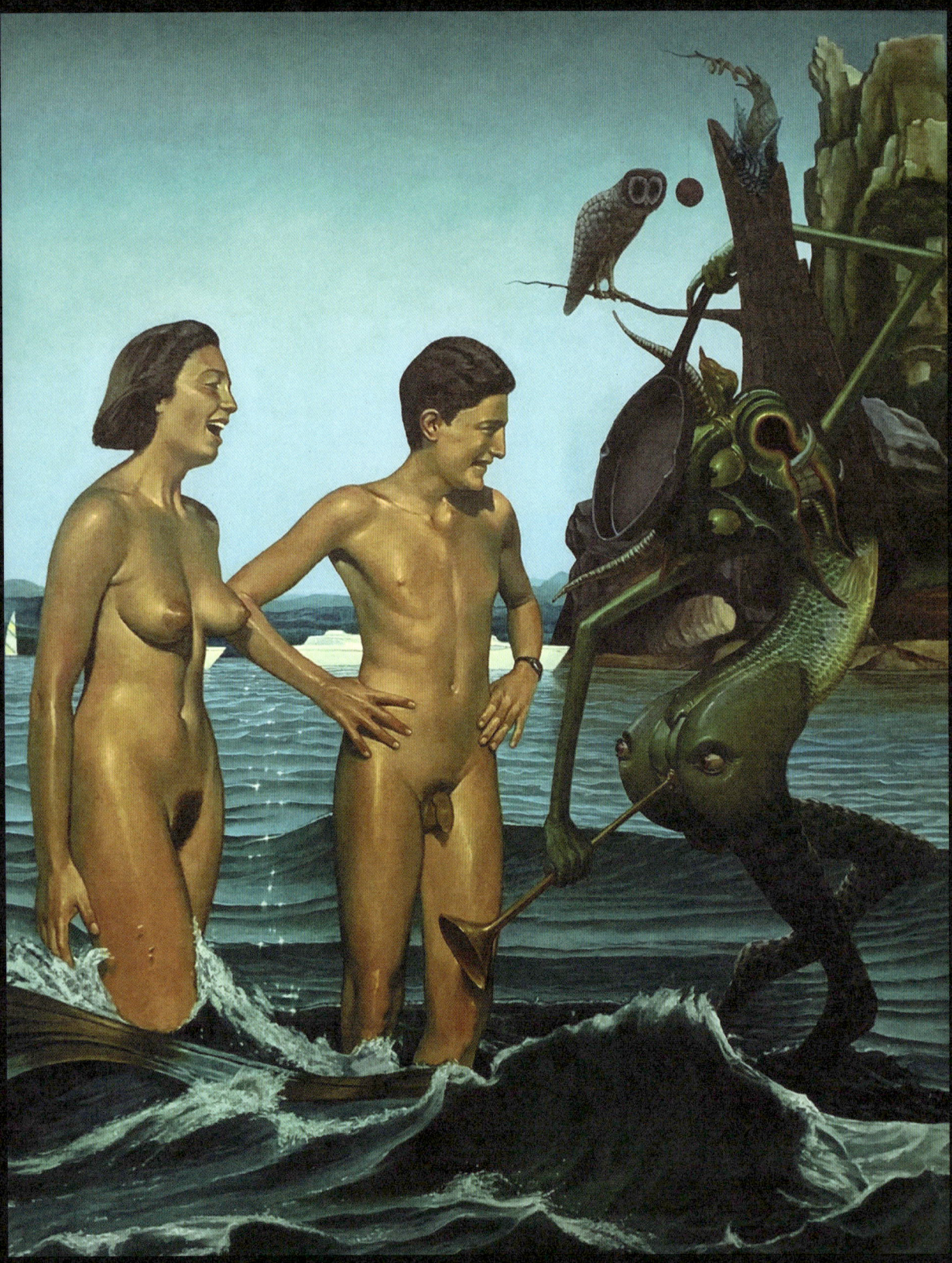

The Soloist, 2020
Oil on canvas 60 × 48 in.

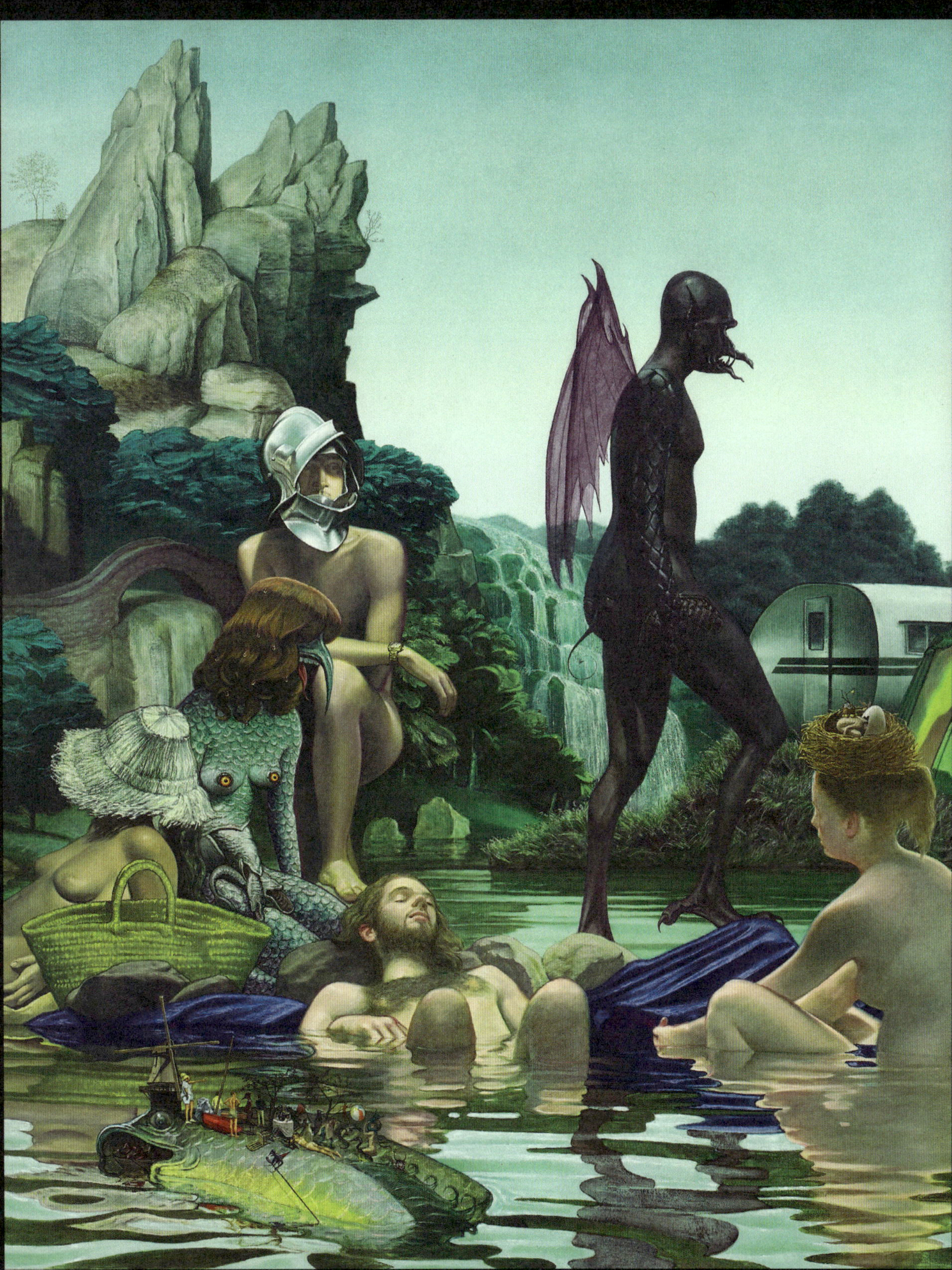

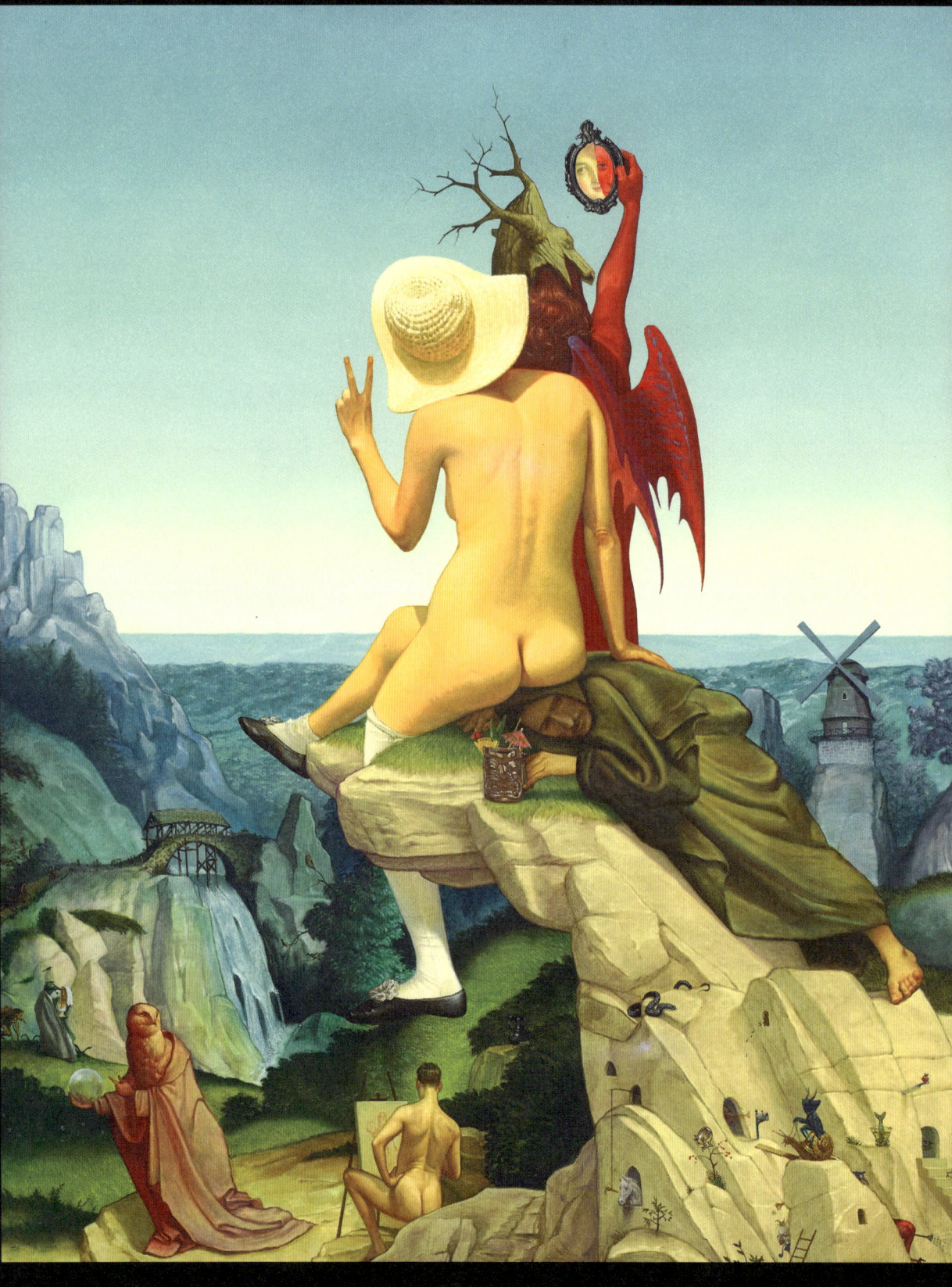

Selfie, 2023
Oil and Flashe paint on canvas 70 × 56 in.

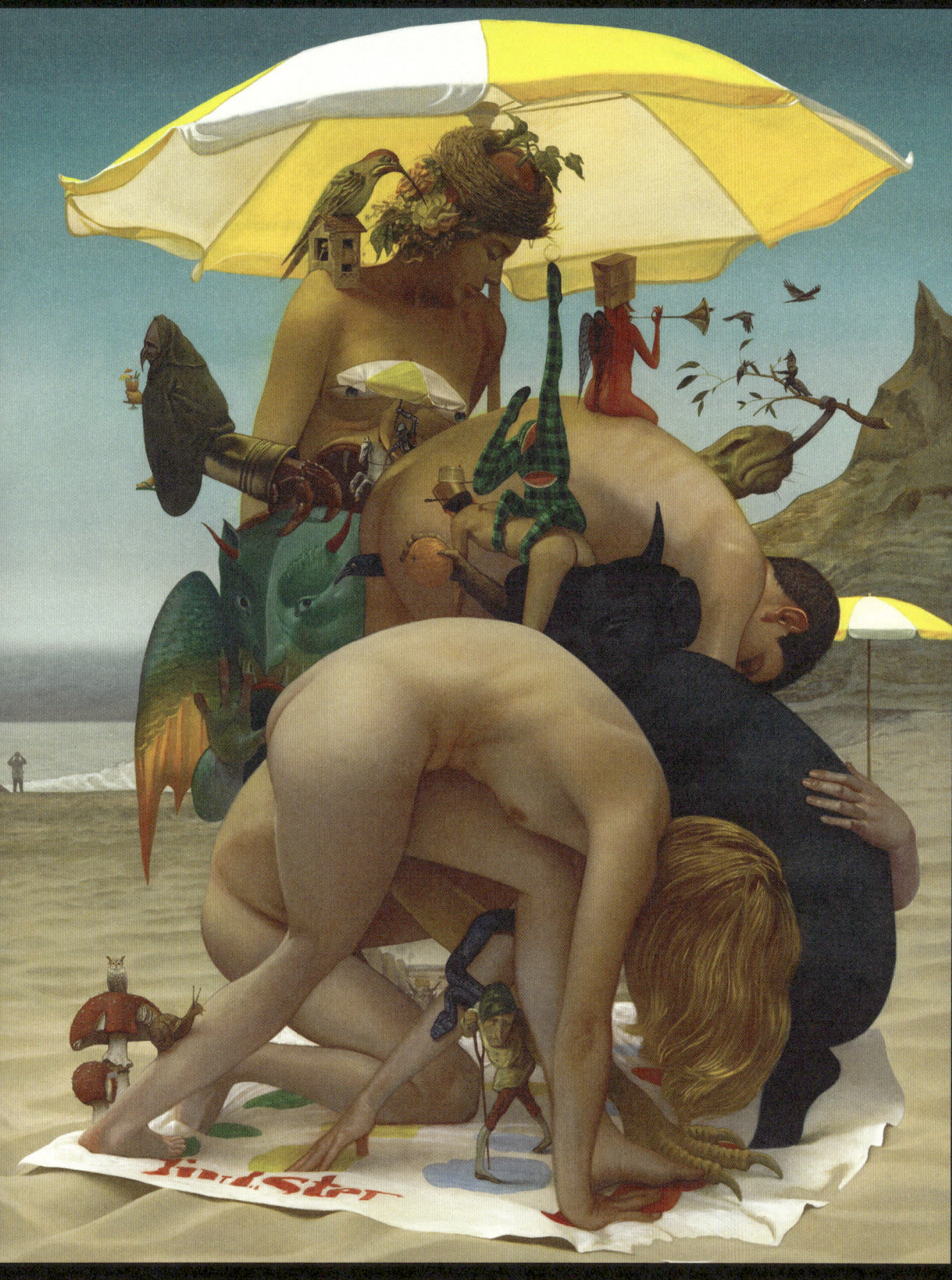

Les Petit Jouets, 2019
Two Framed Archival Digital Prints, Each 18 × 24 in., Edition of 1

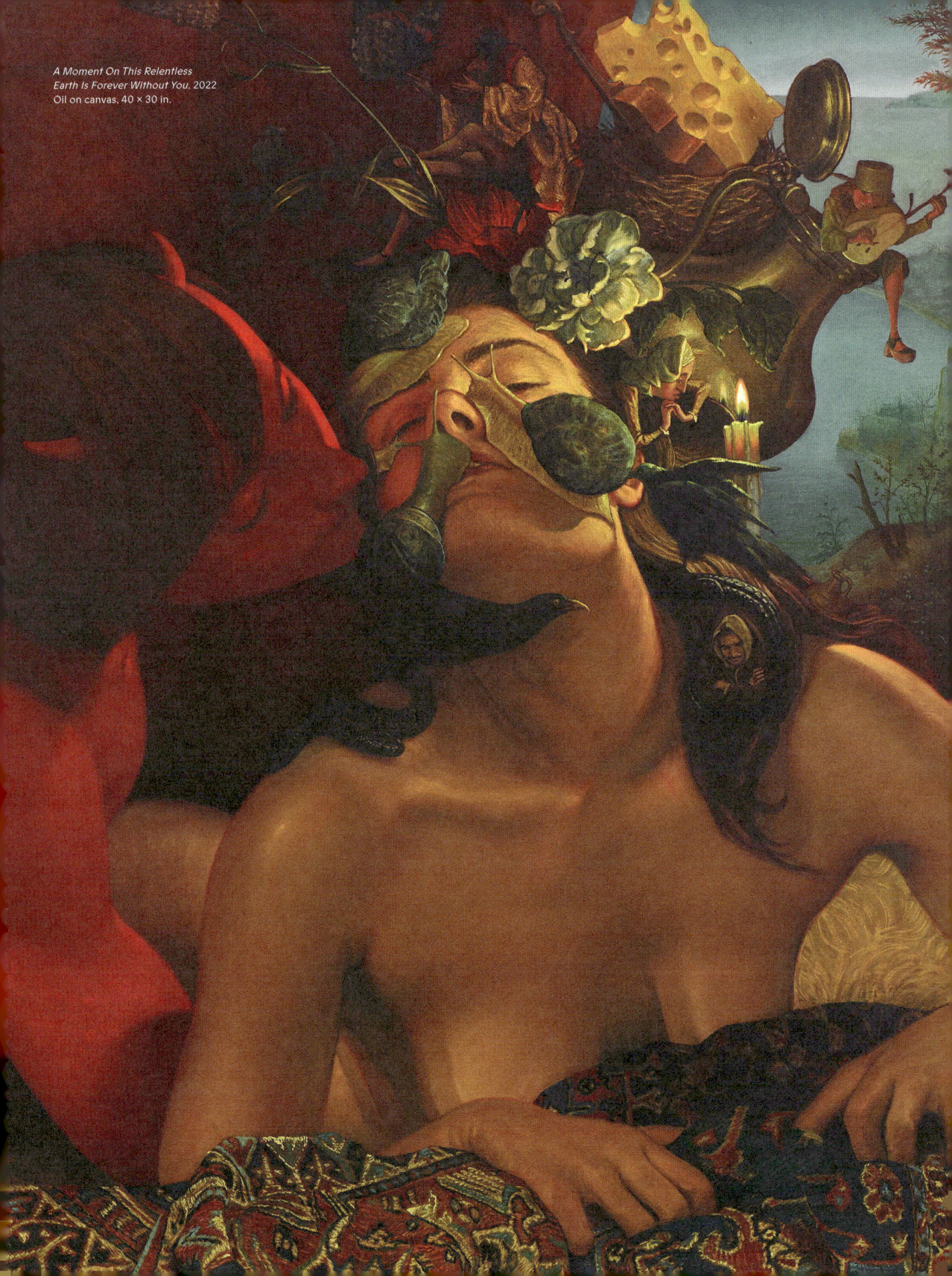

*A Moment On This Relentless
Earth Is Forever Without You*, 2022
Oil on canvas, 40 × 30 in.

W Tell us about your current body of work. What has inspired you as of late?

M It was during the lockdown in 2020 when I first started making my current body of work. We were all at home stuck on our couches and stressed about what was going on in the world outside. It seemed to me that we were all trapped inside with our inner demons. I remember having a vision of a demon sitting next to me on the couch, doomscrolling. I thought that if we could just take our demons out for a stroll or on a trip to the beach, we would all be better off.

So, in an act of catharsis, I made a painting of a young couple splashing in the waves with a demon. It was an odd painting for me and led me to think about the power art has to seduce us, especially when this power is used to present the grotesque in a way that is seductive. The human condition allows for a paradoxical reaction to the grotesque: the dual emotions of repulsion and attraction.

Art as a medium is uniquely adept at allowing us to engage in this contradictory response through what can be best characterized as a type of transfiguration. The traditional idea that art fundamentally seeks beauty seems a rational (if slightly naive) conclusion until one considers that the act of seduction is often decoupled from rationality and that through art we can be attracted to that which if seen in the flesh would repulse us. It's a special power—one of many that art possesses.

W You maintain a commitment to traditional painting methods, but I'm curious if you supplement them with more modern or digital techniques as well? Can you share a bit about your process? How do you go about making a work, from concept to completion?

M Every painting is a dance with the past. When you boil it down, painting is a wonderfully archaic process. You mix colored powders with oil then attach animal hair to the end of a stick. Finally, you find a piece of fabric, and you're off. I doubt there is another method of art making which is so simple yet able to elicit such emotion. Having said that, I can't ignore the advantages afforded to me in the present day. I use photoshop to make digital collages where I can easily build my compositions and quickly make small changes until I'm satisfied. I keep many folders of images that I pull from all sorts of sources: photos, scanned book and magazine pages, drawings, etc.

I usually start with a quick sketch or by simply jotting down an idea. It can be something as innocuous as "Playing beach volleyball with your demons in a snowy landscape." It's then a matter of assembling images. The process of collaging them in Photoshop is very playful and allows me to accomplish a completed composition and make most of the adjustments before I start the painting. I use this process for the main composition. Once a painting starts, I begin adding the smaller figures and tiny worlds. I think of this as creating micro-

cosms within the macrocosm. It's a way of rewarding the viewer who sees the painting in person, as many of these details can't be seen via jpeg or on a phone screen.

W The characters in your paintings, especially from your *Inner Demon Delectatio* series, are whimsical yet eerie. They embody aspects of levity and darkness, indulgence and delight. What do these demons represent for you and what are you trying to communicate through them?

M When left unencumbered, my imagination often veers toward the aberrant. I think of this inclination as a feature not a bug. It's in our unattended moments that we allow ourselves the freedom to contemplate the abject. We allow ourselves to flirt with our demons, to be seduced by them. Pursuant to this point, the critic Pere Salabert wrote, "The redemption of the flesh through the raw materiality present in art can lead the spectator to a state in which his physical or moral integrity is altered. The abject is the process, always in transit, which dominates the obscene instance of the object. That's why the subject is drawn to it, instead of rejected, in a sort of 'seductive disgust'." It is this transitional state between disgust and delight, pleasure and refusal, Eros and Thanatos, that makes the grotesque so intoxicating.

Art persuades us of its beauty and allows us to delight in its paradox. It's this paradoxical world that my paintings depict. Where the freedom exists to fall in love with the unlovable and seek the unknowable. A place where one can eschew the coldness of classical beauty and indulge guilt free in the allure of the repulsive. A hinterland where you can happily live alongside your demons—or at least date them for a while.

W How much of your work is introspective, and how often are you commenting on broader cultural issues? Does the darkness present in your work reflect personal struggles, or is it commentary on the human condition?

M I think it is universally true that we all have parts of ourselves we choose not to show the world. It's as true a statement for myself as it is for anyone else. Which is another way of saying that struggling with our doubts and fears and shame is so pervasive that it is prosaic and banal. Of course, it's hard to read the label from inside the bottle and doesn't feel that way when you're the one struggling. I can fall victim to a shame spiral as much as the next guy. But I think it's important to keep these feelings in perspective, and part of doing that is realizing that they are part of what it means to be human. My work attempts to make that point in a way that portrays our demons as part of our daily lives. Which they are... we just can't see them.

W Your work often blurs the boundaries between reality and fantasy. How do you decide how far to push your imagery into surreal or otherworldly territories?

M The truth is, I can't imagine making a painting that isn't of its own world. One of the greatest gifts of being an artist is that you get to sit in front of an empty white canvas, and you have complete control over the world that will be;

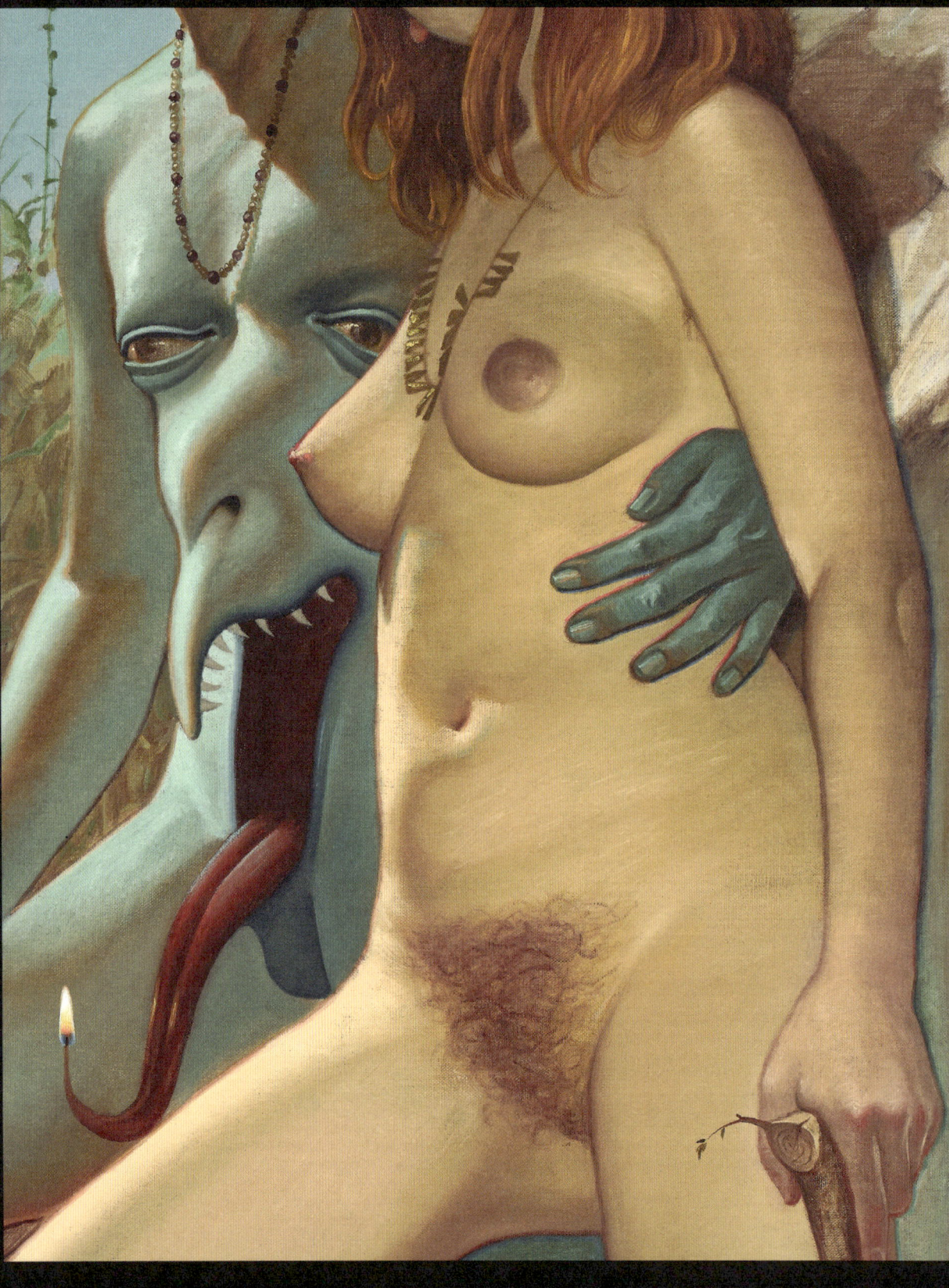

The Couple, 2023
Oil and Flashe paint on canvas, 24 × 18 in.

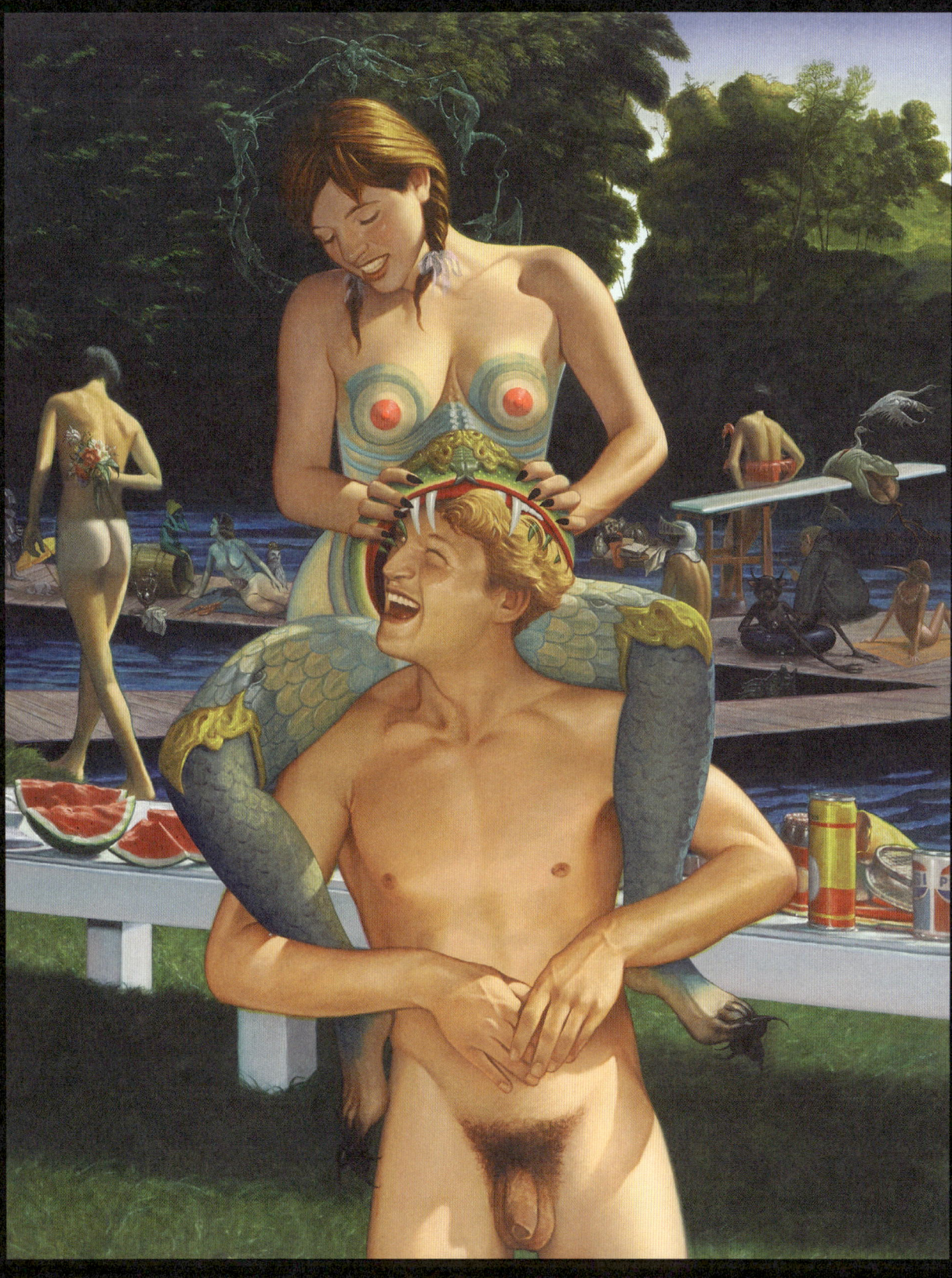

Content Is A Man Whose Pleasures Are Simple, 2021
Oil on canvas, 60 × 48 in.

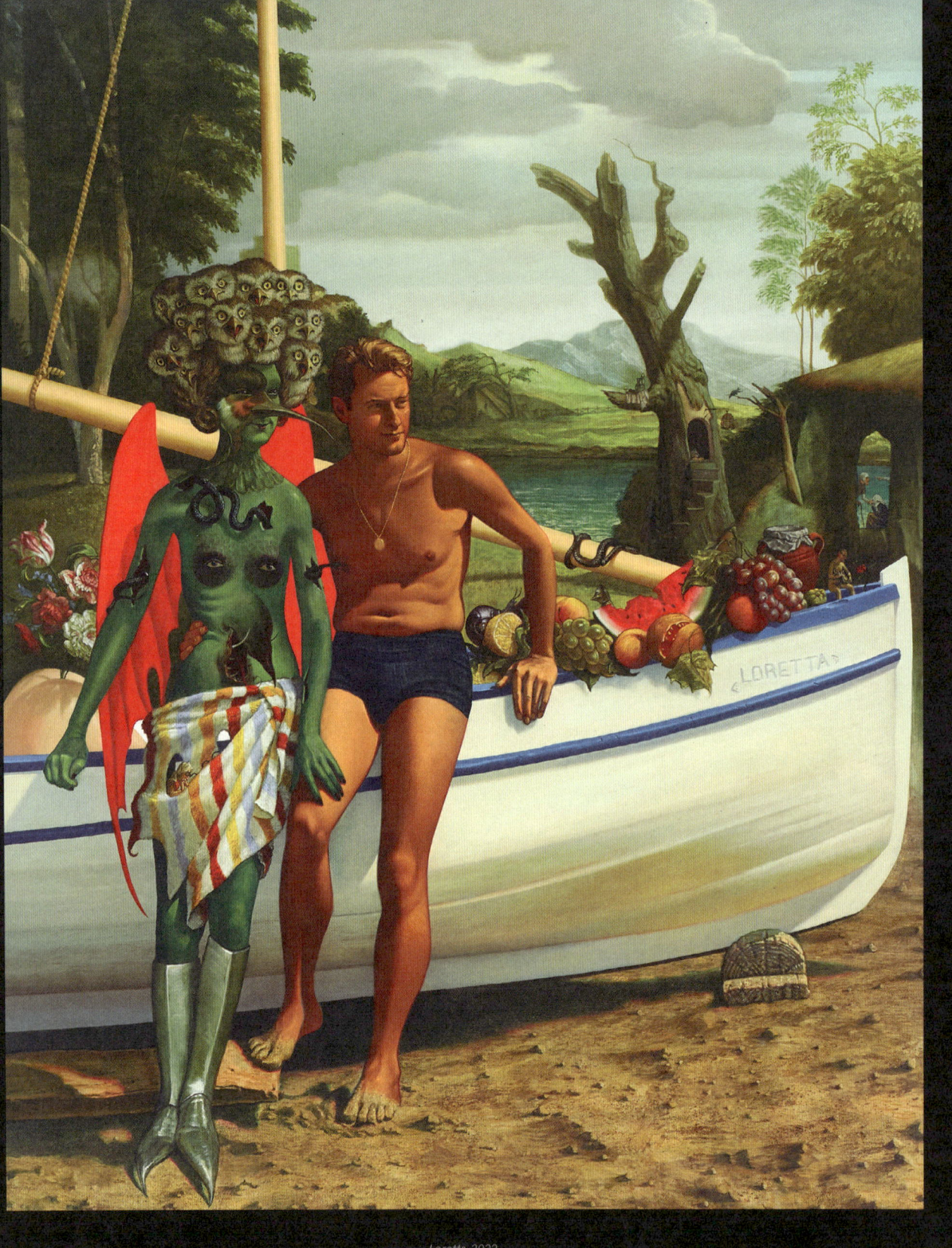

Loretta, 2022
Oil on canvas 70 × 58 in.

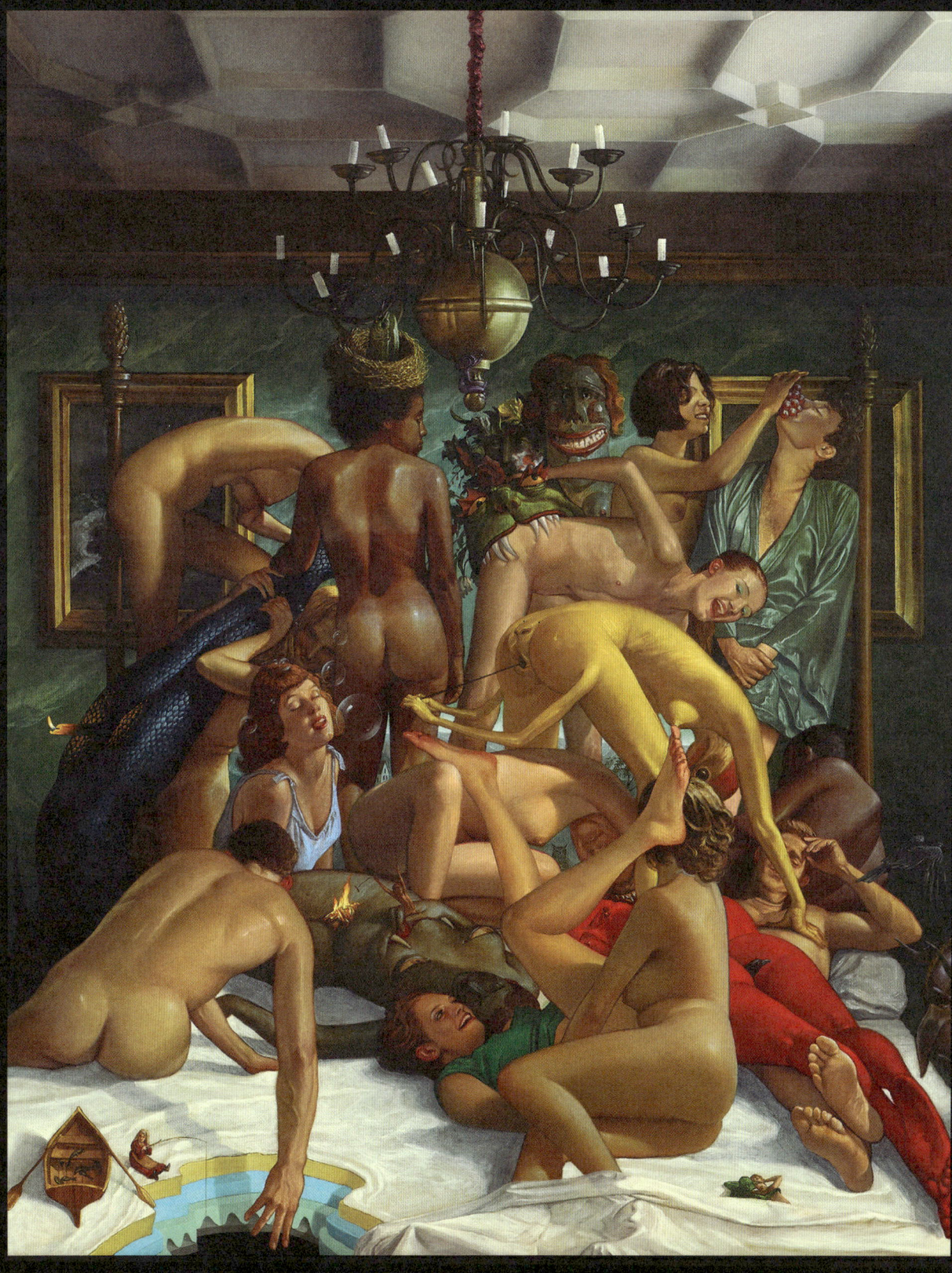

Morning's Light We Can't Forget, It Warms Us Like An Ember, Illuminating With Regret, The Nights We Can't Remember, 2023
Oil and Flashe paint on canvas, 70 × 56 in.

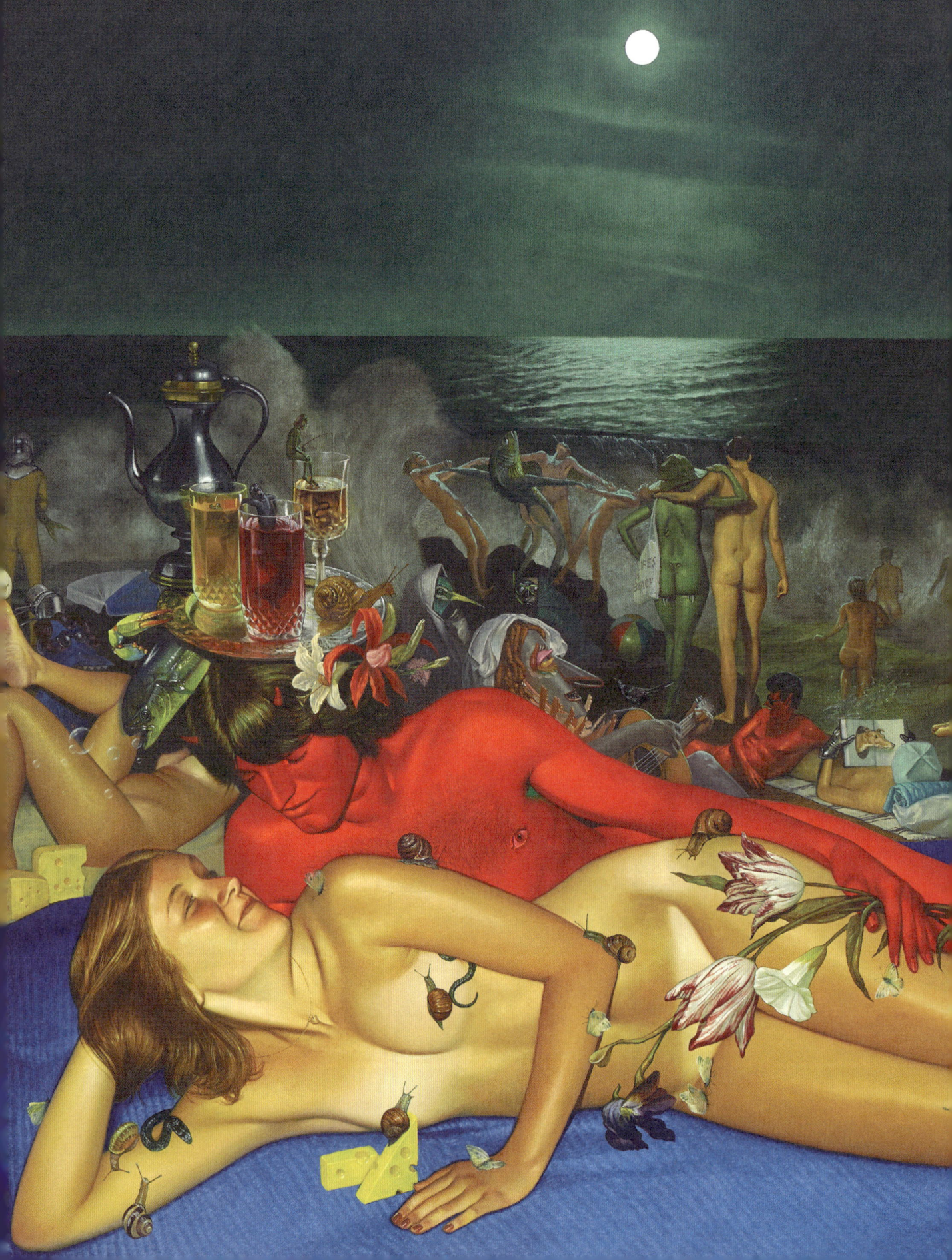

"I'm making a proposal for an alternate reality, which is what my favorite painters do."

its rules, its customs, its structure, its morays, etc. Why anyone would choose to make a painting that adheres to all the same nonsense that we have to adhere to in this world is beyond me. I see many artists think and talk about paintings as if they should, and they make paintings accordingly. This seems like a waste of an opportunity, of a gift, really.

W There's a playful yet sinister edge to your work, which seems to create a sense of irony. Can you talk about the role irony and humor play in your work?

M I think making a painting is a bit like mixing a drink. Like most good drinks, simple is better. A few ingredients in the right proportions seems to work best. When it comes to art, every artist needs to define their own ingredients. First, they need to discover the flavors they want in their world and then play with the percentages. I've narrowed mine down to three main ingredients: humor + pathos + virtuosity. Humor is one of the most enjoyable ingredients, and when used in conjunction with the other two, it makes painting fun. When not tempered by other ingredients, humor can run the risk of being mean spirited or turn a painting into an overly simplistic one-liner. However, there are few things I enjoy more than seeing a complex, well-painted painting that makes me smile.

W Do you see your work as a form of escape, a mirror to reality, or something else entirely? How do you hope viewers respond to the worlds you create in your paintings?

M I'm making a proposal for an alternate reality, which is what my favorite painters do. The trick is to make these realities convincing on their own terms. By doing this, the painted reality allows us to examine by contrast the world around us. I'm proposing a world where the modern notion of moderating or suppressing our natural impulses toward the aberrant is replaced by the freedom to embrace those tendencies and revel in them, flirting with our inner demons instead of hiding them from the world. At the end of the day my work is celebratory and honors a part of the human condition that is often seen

as unsettling or suspicious. While it would be difficult to construct a functional society where this freedom exists, painting allows me to create a plausibly ridiculous fac simile. I don't think a painting should be required to *do* anything. I don't think they should communicate or explain anything, continue a dialogue or have an agenda. However, I do think the best paintings affect the viewer emotionally. Art can alter the viewer's emotional state, if only briefly, without saying a word. And what an amazing power that is.

W How do you see your work evolving in the future? What else can we expect from Matt Hansel?

M Luckily, I have no idea. The process of finding a new door to walk through is always opaque until it's painfully obvious. It's like trying to find a station on an old radio. It's mostly noise and static with glimpses and snippets of voices and melodies which come into focus for a moment or two and then recede. It is the struggle and joy of the artist to suddenly hit a frequency that penetrates the uncertainty; rising up through the noise, emitting a sound so clear and true that the hand must follow it. ∎

Opposite Page:
*How Strange And Unearthly Is Love, How Bold
And Nature-less In Its Ecstasies, 2023
Oil and flashe paint on canvas, 70 × 56*

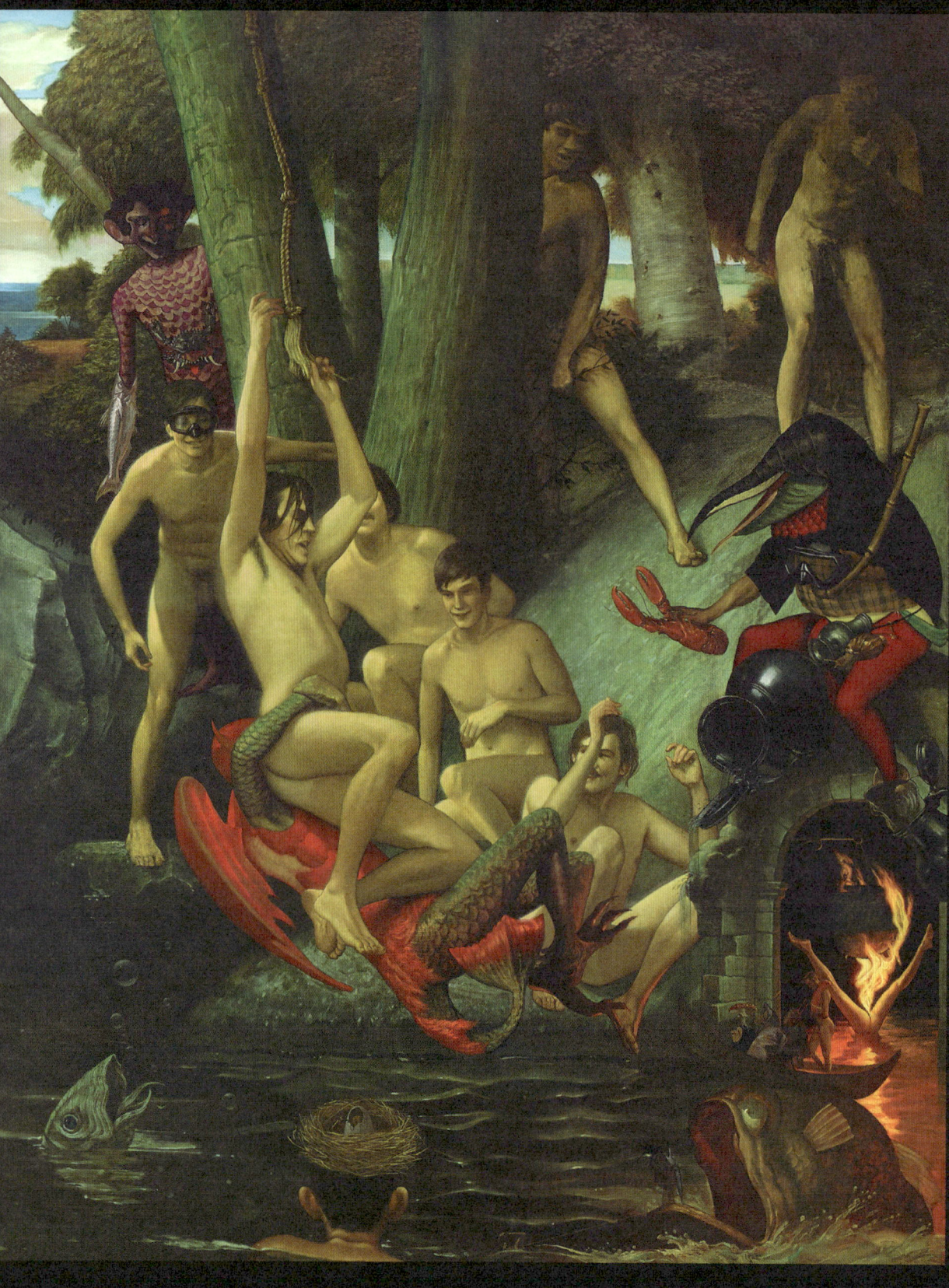

The days of our youth Are beyond our control Those lost joys have drown in the ol' swimming hole I wish in my sorrow To strip to my soul And dive once again In the ol' swimming hole, 2022, Oil on canvas, 70 × 58 in.

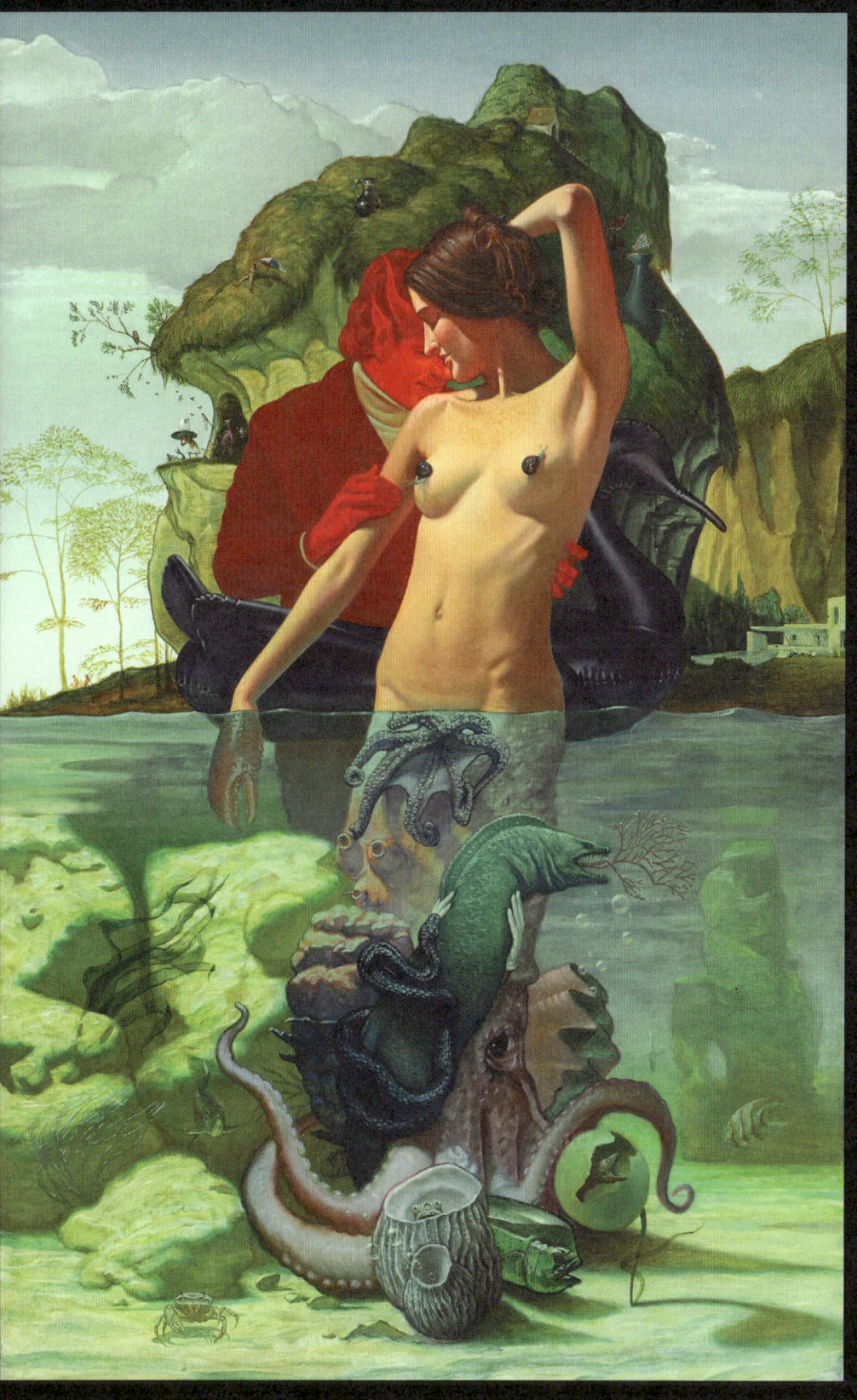

As Above, So Below For Love? No One Knows, 2022
Oil on canvas, 70 × 45 in.

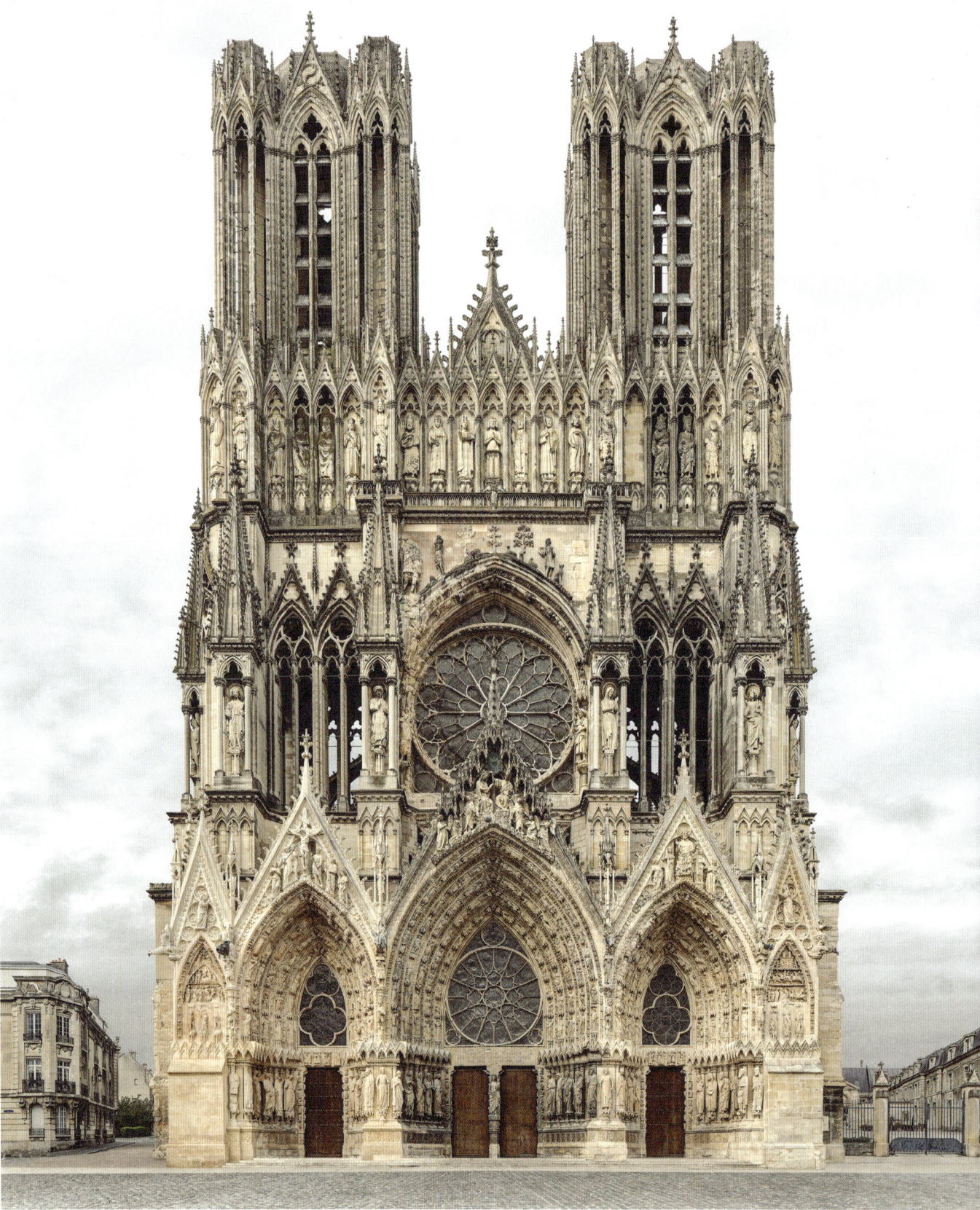

HYPER GOTHIC

—

Gothic architecture as seen through the lens of German artist Markus Brunetti

Gothic architecture first emerged during the 12th century in France and spread throughout medieval Europe into the late 16th century. It evolved from Romanesque architecture, which was known for its many arches, vaulted ceilings, and stained glass windows. Heavily influenced by the power and theological doctrines of the Catholic Church at the time and supported by technical advances in engineering, the Gothic style exaggerated Romanesque's key features, increasing the scale of the arches and the overall height of the buildings themselves, bringing them closer to the heavens. Walls were replaced with massive stained glass windows that depicted biblical scenes and allowed generous amounts of ethereal light into the space. As the style evolved over time, it became much more ornate, boasting intricate facades and window tracery. Through the marriage of artisan craftsmanship and human innovation, these impossible structures became magnificent places of worship that fostered a sense of transcendence and divinity on Earth.

Known today as one of the most sophisticated and awe-inspiring architectural styles in human history, Gothic architecture has literally stood the test of time. Despite centuries of change, it continues to capture the modern imagination, as seen in artist Markus Brunetti's breathtaking photographic works. Much like the buildings he documents, Brunetti's work is known for its extraordinary scale showcasing exquisite details that are both monumental yet intimate at the same time. He achieves this by painstakingly seaming together thousands of large-format photographs taken over the course of several weeks. The result is similar to the finest portraiture. Brunetti reveals every nuance with utmost clarity, allowing the viewer to experience the complexity and character of these magnificent structures as if they were standing in front of them themselves.

Words *Adam Larson* / All Artworks *Markus Brunetti*
©*Markus Brunetti. Courtesy Yossi Milo, New York*

Previous Page:
Reims, Cathedrale Notre Dame, 2013–2014
Archival Pigment Print

Opposite Page:
Vendome, Eglise de la Trinité, 2013–2018
Archival Pigment Print

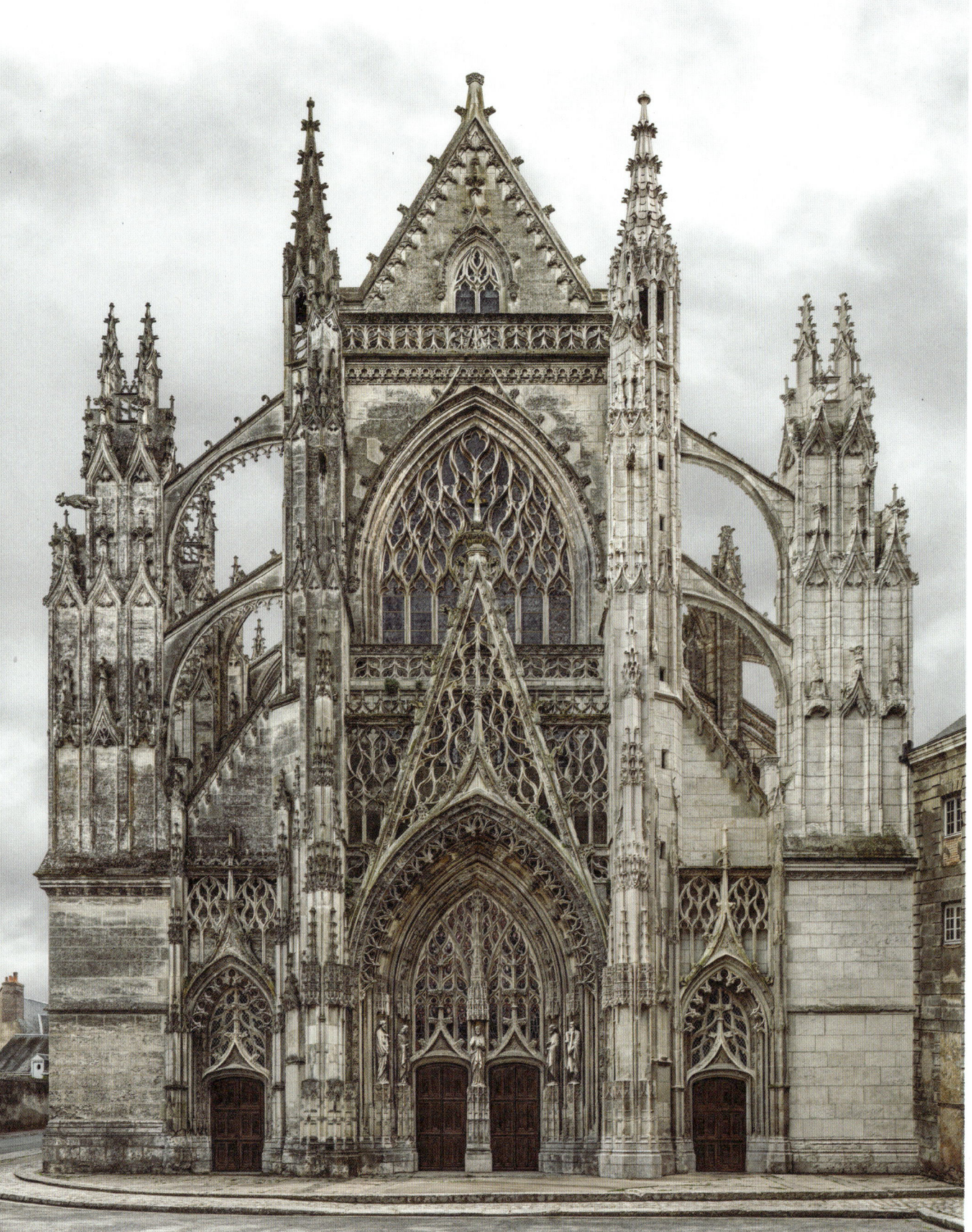

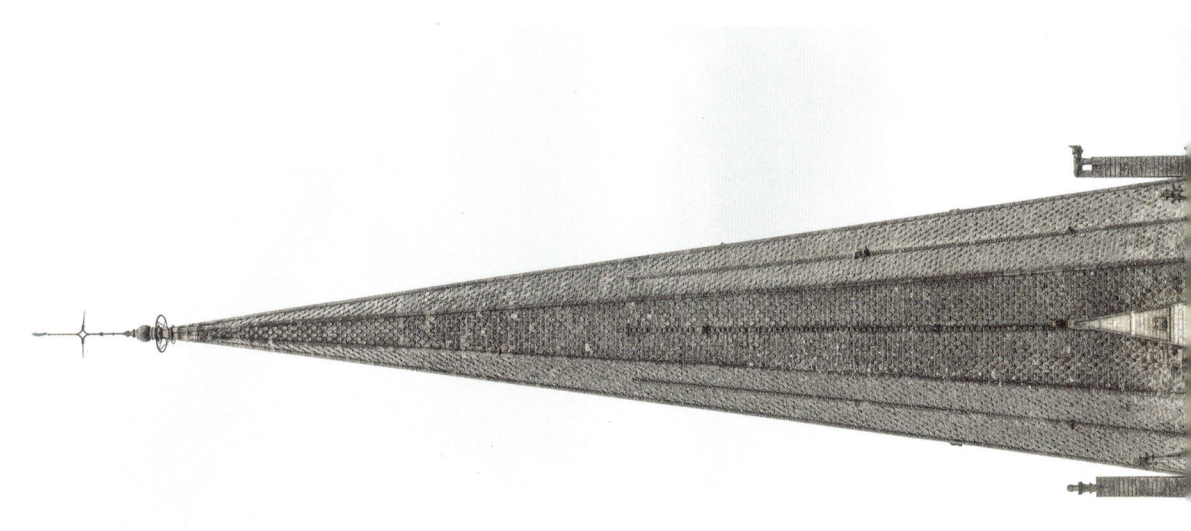

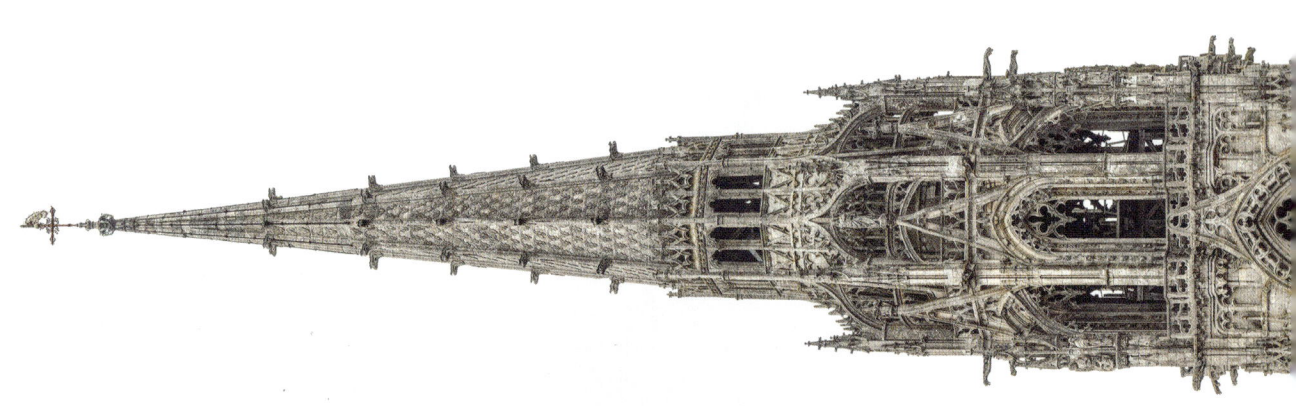

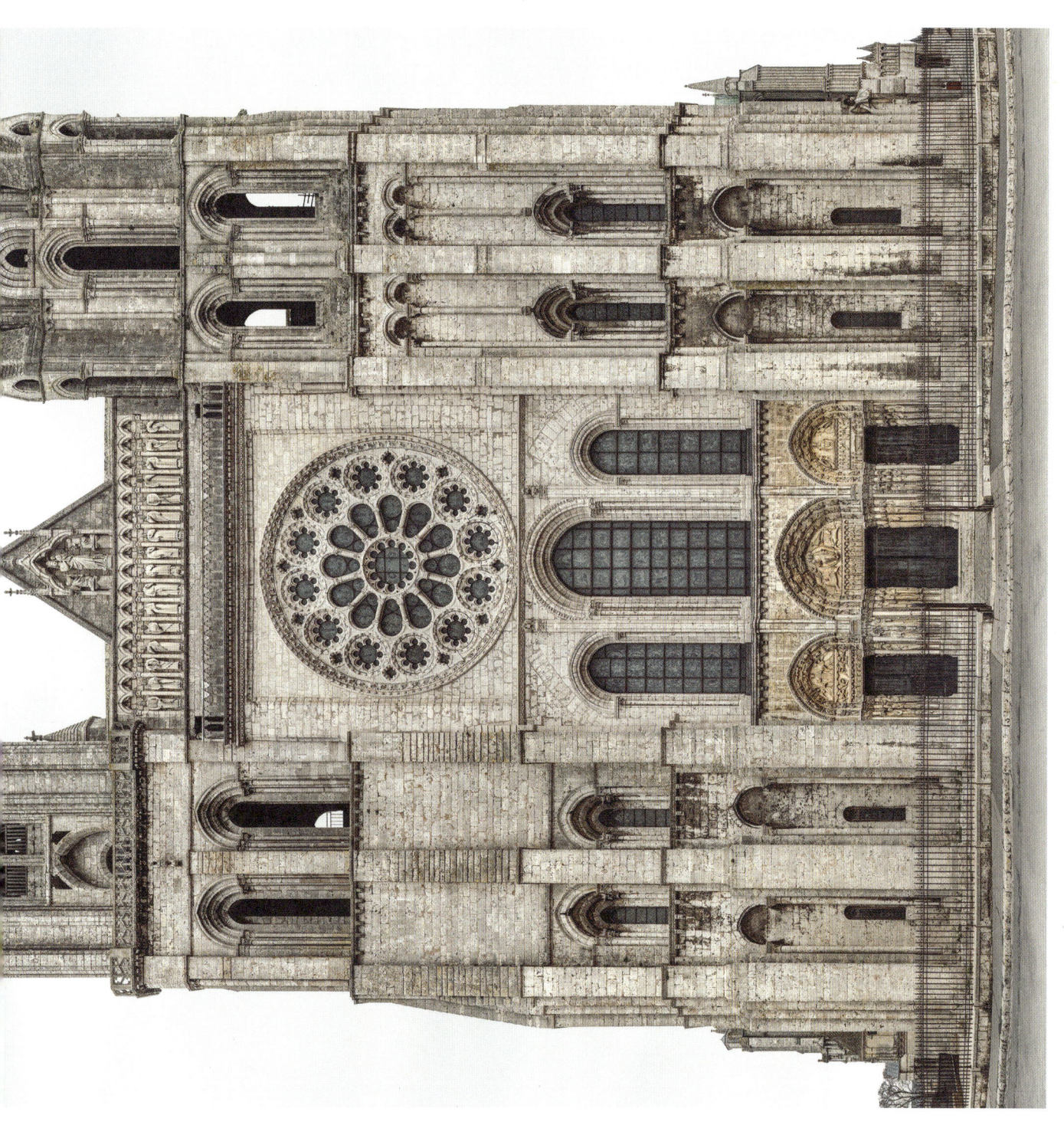

Chartres, Cathédrale Notre-Dame, 2012–2015
Archival Pigment Print

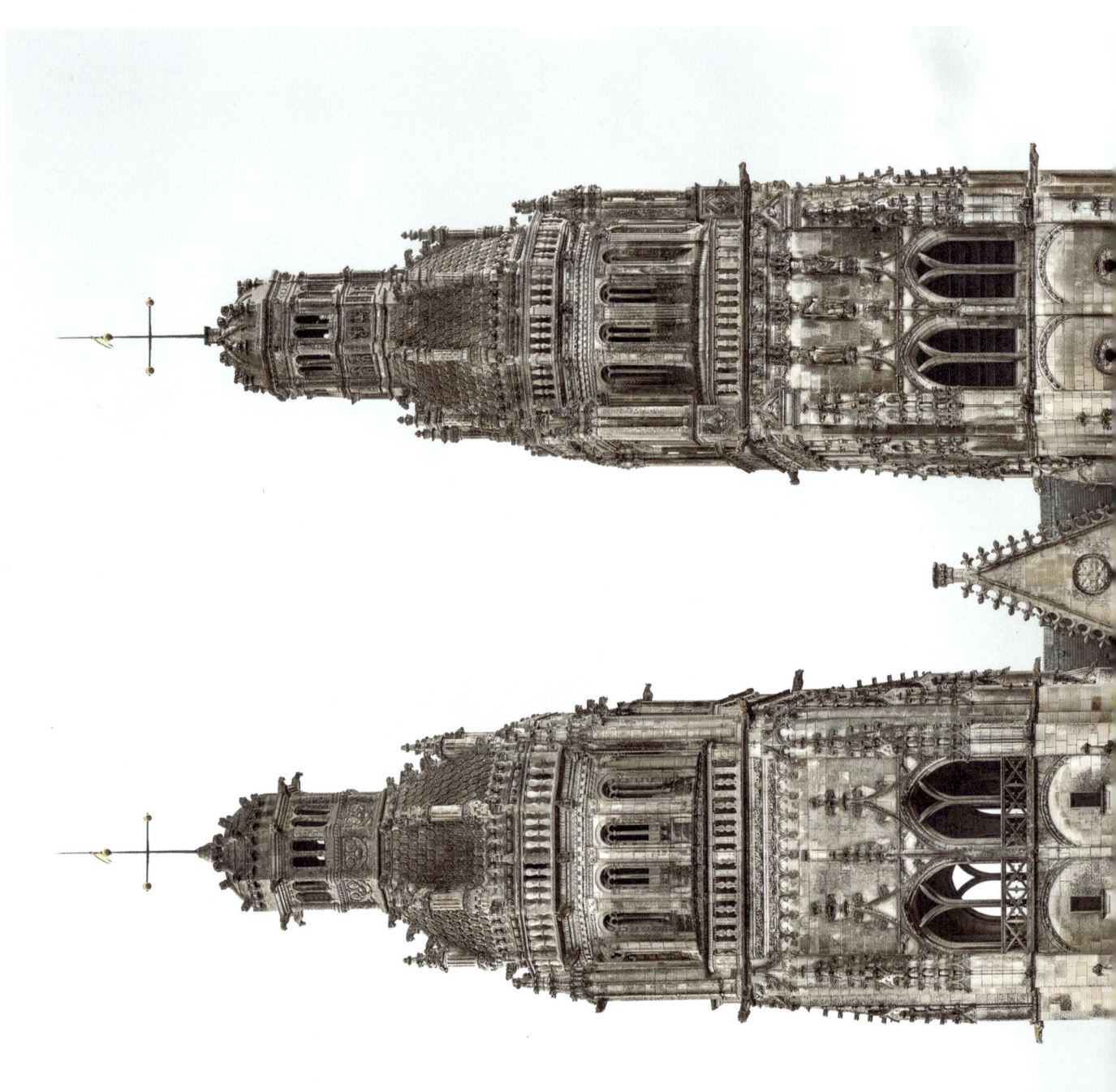

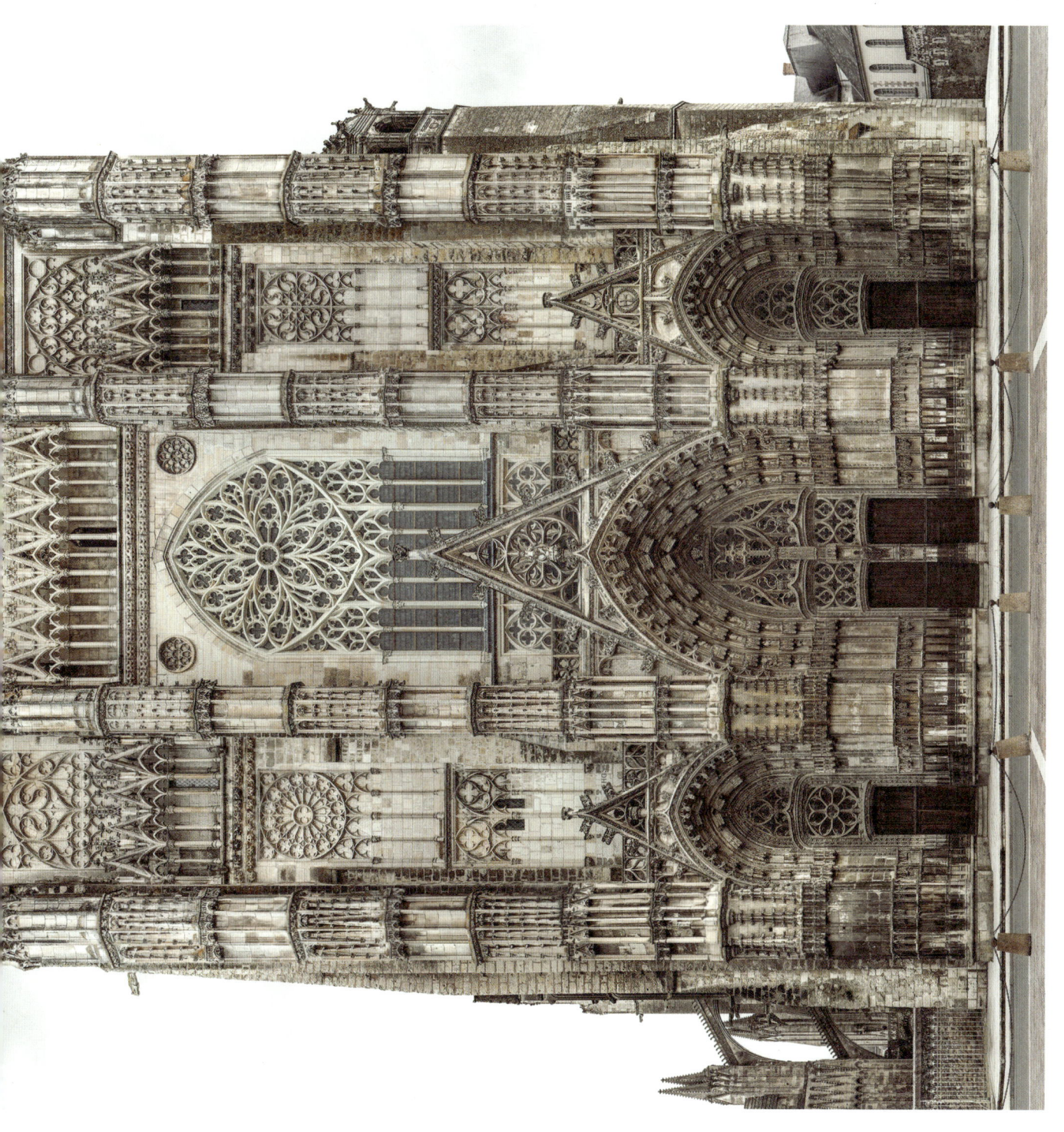

Tours, Cathédrale Saint-Gatien, 2013–2015
Archival Pigment Print

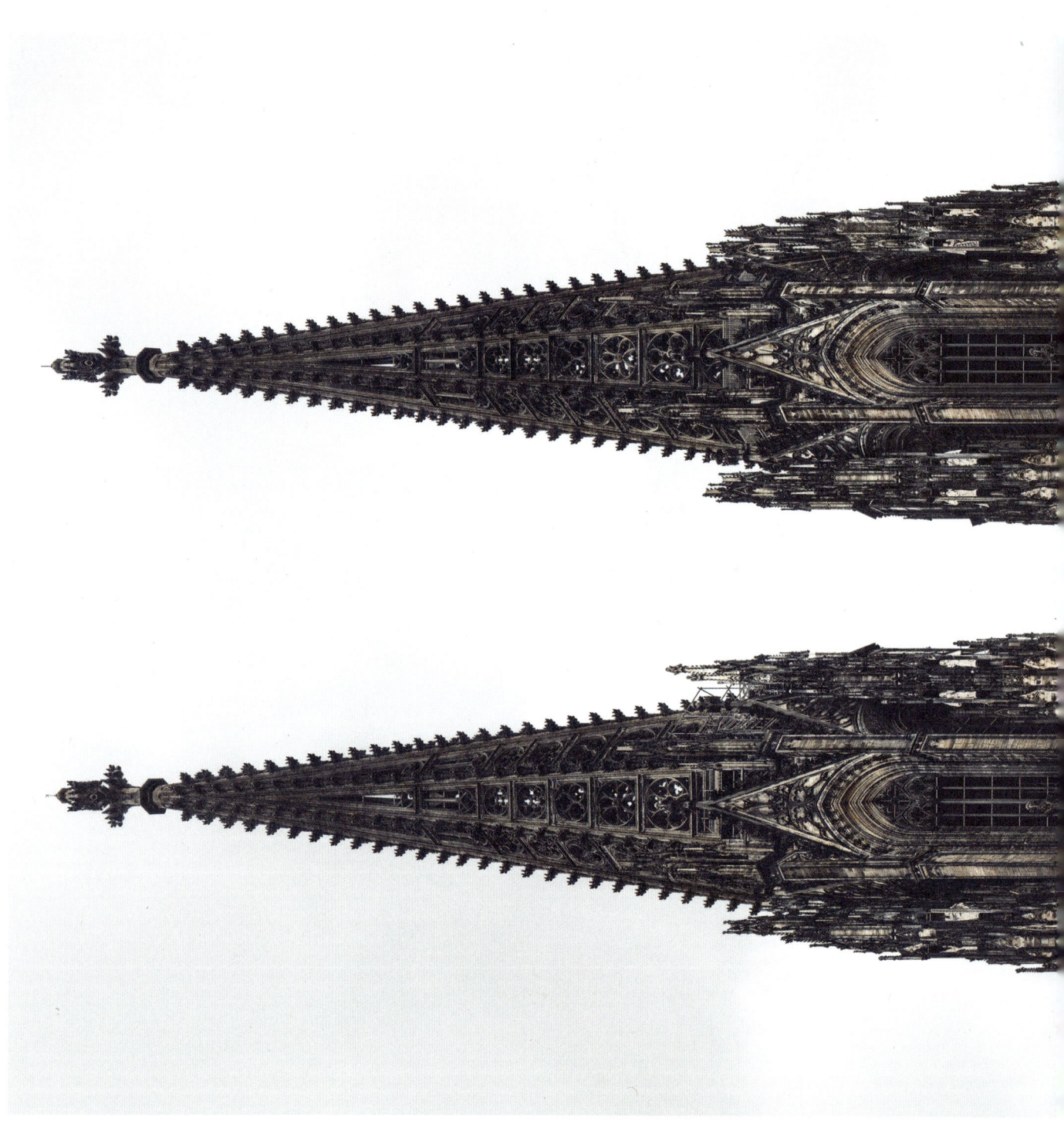

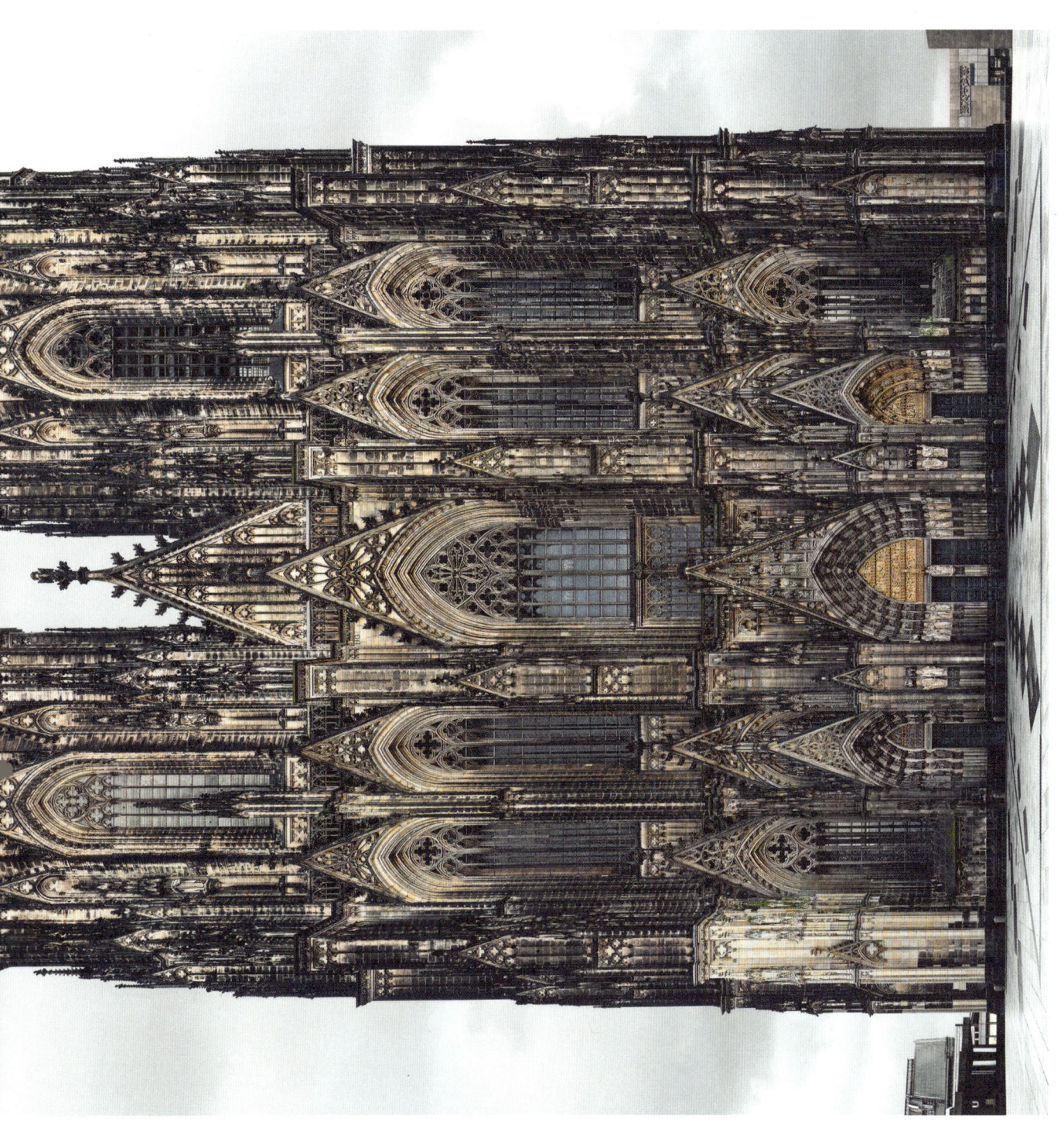

Köln, Hohe Domkirche St. Petrus, 2008–2014
Archival Pigment Print

185

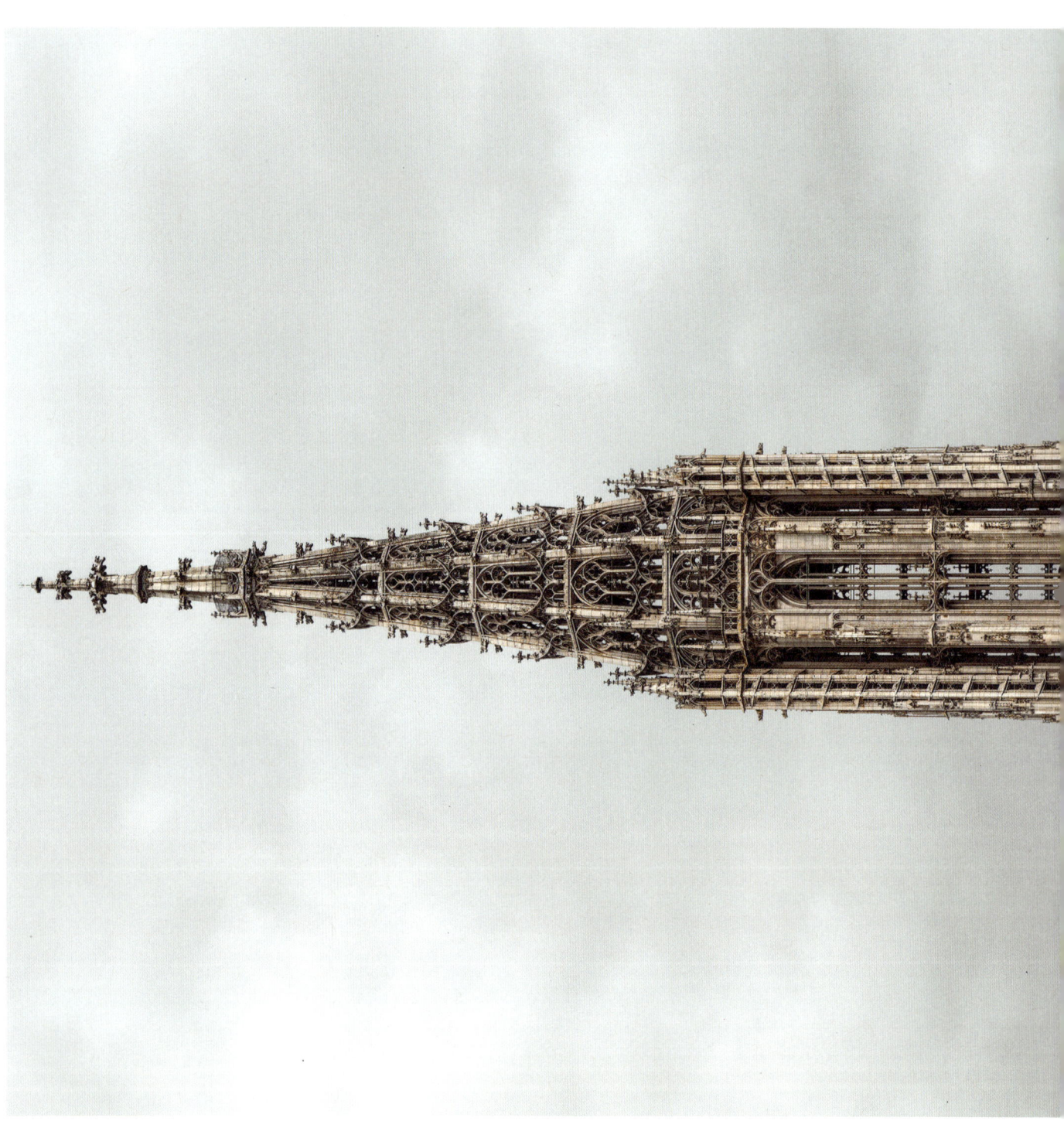

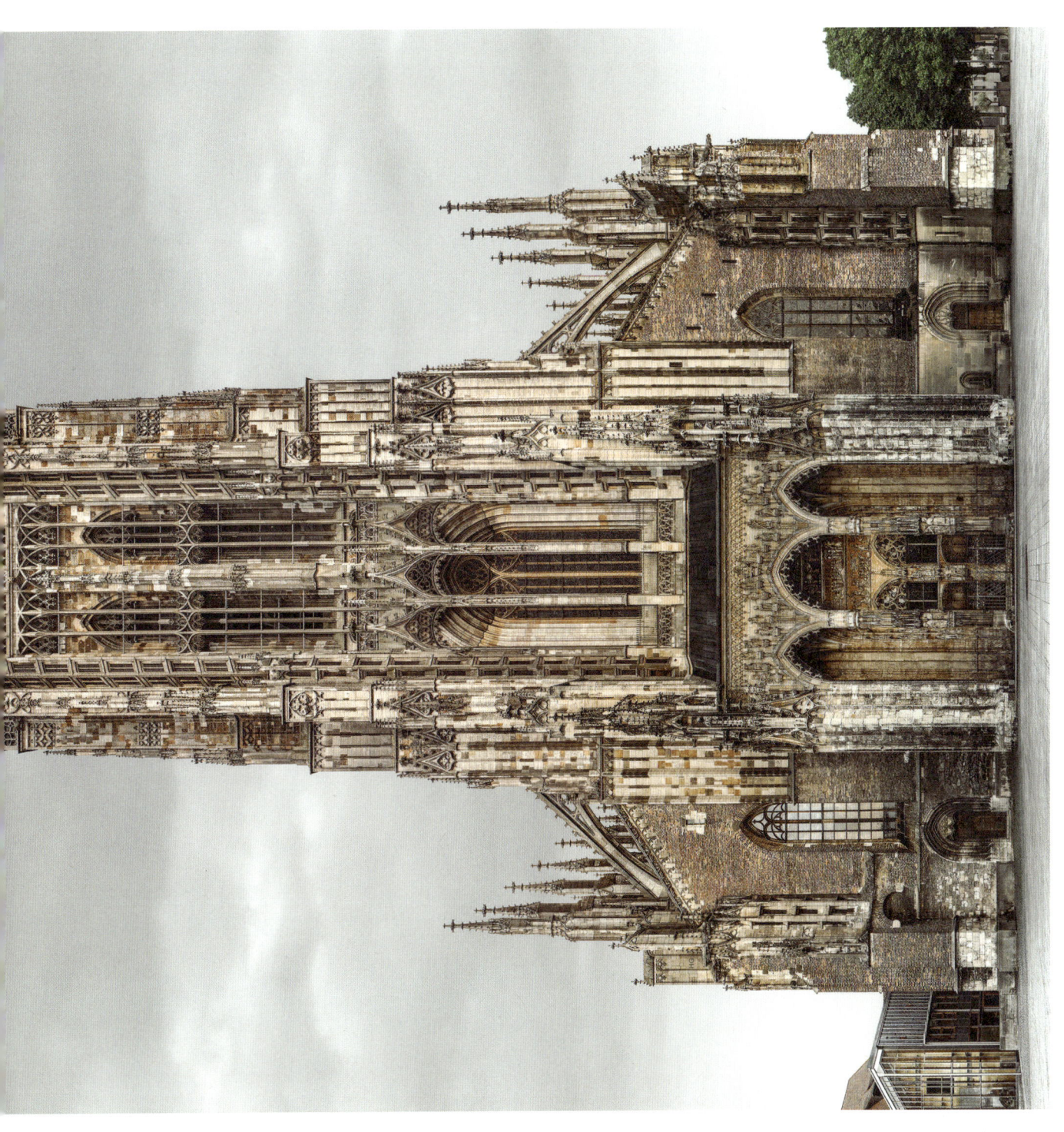

Ulm, Munster, 2007–2014
Archival Pigment Print

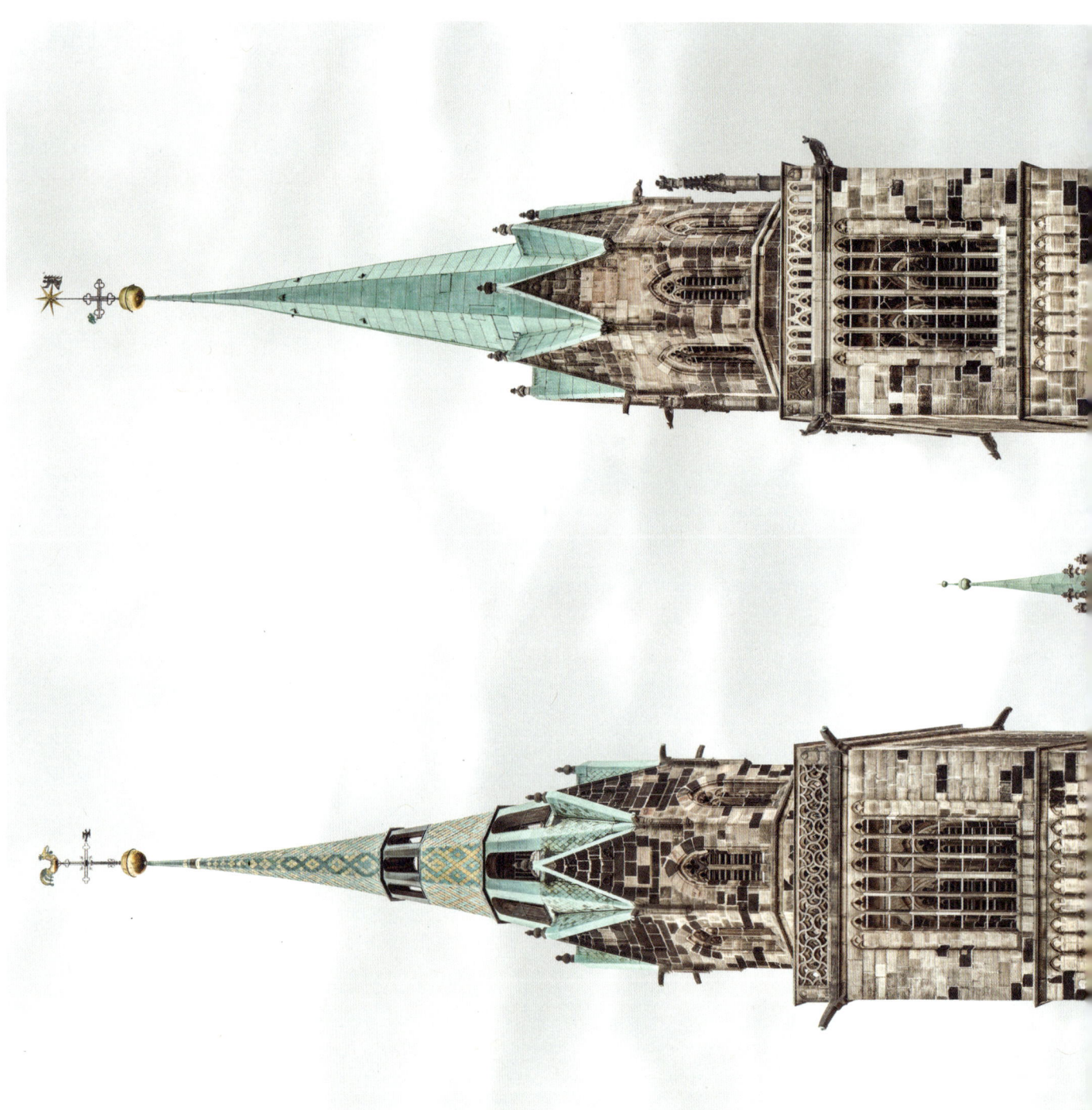

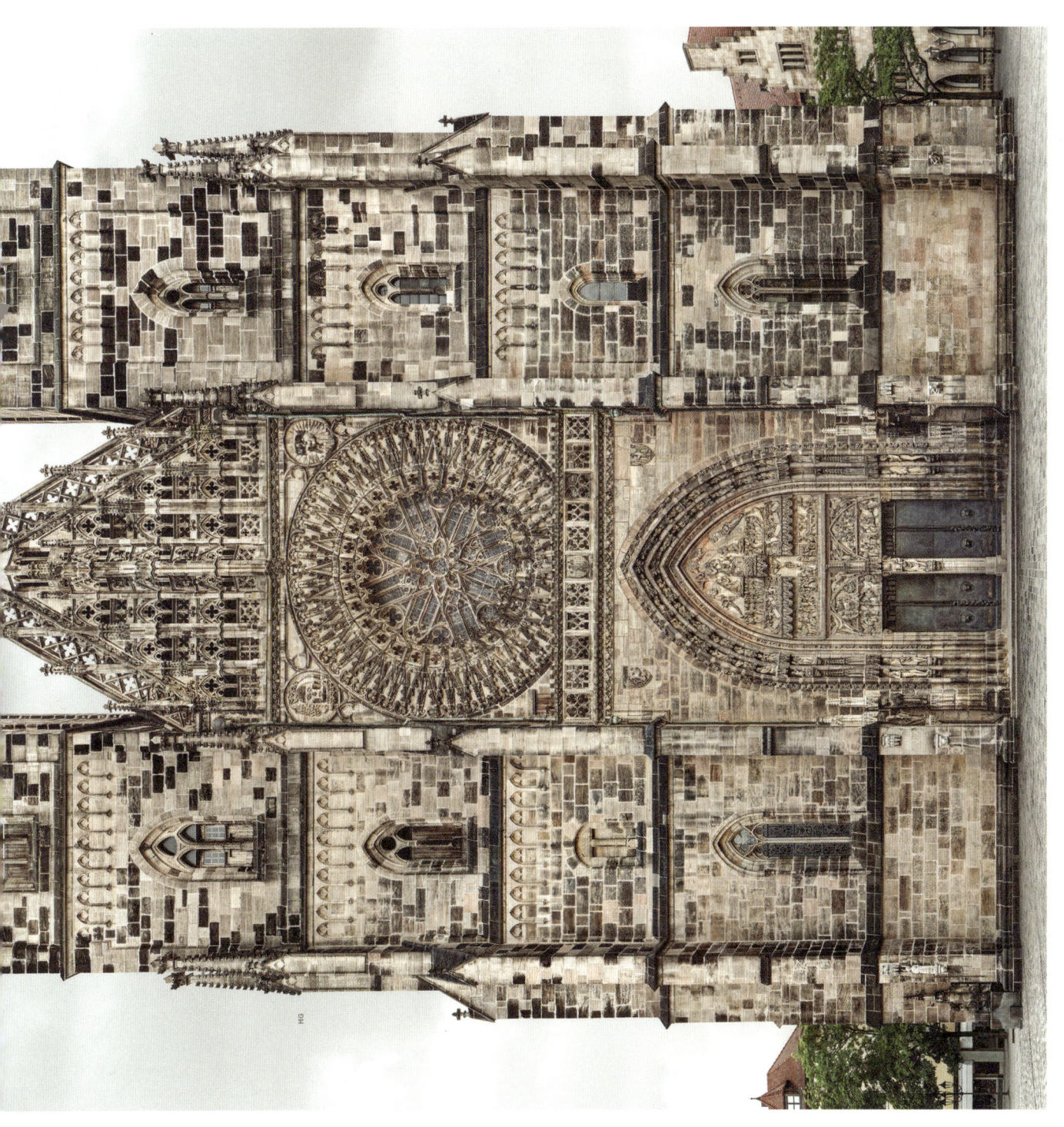

Nürnberg, Sankt Lorenz, 2012–2017
Archival Pigment Print

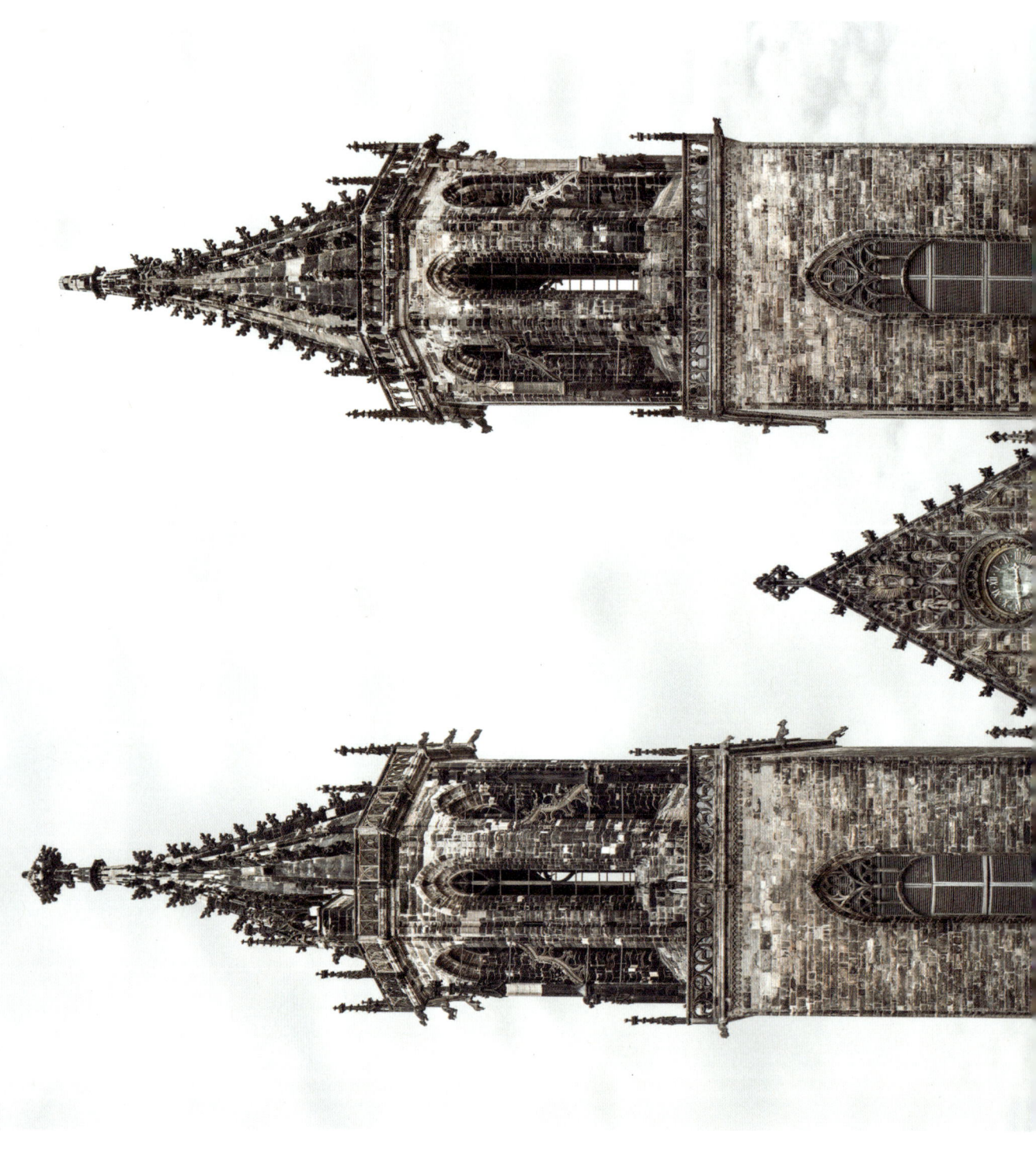

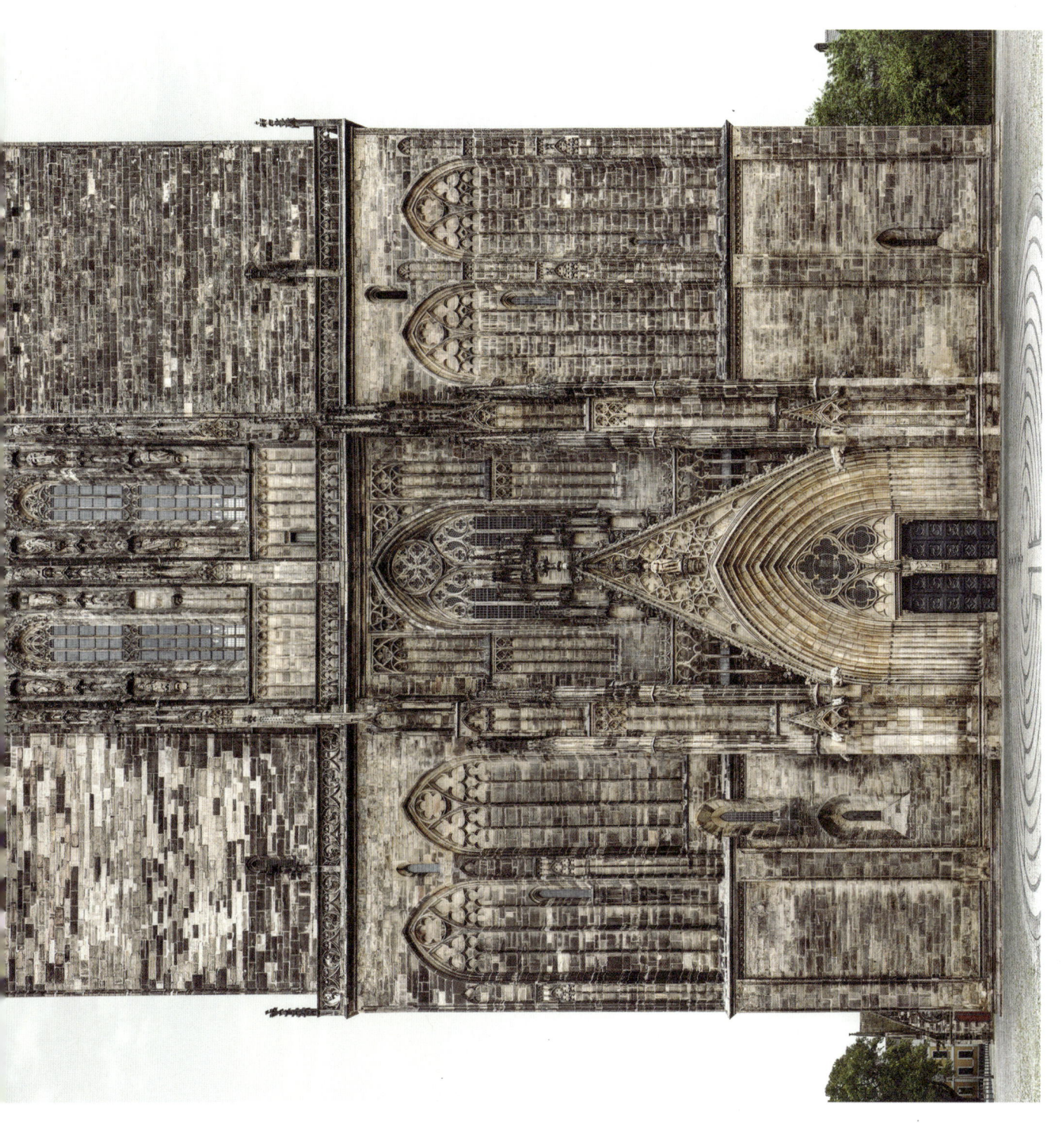

Magdeburg, Dom St. Mauritius und Katharina, 2011–2015
Archival Pigment Print

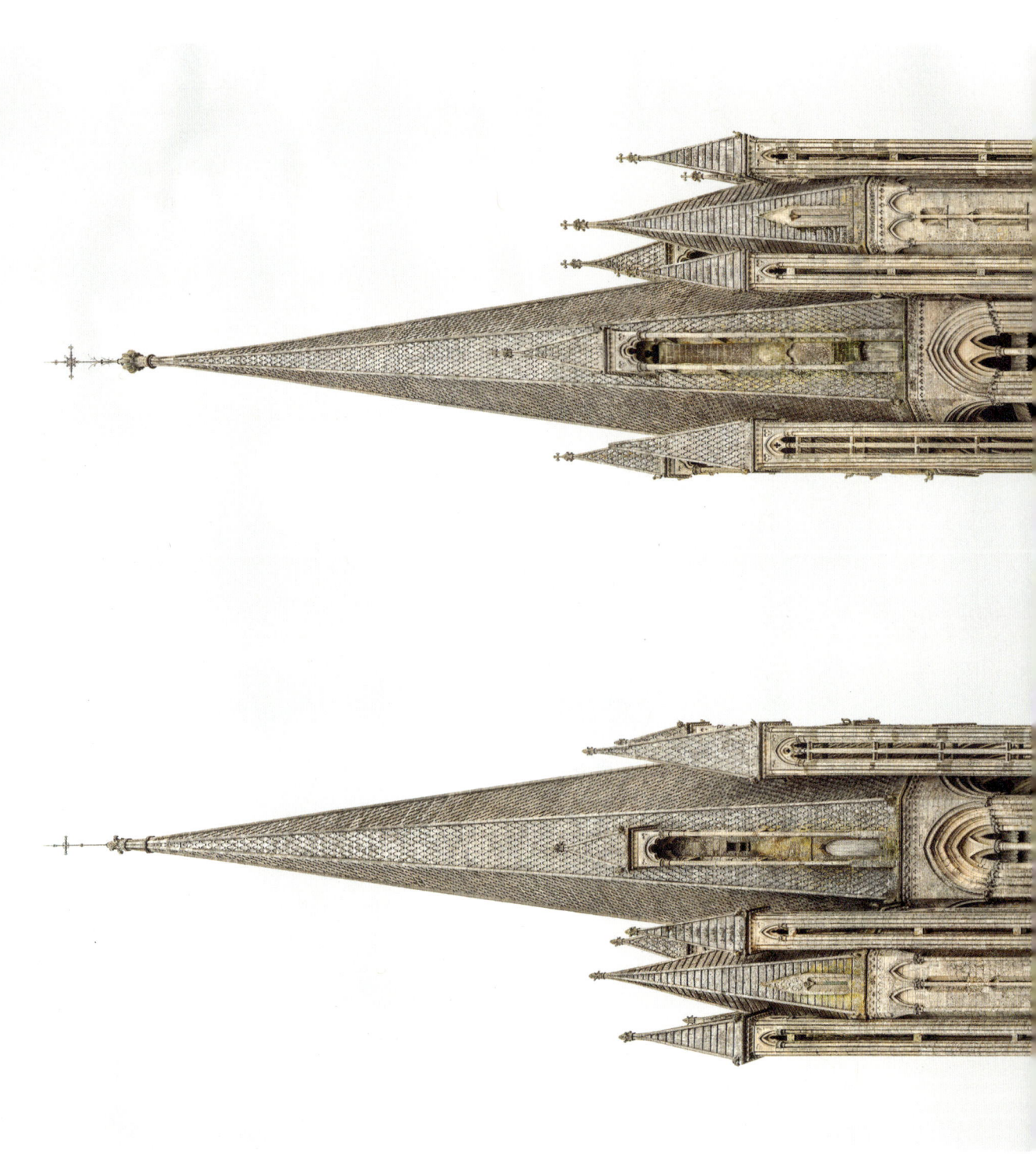

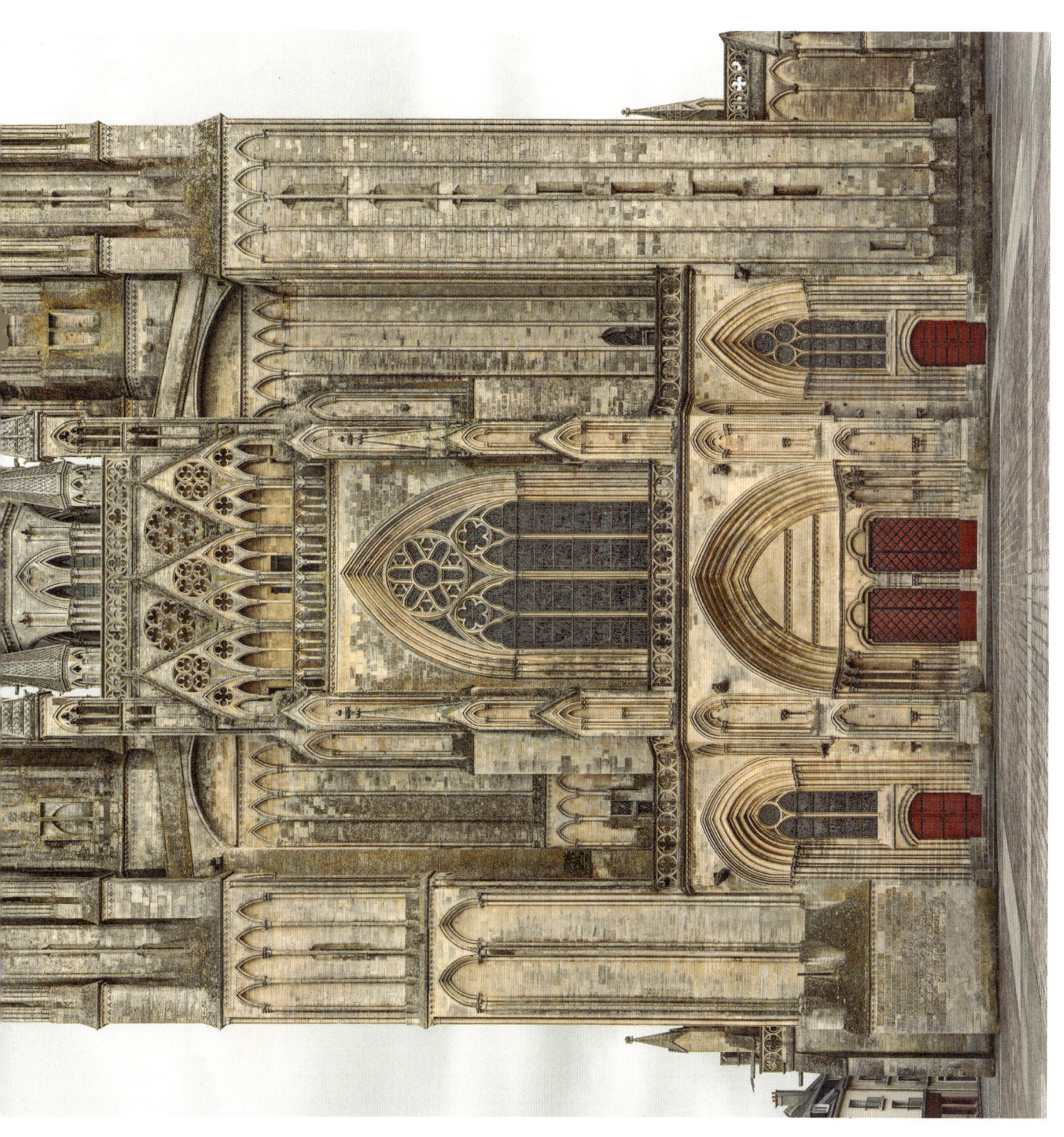

Coutance, Notre-Dame, 2013–2023
Archival Pigment Print

RICK OWENS

Mystery & Majesty

Words *Christopher Stella* / Photographs *Matthew Reeves*

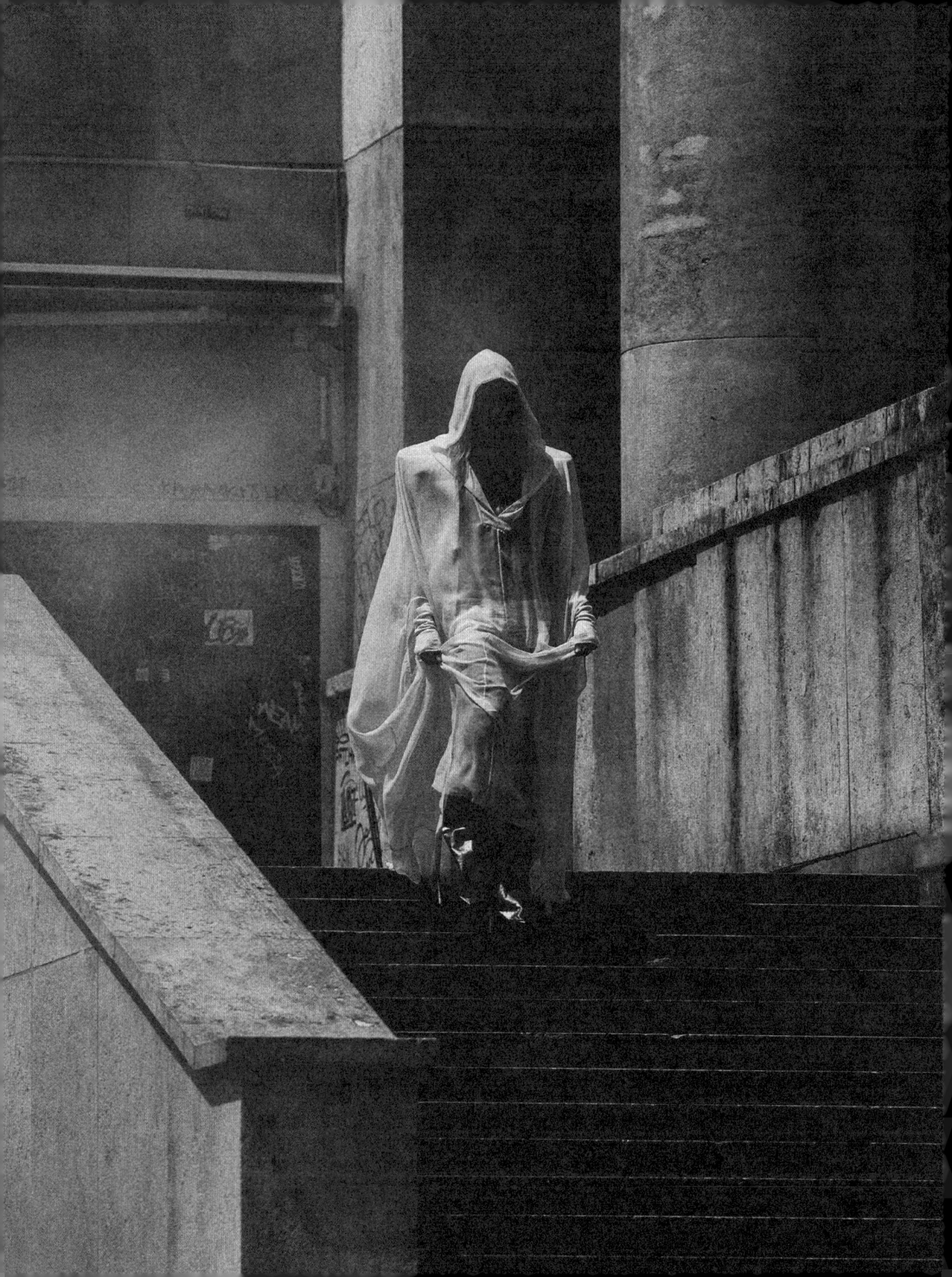

Mythic is the word that comes to mind when describing Owens' Spring/
Summer 2025 collection. The setting alone conjured the epic: Framed
by the soaring Roman columns of Paris's Palais de Tokyo, flanked by
Alfred Janniot's bas-reliefs of the nine muses, and shadowed by statues
of Greek gods, the show unfolded like a living frieze. Over 200 models
streamed up and down the limestone staircases in silent procession—
four abreast, in regiments of sixteen to twenty—forming a kinetic wave
of cream and taupe. Chunky leather and billowing chiffon echoed the
smoke rising at the show's entrance, blurring the line between the ethereal
and the elemental.

Part solemn rite, part military march, the spectacle seemed to float
outside of time. Half-moon headdresses and belted tunics evoked
both ancient mosaics and distant galaxies. Owens' signature aesthetic
remained unmistakable: elongated silhouettes, asymmetrical cuts, and
garments that dissolve the distinction between limb and torso.

Yet in a surprising departure, there wasn't a single stitch of black.
Owens left his namesake noir behind to cast a new light. Why not
brightness? The show, after all, was titled Hollywood—a reference
both to the grandeur of all-caps HOLLYWOOD and the gritty boulevard in Los Angeles where his career began. Setting and concept fused
to create a production already being spoken of as legend—timeless,
transcendent, unforgettable. And while most readers weren't there
to witness it firsthand, *Wednesday* photographer-at-large Matthew
Reeves was—capturing the show's mystery and majesty in a way he
does so well.

Words *Christopher Stella* / Photographs *Matthew Reeves*

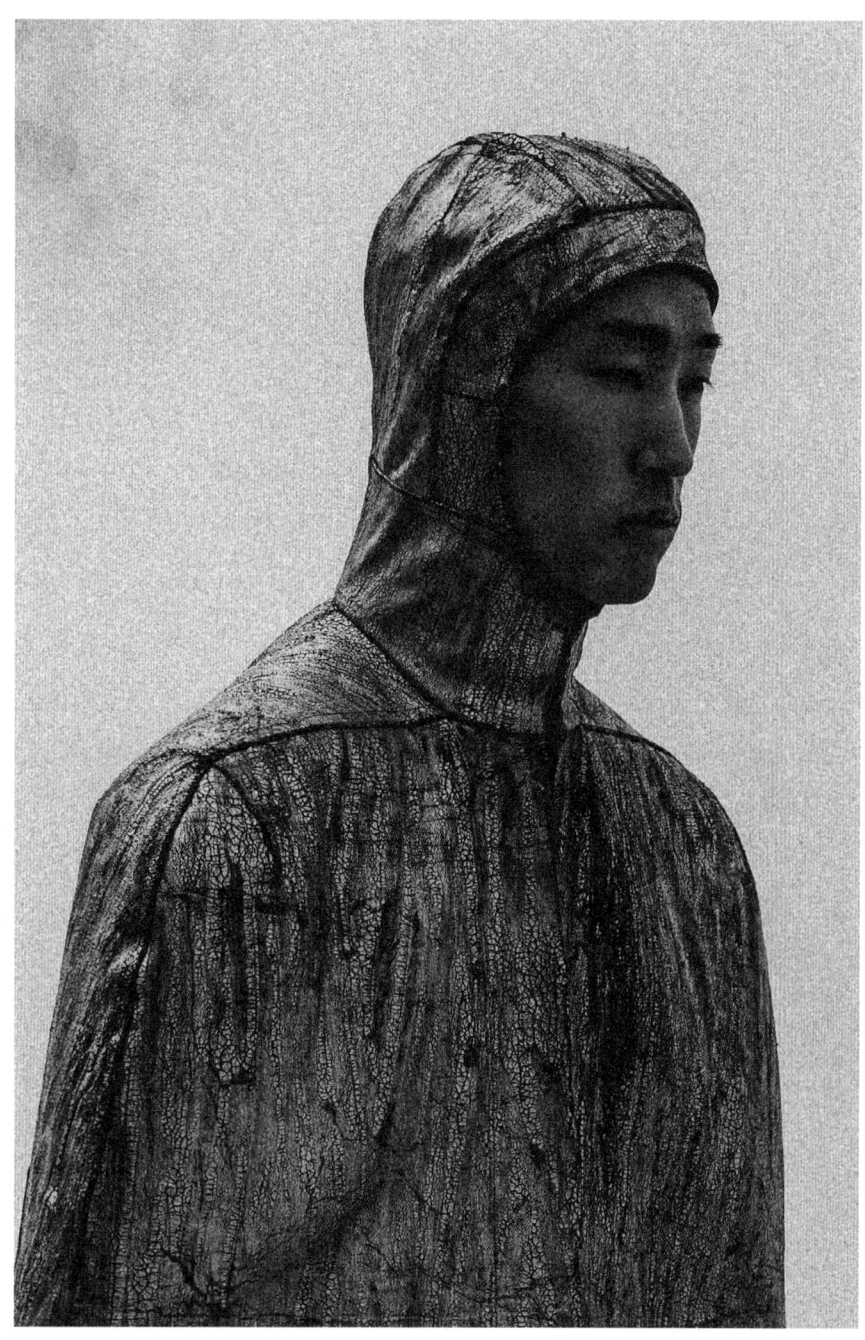

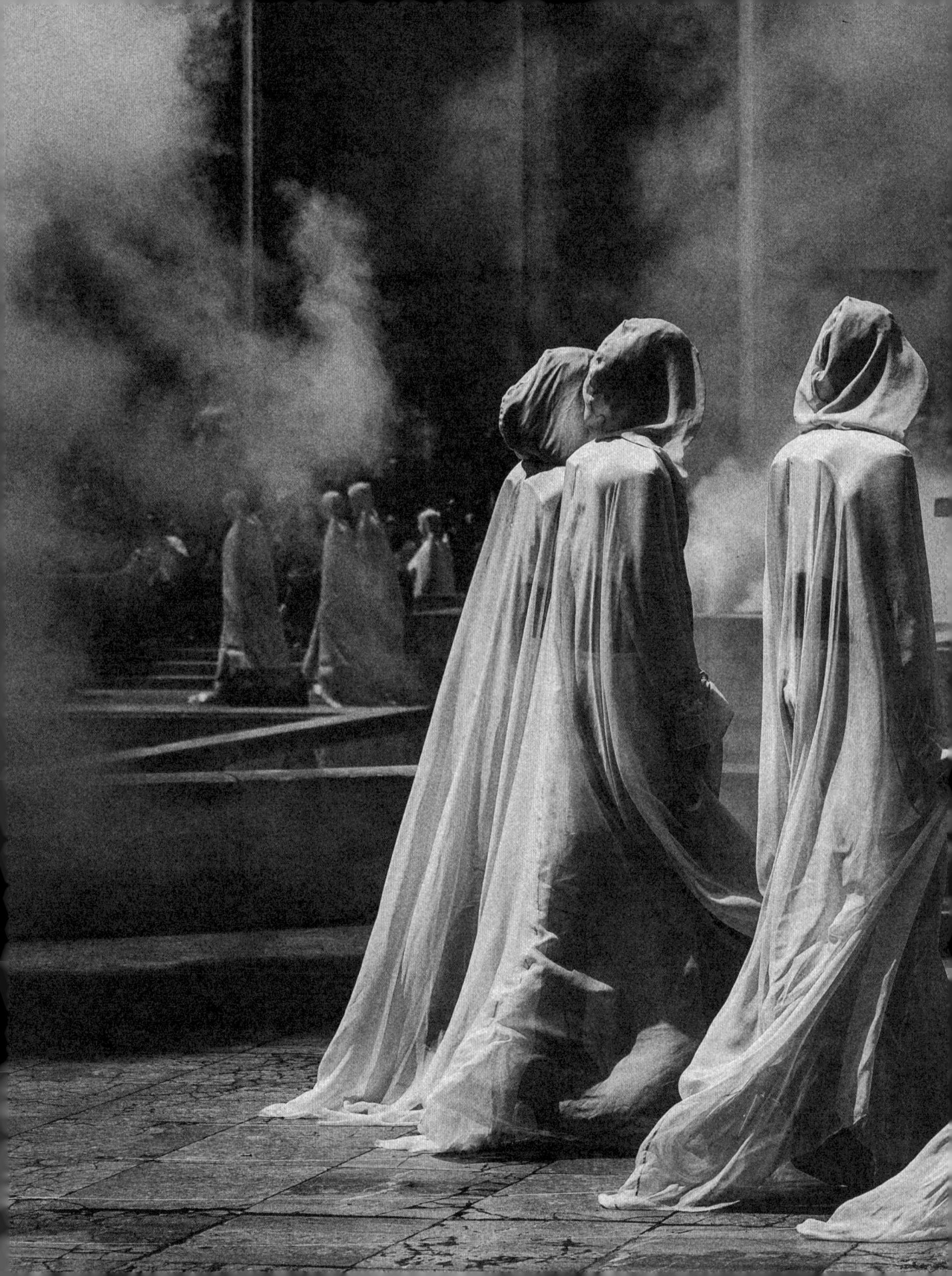

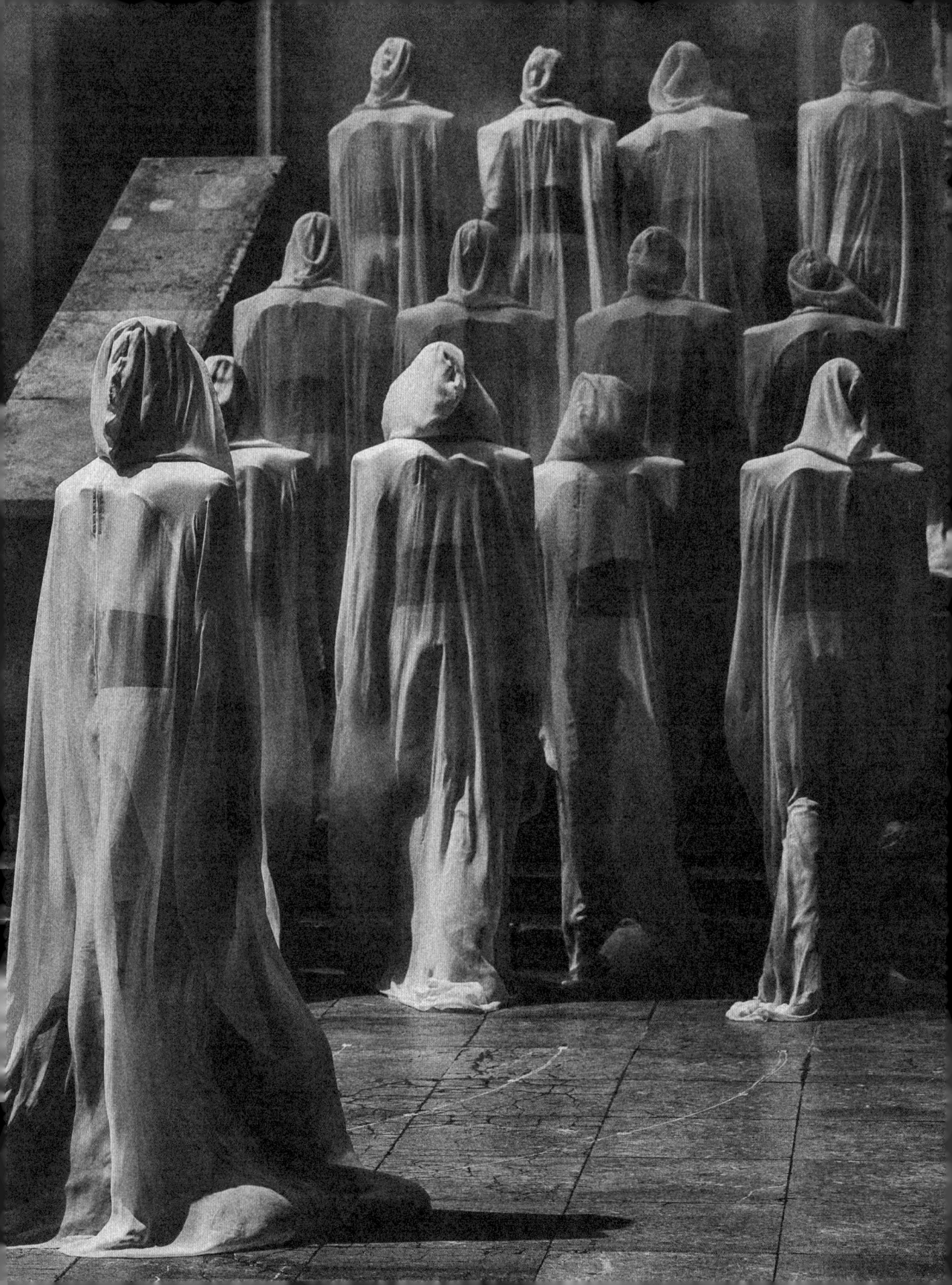

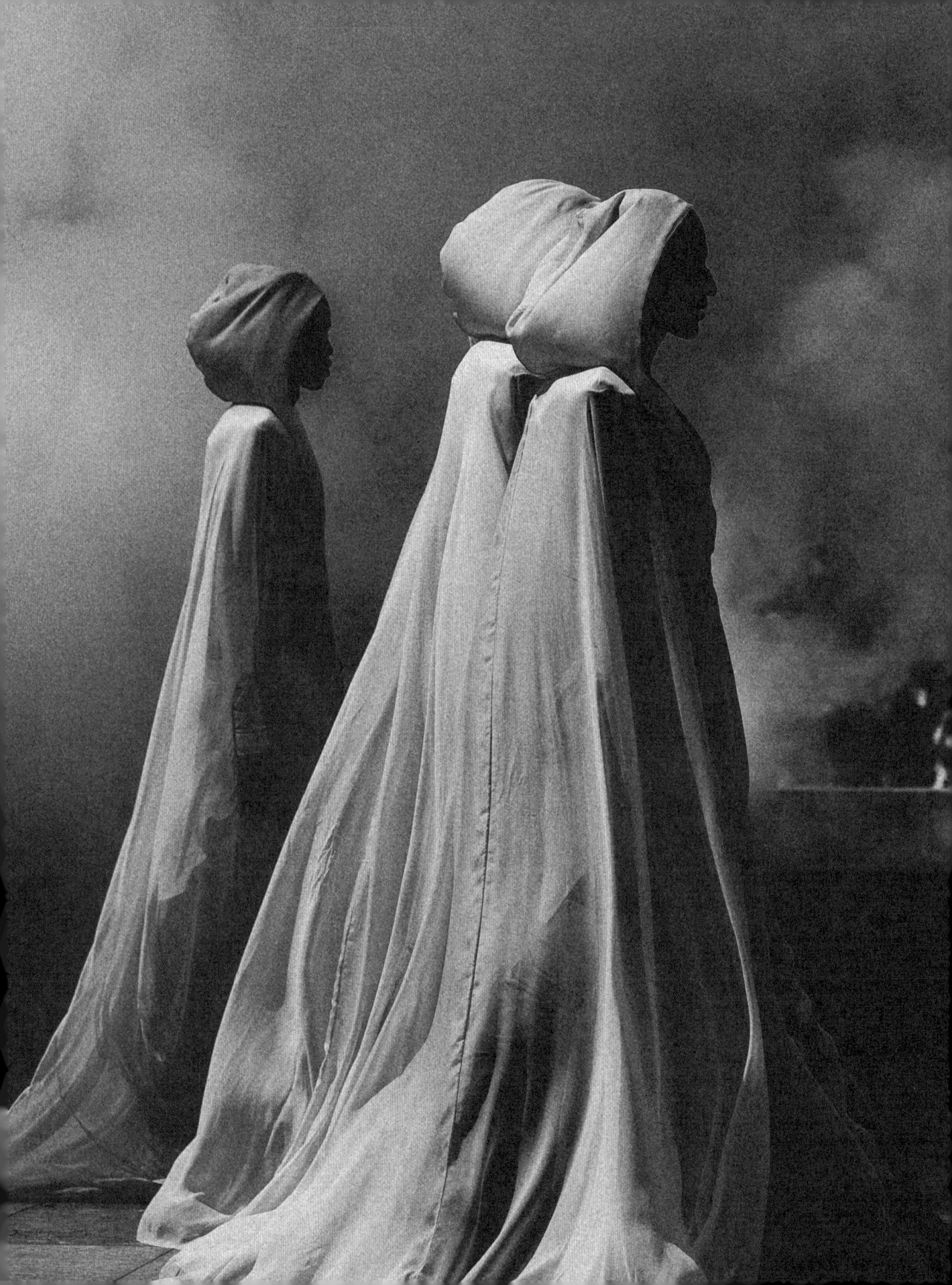

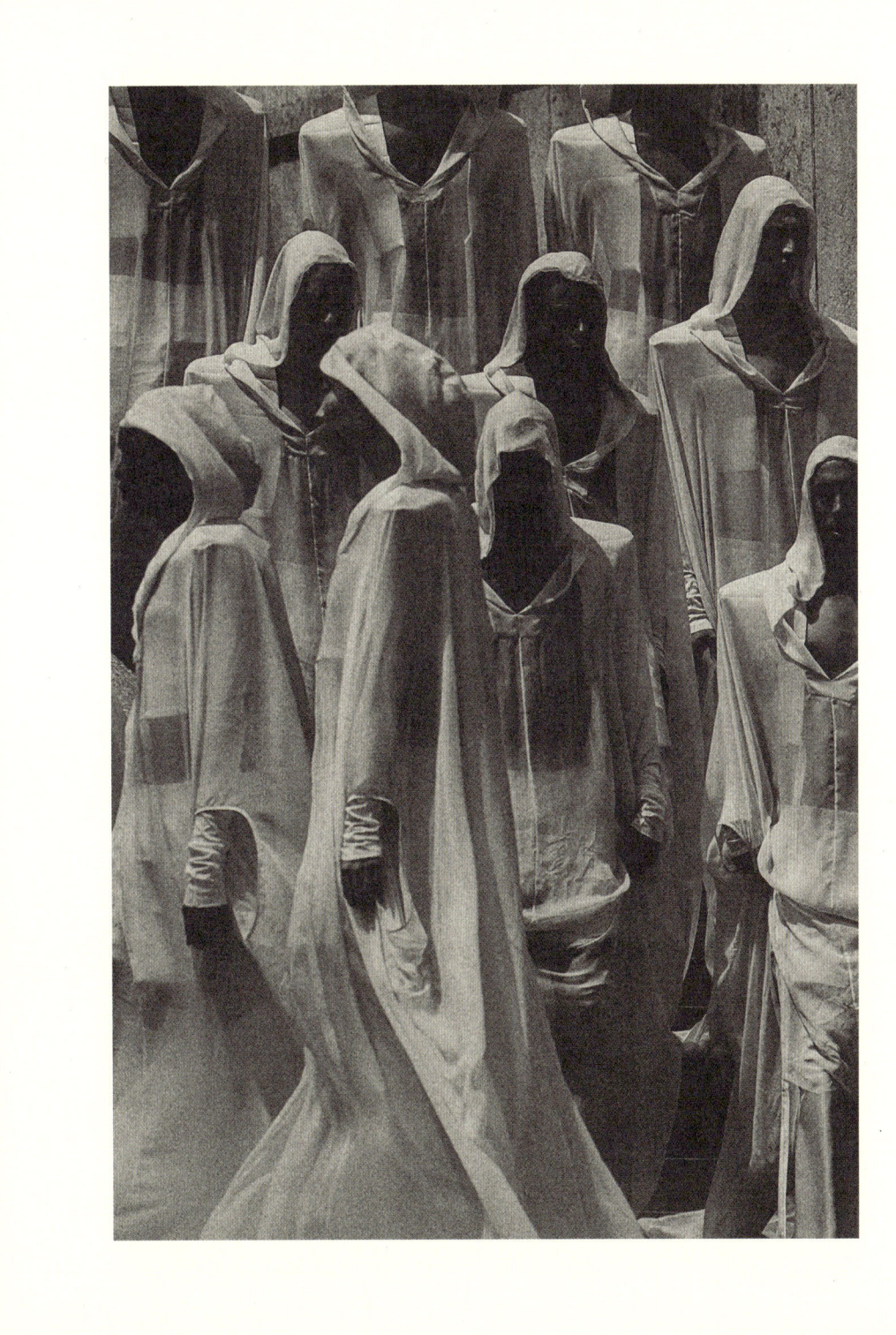

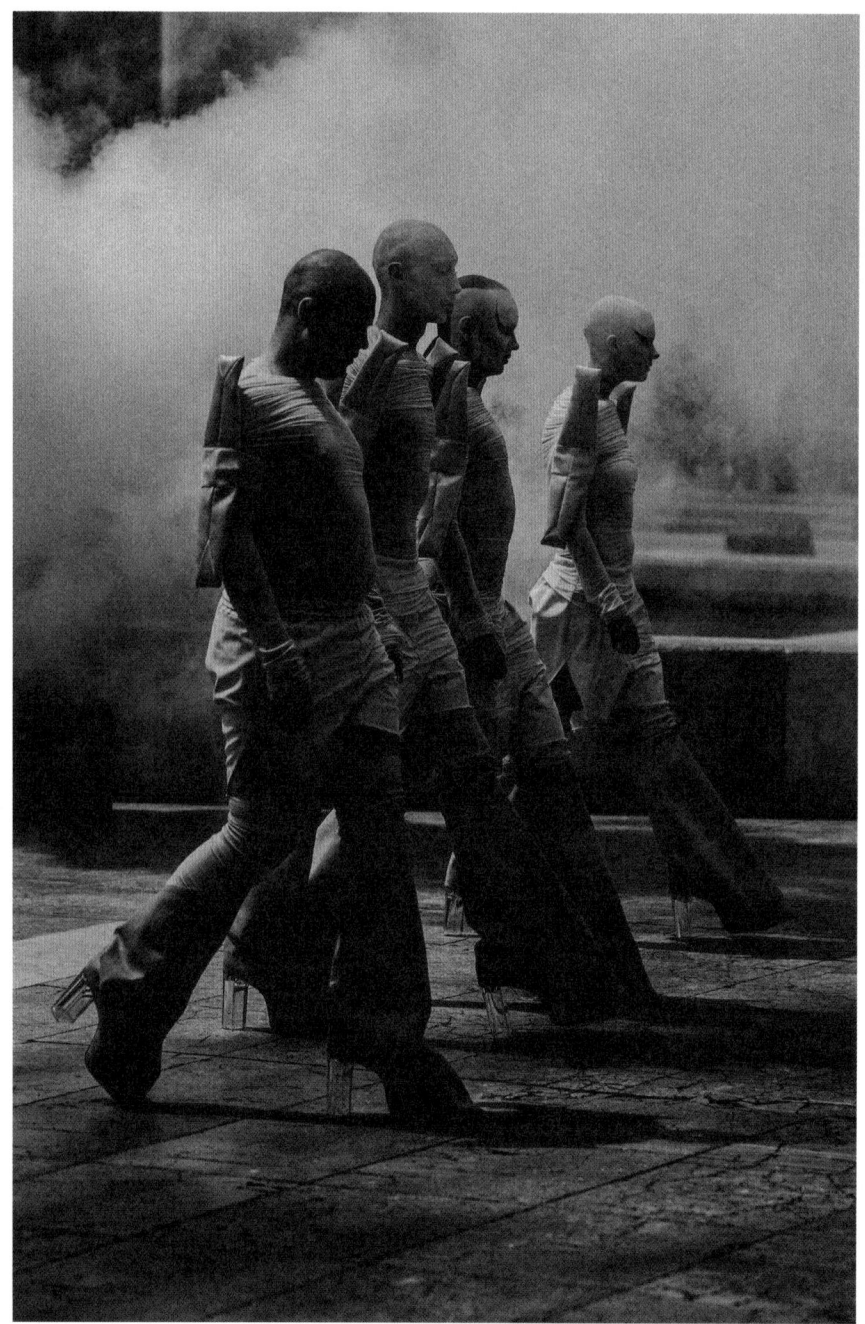

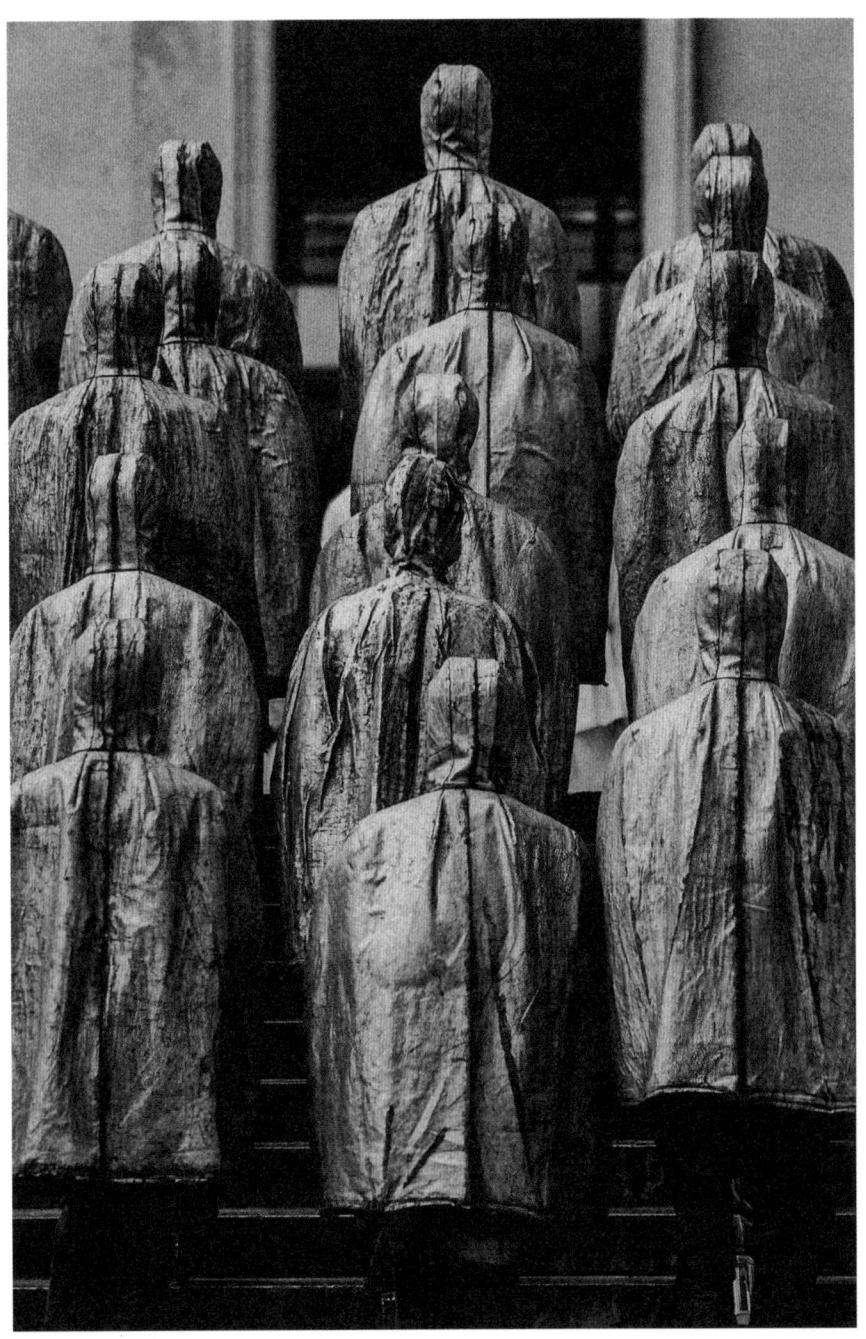

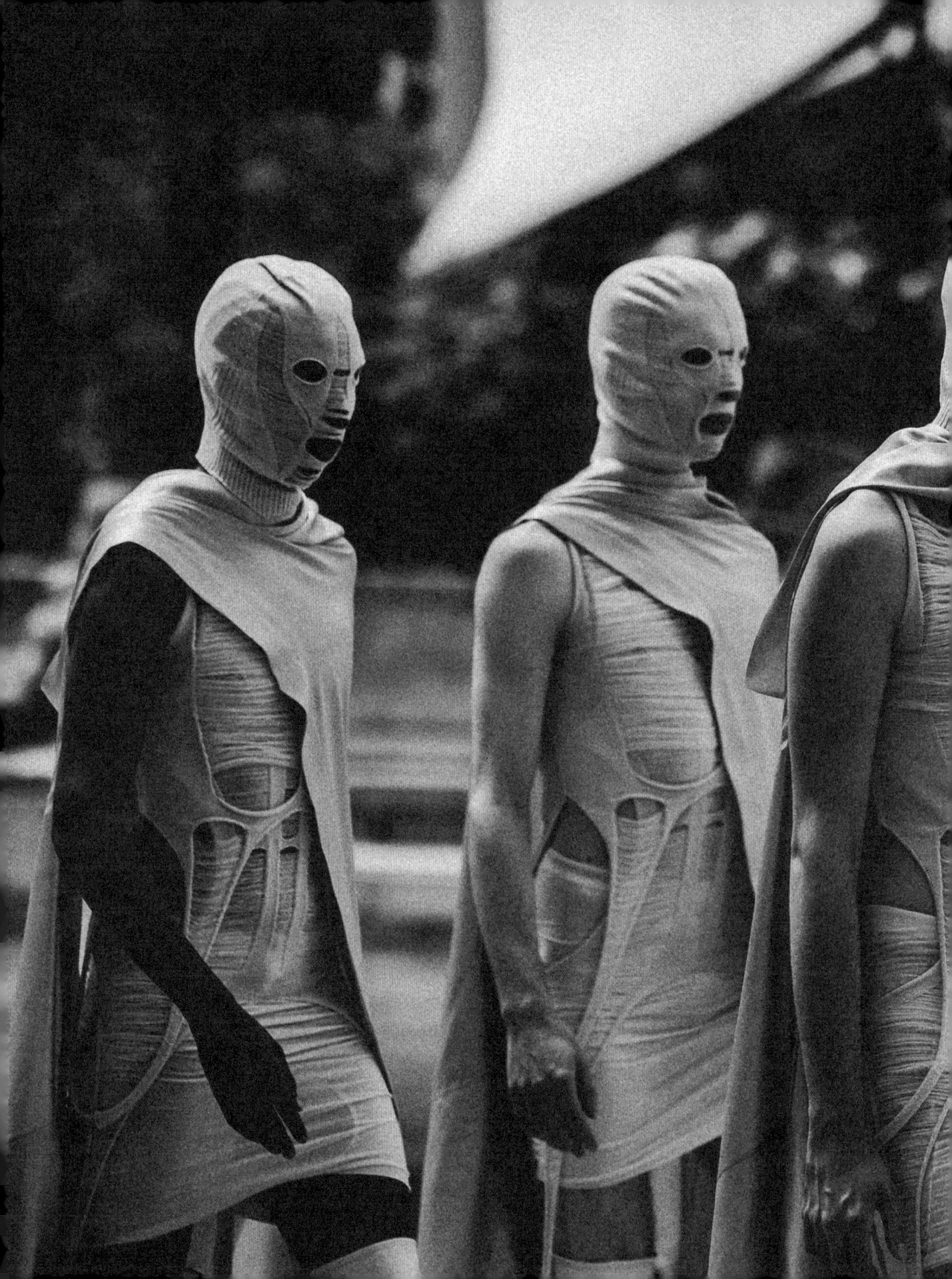

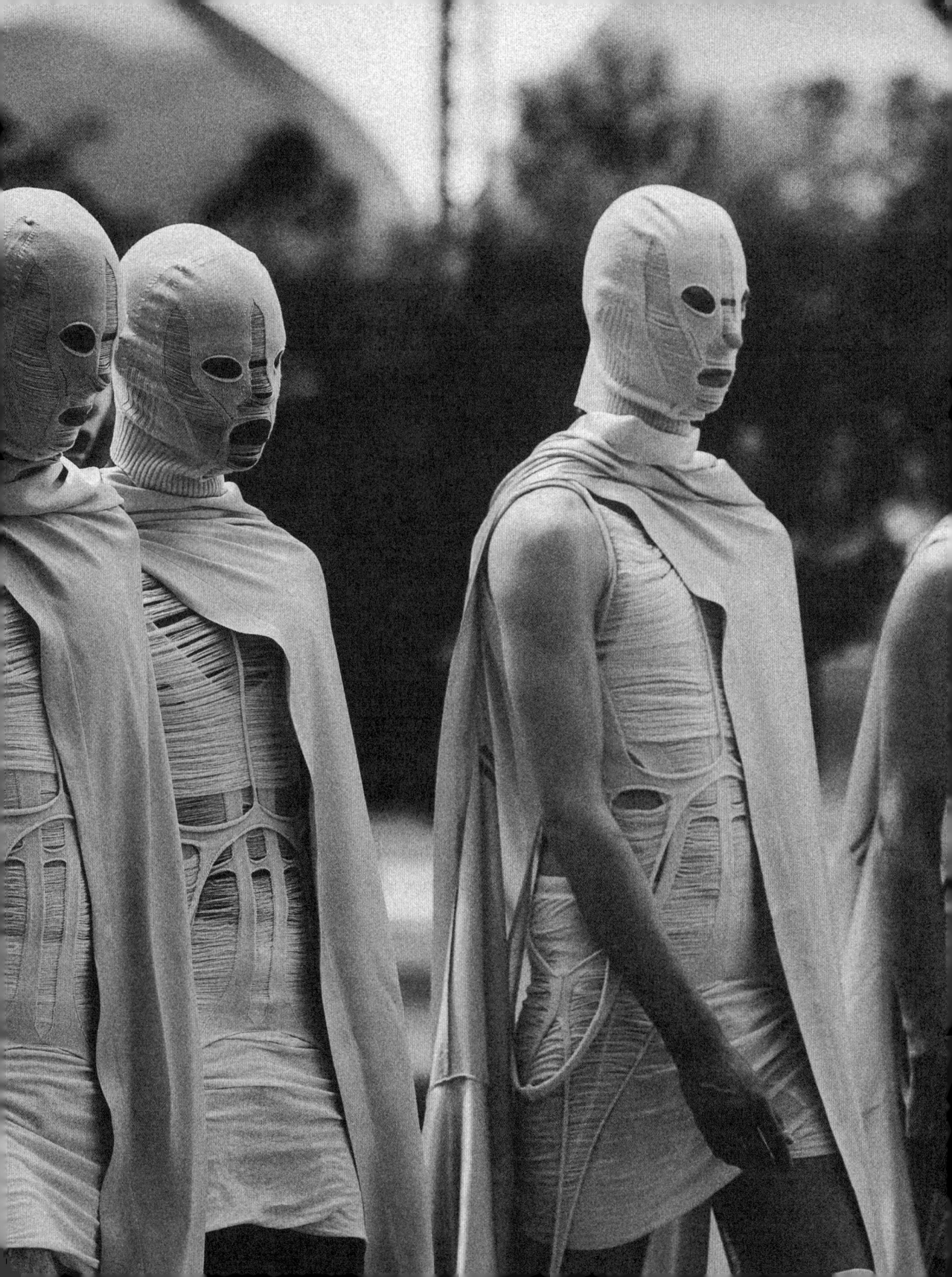

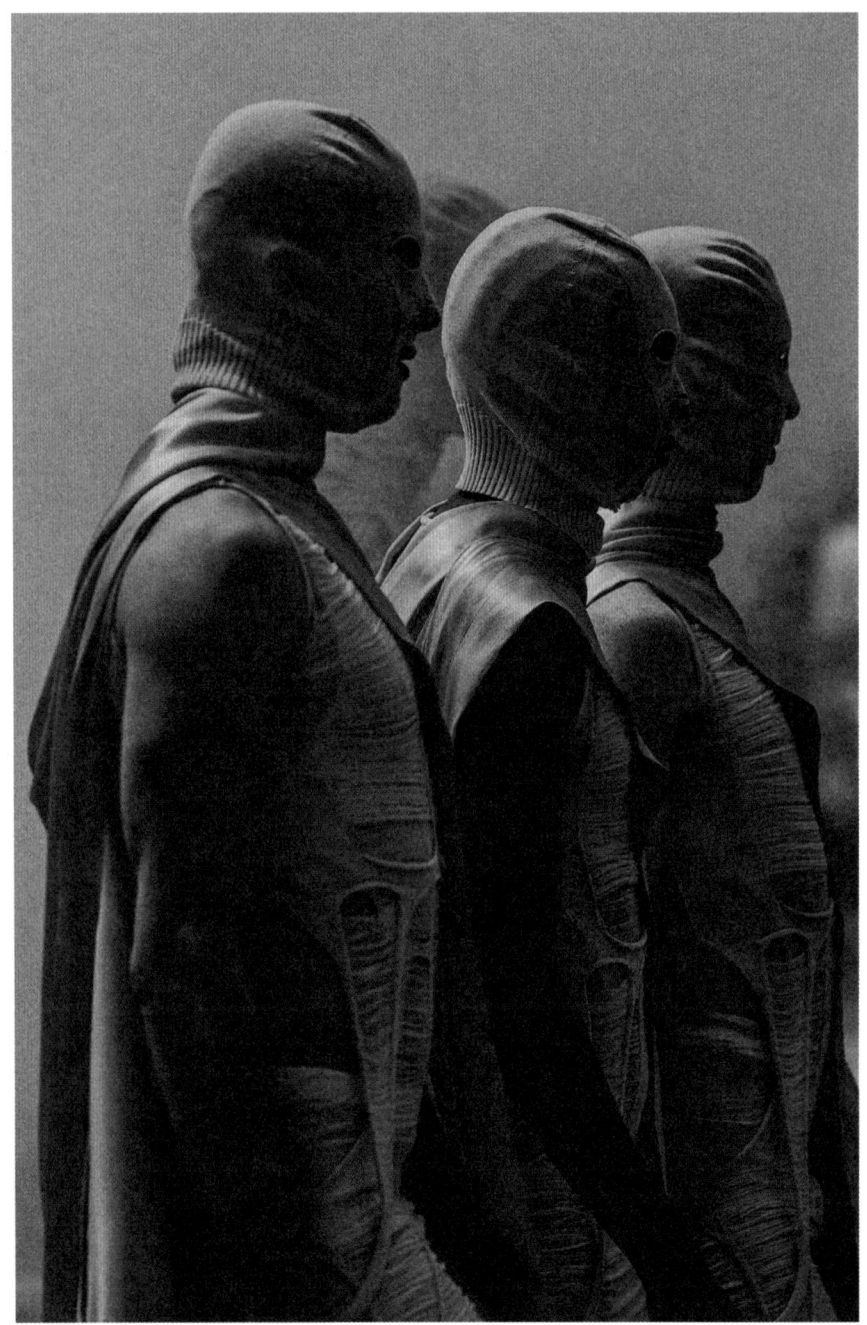

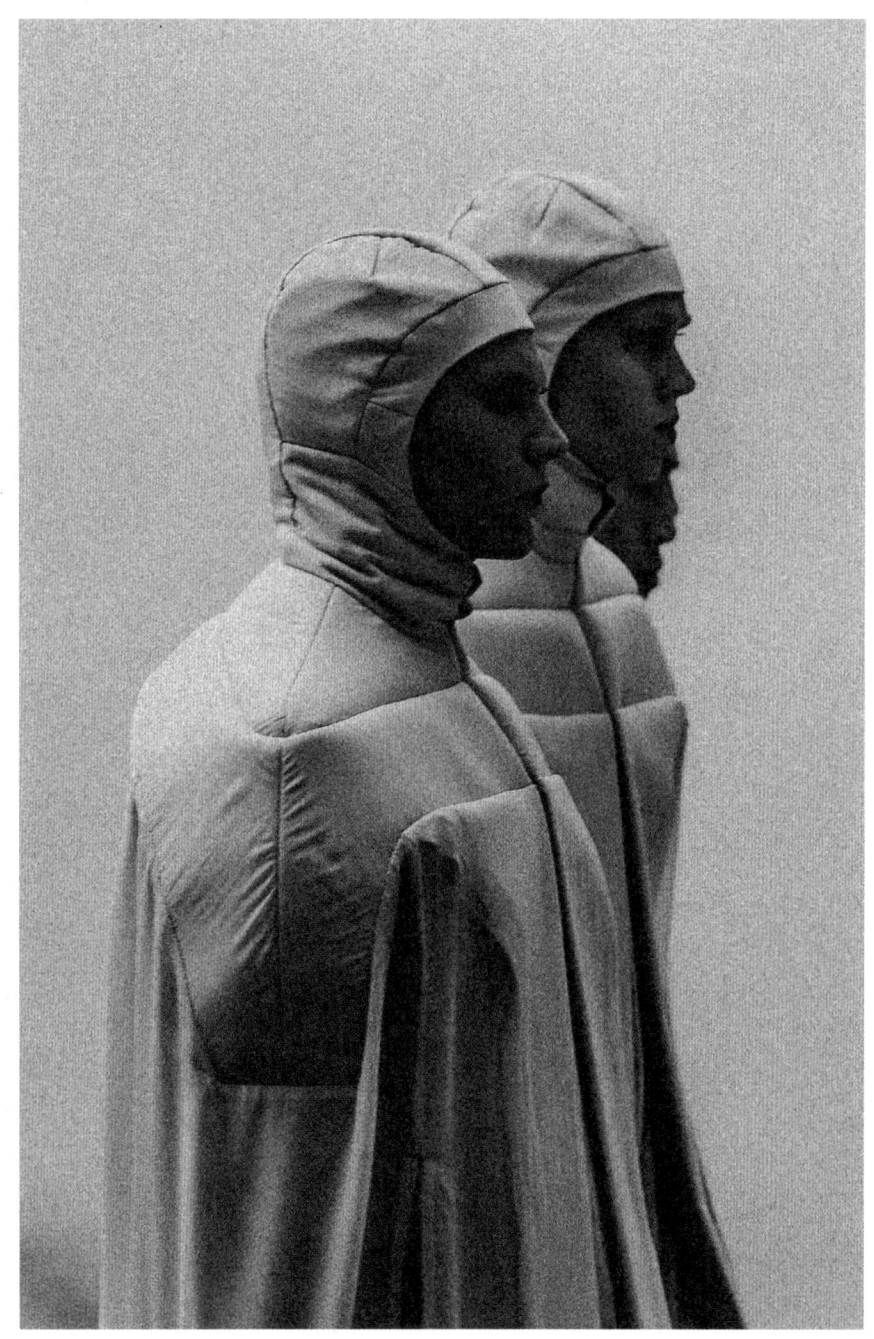

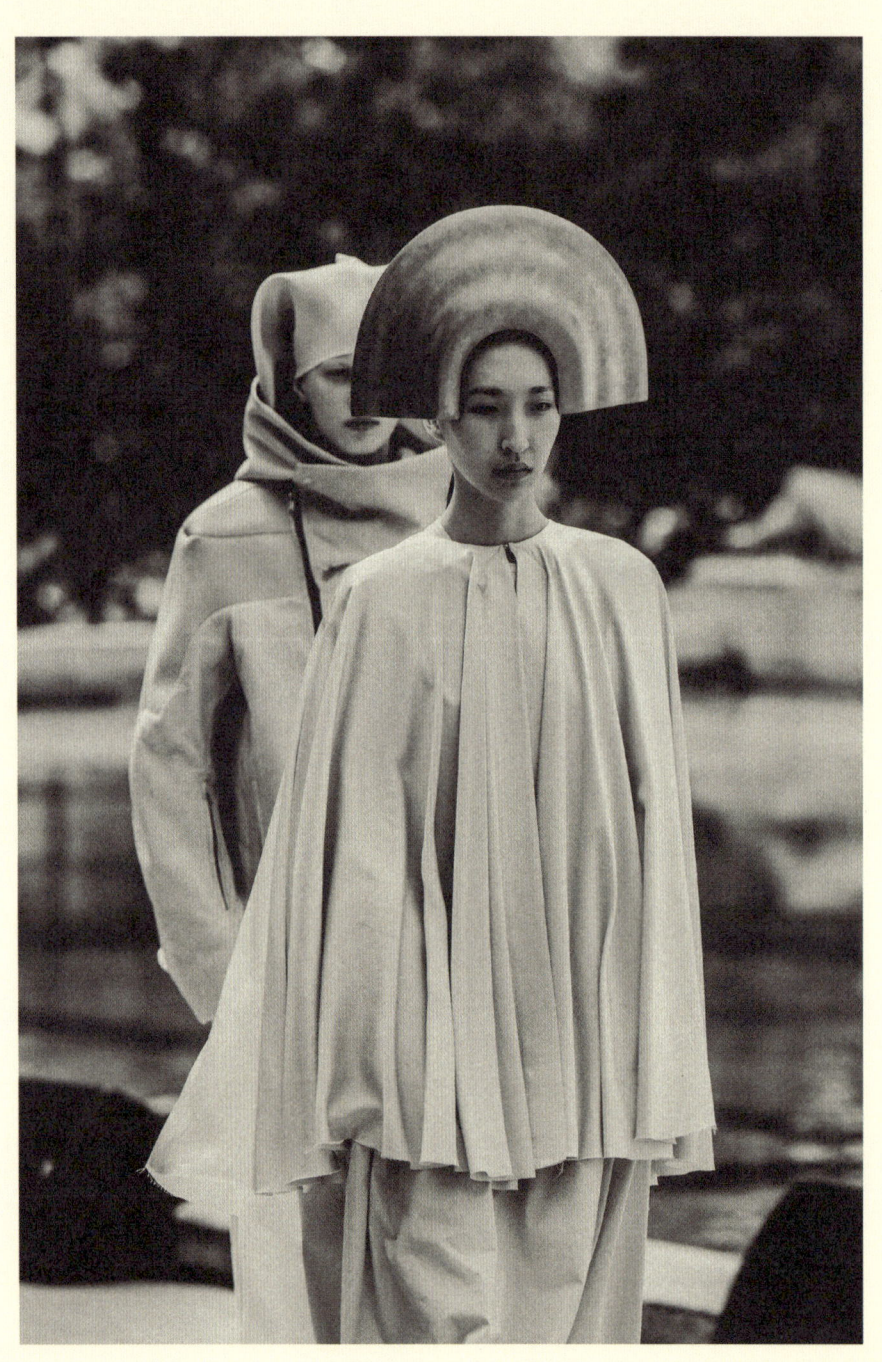

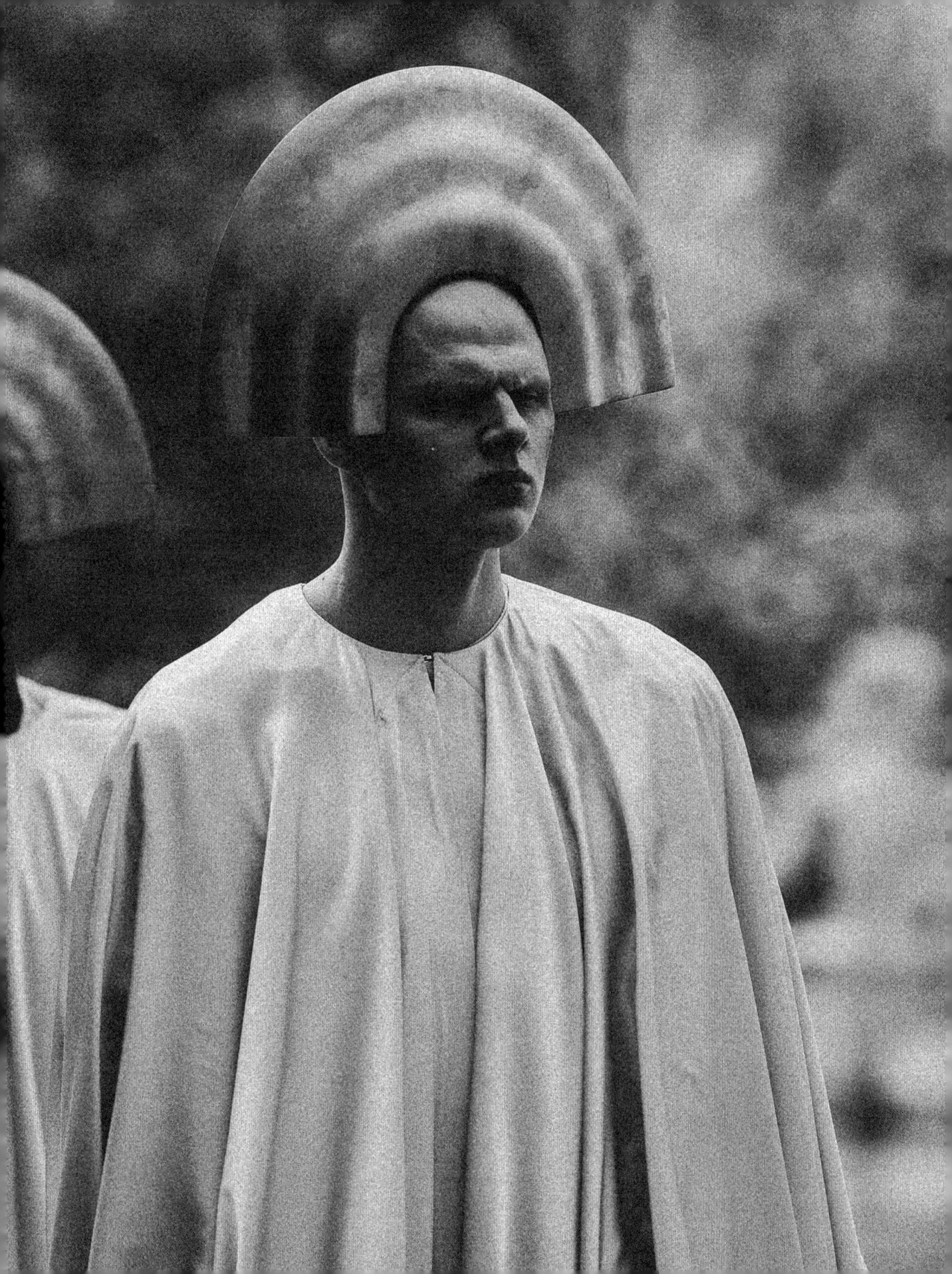

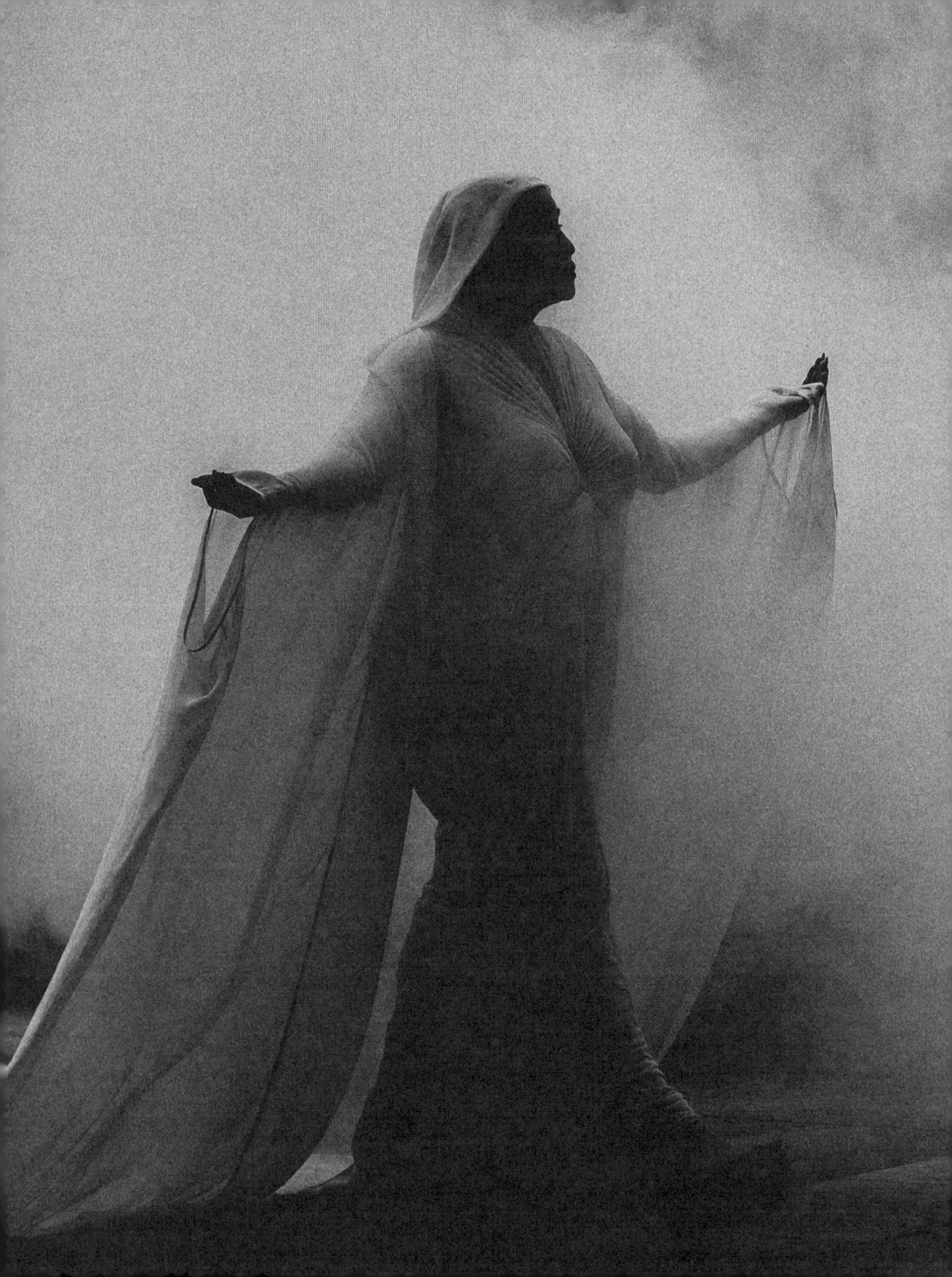

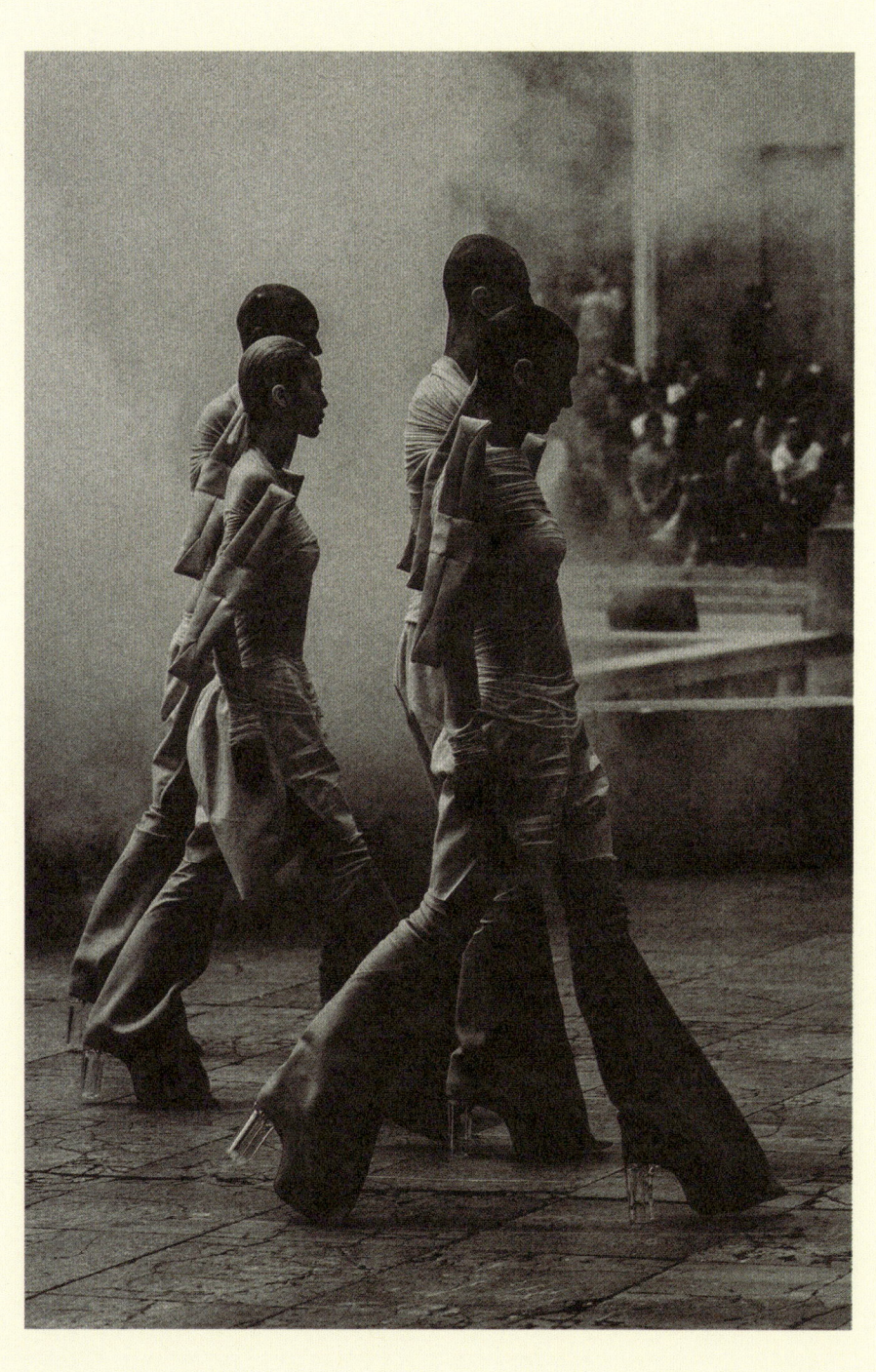

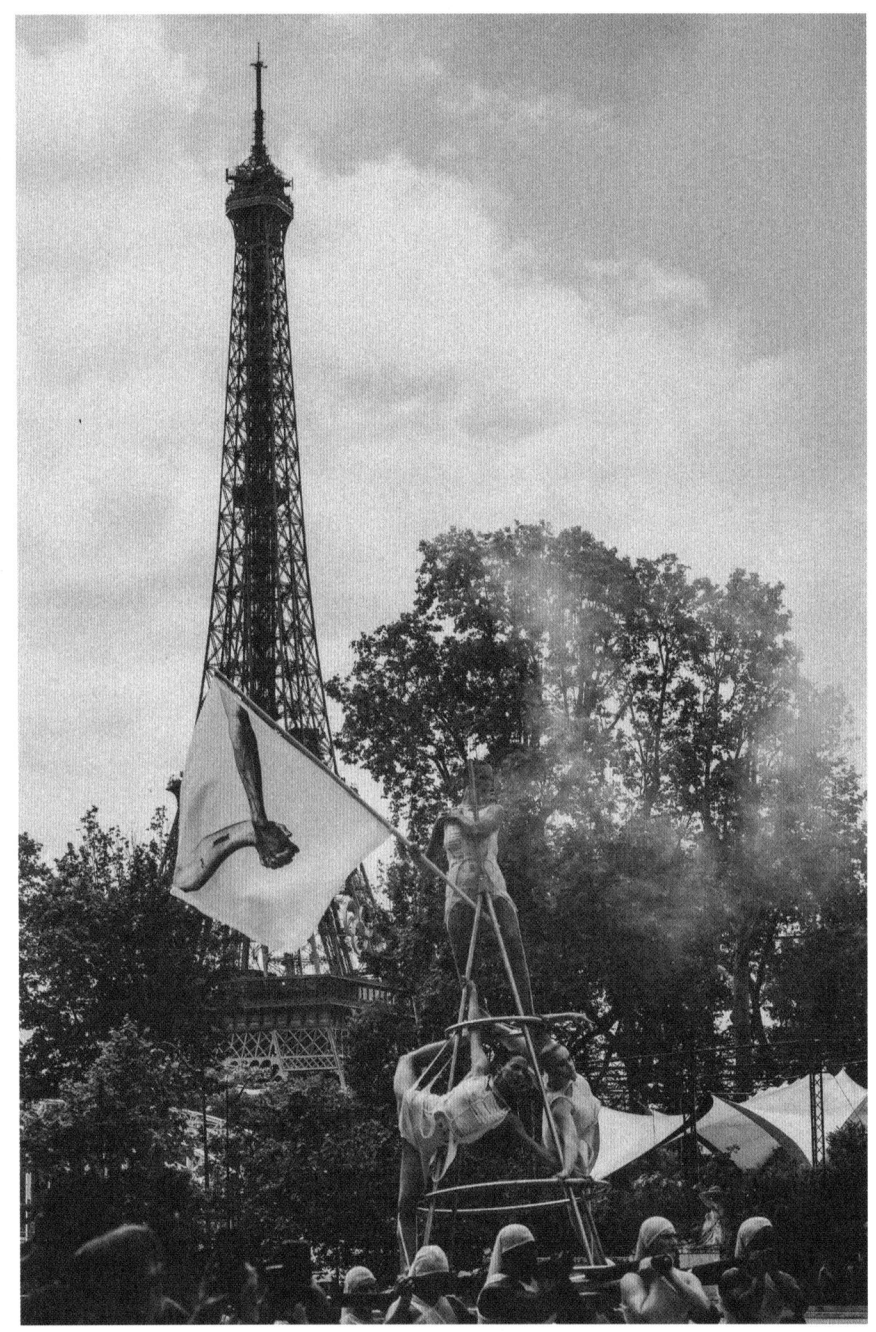

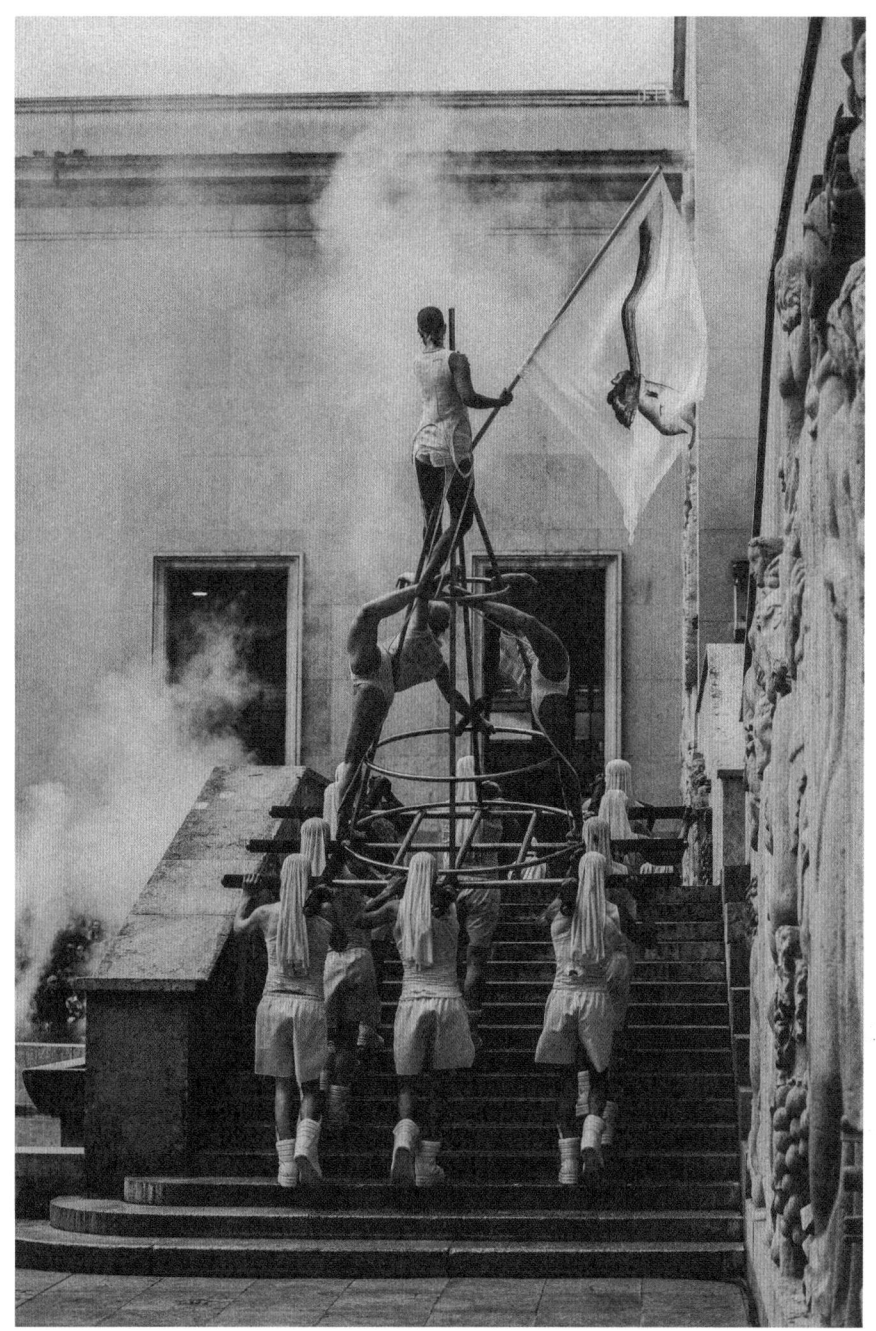

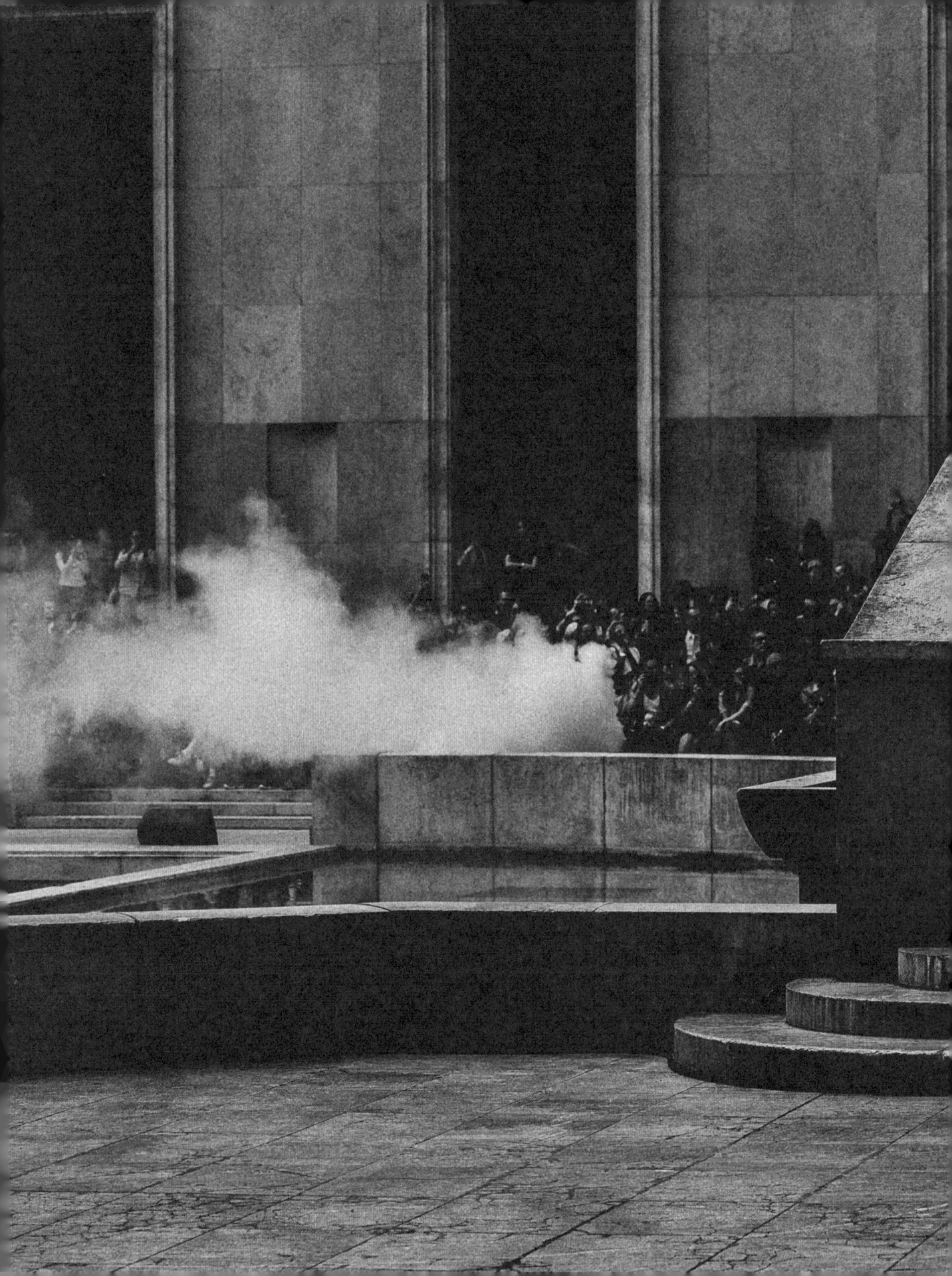

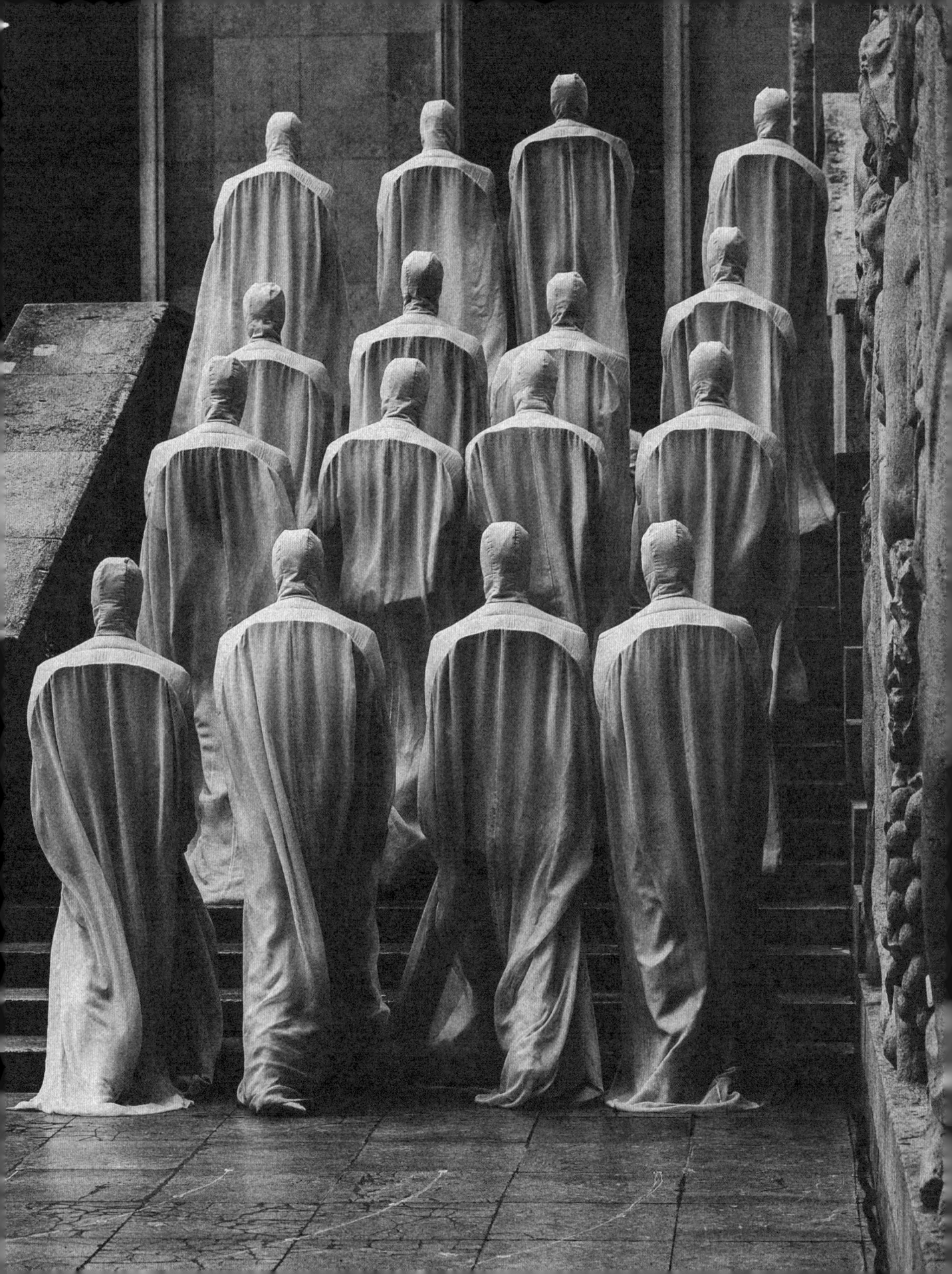

GESAFF

The Dark Prince Returns

ELSTEIN

Photographs *Jordan Hemingway*

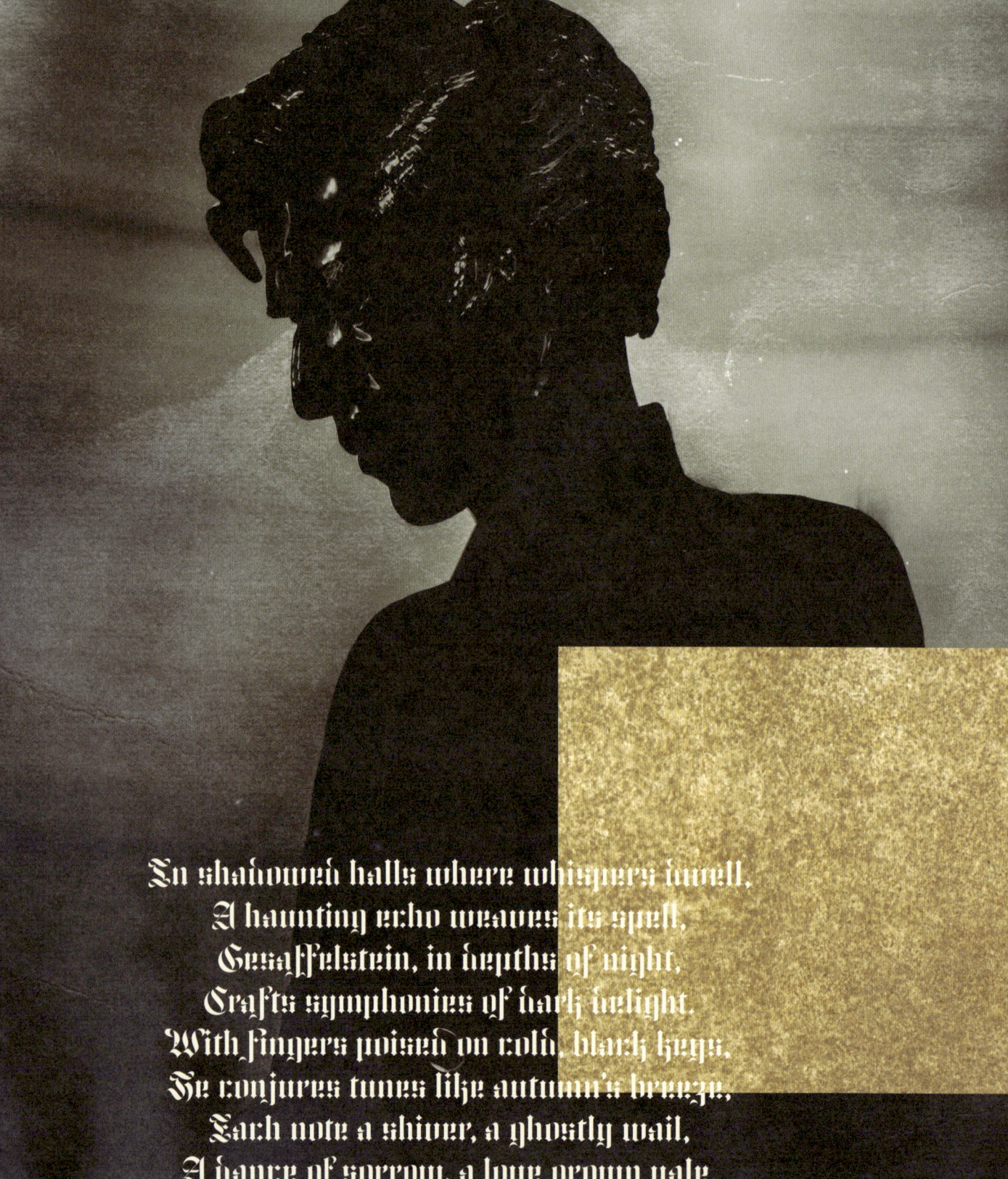

In shadowed halls where whispers dwell,
A haunting echo weaves its spell,
Gesaffelstein, in depths of night,
Crafts symphonies of dark delight.
With fingers poised on cold, black keys,
He conjures tunes like autumn's breeze,
Each note a shiver, a ghostly wail,
A dance of sorrow, a love grown pale.

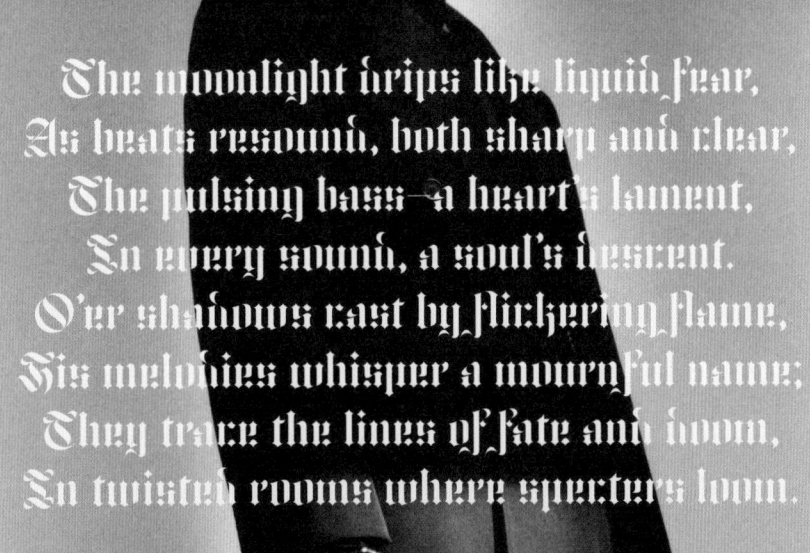

The moonlight drips like liquid fear,
As beats resound, both sharp and clear,
The pulsing bass—a heart's lament,
In every sound, a soul's descent.
O'er shadows cast by flickering flame,
His melodies whisper a mournful name;
They trace the lines of fate and doom,
In twisted rooms where specters loom.

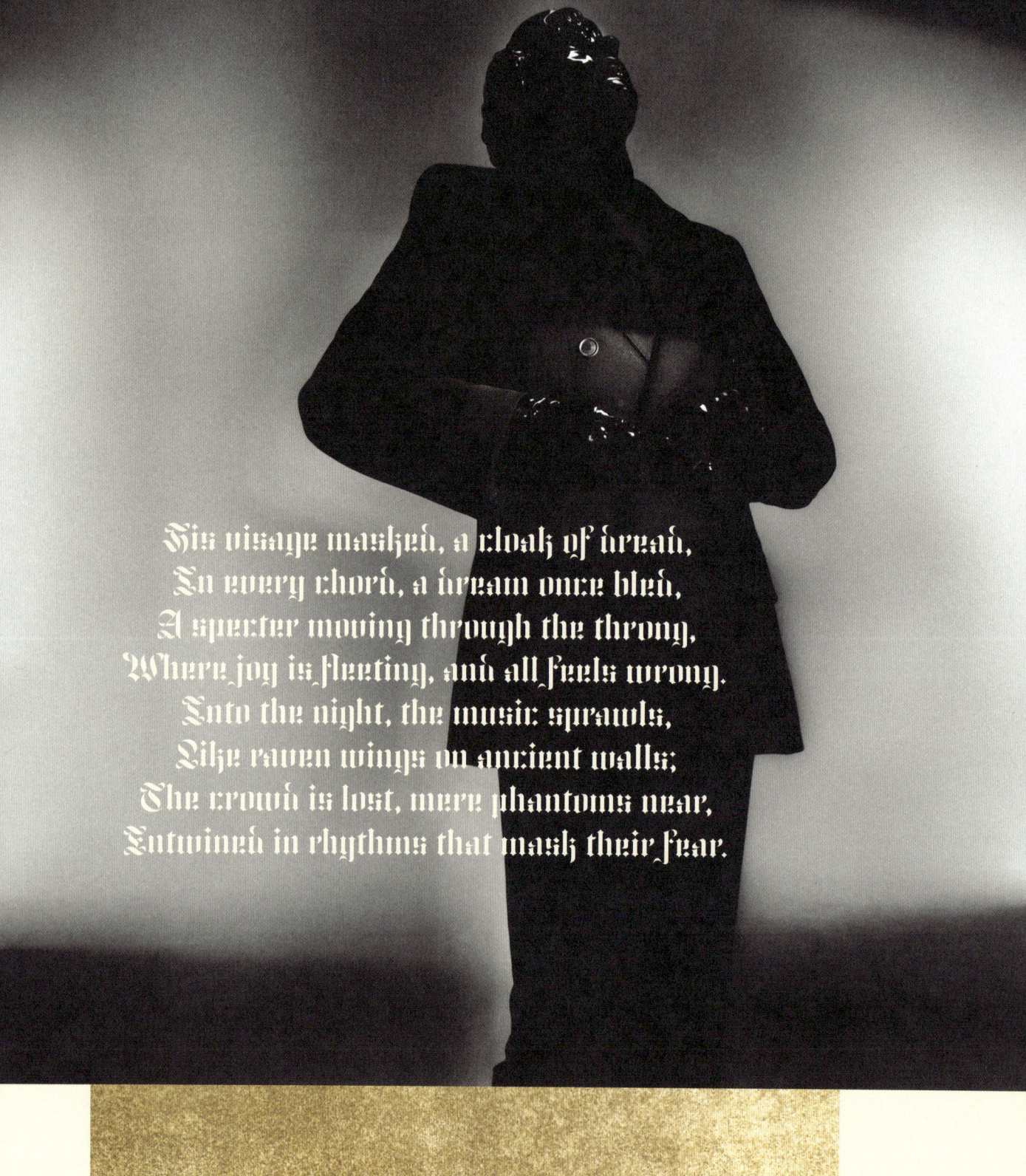

His visage masked, a cloak of dread,
In every chord, a dream once bled,
A specter moving through the throng,
Where joy is fleeting, and all feels wrong.
Into the night, the music sprawls,
Like raven wings on ancient walls;
The crowd is lost, mere phantoms near,
Entwined in rhythms that mask their fear.

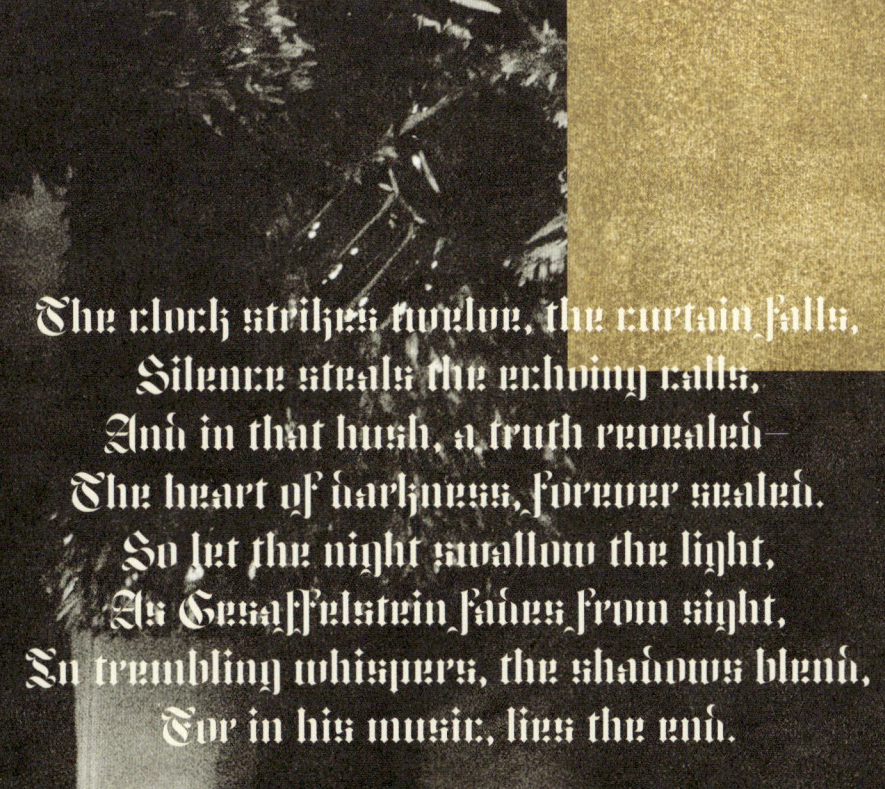

The clock strikes twelve, the curtain falls,
Silence steals the echoing calls,
And in that hush, a truth revealed—
The heart of darkness, forever sealed.
So let the night swallow the light,
As Gesaffelstein fades from sight,
In trembling whispers, the shadows blend,
For in his music, lies the end.

UNDEAD
UNDEAD
UNDEAD

A lively conversation with David J from
Bauhaus and Love and Rockets

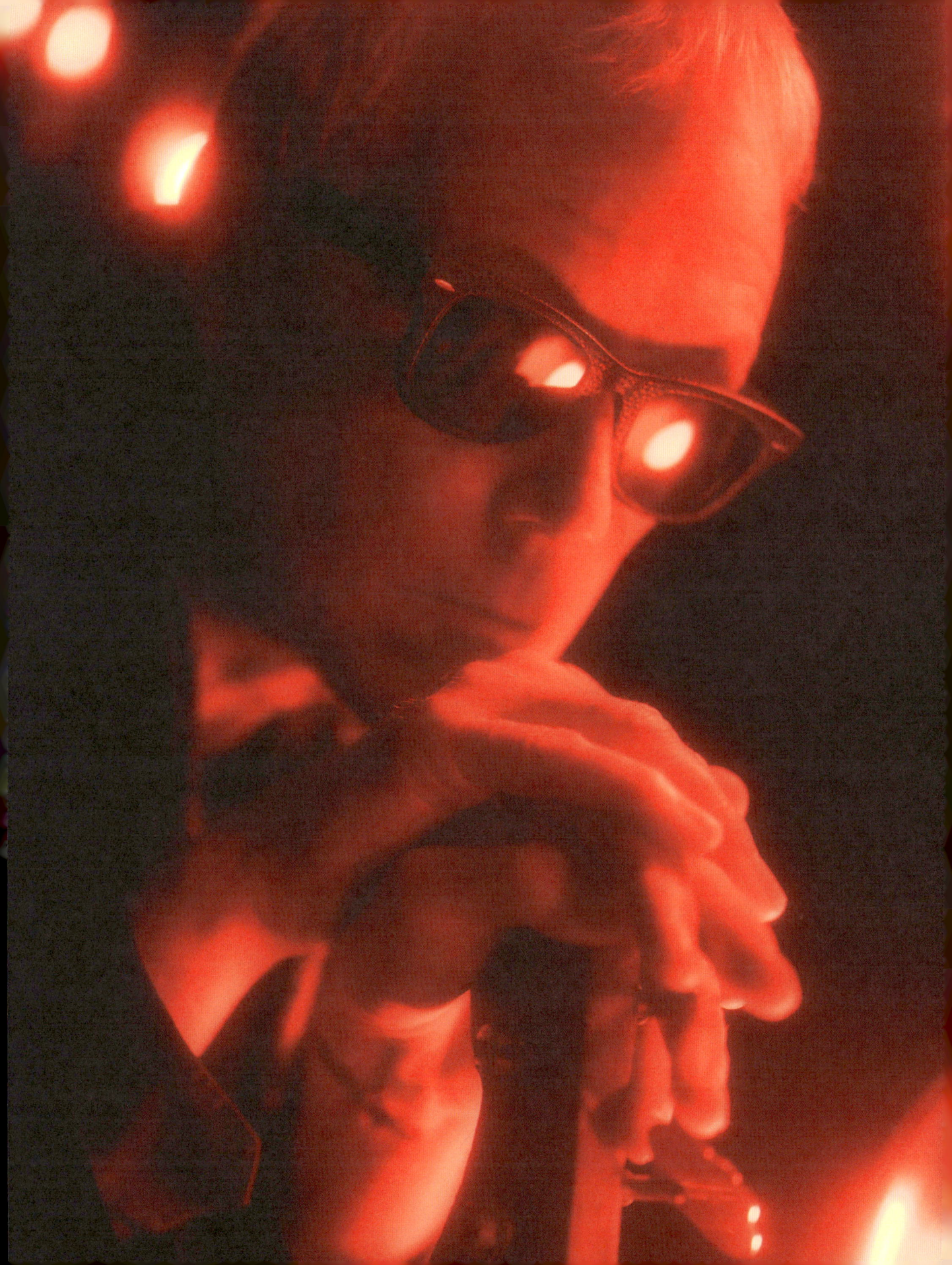

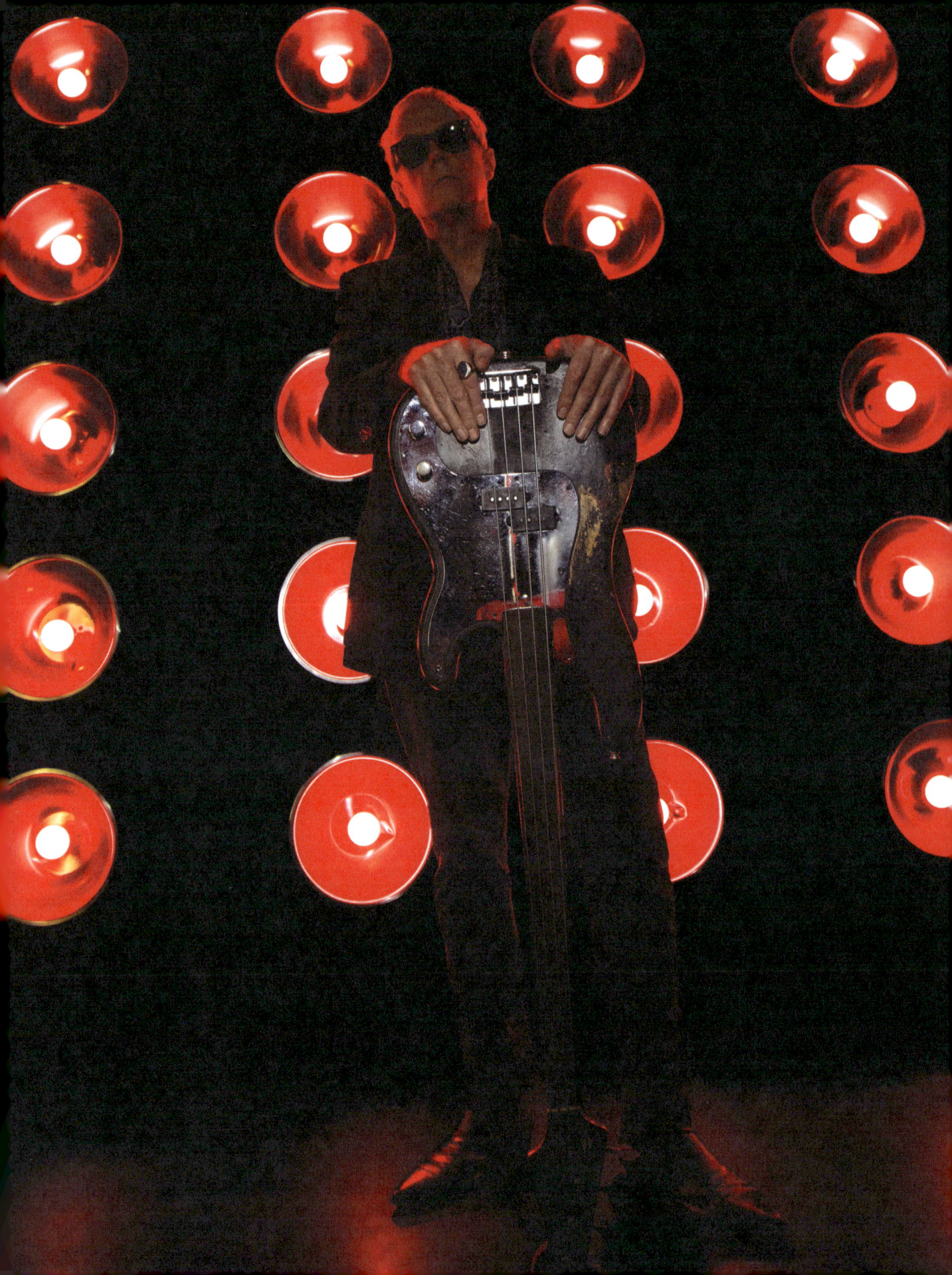

Had David J retired after uttering "rest in peace" at the final Bauhaus show in 1983, his legacy would already have been assured. As the band's bassist from 1979 until their initial breakup, he helped pioneer post-punk and gothic rock, laying the groundwork for countless imitators in the decades to follow. His melodic bass lines and lyrical contributions—especially on the seminal "Bela Lugosi's Dead"—shaped not just Bauhaus's identity but the very foundations of goth culture itself. But Bauhaus's end wasn't a conclusion for David—it was a beginning. Alongside former bandmates Daniel Ash and his brother Kevin Haskins, he cofounded Love and Rockets, which would go on to achieve significant commercial success in the U.S. His solo career followed suit, with the 1989 single "I'll Be Your Chauffeur" reaching No. 1 on Billboard's Modern Rock Tracks chart.

David's memoir, *Who Killed Mister Moonlight?* (Bauhaus, Black Magick, and Benediction), was released in 2014 to critical acclaim. In recent years, he's become a sought-after collaborator, working with a wide range of artists, including Porno for Pyros, Voltaire, and Night Crickets. *Wednesday* sat down with David over bourbon in Los Angeles, captivated as the amiable and engaging icon recounted tales of his musical origins, a surreal encounter with David Bowie on the set of *The Hunger,* dub's unexpected influence on Bauhaus, and some chilling personal experiences with Electronic Voice Phenomena (EVP) recordings.

Introduction *David Moynihan* / Interview *Kevin Grady* / Photographs *Alejandra Guerrero*
Model *Darenzia* / Makeup *Jennifer Corona*

W How did growing up in Northampton, England, impact you and your music?

D Well, it was filtered by being away from big cities like London, Liverpool, and Manchester. It's smaller, and it's right smack bang in the middle of the country. My perception of music when I was a kid came through the radio—bands like The Kinks, who I adored, and The Who, and most of all The Beatles. But generally, the music I was exposed to was very limited. There was also my parents' record collection—they liked things like Burt Bacharach, which also appealed to me. My mother's favorite singer was Ella Fitzgerald. So, there was a bit of that, a bit of Count Basie, Herb Alpert & the Tijuana Brass...

W My parents listened to Herb Alpert as well. *Whipped Cream & Other Delights*!

D Right. And then Johnny Mathis, Tony Bennett, the crooners—Frank Sinatra, of course. Some of my dad's favorites were Django Reinhardt, Stéphane Grappelli, and The Quintette du Hot Club de France, which I also liked. When the '70s came along, that was when music exploded for me. T-Rex, Roxy Music, and David Bowie were the big three. I was secretly delighted by my dad's abhorrence of these glam artists. It made it all the more delicious. He was outraged, especially by Bowie. But then, the very last birthday present he ever sent me was a bio of David Bowie, *Starman*. I was rather touched by that.

When Bowie came along, everything exploded into technicolor. I first heard his music on a TV show called *The Old Grey Whistle Test*. They would show old black-and-white movies, dancing girls, or horror movies, or they would put on *Fritz the Cat* and play a contemporary track with it. One of those was "Andy Warhol" by Bowie, and I instantly loved it. The next day, I went down to Spinadisc Records in Abington Square and bought *Hunky Dory* and saw Bowie's image for the first time, you know, looking like Greta Garbo on the front. I was very intrigued by that.

W I'll bet.

D And then I just remember going on the top deck of a double-decker bus and riding back to my house, poring over those lyrics. I had never read anything like it, and I was taken with the imagery. I couldn't wait to play it, and I literally ran from the bus stop to the house with the album under my arm and made a beeline for my parents' gramophone, this huge piece of mahogany furniture with enormous speakers. I cranked the volume, and it's, you know, "Changes" and "Life on Mars." I was completely gobsmacked. Later, my brother Kevin saw Bowie performing on a kids' TV show, and he wasn't sure about this bloke. He said, "He looks weird; I don't know if I hate it or love it. I'm really confused!"

Bowie appeared on *The Top of the Pops* later that same night, and we watched it together. I was in awe! I loved the skintight clothes and wrestling boots, that

spiky red hair, and his eyes were just so weird because of the injury to his one eye, where the pupil is permanently dilated, you know?

W He'd injured it as a child in a fight over a girl.

D That's right. There was just something alien about him, the way he held himself. It made you feel a little uncomfortable. But also, you really liked it. At the same time there was Marc Bolan. He preceded Bowie, and I fell in love with his music and his image to such a degree that I joined his fan club, the only fan club I've ever been a member of. There was Roxy Music as well—it all transported me to another place.

W Where were you when David Bowie died?

D I was in the Crystal Hotel in Portland, and I wrote that song ("Where Were You The Day That David Bowie Died?") on the actual day. I'd picked up a copy of *Blackstar* the day it came out on CD so I could play it on the road. Then I played in Seattle that night, and after the gig, I invited a few attendees and old friends down into my basement area where I was staying overnight. We lit some candles, and we had some oil lamps glowing away in the dark. And we all sat there It was like the old days when I used to get together with my mates and we'd play, you know, like *Heroes* or *Scary Monsters*. We all sat down in anticipation of this brand-new Bowie record. We listened to it, and we were all just completely wowed by it. It was beautiful.

W It didn't disappoint, did it? I got it the same day, too. I thought it was one of his best albums. I still do.

D I think it's up there with the best of them. And it was also treading new ground with the jazz influence coming through. So that happened, and then I went back to Portland because I had a recording session booked the next day at Revolver Studios, which is owned by Collin Hegna from Brian Jonestown Massacre. The night before I went out with this young lady, and we had a nightcap sitting downstairs on the patio of the hotel. I refer to all of this in the song. We were discussing who we'd want to meet if we could meet anybody in the world. She was taking her time thinking of who that would be, and I knew she was a huge Bowie fan, so I ventured Bowie She goes, "Oh, no, no, that would just be too much." I said, "I get it. It's kind of like me with Bob Dylan." That was the last thing we said before saying goodnight I went up to my room, and the phone rang. It was my son, Joe, and he said, "Oh, Dad, it's so sad about Bowie." I didn't know what the hell he was talking about. And he explained, and I was just completely devastated. I intended to play *Blackstar* just to myself on headphones that night, and I was really looking forward to doing that But now it would be with a whole different context.

W I know several people who couldn't play it at all.

D I had to play it. I knew it would be a kind of elegy. I got a sense when I heard it that first time that he was alluding to not being around much longer. It was so very conscious. I played it with that mindset, and it got to the last song, "I Can't Give Everything Away." And what he's musically alluding to on that is very personal to me because it relates to the time I met Bowie on the set of *The Hunger*.

Going back to that day, we had a break in filming, and Bauhaus's little holding pen *(laughter)* was right next to Bowie's dressing room. And in our area, there was an old jukebox, stacked with old singles. Nobody was around, just me. And I was choosing a record to play, when I became aware of a very strong, looming presence behind me. Then I hear this voice, a very distinctive voice, "Do you mind if I pick one?" It was Bowie! I said, "Oh! Please do!" So, he punches in a number, and what he plays is an instrumental called "Groovin' with Mr. Bloe" by Mr. Bloe from 1970. I have it here! *(plays track on a tape recorder)* Can you hear that?

W I can't. It's not coming through…

D Really? You can't hear that? That's weird. I mean, it's much louder than my voice…

W So strange. David, are you here?! *(laughter)*

D It's kind of spooky. It's just actually physically playing on a tape recorder. Why can't you hear that?! Anyway, so he starts dancing, and he's dressed in that shiny black suit he wears in the film. Just smiling that big, beaming smile and making eye contact with me through his blue-tinted shades. Just me and him, so surreal, and I'm just standing there, nodding along. Now, the thing is, when *Low* came out, there was the track "A New Career in a New Town." And the first time I heard that, I thought, oh, he's cribbed that harmonica line from "Groovin' with Mr Bloe." I always thought that. So, I said to him, "This reminds me of something." He goes, "Oh, what's that?" I said, "It's one of yours." He goes, "What?" So, I said, "A New Career in a New Town." And he goes, like this—puts his finger to his lips, winks, and then carries on dancing, smiling.

W I can picture it.

D Anyway, fast forward. Hotel room, Portland, the night he left us. And that track comes on, and I hear the same allusion to Mr. Bloe. And the title: "I Can't Give Everything Away." I just lost it. I was sobbing. It was just so emotional.

W That must have been incredible, to piece that together.

D Yeah, it just came like a lightning bolt. Then I thought, is he saying with that track that he knew he was going to die? And by alluding to "A New Career in a New Town," is he suggesting that the new town is the afterlife? And the new career is whatever the hell he's going to be doing there?

W That just blew my mind.

D Yeah. So, that was the last song on the album, and I sort of pulled myself together. I saw my guitar over in the corner, and she's calling to me, you know? I knew I was going to write a song, and I just started writing those lyrics, "The Day That David Bowie Died," in one flow. Then picked up the guitar and came up with the music.

We recorded it the next day, with a revolving door of musicians coming in and doing takes. And at the end of the day, we got in a couple of nice bottles of wine and called everybody back because we'd mixed it and it was finished, and we had this wonderful shared playback. It became this sort of vigil and a wake. Everyone was crying.

W What a lovely tribute. I was living in New York at the time and was one of those people gathered outside of where he lived in Soho, you know, burning candles and making a sort of altar. Bowie had personally blessed and contributed artwork to my previous publication, *Lemon*, which was such an honor. It was impossible to imagine he was gone.

How did Peter Murphy interact with Bowie when he met him on the set of *The Hunger*?

D He hid. As I said, sometimes it's just too much to meet your heroes, and it was too much for him. But we all met him at the end of the shoot because he came back to say goodbye. We thought he'd left and were getting our things together, and everybody else had gone. And we thought that it would have been nice to say goodbye, oh well. Then we hear these footsteps, and he bursts through the doors and goes, "Oh guys, I'm so glad you didn't go I wanted to say goodbye and how great it's been working with you. I'd like to see Bauhaus play live someday—good luck with everything."

W That's wonderful.

D Just nice that he made that effort. I think he was relating to us on the level of being like boys in the band, away from all the actors, you know?

W I'm trying to picture the timing of that relative to when your "Ziggy Stardust" cover came out. Was that before or after?

D It was just before.

W Did you ever hear what he thought about that?

D I didn't hear it from the horse's mouth, but a couple of people told me that he said, "I should have done it like that!" I hope he did say that!

W It's one of those rare covers that enhances the mythology of the original song. What are your thoughts about the modern music scene?

D I just think there's too much choice, accessing music through the internet. It's overwhelming. Back in pre-internet days, the good stuff just kind of filtered through like the cream rising to the top. But you had to track it down. It's just a completely different world now. Back then, there was far more mystique, and because of that, more potency. To be honest, I don't think music is anywhere near as important as it used to be. Compared to now, the '70s were quite bright and breezy. There was all that "no future," but there was still more hope back then. Far more.

W The darkness today is truly overwhelming. That's the impetus for this magazine. Speaking of darkness, I'm fascinated by how you injected a dub sensibility into dark songs like "Bela Lugosi's Dead." I know there'd

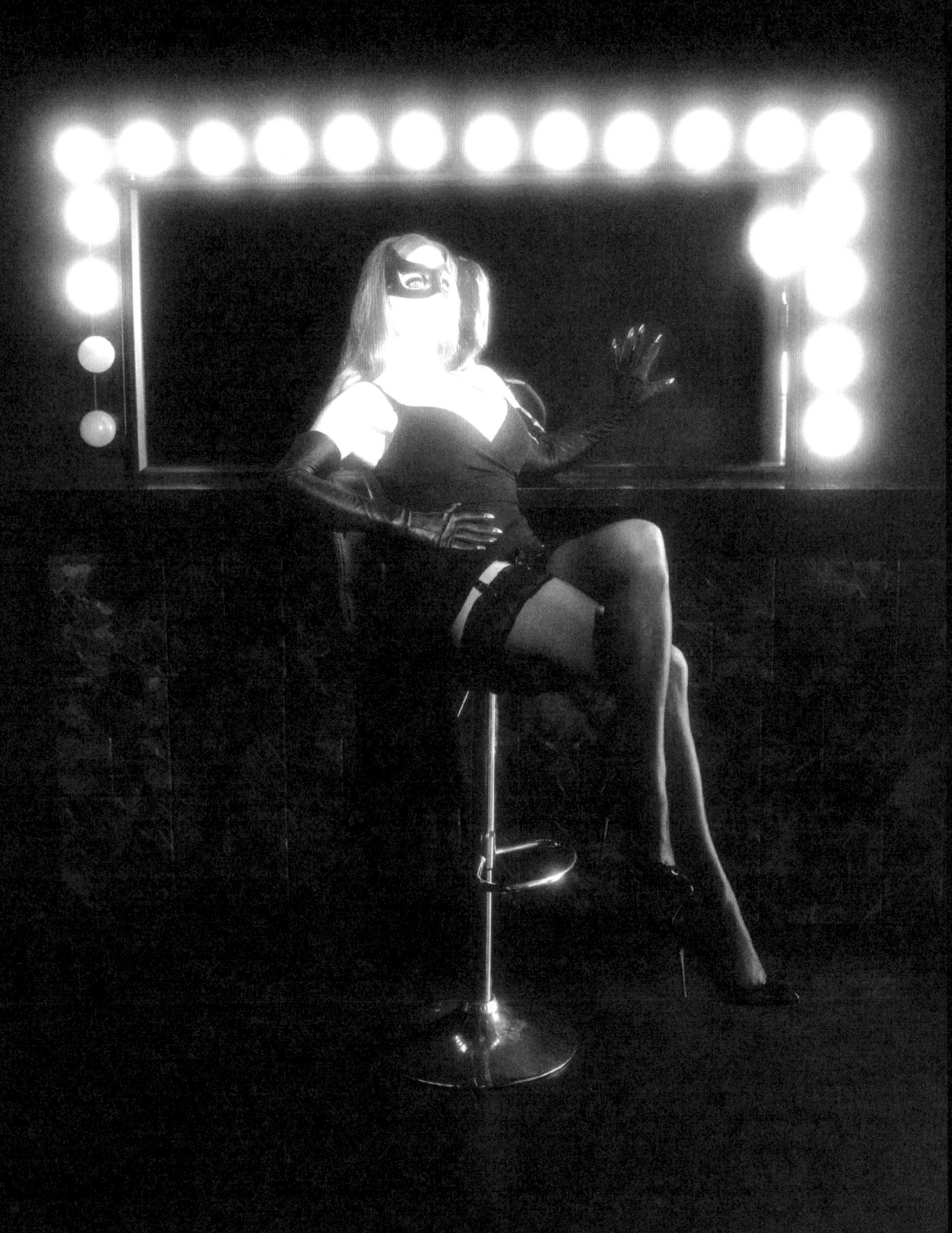

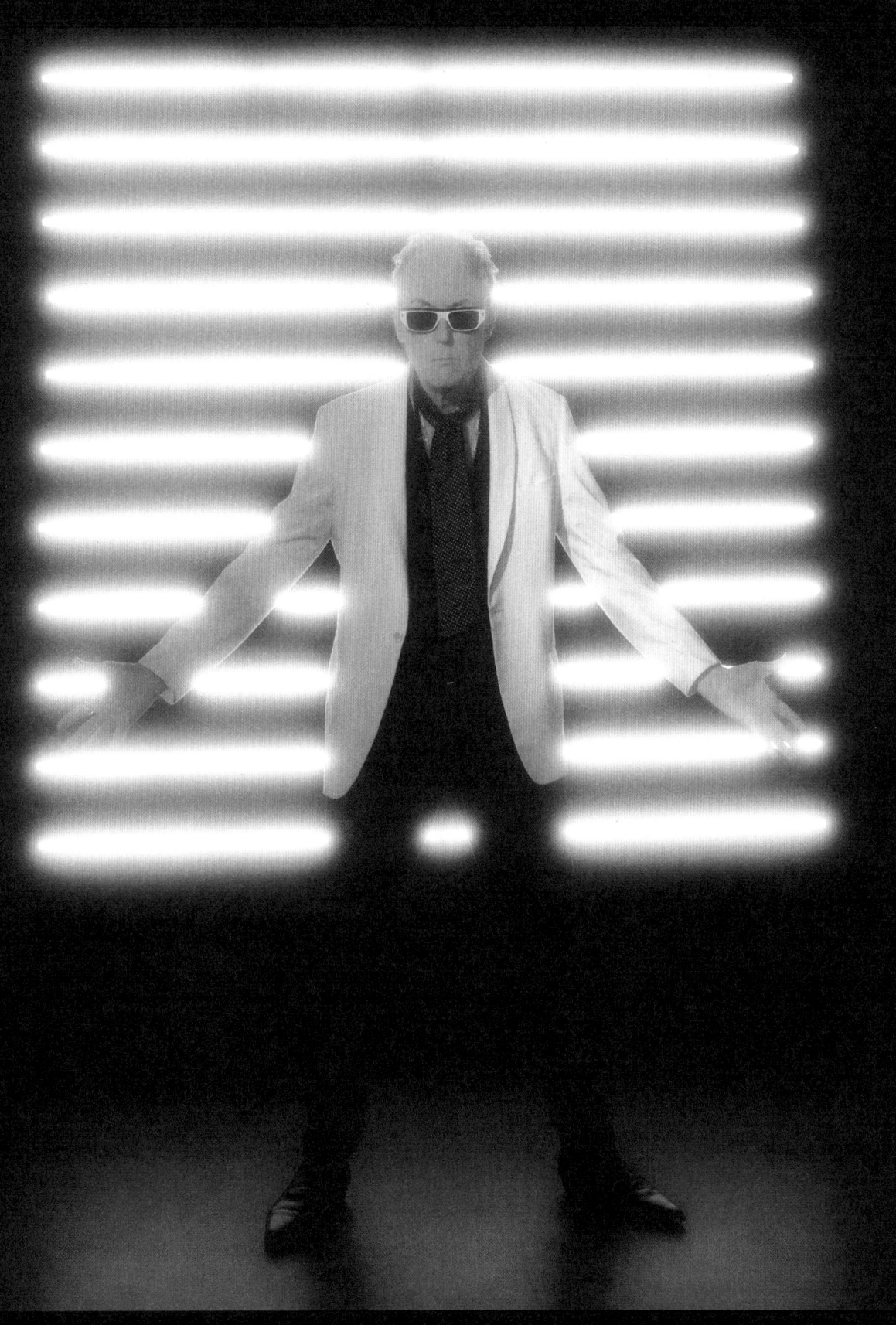

been this connection between reggae and punk in the UK. When you were producing that track, were you aware you were making something iconic?

D No, but we were aware that we were making something bloody good! And we were aware that we were drawing from dub. That was very conscious. And there was also the use of echo as a tool, as another instrument. We loved that music. In Northampton, there was a big Rastafarian community. We'd go to the sound system events. There was one place downtown that the police would leave alone. There would be ganja smoking, and they'd have these huge speakers right up to the ceiling, and they'd pass the mic around, toasting. We were regulars—me, Kevin, and Daniel—and the only white faces there, along with a few beautiful women. And we were completely accepted. We loved the music. So, it just seeped into what we were doing. And certainly, that came to the fore with "Bela Lugosi's Dead," although that bassline isn't really a dub bassline as such. The bass on the end of "She's in Parties," now that is pure dub!

W I get the sense, from various times I've hung out with you, that you're quite a spiritual person. Would you say that's true?

D Very much so. That recalls a recent songwriting experience I had while staying at the Chelsea Hotel. Do you remember Jobriath, the American glam musician?

W Yes. He died there when he was quite young, right? I first heard of him through Morrissey's fascination with him.

D That's right. He lived in a rooftop pyramid apartment on top of the Chelsea Hotel, and that's where he died of AIDS. It's the gym now, but it's still very vibey. He had his piano in there, and he was playing it right up to the end. Anyway, I was staying at the hotel recently and spending some time up there. There's a patio adjacent to what was once his room. And I just felt something there, a strong presence.

W I love a ghost story!

D He's always fascinated me. I think his story is one of too much too soon and all that. Anyway, I just knew I was going to write a song about it, and I did. It's called "The Lonesome Death of Cole Berlin," which was his alter ego. In his later years, he would play old-timey cabaret and wear a tuxedo and a little Clark Gable-style tash, very 1930s matinee idol-esque.

So, I was in New York to perform at a tribute for Genesis P-Orridge, put together by ex-members of Psychic TV. I had had a vivid dream about Gen on the night they were buried, although I wasn't aware of that synchronicity at the time. For my performance, I read this piece describing my dream. I did it with the brilliant writer Douglas Rushkoff, and I wanted to incorporate an element of necromancy, to try to commune with Genesis. I've got this device, a ghost box—a variation of the traditional Frank's Box—which psychic investigators use to record electronic voice phenomena.

It works by tuning in radio frequencies and applying a fast scan where you can vary the speed of the scan, and it creates a static field. And the theory is that entities use it as a medium for their voices. Indeed, strange voices do seem to come through. I wanted to use this for the performance, so one night I went to Jobriath's pyramid room on top of the Chelsea, and I tuned it in just to see if I could get something. Playing it back, I heard the word "free" two times. "Free! Free!"

W Goosebumps...

D It was a bit chilling. We tried it in the rehearsal for the Genesis concert, and we heard "breathe, breathe" two times. Douglas was a bit freaked out by this because he had just been having a conversation with Alice, the bass player, all about breathing and Gen's acute asthma, and there's a piece that Gen did called "Breathe." Very strange. It seemed like something supernatural was going on.

W I'm so fascinated by these experiences that people have, but mainstream science tends to dismiss them outright. Yet several people I know and trust have had inexplicable experiences.

D Yeah, I think it's all there to be explained scientifically eventually, you know.

W Agreed. "Supernatural" and "paranormal" seem like the wrong words. It is natural, and it is normal—we just don't understand it all yet. There's no scientific consensus on the nature of consciousness, for a start. Perhaps there are connections associated with that. Speaking of connections, what's it like playing with your brother Kevin all these years, as opposed to other drummers?

D Kevin and I don't converse that much. Kevin's a bit taciturn, to tell the truth, and we haven't got that much in common. But we have the most wonderful, deep conversations through music. That's how we converse. And we have a real psychic rapport. We always have, and it has evolved through working the muscle of that psychic connection through playing together. I love playing with Kevin. I mean, he's a brilliant drummer—I think he's one of the most innovative drummers on the scene. He's very unconventional. Highly nuanced, subtle yet at the same time powerful. He uses dynamics so well. He's a drummer who was schooled in jazz, like Charlie Watts. It comes from that. He's so imaginative. When we get into this unthinking Zen zone, when we lock in together, it's very powerful.

W It is indeed. I'm sure you get asked a million times about Bauhaus reforming, and I'm not going to ask because I already know the answer. But will The Bubbleman return to save the planet as goodwill ambassadors?

D One can only hope! ∎

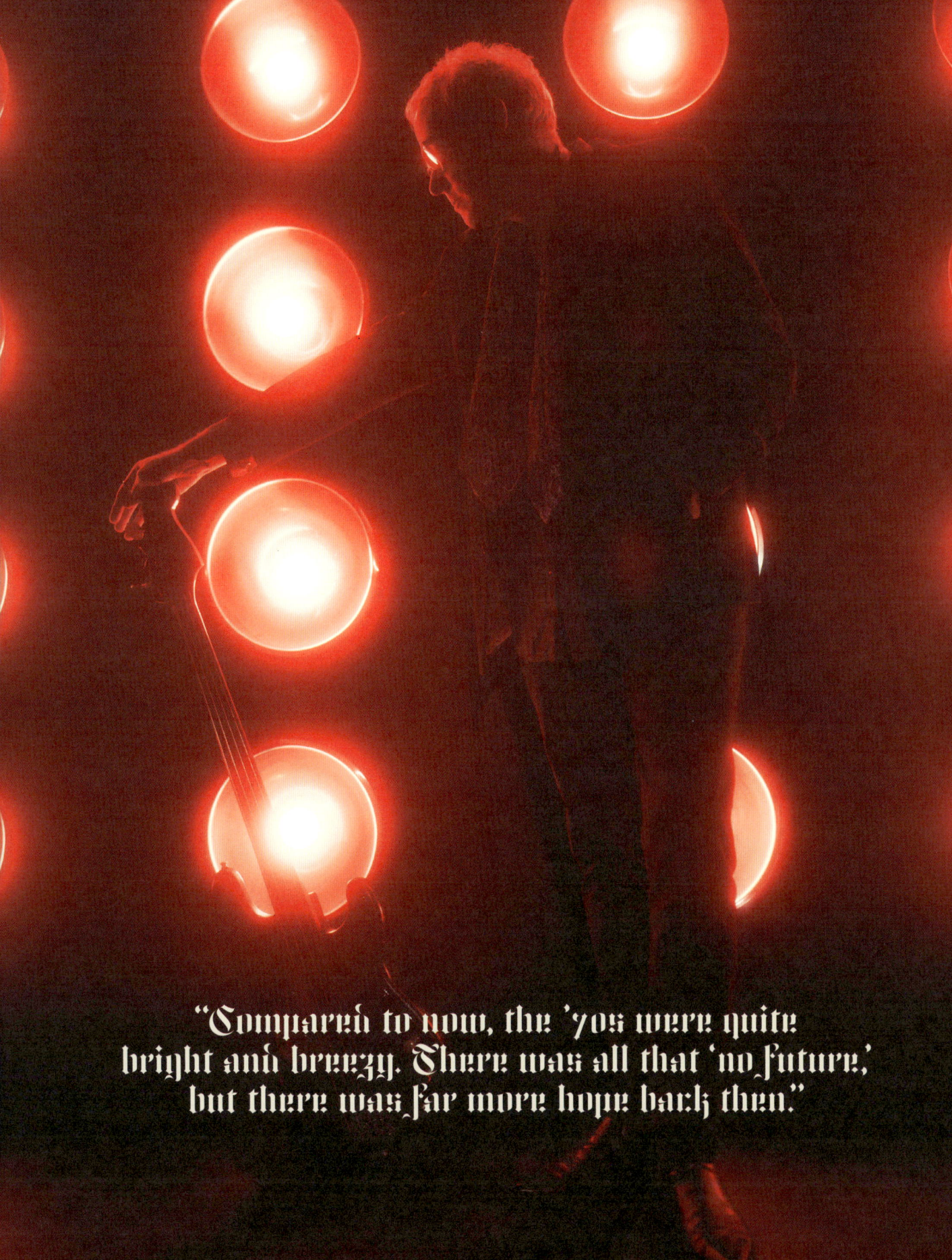

"Compared to now, the '70s were quite bright and breezy. There was all that 'no future,' but there was far more hope back then."

BLACK ASTEROID

—

From the depths of dark techno to the heights of high fashion, Bryan Black—the artist known as Black Asteroid—thrives on extremes. Wednesday sent some prompts; his answers sketch the contours of an extraordinary life.

Photograph *Stephen Rutterford*

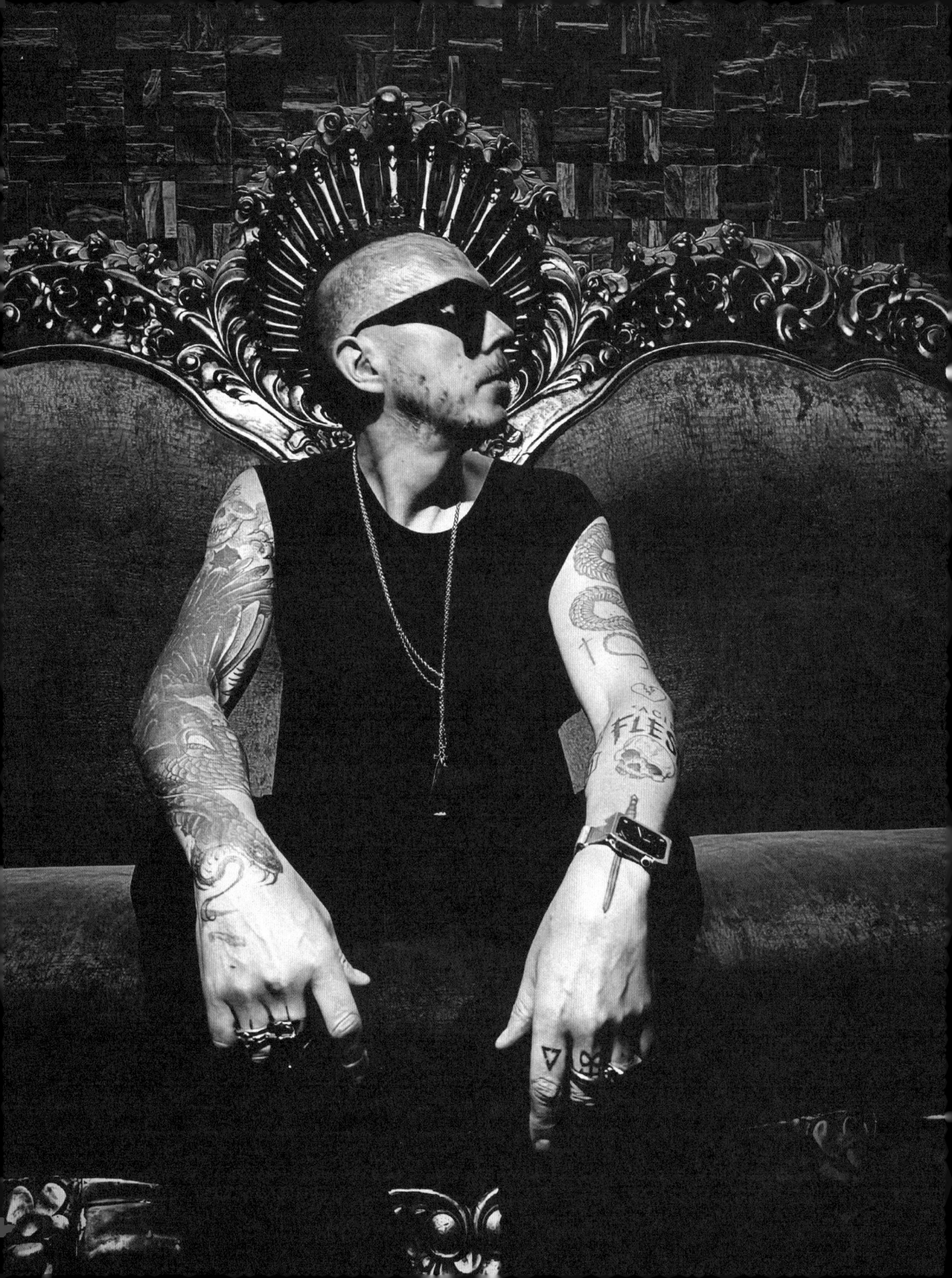

Minneapolis

I was born and raised in the suburbs of Minneapolis.
As soon as I graduated from high school, I took my first job
as a gallery guard at the Walker Art Center in Minneapolis.
My appreciation for modern art was mostly shaped here.
I also spent my first summer in Minneapolis teaching myself
how to use computer sequencers and MIDI instruments.

Rick Owens

I knew Rick's work, and it was out of my price range.
I watched his shows on YouTube. It was 2011, and his latest
show featured a song I produced with MOTOR.
I reached out to his publicist. Rick wrote me back almost
immediately and invited me to Paris. I spent many nights at
his house with Michele Lamy, and the three of us have since
been collaborators sporadically.

Rick and Michele invited me to Venice for the Biennale, and
we set up a studio on a barge. A$AP Rocky joined us. A$AP
and I spent days walking around the island. Michele decided
to recite a poem over one of the songs I was producing
in the makeshift studio. This became "Tangiers" and was
included on my first album. We eventually shot a video
in Brooklyn with longtime collaborator Timothy Saccenti,
probably the biggest video production I've been a part of.

Black Asteroid

Around 2010, after three MOTOR albums, I was now
living in NY, having left London after nearly 10 years. There
was some distance creatively and physically from my
MOTOR partner, who was in EU. We didn't agree on much,
mostly because we weren't hanging out in a studio getting
drunk and having fun as we were before.

I discovered he was already recording some music
with one of our fans, so Black Asteroid was born out of anger
initially. I felt betrayed, but it inspired me to write
a massive techno hit to show everyone I was going solo.
I sent the first song, "Engine," to Chris Liebing.
I didn't even know he was running a label called CLR.
Unknowingly, it was the hottest techno label,
and he signed me immediately.

My first EP was a massive hit and took me around
the world. I was still shaking off my MOTOR days, so I
performed live with neon lights, hardware, and vocals.
I gained a strong fan base and upset a lot of techno purists.
Eventually, I discovered that DJing would
allow me to play more diverse sets and open more
doors. Shortly after, I was playing Berghain and
all the major festivals in Europe.

Prince

When *Purple Rain* came out, I was obsessed. Seeing
Prince slither around the stage singing "Darling Nikki"
was the defining moment that I wanted to be a
performer. That movie and film totally changed me.

When I started my first band, haloblack, I was underage and
had to sneak into my own gigs. Prince was having parties
at Paisley Park, and one of his people invited my band to
perform. I didn't see him there, but he saw the show, and his
people approached me afterward and asked if I could help
Prince with his keyboards and samplers, as a keyboard tech.
I honestly didn't know what I was doing; I was self-taught. I
knew enough to make my home studio work. But
the pressure and intensity working for him and the
band taught me everything I know about music
production and live performance.

He was always really nice to me; we were both very
soft-spoken. In all my time there, I took only one photo. Of
his cat. The things I saw and the people I met still haunt me
to this day. I can't believe that all happened.
My first job in the music industry.

haloblack

I randomly bought the first NIN single, "Down in It," because
it had a great cover. I thought it was cool but quickly forgot
about it. Then I got the album, *Pretty Hate Machine.* I
remember listening to it on my waterbed as a teenager and
being transformed. I was into English acid house and indie
rock bands. Baby Ford, Love and Rockets, etc. NIN was the
first band to really mix rock energy and electronic music in
a song format. It was aggressive yet poppy. I modeled my
early work on that formula and quickly found my own sound
by the second haloblack record, "Funkyhell," which is to this
day probably the best album I've written.

Motor

MOTOR was started as a reaction to a dull moment
for techno. It just wasn't pushing forward; there was no
excitement or danger. We injected techno with punk energy.
We showed up to the Mute Records office with our first
demo. They signed it immediately because it was so bonkers.
We were commissioned to remix Throbbing Gristle at the
same time. It was just a piss take but became popular
very fast. We were selling 20,000 pieces of 12-inch vinyl
and pumping out EPs.

I later found out that Boys Noize and Justice credited
MOTOR for inspiring them to make crunchy electro.
We were pioneers, and because our relationship was
so hostile, we never realized our full potential.

New York

I always saw myself living in Europe. I left Minneapolis and moved to London in the early 2000s to study visual arts. London was the place to be for music and fashion. After failing to get an artist visa in the UK, I moved to New York. I wasn't happy about it.

For the first few years, I worked as a creative in the city, but when I moved to Brooklyn, it all started to make sense. I fell in love with the city. I now regard New York as the best city in the world—there's no other city like it.

Time

I am fascinated with the vastness of space. The incredible history of Earth as well as the evolution of humans. It's incredible that we don't have the most basic answers to the biggest questions in life.

The fact that time is relative and not absolute is mind-boggling. Time, as we use it, is a man-made concept. The past, present, and future are all represented in spacetime simultaneously, yet we only experience the present. Science and Ccosmology fascinate me endlessly.

My goal now is to work at the intersection of art and science. I've given myself to music, and I'm ready for the next challenge.

Depeche Mode

After MOTOR signed to Mute Records, I learned that Martin Gore was a fan. As soon as I found out, I asked Douglas McCarthy from Nitzer Ebb to make an introduction. Douglas had just featured on the first MOTOR record. Depeche Mode asked us to remix their big "comeback" single, "Precious." After that, I asked Martin if MOTOR could be a future support act. They invited us to tour with them in 2009 as the main support act. It was all outdoor football stadiums in Europe. It was such a rush.

Thrust

After a string of EPs on CLR and Electric Deluxe with Speedy J, I wanted to release an album. I grew up with albums, and it was generally not easy to do as a techno artist. I connived a label to sign it and fund an expensive music video featuring Michele Lamy. I played a few shows with Zola Jesus and asked her to be on the album. Also crossed paths with Cold Cave and extended the same invitation. Cold Cave and I produced three songs together. Our song "Black Moon" was a hit. I got hooked on vocals and a little melody at this point. There was no going back to instrumental techno.

Raf Simons

Raf had used one of my songs in a show in 2009, before Rick Owens. We met in Antwerp, and he was soft-spoken and kind. He designed a MOTOR t-shirt that we sold on the Depeche Mode tour. I am still working with his team on projects. I guess this was the first foray into the fashion world, a precursor to what would come with Rick Owens a year or so later.

Infinite Darkness

Most of the music for my second artist album was recorded during COVID. I had gone back and listened to my whole catalog, and the records I made as haloblack stood out. I missed the energy and experimentation. I felt there was no soul in dance music and spent COVID writing more emotional pieces.

Infinite Darkness became about maximalism. As a minimalist, this was something I fought against my whole life. Less is almost always more, and up to this point, I had a rule to keep my music limited to 8 channels of audio.

I discovered ACTORS at this time and sent an instrumental to the singer, Jason Corbett. He came back with an amazing hooky vocal and a guitar riff. I arranged it into a song, and it became a crossover record. The song "Ashes and Dust" is right at the edge of what is acceptable for a techno song—I love pushing how far I can go with a techno song.

Ian Astbury started following me on Instagram. I sent a little drumbeat, and he eventually replied that it was bombastic. I suggested we record it together as I was going to DJ in Los Angeles in the coming months.

I booked a studio in Hollywood; I had no idea if he would show up. Or if I was being trolled by an impersonator online. We saw a black SUV arrive at the studio, and Ian came in with a bag of pens, art books, and stories. We spent hours just talking about life and art, and with only minutes left in the session (the engineer was asleep at this point), Ian went into the vocal booth and nailed a vocal in one take.

I took this home to New York and spent some days arranging different versions. The first version was guitar-heavy, and over time it became more electronic. The whole experience was a rock and roll fantasy come to life for me.

Rhys Fulber from Front Line Assembly and I always chatted online, and eventually FLA invited me to remix a single. Bill Leeb loved the remix so much that he included it on the album. I sent him an instrumental, and we recorded a song for my album. The original featured on my *Flesh* EP, and for my album, I decided to include a reworked version of "Methane Rain." ▮

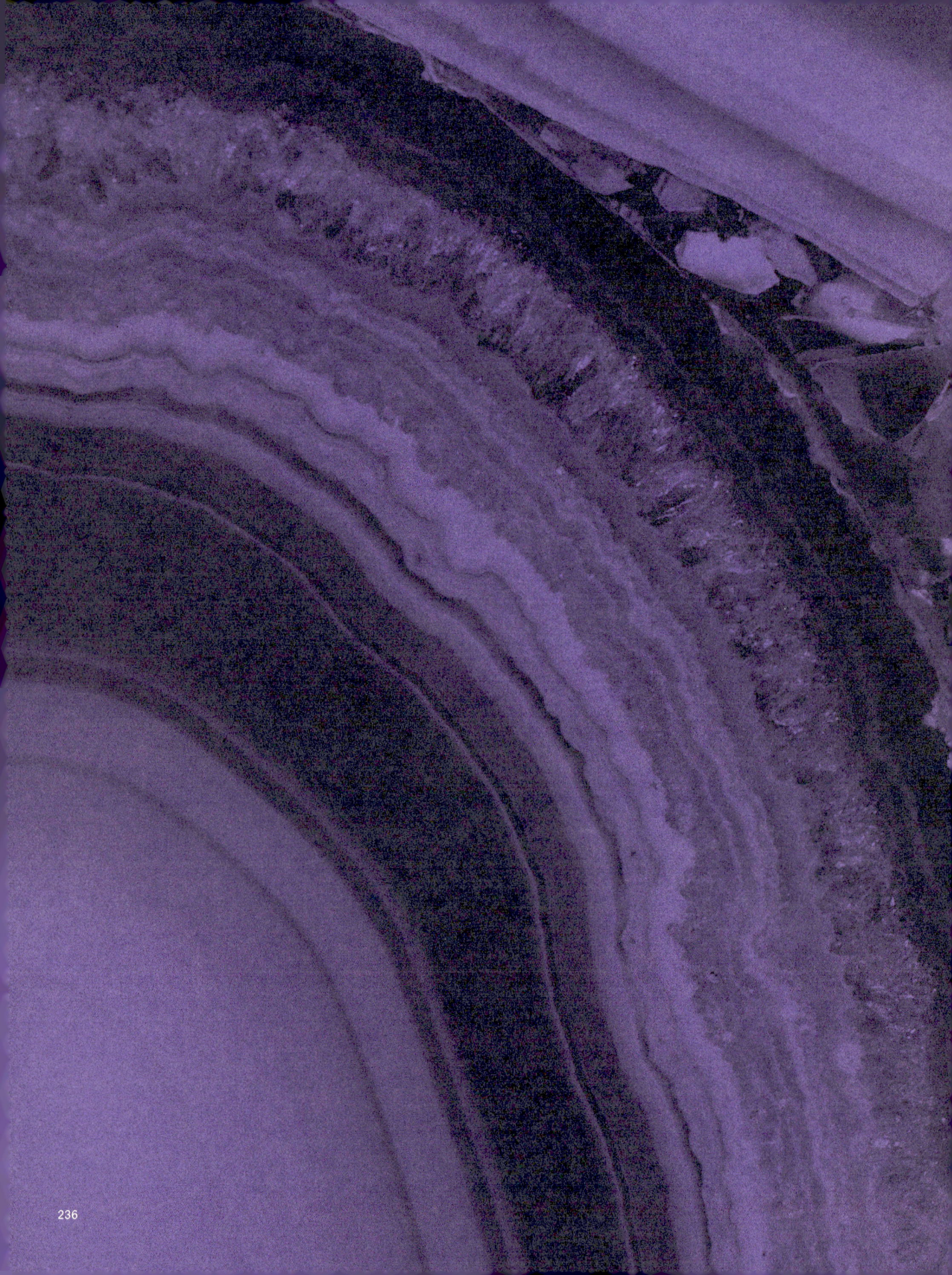

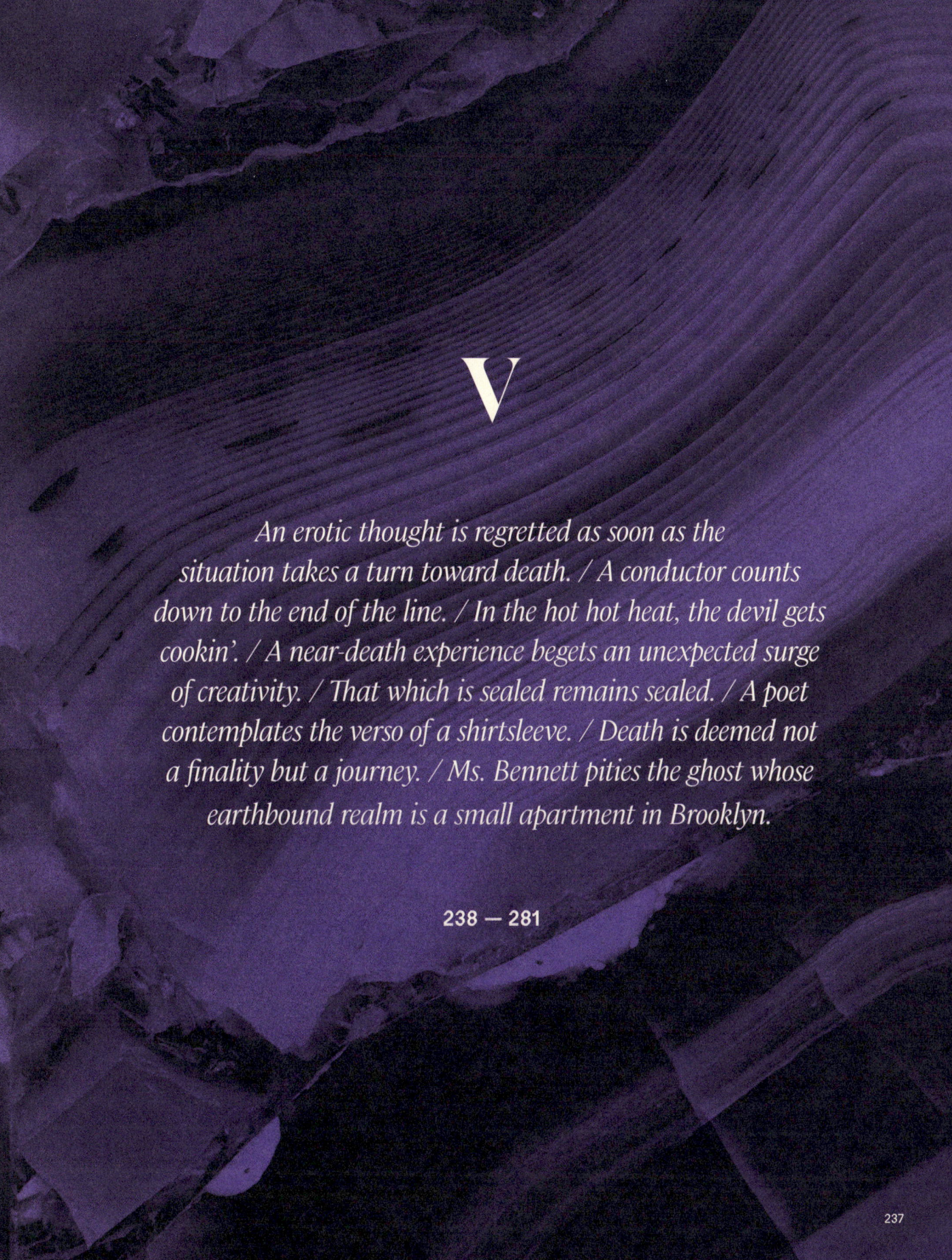

V

An erotic thought is regretted as soon as the situation takes a turn toward death. / A conductor counts down to the end of the line. / In the hot hot heat, the devil gets cookin'. / A near-death experience begets an unexpected surge of creativity. / That which is sealed remains sealed. / A poet contemplates the verso of a shirtsleeve. / Death is deemed not a finality but a journey. / Ms. Bennett pities the ghost whose earthbound realm is a small apartment in Brooklyn.

238 — 281

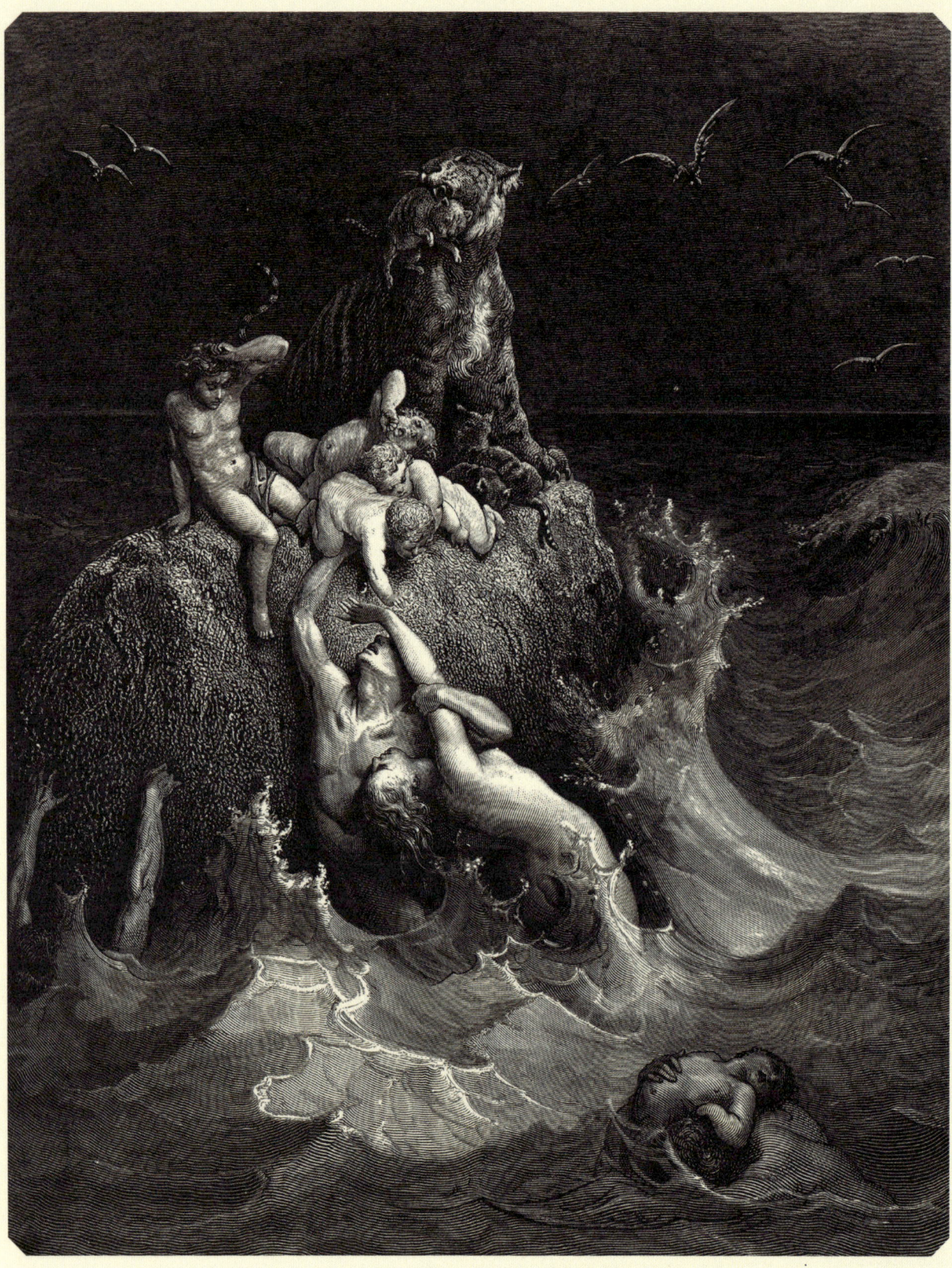

FLESH & METAL

Charles McEnerney

Charles McEnerney was born and raised in Flushing, Queens, in New York City and has lived in Seattle, Los Angeles, and Boston. He is a dad to Adacie and Declan. He was the singer/songwriter in the New York post-punk band Falling Stairs and is now a solo artist. Charles is co-author of the gift books Dear Graduate, Dear Love, *and* Dear Newlyweds *for Clarkson Potter (Penguin Random House), and is currently working on a novella and a collection of short stories.*

"This is the number seven train to Flushing," the conductor always says as the train gets ready to leave 42nd Street at Times Square. Times Square is a big place, known around the world as the crossroads of culture, business, and entertainment. Well, that's what the tourist brochures say, anyway.

"This is the local train to Queens," he says, as monotone and dull as you could imagine. "Watch the closing doors."

It was a daily ritual to him. All right, granted, it is part of his job, but you gotta get tired hearing it. He must have said that ten dozen times a day. Probably hundreds of times a week, thousands of times every month. That had to add up to millions before he'd retire. Can you even imagine that? Can you imagine saying something over and over again until you're not even aware you're saying it?

Thank God I'm not back there anymore. I like being up front, but I worked there long and hard enough to deserve moving up. Back there, I felt like an idiot, opening and closing the doors on people and poking my head out the window to see who we'd left behind. They'd be there on the platform shaking their heads or looking at their watches with anger or giving me the finger. I used to pull my head into the train, lock my window, and just laugh. Sometimes you just had to.

You always have to tell people what stop they're at, but of course they knew where they were! They've been taking this train along with us every day of the week. They'd memorized the names of the stations years ago and tried to forget them. You can't, though. I know. Every kind of person in the world takes this train: Spanish, Black, Indian, Oriental, White... any kind of person you could imagine. It's a strange town at the end of the line, but it's always suited me and mine okay. Me and my wife grew up there, and we always wanted to raise our children close to our own roots. Some people think they should try and do their kids better than they'd had for themselves, but what was so bad about what me and my wife had? I don't think we had it so bad, and so I don't see the reasoning behind trying to move off to somewhere new where things are supposed to be better. They're fine right here. Besides, I think it's good to be around so many different types of people. This is the place you should be if you want to seem 'em, too.

In by nine, out by five. It was a never-ending cycle for them, but at least they got to get off the train and see something else. I used to envy that. They see sunlight and breathe the air, as dirty as it might be here in New York. Instead, I see it all from the inside this booth made of metal, glass and plastic, and all I have is an ignition key, a pedal and an intercom for company. Still, these subway riders take this train almost a dozen times a week. Near fifty times a month. They'll be adding up to the millions before they knew it, too. I don't mean to complain to you. It's a job. It's no great career, not anything I boast to relatives or friends about, but I perform an important service, right? Something you might take for granted, but you need it all the same. You or someone you know couldn't live without this. It's a necessary and powerful job. The world couldn't function without me. Look at is that way.

Someone, I think it was Ben Franklin maybe, said that it didn't matter what job you did, so long as you did it well. I agree with that, but he, after all, was an inventor and a politician and an important figure in history. I don't know if he was thinking of train conductors when he made that statement, but I like to think so. I don't mean to get defensive, but sometimes I get the feeling people don't respect a man for doing a job and doing it well. I take honor in something that serves a purpose. At the same time, I know I couldn't do much else. It's not that I'm dumb, but I barely finished Flushing High School and didn't go to any ritzy college. Who would hire me? I've always been proud of what I do, especially being a good husband and father. I know those things are supposed to come naturally, but look around you. You don't see much of that these days. I think I've done a good job at home, but, then again, I might be the only one who thinks that. Fathers aren't usually commended too much for being dads. So, some days I thank God for the Mass Transit Authority. Other days, I just wish I could take this train to somewhere beyond the end of the tracks.

"Fifth Avenue. Change here for the F, D and B Trains." There he goes again. Well, I suppose that is his job, but I'm glad I don't have to do it. I spent my time opening and closing those damn doors and telling people to watch them. Now I can sit up front and drive this rattling train in my own little booth and no one disturbs me.

People ask me how I can take it sitting up here for hours on end hitting the ignition and brakes. At first it did make me a little crazy, but I started to find ways to amuse myself, like watching how the neighborhoods along the elevated line changed or making up a scene in my head where I'm trying to get control of a runaway train. Don't tell anyone about that, though. I'd hate for someone to get the wrong idea. Mostly, I just listen. The people standing outside the conductor's door talk just loud enough for me to hear. I've heard everything from gossiping to bragging to complaining to nothing at all.

A lot of people don't like to talk on the subway; that's what I've heard, anyway. People tell me they don't like to talk because if no one else is talking, then people are listening to them. I suppose it's true. Here I am in my booth listening to people outside talk about how they hate their job or how they cheated on a test in school or how they want to move out of New York or how they flirted with a guy they met last night at a bar. I'm guilty of listening, too. It's a natural thing to want to eavesdrop, don't you think? I mean, most of us are pretty much the same, but it's interesting listening to what someone else has to say and not have to say anything back. You can just listen to their conversation and pretend like you're not. Though, I don't have to pretend much. They can't see me.

"Grand Central Station. Change here for the 4, 5, 6, and Metro-North trains. Last stop to transfer in Manhattan."

Don't get me wrong, though. I'm not compulsive about it or anything. I listen when their voices get loud enough and they mention something that interests me. On the other hand, my wife, Julia, is the queen of eaves-dropping. She's gone as far as to turn off the television or radio so she can hear the neighbors arguing. Drives me nuts sometimes because she wants me to be quiet so she can hear every word they say. She doesn't pay that much attention to me a lot of the time. It's not as if we hadn't been happy, because we were. We were. We had a lot of fun together, and I'm glad we got married. We had been together for six years when she asked me what was going on.

"What do you mean, 'What's going on?'" I asked. She came back at me with those squinting eyes she's got.

"Are we gonna get married or not? We can't just date forever. It's got to progress. We've got to move forward. Do you think we're going to just stay in one place forever?" she asked me the way she will.

"Well, I don't know. I hadn't thought about it."

"Well, think about it," she yelled at me. And I did.

I thought about standing on the altar in front of that priest and what it would be like to devote my life and love to another person. For better or worse. For richer or poorer. In sickness and in health. it felt like I was donating blood instead of committing to marriage. Now I know a lot of women think that they want to make a commitment and men don't, but don't you be fooled for a minute. Julia and I loved each other like no two people naturally could, but the thought of thinking about such possible adversity, when the chances were that we'd just not get along occasionally, scared me.

What if we did turn poor or she got sick? Could I handle that? I still don't know. It's not that I feared commitment, I just feared what would come next. I feared what she would ask for that I wasn't up for giving.

I don't mind giving away some freedom so long as I think there's something to get in return. That's just the sort of man I am. I don't ask for much but I get a little weary when someone does.

"Vernon Jackson Avenue."

So we got married. I got to see the reasoning behind it and most of my friends told me it wasn't so bad. They told me that it was nice to go to bed and to wake up with someone beside you and know they would be there forever. Sure, some of them took advantage and had a bit of variety on the side, but what the hell? They're men. What the hell can you expect?

I really do believe that we're more animal than intellectual. We don't get mad when someone fucks with our head, but when we're physically threatened in some way, we get angry as hell. And look at how men and women feel about each other! We're not looking for some genius, just someone who gets us excited and keeps us there. That's the way I see it, anyway.

Julia did that for me and more. I knew she's always keep me interested and I didn't think we'd ever feel separated until last week. I'll tell you what happened. We'd gone to a party a friend of mine from work was having. It was no big deal, just a bunch of guys and their wives. I thought we'd have a good time and relax and enjoy ourselves. Julia even seemed to be looking forward to it. She went out and bought a sexy blue dress with slits up the side. I loved her legs, and she knew it, so if a dress had slits up the side, I liked it. That's the kind of woman Julia is.

"Hunters Point Avenue. Change here for the Long Island Rail Road."

So we got there, and I introduced her around. We were early, but I didn't mind. After people started arriving, I caught a few guys giving her the look. You know, the I-can't-believe-his-wife-is-such-a-looker look. It made me feel good. Made me feel like I'd done okay in their eyes, and maybe I'd be looked up to from now on. It's not like the guys don't respect me. I think they think I'm okay, but I've had my problems making friends at work. When I started this job fourteen years ago, it was because my friend Jonas talked me into applying. Jonas left the MTA a year or two later for a job with the sanitation department, but I stayed. I liked it okay by then. All except that it was kind of tough facing friends. People must have thought I was weird or something, but that's really nothing new.

"Court House Square. Watch the closing doors."

People have been thinking I'm weird for the longest time. When I was in grammar school, they used to call me captain strange. I took that as a compliment for a while. I thought, "How different could I be from Captain America or Superman?" That wasn't the way they saw it, though.

In high school, I had a couple of good buds, but I never figured out how to keep them. At first we'd find things to do together, and it would be great. I was never much of a jock, as you can probably tell, and I didn't hang out with the hot-rod kids, but I had my interests, and I had some friends. Eventually, though, something would happen, and they'd tell me off. "Shit, you're crazy," I heard more than once. You're probably thinking this is a regular way for kids to treat each other, but there wasn't anything regular about it. Maybe you had your problems in high school, but I can tell you right now that mine were worse. I can guarantee it. The thing is, I don't even think I'm all that strange or weird. I used to be quiet, and I think that bothers people. I think folks don't trust people who don't talk. It makes 'em uncomfortable. Makes 'em wonder what this quiet person is thinking. Then again, it doesn't take much for most people to become untrusting.

I'm not so quiet anymore, but you may have noticed that. Actually, a lot has changed in me. I barely recognize myself. I've become a husband and a father and a good provider. I know how to be a good man, I'd say, but some would probably disagree.

"Queensboro Plaza. Change here for the N to Astoria. Please take all newspapers and debris and deposit them in the receptacles located on the station platform."

What's so strange is that after all of this, I can't understand how I've come to this decision. I guess I started thinking about this after I fought with Julia the other night. I wasn't mad because she was talking and laughing with my friends at that party. I thought that was nice. She was trying to make friends with my coworkers and I appreciated it.

I thought she was doing me a favor and making us look like one of those couples that has everything in the world. The kind of couple that has no problems and everyone admires for keeping it together and making it look real easy. The kind that you want to be friends with.

I started seeing her give them these looks, though. She was drinking vodka tonics and laughing and sort of flirting with them. At first I wasn't sure, so I paid close attention to her. She was laughing at stupid jokes that, if I had told them, she would have just said, "That's stupid." She was giggling and touching their arms and saying, "Oh, how funny!" I couldn't believe it. So, I told her I didn't feel good and that I wanted to leave.

She looked annoyed, but I didn't care. I grabbed our coats and said good-bye. She put hers on in the hallway, and when the door closed, I looked at her angry face. It made me realize that she wanted to stay. I hadn't seen her that angry in a long time.

"What the fuck?" she asked me. "I was having a good time. You said you wanted to come here and have a good time and make some friends! That's what I was doing." She poked the elevator button hard a couple of times.

"You said you wanted to make friends with some of the guys at work, and that's what I was doing and then you want to leave. I can't figure you out, Daniel." I told her what I thought she was doing, and she denied it. I suppose they always do. It's not as if you could say, "I think you were flirting with so-and-so," and someone would admit it and say, "Yeah, I was." I can't see something like that happening.

"33rd Street. Rawson Street."

So, we fought all the way home. She was crying in the car and looking out the window away from me. She kept saying, "Why don't you trust me? Why do you think I was doing something terrible when I was just trying to help you?" I thought she was trying to make me feel guilty, and it bothered me even worse. She thought I would just fall for her stupid story, but I knew better. I knew what she was looking to do back at that party.

"What do you think? Do you think I was going to just sneak off with three of them and fuck 'em on the bathroom sink? Give me a break, Dan!"

There's been times in the past when I didn't trust Julia, but never like this. I've never suspected her to be fooling around behind my back, but this whole thing made me think. What if she'd been flirting with the kid behind the counter at our local supermarket? What about the Newsday delivery boy? The Con Ed man? I hate to think of Julia like that, but people are capable of doing a lot of things you don't expect, right? It was all too much to take, and I didn't want to. I wanted to forget about it and just never go to another party. The guys might ask why I didn't come to their parties anymore, but I could make up a good lie, and they'd believe it. It's not as if they want to see me, anyway. It's Julia they want to see.

"40th Street. Lowery Street."

She wouldn't talk to me for a week. The first thing she said to me, just the other day, was that she was hurt and upset that I didn't trust her. She had thought long and hard about it and believed we would never be the same. I couldn't believe her. All I did was question one night at a party, and the next thing I knew she's talking like this. I didn't do it to make her feel bad, but I can't live with her thinking she'd rather flirt with a stranger than sit down and talk with me.

"46th Street. Bliss Street."

So, I went home last night and decided to make a go of it. I'd tell her I forgave her and that I wanted to forget the whole incident. I had mapped out the whole conversation in my head on the way up in the elevator. I knew I could make it work. She would give me a dirty look when I entered. I'd follow her and pull out the bouquet of flowers I'd bought and put them up near her nose for her to smell. Her eyes would light up and she might cry. I would smile and tell her that everything would be all right, and maybe we would hug for a few minutes.

"52nd Street... Lincoln Avenue."

I opened the door and looked around the apartment, but it was dark. That wasn't unusual because sometimes Julia would take the kids down to the park and let them play before suppertime, but it was cold out tonight, too cold to be playing on the swings and seesaws. I turned on a couple of lights and put down the flowers. I went to the refrigerator to see if she'd left me a message. There was an envelope there with my name on it, sealed up and hanging from the refrigerator with a Big Bird magnet. I opened the letter and pulled out the letter. It was a short note, barely a letter at all. It just said, "I've left you. I can't be in this marriage anymore. You have just pushed me too far. I have given you all I can, but it's never enough in your eyes. The kids are at Mrs. Morrow's. Please explain this to them as best you can."

"61st Street, Woodside. Change here for the LIRR."

That was it. Just a little note to let me know that she's left me and left me with two children. There wasn't a bit of feeling in it. Just this cold-hearted, mean tone of, "Oh, well, I'm outta here. Goodbye." Can you imagine this? Can you even fucking imagine this? I thought I would kill her if I could find her. How could she do this to me? I had taken care of her and those kids for years. I'd given her everything in the world that a man can give a woman, and all it took was one small argument to make her want to walk away.

"69th Street and Fisk Avenue."

I have to tell you… I didn't really take it too well. I fell on the ground and started breathing weird. The apartment was so cold and dark, and all of a sudden I couldn't hear nothing but the sound of my hand crumpling this letter. It took me almost an hour to get to my feet and start breathing right again.

That bitch. She didn't even have the balls to wait 'til I got home to tell me face-to-face. That was just fucking like her. She always was a coward. She always knew how to hurt people. I think she'd always wanted to leave me. She was just waiting for the right time so it would be my fault. That fucking bitch.

So, I went to get the kids. I heard them through the door and wondered what the fuck I was going to do with two little kids. Mrs. Morrow was an old woman. I couldn't ask her to take care of them every day, but I didn't make enough money to put them in daycare or anything. What was I going to do?

"74th Street and Broadway. Change here for the E, F, G, R, and the shuttle bus to LaGuardia Airport. Watch the closing doors."

Mrs. Morrow didn't know what was going on. She muttered something to me and smiled and waved as the kids came into the hallway. I thanked her and took the kids.

"Did your mother say where she was going?" I asked.

"No," the youngest one said.

"She did so. She said she was going out for a walk," the older one said. I could see they didn't know what was happening. I didn't even know what was happening.

"82nd Street, Jackson Heights."

I've barely slept the last two nights. I tried, but I kept thinking, "What am I going to do? How am I going to take care of two little kids? How am I going to explain to my family what happened? What if someone calls for Julia? What do I say? Do I lie, or do I tell the truth? Will they believe it if I lie? Will they laugh or cry if I tell the truth? Will they react at all?" I started to think of ways to find her. I could hire a detective or take some vacation time and go looking for her myself. She might be staying with her sister in Dallas or maybe her mother on Long Island.

I could track her down and drag her back here and tell her, "You made a promise. You promised to stay with me in sickness and in health, for richer or poorer, in good times and in bad. Maybe they hadn't said, 'in times of trusting and untrusting,' but it was the same idea, right?"

"90th Street. Elmhurst Avenue."

It was just too much to take. The next morning, I had to ask Mrs. Morrow to watch the kids again. She didn't seem to mind, but I don't understand Hebrew, so maybe she did. I just knew I couldn't start missing work. If I missed work, they'd fire me, and I'd have no money coming in, and then I couldn't pay the rent, and then I couldn't live here, and what would we do? What would the kids have to eat? I thought she might come back eventually, but I had to teach her a lesson. I wanted to show her that you don't make a commitment and then walk out on it. I wanted to leave her with something that would make her regret ever writing that note. I started sleeping okay again. My problems would be over soon.

"Junction Boulevard."

I bought the kids tickets to fly down and visit their Aunt Susan in Texas, but I didn't tell her that they were one-way tickets. I told Susan that Julia and I were going away for a few days for a little second honeymoon and asked if she would mind watching them. She said yes right away and asked if she could speak with Julia.

"Sorry," I said, "Julia is sleeping. This is kind of a surprise."

Susan said she'd go along with it. She said it was so sweet and romantic of me to surprise Julia with the trip. She said that Julia seemed sort of overworked as of late, and a vacation would do her good. I thanked Susan again and told her to take good care of the children.

"103rd Street. Corona Plaza. We have a red signal against us. We should be moving shortly. Thank you for your patience."

So, I brought the kids to the airport this morning and asked the stewardess to watch out for them until they landed in Dallas. I kissed the youngest one on the cheek and gave the older one a hug. They didn't seem upset at all, but I guess they were excited about being on an airplane. They'd always watched them coming in for landings with such interest. They didn't even see me leave as I stepped away and out of the airport.

I found myself crying on the way to work today, but I don't know why. I'd made up my mind, and there's nothing so consoling as having made a tough decision. Julia had made her own decision. She had walked out the door and left her family behind. Perhaps she would come back today with tears in her eyes and an apology, but for me it was too late. You only get one opportunity in life to prove your trust. After that, it's just a word you throw around and abuse, isn't it?

"111th Street."

You might think that what I'm doing is sick, but who really knows? It's the perfect out for me, but I know other people will be affected. There's a lot of people on this train, and I wish they weren't going to get hurt, but what else can I do? There's no other solution to my problems. If I do this any other way, people will say I was a coward and bowed out of life without dignity. I'd be called strange and weird all over again, and that's not something I can bear, even if I'm listening to them from heaven.

You probably think I'm nuts, but Julia was everything to me. I stayed in this job fourteen years to keep her and the kids fed and clothed. I could have done other things in my lifetime. Maybe I couldn't have been an inventor or changed the course of history, but I could have done more. It's not that I'm not proud of being a conductor. I am, but what good is pride if a woman can take your whole life and make it feel so worthless?

"Willets Point. Shea Stadium. Next and last stop, Flushing, Main Street."

When you reach Main Street, there's a big ceramic and concrete wall and a couple of railroad ties to soften the blow in case a train loses its brakes and crashes. I don't know how fast I can come into the station without alarming someone, but I don't think I'll have to go too fast to make it happen.

I imagine this is going to get a lot of television coverage, and it's funny because this is just the kind of thing Julia would love to be a part of. She always loves a good fuss. Too bad she had to miss it. I think she'd enjoy being the wife of the man who drove a speeding train into the wall and killed himself. It might make her proud.

I thought about leaving a note to explain all of this, but why tell the whole world why you're hurting? I don't want to lie there dead with people over me saying, "He did it because his love went wrong." It's really none of their business, anyway. Most folks will just think I was crazy. Why complicate it with an excuse? Julia will understand why I did this. She won't need any letter to explain.

"This is the last and final stop on this train." ▮

MAY

Roger Rueff

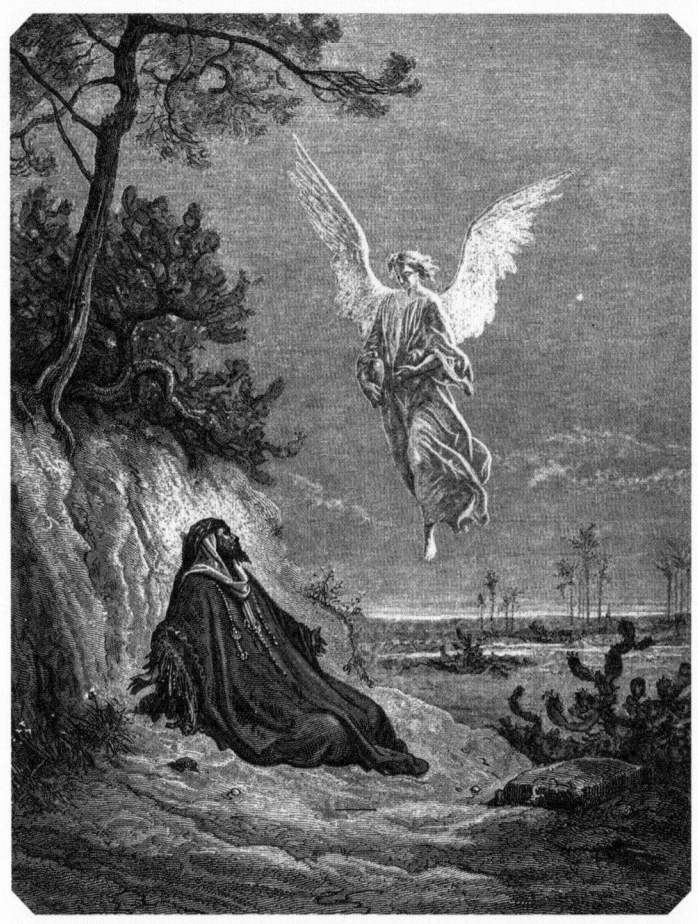

Roger Rueff is an engineer/artist/writer/dramatist whose written works include the internationally produced play "Hospitality Suite," its screenplay adaptation for the film The Big Kahuna, the collection of poetic proverbs Fifty Things I Want My Son to Know (Andrews-McMeel), and a unique approach to story creation and analysis called "Discovering the Soul of Your Story" (www.soulofyourstory.com). His visual artworks in his chosen medium—stained glass—reflect a lifelong obsession with the spiritual effect of lighting, the deep efficiency of symbolism, and the emotional power of design.

When you're plummeting to the ground from thirty thousand feet in the air, your religious convictions, however strongly held, suddenly come into question. There's a headiness that overcomes you, if you survive the initial gut-wrenching jolt when your seat drops away from beneath you and your stomach rams high into your throat. You become suddenly flushed—not so much with blood as with the dynamism of life. You feel its currents rush past you with an agonizing swiftness that seems bent on tearing away your skin. Everything that ever mattered to you pushes up against some kind of invisible wall rushing toward you, and you feel the pressure building as it nears.

I've heard it said that when you're about to die, your life flashes before you in its entirety, as if for review. If that's true—and I can't really say one way or the other at this point—it strikes me as little more than a frantic scrambling for escape. As if you could somehow clamber backward down the ladder of episodes that has led to your demise and jump off at some safe spot.

Barely two hours ago, I allowed myself a brief erotic thought involving the stewardess who greeted me as I boarded the plane. A part of me regrets that now. The sight of her caroming past me, as she did just moments ago, flailing about for a handhold, has left me with a sense of loss at never having known her hopes and dreams. And since it seems likely we will share the same fate, I think of her now as a sister.

Not surprisingly, I'm hurtling toward the ground without my shoes. My feet swell when I travel by air; I'm not sure why. So, I take off my shoes as soon as the plane levels off. And always, as I untie the laces, something inside me thinks to itself, "What if something happens? You'll be found without shoes." It's afraid of being judged by those who will discover my remains. But that something is gone now. It floats high above, where I was before we started falling, and looks down, shaking its head, saying its final, "I told you so."

The woman beside me crossed herself before we took off. I remember thinking, "How quaint." Now, I don't know whether to commend her foresight or upbraid her because it didn't work. The point is moot, I guess. I can't bear to look at her, anyway, except from the corner of my eye. She's caught up in a private terror. Swallowed whole by the collective scream that we all want to utter but can't.

Confessions and petitions are pouring out of us now—faster than the gods can say, "No." Maybe one will slip past the filter. The powers that be will have to say, "Oops! Here's one we forgot to deny." And something good will happen somewhere. To someone. But it won't be any of us.

We're slicing now through thick, white clouds that seem from above as if they should embrace us gently, like great big pillows of foam. There's a rush of disappointment with each one we pass through. It's like finding out there's no Santa Claus over and over at three hundred miles an hour.

Maybe I'll leap through some kind of door when we hit. Maybe there's a thin, glassy film that hides one world from the next. And maybe, when we strike the ground, that film will shatter, and its glass will go flying. Maybe the impact will prove to be nothing more than someone's sharp slap across my face to rouse me from a very lucid dream. Maybe I'll awaken at last to find that my whole life has been a dream and that the world I've always clung to as real is actually just a grand and lovely illusion.

May— ▮

HERMETICS

Jason O'Toole

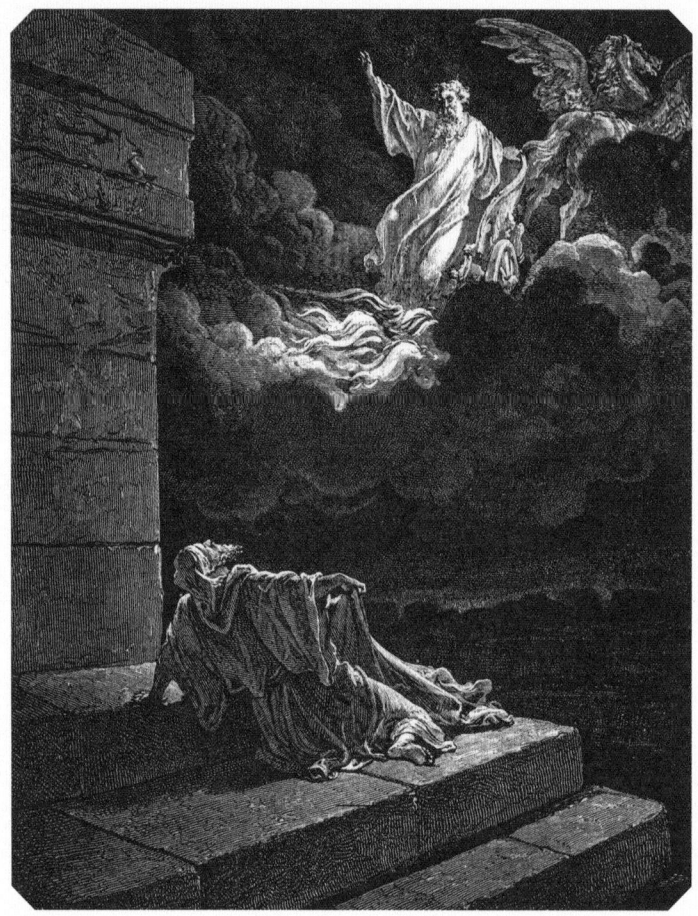

Jason O'Toole is Poet Laureate Emeritus of North Andover, MA. He serves on the advisory board of the New England Poetry Club and as treasurer of the Independent Living Resource Center San Francisco. His newest collections are The Strange Misgivings of the Sadly Gifted *(Dead Man's Press Ink) and* Wait Out the Burn *(Ghost City Press).*

Do not think of here
And there.
Think of here to there,
and back again.

Time is a circle, says Nietzsche,
Be an optimist, a realist, but never a nihilist.
There is no demarcation
where light ends and darkness begins.

Eternally is here, croons Jeffrey Lee,
dead, yet rambling.
As above, so below –
an effervescent spectrum.

Here, there, and everywhere
sing the alchemical Beatles,
two now dead,
yet everywhere.
omnipresent, immortal –
bullets and cancer, notwithstanding.

Am I with you, my son, in eternity,
though linear time is all I see?
There are more colors in the rainbow
than stars in the sky.

UP ITS SLEEVE

Richard Herstek

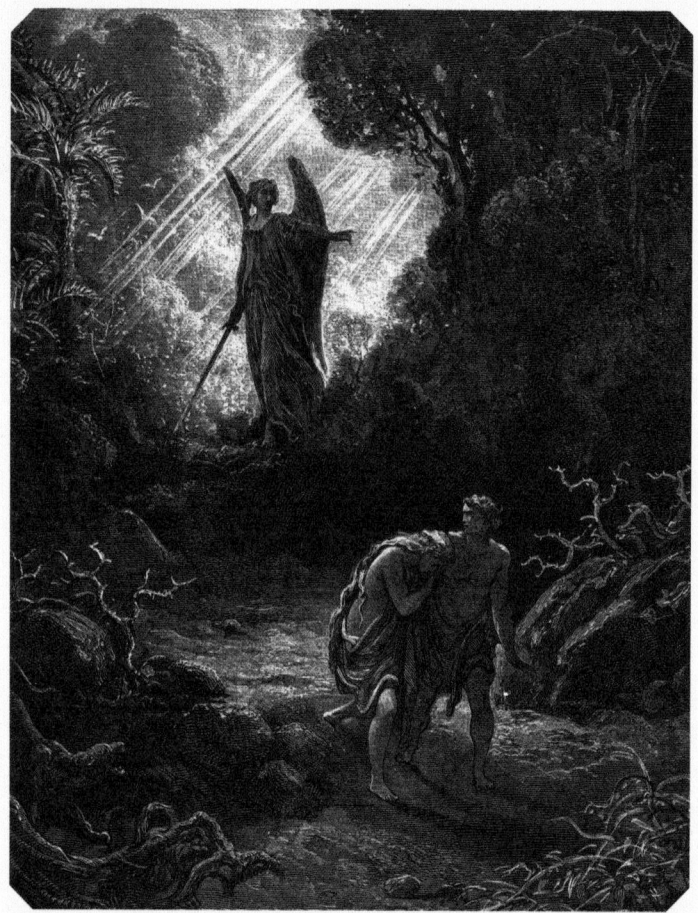

Rich Herstek has been an advertising creative director, poet, travel writer, playwright, and screenwriter, having earned his MA at the London Film School. His work has appeared in GUM, Lemon *magazine,* The Paris Review, Travelers Roundtable, NPR, *and* The Book of the Prague Marathon, *as well as dozens of other publications.*

So far, everything looks alright.
But looks do tend to deceive.
The future may be cloudy but
at least the day is bright.
Wonder what the world got up its sleeve.

If one hand holds money
you know the other holds a knife.
Is there anything or anyone you can believe?
Ain't that a hell of a way to go through life,
Always wondering what the world got up its sleeve?

Ten gigs come in. Nine disappear.
And you're just waiting for the last one to leave.
No surprise that you learn to live with fear.
Always wondering what the world got up its sleeve.

You feel like you're the butt of every joke.
Of every dirty trick they can conceive.
Sometimes you get so mad you could choke,
wondering what the world got up its sleeve.

Snake pits ahead, lions at your back.
You could die and not a single soul would grieve.
Sometimes you freeze right there in your tracks.
Wondering what the world got up its sleeve.

A dime's worth of luck buys a buck's worth of hope.
The death sentence stays, but you get a reprieve.
It's a bad way to live, but a good way to cope.
Always wondering what the world got up its sleeve.

If you wake up feeling good, you give yourself a slap
and ask how you can be so naïve.
You know good feelings ain't nothing but a trap.
And the world always got something up its sleeve.

But so far, everything looks alright.
Though looks do tend to deceive.
The future may be cloudy,
but at least the day is bright.
Wonder what the world got up its sleeve.

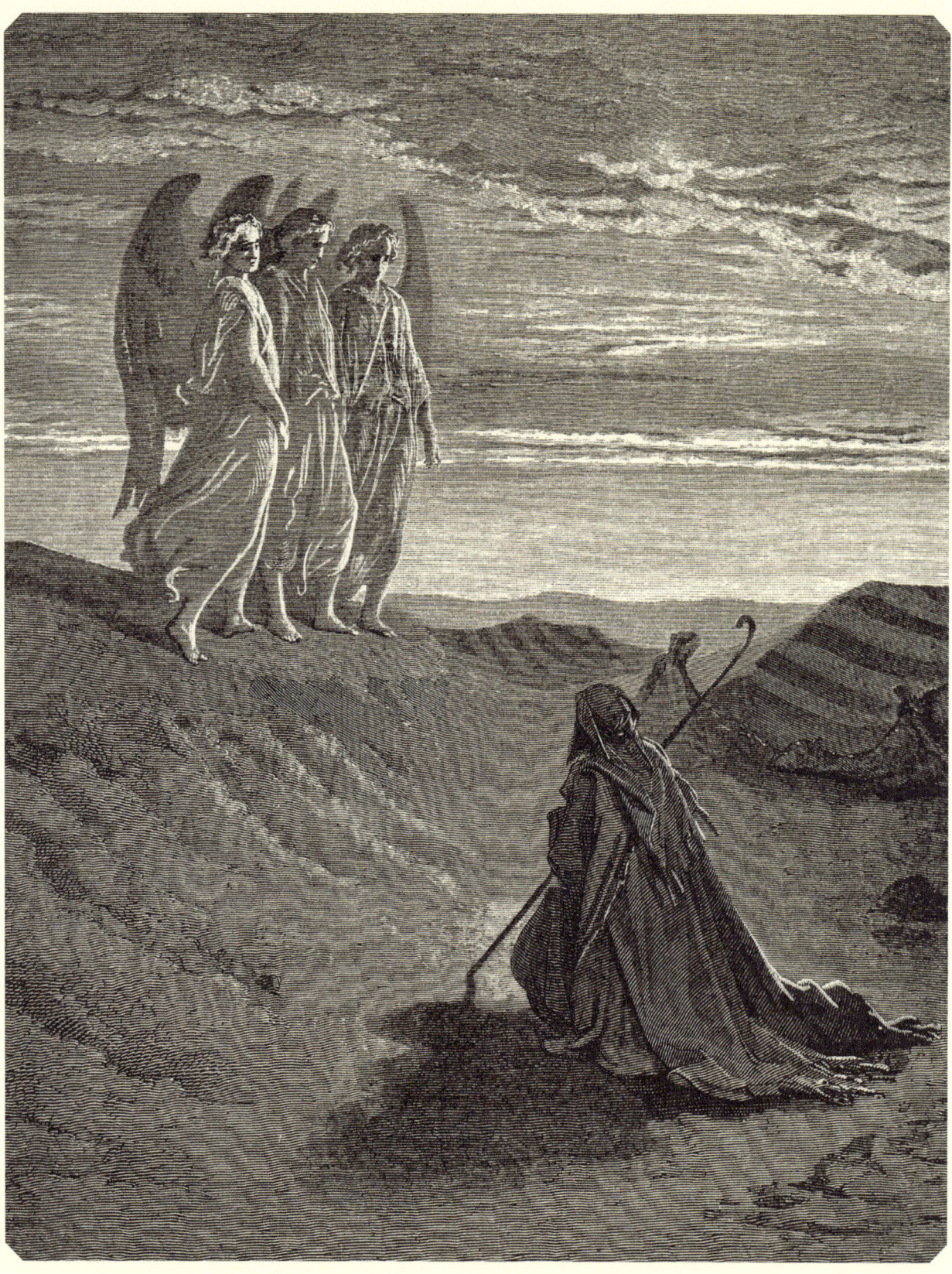

THE THIRTEENTH CELL

Brittany Raglin

———

Brittany Troye Raglin is a Black narrative fiction author and screenwriter from Nyack, New York. She has her BA in screenwriting from Brooklyn College School of Visual, Media, and Performing Arts. She specializes in writing horror, cerebral drama, fantasy, and sci-fi works. She has worked in commercial, TV, and film production for over ten years across several departments. She currently resides in Flatbush, Brooklyn, where she has lived for fifteen years.

I

Demon heat, the type that slips in under your skin and wears you. It gets caked under your fingernails and seeps into your pores. The kind of hot that *possesses* people.

On nasty days like this, when the temperature is climbing into triple digits with a humidity to match, I expect there will be a phone call. It would be a case unlike the ones populating every corner of my office. The towering piles of missing girls, petty drug deals, gun possession. The call I was anticipating on this day would be from the devil himself. You get to a point in your career where you know, you could feel when the bad ones were coming—the ones you never get over.

I sat boiling in my tiny corner office, melting away under an ancient and broken ceiling fan; a sudden chill ran down my spine. There it was—that old and terrible reflex. Instinctively, I moved my hand to my office phone. I held it to my ear and waited in near silence. The fan above my head was squeaking a rhythm I had memorized over the last ten hours.

After about a minute, the phone rang.

II

Detective Andy Delroy, my six-foot-four chain-smoking partner. He was ruminating like the heavy rain clouds crawling toward us. Nicotine hung low around his head. Del was a pack-to-pack smoker who found his habit after working a particularly nasty case in this very town. It was something I had tried very hard to block out of my own mind—this assignment was the first time we'd been back after vowing never to return. Del's vice was one of the many emotional consolation prizes received after being marked national heroes. Since that case closed, Del has been lighting one cigarette with the other into infinity. It was an Olympic torch procession that led

back to fifteen of the smallest caskets we'd ever seen.

Delroy's eyes studied the darkening skies; the embers of his square were crawling down to the filter. I slammed the car door, and he returned to Earth. His face lit up, and he flashed me a smile.

"Nasty morning." He spat and crunched the butt into the gravel, a ritual greeting.

"You eat breakfast today, Del?" Delroy, *Big D,* never skipped a meal unless there was something in the air. He was a titan of a man, but you wouldn't know from looking that he was sensitive to things—*energies* and the like. He seldom talked about them outright, and I don't have the words to describe the things he could do. I didn't have a touch of the divine like Del, but I could read him like tea leaves.

Delroy shrugged. "Nah, didn't want to. Couldn't sleep much neither." That confirmed something for me.

We turned our heads toward a sudden commotion. An old NOLA-style trolleybus appeared, chugging down the county road. It was gaudy—purple, green, and yellow. The colors clashed against the grey blur of swamp forest that wrapped around the road. As it got closer, we could hear a chorus of voices. A dozen passengers were crowded on wooden bench seats, laughing in unison. They were taking cues from an enthusiastic host with a microphone.

SWAMPLAND MURDER TOURS was painted along the side of the hideous thing.

"—AND OUR NEXT STOP WILL BE THE INFAMOUS LOCATION AND MASS GRAVE SITE OF THE MAGNOLIA MUR—"

"Can't believe people pay money for that shit," Del hissed. He hated all things true crime for obvious reasons.

"That's one way to keep the lights on, I guess." I bit back the sudden urge to take my gun out and shoot the back tires. We watched the thing disappear down the road in silence. It felt like a bad omen. There had been a jailbreak at a tiny town precinct. Nothing but swampland and forest on all sides. A young male, Black, was brought in for questioning in the night and had vanished from custody by morning. The peculiar thing was how clean the job was. There was practically no evidence; the cell door wasn't even left ajar. In fact, it was still locked in the morning. A couple of night shift rookies guarded the only possible exit in the place and were awake all night, confirmed by security footage.

"Where's the footage from the holding cell floor?" I asked.

"Gone, deleted. Figured the perp done it." The slack-jawed twenty-year-old deputy, Jenkins, was clinging onto what was surely his last brain cell. I could practically hear it frying.

"How'd you figure that, son?" Delroy was already getting impatient. Ten minutes in, and I knew he wanted to smoke another square. We both knew this boy was green and meant to stall until we got to asking after the two cops who were on the night shift last night. To our surprise, neither was here at the scene. It was just the nematoid here. Odd, since they undoubtedly got the call that two BCI detectives were coming down to "aid" the investigation.

"Cuz it's gone, sir."

"What time did you bring the suspect in and what for?" I gave him a thorough up and down.

The kid squirmed. This was probably the most police work he'd ever done, and all he was doing was stalling.

"I'm not sure, ma'am, you'd have to ask the sheriff."

"And *where is* Sheriff Towns? Don't you think he would want to be down here if he's got suspects breakin' out of his jail?" The deputy paused. He was running out of script.

"I called him, miss; he should be comin' down any minute."

"Detective is fine; I figure you don't need to trouble yourself with the *state bureau of investigations part,*" I shot.

"We'll need to talk to them boys that were working the night shift as well," Del said.

"I'm sure they gonna be with him, sir."

"And why's that?"

"On account of 'em bein' his kin, sir. They're his sons." *And there it is.*

I gave Delroy a look, and he knew. His jaw pulsated, agreeing.

Del put an unlit cigarette behind his ear and gave me a look. More of our unspoken phrases.

III

—

Del didn't have any family in the world save for his Abuelita, and she was a *bruja,* a witch. It was always my belief that he had a touch of whatever his grandmother did. Del never called her a witch, though; something about speaking on it was bad luck. Del knew things, and he felt them even more. His talents made Del an amazing detective, and I admired him for it.

"Something ain't right. How'd the guy manage to delete security footage? I saw the console near the center desk. Them boys were posted a couple desks down all night." Del was already lighting another port with the cherry of the first.

"Nothing was stolen, it seems."

"Not a paperclip."

"*Even if* the security system was easy for him to get to, which it wasn't, why would you need to delete security footage? You already got booked, and you're already in the system."

Del's cigarette crackled as he pulled.

"Right, *you wouldn't.* Too risky; an escape is all about speed," Del grumbled.

"This precinct... I don't remember it from our last visit, but it feels so familiar," I pondered.

Thunder was stirring above our heads.

Then I found the memory.

"... The Blanche case," I replied. I remembered her face all over local headlines in Chicago. Her hometown and mine.

It was one of those tragic cases involving police stops, arrest, and a dead Black body by the end of it all. That night got its start in ways that weren't unlike the incident we were investigating now. The Blanche case was colder than the morgue, and all questions were shut behind locked doors, and here we were, two Black officers caught up in the spokes of the eternal wheel.

"Our friend Sheriff Towns was a rookie back then. His daddy was sittin' where he sits now," Del reminded me. I kicked the gravel with my boot.

IV

——

There were six private holding cells enclosed with cast-iron bars. They were decades old, but sturdy. The bars were about two inches apart, impossible for a grown man to slide through. I wrapped my fingers around one of them. The iron was ice despite the boiling and stuffy air down in the basement floor.

"We put him in that one and went back to our posts. Strangest thing."

Jenkins was pointing at cell thirteen.

Del's grip tightened around his notepad, crushing it.

"Open it," I ordered Jenkins.

Jenkins turned the lock with a key. The lock was heavy and looked about as old as the iron bars, but it was in good condition. It showed no signs of tampering, no scratch marks near the keyhole.

The air inside the cell was even more stale than the outside. It was a tomb.

The cell contained one metal cot-bench and a sink that recycled the water from the back of a toilet—nothing out of the ordinary.

"He was only in here for a couple of hours. He coulda had a plan already." Del was spooked now; he eyeballed me from the other side of the bars.

"Gas station cam outside didn't catch a single person or car outside the place during the escape. If he had a partner, we would've at least seen something on the CCTV." There was nothing but thick forest out back, and beyond that... the swamp. The only road through town was in the front. *No getaway car, no tracks.*

I went and laid down on the frigid metal slab that was attached to the wall. *Nowhere to go. Mind racing. He had to come up with a hell of a plan.*

My skin began rippling. Something was on the tip of my mind's tongue, beckoning to me in the dark.

My eyes fluttered open. I hadn't realized they were closed.

"Sadie Blanche." It was the second time today I blurted out her name like a recovered memory. Jenkins and Del ogled me from the other side of the bars.

"What about her?" Del murmured.

"Ain't this the exact place where she—"

"—Where she was held. Sure is." Del was almost whispering. He took his crucifix and tucked it back underneath his shirt so it made contact where his heart was beating. I knew he was reciting old words in his head. Del was too superstitious for this much coincidence.

"Blanche, ma'am?" Jenkins seemed to be suffocating under the invisible weight of our trauma and superstitions.

"Would've been before your time, but someone died down here. Her name was Sadie." I was hit with an urge to run up those cement steps and smoke one of Del's squares down to the filter. Reading my mind, Del started toward the exit.

"Allegedly. Case is cold," Del grumbled over his shoulder.

"You got a face that looks like you knew her, ma'am." Jenkins trailed along at our heels as we went back up for air.

"No, I didn't know her. But I—" The words caught in my throat; my mouth was filling with the taste of salt.

Out of the corner of my eye for only an instant... I thought I saw someone lying on the metal bench in cell number thirteen, facing the wall.

V

——

I spit a mouthful onto the gravel as soon as we reached the surface. Whatever had just come over me went in the dirt. The smell of the coming rainfall purged the staleness from my lungs.

"Break-out mystery aside... If he didn't head for the road, there's only one other way out." I tilted my head toward the tangle of wilderness. Del was smoking again, and the tension was evaporating from his body.

"We don't know nothin' bout the kid and what he is capable of. I don't see no reason to count him out."

"Well then, let's take a look. Jenkins, you can give the sheriff a call and let him know to stay at the site. We'll be joinin' him and the boys shortly." Jenkins shot us one more curious look before heading inside.

The precinct was the last stop before hundreds of acres of swampland, positioned at the edge of a green abyss. Only a few yards away, the wall of lush darkness called out to us by way of thousands of species of bug, amphibian, and *creature*. It was a gaping, screaming mouth.

Del hated the great outdoors but especially the swamp. He grew up being told the stories of *La Llorona* by his primos when he was old enough to stay up late. The real reason why he hated this swamp, however, was the same reason he smoked two packs a day for the last few years. Every step toward the trees shook loose memories of pulling small, bloated corpses from the muck. The sucking and squelching of the swamp bed. Tendrils of alien mosses and aquatic plants wrapped around rotted arms and legs. Del and I knew that the true *La Llorona* was the swamp itself. If the riverbeds hadn't flooded an unseasonable amount that year, she would have never let them go.

I could hear Del self-soothing by clicking rosary beads in his pocket. I knew he wouldn't sleep tonight or any night spent in this town.

Thunder growled louder overhead. It wouldn't dump on us yet, but the beast was showing its claws.

SST! Del fired up another square. He crouched down and traced his lit finger along the ground, following hidden footprints.

"Hm," he grunted. It was a good grunt.

"I was startin' to worry." Another drag. The embers were alive and dead before they touched the ground.

"What, worried that you'd have to get in the water again?" I was being playful, but the sentence knocked loose more visions of swamp-rotted flesh, lying against the satin lining of a casket.

"I was startin' to think the perp wasn't human... Its footprints goin' straight back. Someone was with him." Del pivoted and began heading back toward the precinct.

Moments later, Del picked up a rock that was flecked with fresh blood. It was halfway between the precinct and the tree line.

"It ain't a lot of blood, wasn't life-threatening." That wasn't much to go on, but it was something. We bagged it and took photos of the spot without drawing too much attention.

We put our backs to the swamp and walked quickly to the car. I could not help but feel her curling green tendrils reaching out for us and searching with a hundred eyes.

VI

—

The county road made a miles-wide loop around the swampland. There was a search team set up at a site north of the precinct. Local police were hoping to catch him on his way out. They knew he wouldn't last in there.

Del liked to ride in my car with the seat way back— plenty of room to stretch those weathered tree trunks. His arms were folded behind his head, a port stuck straight up from his lips like a steamship funnel.

"Those men grew up in these swamps. They know he ain't cutting through that. Not in what—a few hours?"

"Nope. Maybe they're getting him good and lost. He's less of a problem if he disappears."

"You're bein' cynical. Ain't no evidence of foul play, let alone police corruption. Not yet, anyway."

He was right. I was cynical.

The corpses of the children weren't the only bodies found in the swamps. Blanche's body and car had been pulled out of the water a couple decades prior.

"They don't call us down from the state bureau for no reason. I think we're here to make sure they don't have a national PR situation like they did all them years ago... with Blanche." She had only been in the water two days, but that was plenty time for the gators and fish to eat most of her. Still, the M.E saw signs of severe post-mortem trauma. Her actual cause of death was inconclusive.

Del flicked his cigarette with precision through the crack of the window. He never missed the shot. He raised his seat vertical again, and I felt his eyes trying to penetrate my skull, brain, thoughts.

"One case at a time. Gotta keep a clear head and look at the facts. *That's* why we're here."

He was right.

Del slammed the car door.

"How you wanna work this?" he said, sliding on a pair of dark sunglasses. He patted his coat down, searching. I handed him his lighter that he left on the seat. *You need to quit smoking.* He shook his head and grinned.

"The sheriff is your man, so treat him like it."

Walter "Wallie" Sr. and his sons Donnie and Wallie

Jr. were the fourth and fifth generations of Towns men. Despite the bootlegging history that was their family's origin story, the sheriff's badge stayed in the family since prohibition ended. They probably switched sides when the other stopped being more profitable. The Towns men were despotic and proud.

"Del, it's good to see you again." Wallie Sr. clapped Del on the back. He was almost six-foot himself, slim with a thick head of silver hair slicked on the sides. He had changed since he received his own dose of national acclaim. He looked different, changed. His teeth were whiter.

"… And Detective Carter. I was so relieved when I got a call from state that they were sendin' you both. Thought I'd never see y'all again."

"We were hoping you wouldn't have to, Sheriff," Del remarked.

"Please, you know to call me Wallie. This way—" Wallie Sr. turned on a heel and led us through the taped perimeter. I was surprised to see the scale of the manhunt. There was a K-9 Unit, at least fifty search team members, and twenty tactically armed officers. At the edge of the swamp, there was even a watchtower. All units read local. DELITH P.D.

"I guess state finally got you that funding you been lookin' for," I shouted over the commotion.

"Yes, ma'am, guess they didn't want to get caught unprepared like they did with the Magnolia Murders." The mention of that cursed moniker tolled somewhere deep and dark.

The sheriff led us to the foot of the watchtower. Working the spotlight in the small booth were his sons, one dark, one light. Two sides of Sheriff Towns' coin. Their father let out a sharp, bright whistle, and the young men reacted. They waved to us.

"Officer Jenkins showed us the cell; strange thing, no signs of a struggle or a breakout," I pressed. The sheriff didn't hear me. He was waving for his sons to come down.

The boys hopped off the ladder in unison and greeted us with nervous smiles. They looked like they hadn't slept in days. I would be nervous too if the escape had happened on my watch; the eyes of the state were on their father.

Del gave me a look that drew my eye to Donnie Towns' freshly split brow. A small bruise was still fresh, and the wound had just begun to scab over.

"What happened to your head, Donnie?" I asked as casual as I could muster.

"Searchin' through the woods that night, tree branch cracked me good," Donnie lied. Wallie Sr. was stiff.

"Once we realized he was missin', all hell broke loose; we went crazy tryna find him," Wallie Jr. piped up.

"Naturally, and where were you all stationed when this went down?"

"Upstairs office, main floor. He couldn't have gotten past us—"

"You're right, Detective Delroy and I saw… only one way in and one way out."

"Guy could've had a lock pick," said the sheriff. *He can't be serious…*

Del was scribbling in his notepad.

"I have half a mind to drain that swamp, make it a damn parking lot," Sheriff Towns grumbled with his eyes fixed on the forest.

"Cell thirteen… do you remember the Blanche case? Would've been your father's time," I asked the sheriff. His jaw tightened.

"Vaguely. I wasn't real serious about the badge back then."

Conveniently, the sheriff found an opening and was pulled away on another matter. I soon found myself alone with my questions. Del was off with Wallie Jr., following him through the scene, scrawling notes. Donnie was climbing back up the watchtower.

I waited for Donnie to disappear into the booth before scurrying up the ladder after him. Donnie watched with wide eyes as I climbed in and placed myself in front of the only exit.

"Tree branch clocked you pretty good, huh? Bet the blood got everywhere; forehead cuts are the worst."

Before Donnie could lie to me, I revealed the evidence bag and silently placed it on the booth's dashboard. Donnie's eyes got wide before he dropped his gaze to the floor.

"Did he hit you, Donnie? While he was running away? We saw the two sets of footprints."

He flinched when I mentioned the footprints. *Got him.*

"No. I-I couldn't go *in there*… I wouldn't." I knew he meant the woods; I shared the fear.

"Is that why y'all are so hell bent on catching him on this side? Because you saw him running this way? *When you were just standing there watching?*" I spoke in a tone that mimicked his father's; I cornered him with his shame. Wasn't long before his guard broke. Donnie started trembling; he shrank inside himself. The subtle sourness of his rising cortisol levels twinged the air in the booth.

"Please... don't make me..."

I placed a hand on his arm, an attempt to lure him back to me. He recoiled at the lightest touch.

"I-I went down... to check on him. And he... *she...*" Donnie's voice withered to barely a whisper.

I leaned in closer; his lips mouthed the words in a single breath...

"She let him out."

Lightning tore through the sky and obliterated the shadows. The crooked bones of the magnolia trees flashed white.

It finally started to pour.

VII

——

Sleep could not find me that night. Instead, I spent hours going over the Blanche case. The file wasn't as large as I had hoped. Very little policework had been done by the locals.

Sadie was the daughter of an alderman who was able to keep her case in the media and send a private investigator down here.

The two theories proposed by either side were completely at odds with each other. The local theory was that Sadie fell asleep at the wheel on her way down south to visit her grandmother. The land of her maternal roots. Her car and body were pulled out of a shallow creek just off the county highway near town.

The private investigator's theory was based off the testimony of a questionable eyewitness. He was an old man with one eye that ran a fan-boat rental shack. It was just down the road from our precinct. The man was a war veteran, a local kook and conspiracy theorist. He showed up to the precinct to "serve his civic duty" and report an incident he witnessed one night after closing the shop. He saw a man dragging something heavy into the magnolias a few yards away from the

precinct. He also saw a police cruiser parked out front of the precinct that night. The officer that took his statement was on his first day of the job, however. The rookie took the statement, not realizing the implications of putting something like that on the record. Despite the report's mysterious disappearance, the private investigator dug it up. This quickly led to an investigation of the precinct from top to bottom.

The crime scene photos taken of cell thirteen were spread out around me. The PI's notes indicated that upon arrival he found the basement floor to be under construction, with a fresh layer of concrete still wet and drying. I was no expert, but the concrete couldn't have been poured more than a few days prior to when the photos were taken. Other than that, there was not a single sign or trace of Sadie in the precinct.

Before long, I felt a familiar tickle in my brain urging me to get up and go out. The biblical rain of the earlier hours had died down to a light drizzle.

I pulled on my knee-high rubber boots that had been in the back of my closet since the last case closed. I was hoping to never again slide into the footprint that was worn into the sole. The familiarity of those boots triggered another wave of memories that I had to shake my head to remove. Swamp rot. Satin lining. Screaming mothers.

The light under Del's room across the hall was dark, but I could hear him whimpering in his bed.

I arrived at the address of the fan-boat shack. The shack had long since been renovated. To my horror, it was fixed with a giant painted billboard that read: SWAMPLAND MURDER TOURS.

Damn.

VIII

——

The young deputy Jenkins had been replaced by three bright-eyed officers who looked busy when I knocked on the precinct glass. They gave confused looks until I flashed my shield.

Warily, they let me in.

I descended once more down into the dank, dead air. It seemed even worse this time. I used a penlight to look underneath the metal bench. Nothing but gum. I checked where the cement floor met the wall: nothing. Dust. I found myself thinking of Del and trying to will myself into clairvoyance. Nothing.

Defeated, I decided to once more lie on the bench and conjure an idea. But when I looked up, *I saw her in the ceiling.*

Her limbs were contorted like the roots of the swamp mangroves, skin grey rotting bark. CRACK— CRACK—her neck twisted until her dead eyes met mine. She reached down for me. As she broke free of the concrete ceiling, I could taste the wet muck of the riverbed. Water and algae rained down on me as she stretched down... down... until her cold claws met my throat. I was pinned to the metal slab like a corpse on a gurney.

I'm in my hotel room. I'm asleep; this is a nightmare.

I felt the metal slab falling away from me; my feet dangled in the air. My throat cracked and imploded in her slimy grip; blood vessels burst in my eyes. She lifted me higher... and higher still.

The room faded away as the black crept in corners of my eyes. I wasn't sure if it was my consciousness that was leaving me or if it was ME that ceased to exist...

Thunder stirred overhead again. The encore was beginning. I felt a chorus of droplets light up my face and hands. My eyes opened. It took me a moment to realize that I was outside on my back staring up at the sky. *Alive.*

I was hit with a wave of discomfort when I became aware that my socks were wet.

Thunder rumbled overhead again. I sat up and strained to see the dark shapes around me.

I was on the roof. I clambered to my feet, nauseous.

"Detective?" A rectangle of light glowed behind me when an officer opened the roof access door.

He was carrying my boots.

IX

—

Everything was wet and raw from last night's storm. It had been much worse than the first. Broken petals lay strewn across gravestones pummeled by downpour.

The air was pungent with freshly turned dirt and wet sod. One hour outside of swampland, and I realized I preferred the neat rows of gravestones to the tangled chaos of the mangroves. There was less humidity here. I could breathe.

I found Del among the sleeping dead with his abuela's rosary wrapped between his fingers so tight they were turning white. The wick of a fresh black candle was snuffed out and sizzling at his feet. He was praying. I waited.

When he finally greeted me, I saw his weariness. His eyes were bloodshot with dark circles. He reached into his jacket pocket and pulled out his squares but— *a blue pack?*

"Spirits? You don't smoke spirits." He hated them in fact, didn't like how long they lasted.

"Got 'em on account of the fact they pure tobacco. This pack ain't for me... technically." Del turned to reveal the name on the gravestone. Her. Sadie Blanche.

Del lit a square for himself and another for the grave. He put a coin under the plastic of the pack and placed it next to the candle and then put the lit cigarette down. He blew a few quick puffs over the gravestone. I'd never seen Del do this much *conjure* out in the open.

"Night terrors?" I asked. Tension rippled through his jaw. He didn't humor me with a response; I didn't need one. Something in me was devastated to see years of therapy regressing so quickly. The night terrors almost killed him back then.

"I wanted to pray for her and ask for her guidance," Del muttered.

Del took a pull with the rosary hand. Then another.

"... Well? Did you get anything?"

Del took a step closer to me; smoke swirled between us. He held my gaze long and unblinking, waiting for me to admit the truth.

"I think you know."

I could feel what I wanted to say bubbling up from my guts until I blurted it out.

"She did it, Del. I know she did." He nodded, unsurprised.

"She pulled the kid through the wall, and Donnie must've caught him in the act. She pulled them both through the *goddamn wall.* The kid hit Donnie on the head before escaping out back."

Saying it out loud, I felt like a dam had burst. Del was unmoved. He had known all along.

"This thing with the missing boy ain't the real reason we're here, Carter." He was right. The jailbreak was just a way to get us here in this town. In this moment. I was beginning to feel that something unnatural set all of this in motion.

"There's one more thing we have to do," Del grumbled. He kissed his rosary once more and beelined for the cars. I followed swiftly behind. I did not look back, carefully averting all corners of my eyes. I knew that if I looked back, I would see her standing there beside her grave.

X

—

We were back in town and on foot, weaving along a wooded path beside the lush county road. We moved quick and silent until we reached the mile marker where Sadie Blanche's car had been found. It was at the mouth of a creek. It was one of the many small tributaries that ran into the swamplands. I watched in horror as Del clambered down the side of the creek bed and into the murky water. He waded up to his knees without a word.

"Del, what is it? What are we looking for?"

Del turned to face me, but before he could answer, a bone-white hand reached up from the depths and pulled him down into nothingness.

He was gone without a single ripple or scream. A terrifying stillness befell the creek that had just been frothing and flowing moments ago. Even the birds in the trees held their breath. I tore down after him and flopped in. The thrashing disturbed the mirrored surface. Muck and algae leaked into my boots as they sunk in. I called out for him, and nothing answered.

I found myself longing for the comfort from believing in a higher power. I never had a crucifix resting where my heart was beating. I never knew the consolation that came from rosary beads interwoven between fingers and always within reach.

I tried to move back to the creek bank, but I was numb. I tried screaming again, but all was silent. Even the rush of blood that throbbed in my ears was mute.

I used the last of my strength to turn my head.

Before we locked eyes, I could feel her standing there, watching me.

Sadie Blanche.

She was different than when she appeared in the cell. She was human and alive. She watched me for a moment then walked closer to the edge of the creek.

"Now do you see me?" Her voice was doubled and multiplied with the voices of a dozen dead children. I had never heard those voices before, but I somehow recognized them.

She crouched at the creek bank, and I caught a glimpse of her bleeding, collapsed skull. The back of her t-shirt was soaked and dripping red.

She reached out for me, but this time it felt like a helping hand. Without hesitation, I took it.

White-hot pain radiated from the touch and shot through my entire body. It was almost too much to bear, but I managed to hold her.

She pulled me to the edge of the creek and released me. Sadie and dozens of little eyes stood over me, watching. The dark began to creep in again.

They were all of them looking down at me, smiling.

XI

—

Long ago, I made peace with the fact that I could never be romantic with Detective Andy Delroy, but I still held onto the secret that I wanted to wrap my arms around him *just once.* I knew deep down he always wanted the same, if even for a moment. I was certain that I loved him, though no longer in a romantic way. After the magnolia murders, when we unearthed that serial killer's trophy case, something inside me broke. Del's presence was one of the few things that brought my spirit any peace. There was nothing so shallow as sex or romance that could corrupt that.

I woke up on that creek bank in his arms, his head buried in my neck, warm wet tears rolling down my neck like sweat. I felt giddy like a child because I had gotten my wish. He smelled like smoke and rain and palo santo.

"Got a port?" I said through the smothering.

"...Carter, I thought you were going to drown. Something pulled you under," he said as he helped me sit up. I realized the tears weren't his; they were mine.

My senses returned. Something was biting into my palm—my fist was clenched around something small and hard.

It was a metal ring fixed with a large red birthstone. The stone was cracked and chipped but still in place. Engraved on each side was the year 1985. A class ring.

It did not take long for forensics to pull Sadie's DNA from inside the cracks of the chipped stone. Years of being buried in the creek bed did not eradicate the traces of her blood trapped inside. The custom class ring belonged to a long dead former officer. He fit the description given by the witness. The jackhammer didn't need to break up much concrete to find the blood stains hidden in the foundation of cell thirteen. Despite all of this, however, there wasn't any evidence to prove the Towns men were involved with the murder or the cover-up.

In the end, it wasn't a conviction that motivated us to the truth. It was relief from the madness inflicted on us.

Epilogue

—

Two double cheeseburgers with extra pickles, one with fries, one without, a diet coke, and a water. *Been way too long since I've eaten this shit; it'll probably kill me.*

Del and I were so far down the rabbit hole with this case, anything seemed possible. So, I decided to fall off the wagon and end my two-year fast-food sobriety. Del hadn't eaten a single thing on the case. Maybe fasting was his way of inching close enough to death so communing with spirits was possible. I had enough of it and hoped a belly full of meat and cheese would anchor us firmly in reality.

I plopped the tray down, and we chewed in silence.

After everything, we were back at zero. The Blanche case was solved, but our main assignment was still open. The capital wasn't pleased about the way we unearthed another skeleton in this god-forsaken town.

"You shoulda let me get bacon on mine."

"You can't have bacon *and* four packs of Newports a day, D."

"Ain't right keeping a man from his ba—" Del froze. I saw goosebumps forming on his arms. Icy fingers were clawing at my gut again.

A flash of purple and yellow reflected off the windows. SWAMPLAND MURDER TOURS was unloading the afternoon lunch crowd in the parking lot. All that "true crime" and sunshine surely worked up a furious appetite. We were all drawn to the crackling fluorescent burger sign for our fill of grease and flesh.

The burger joint was soon swarming with the group of macabre tourists and their matching t-shirts. Within the crowd, my eyes were drawn to an outlier. He was a young man with wild, searching eyes. When his gaze found mine, he beelined for our table.

Del dropped his burger and got to his feet. Reflexively, he slipped his gun out of the holster and pointed it down at his side without alerting the diners.

"Del, no—it's him." Trevor's clothes were dirty tatters. Dried mud was caked up to his knees. Del put his gun back, and they both took a seat. The food sat between us, still hot and half-eaten.

"Are you two the detectives?" he asked quietly, eyeballing my fries. I pushed them over to him. He instantly began devouring.

"Yeah, we're them. We were sittin' here trying to figure out how you did it."

"The story is gonna sound crazy—" he mumbled.

I felt that icy claw again. I swallowed back the nausea. I turned to see a woman exiting through the door. She looked back at me, staring with a dozen eyes. ∎

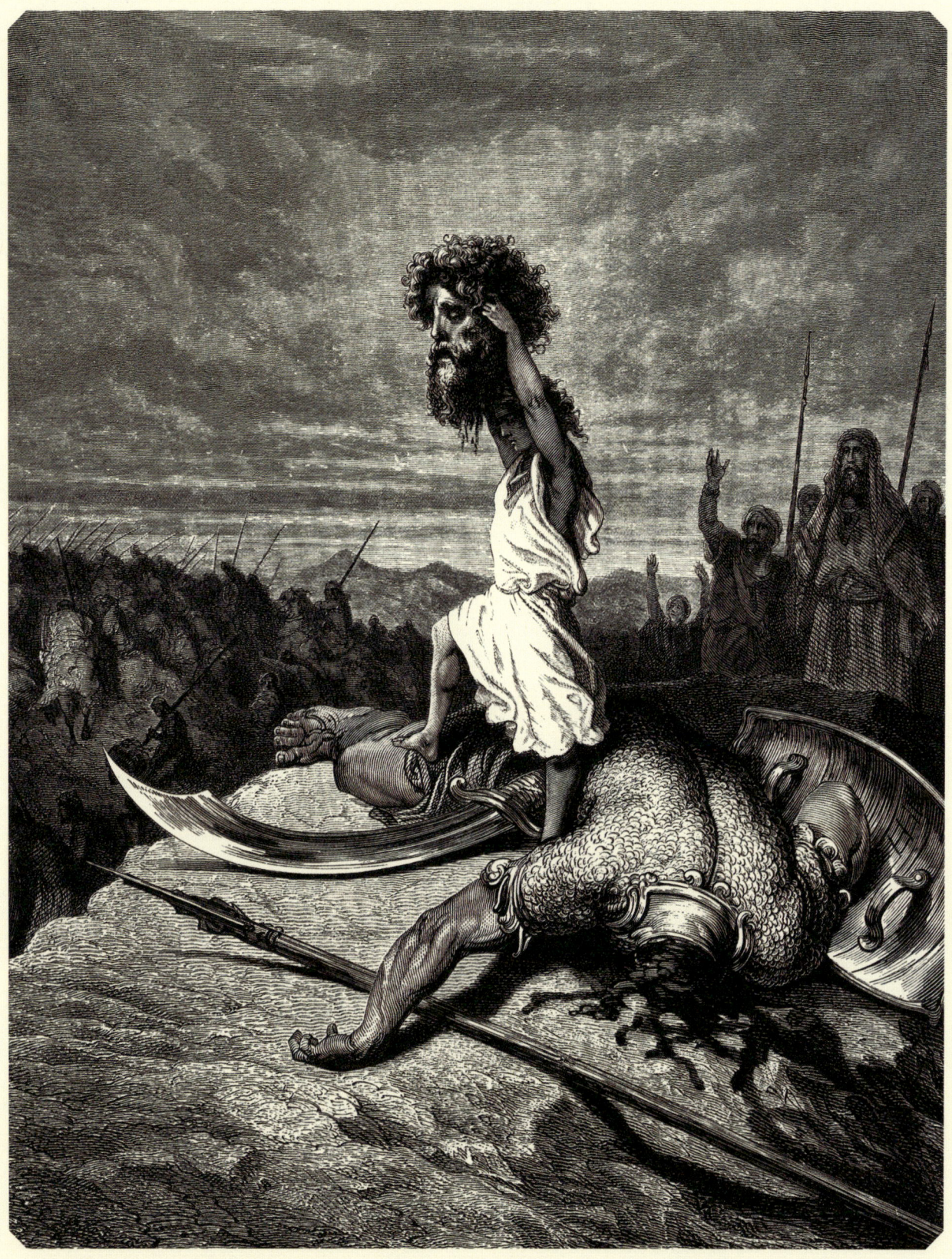

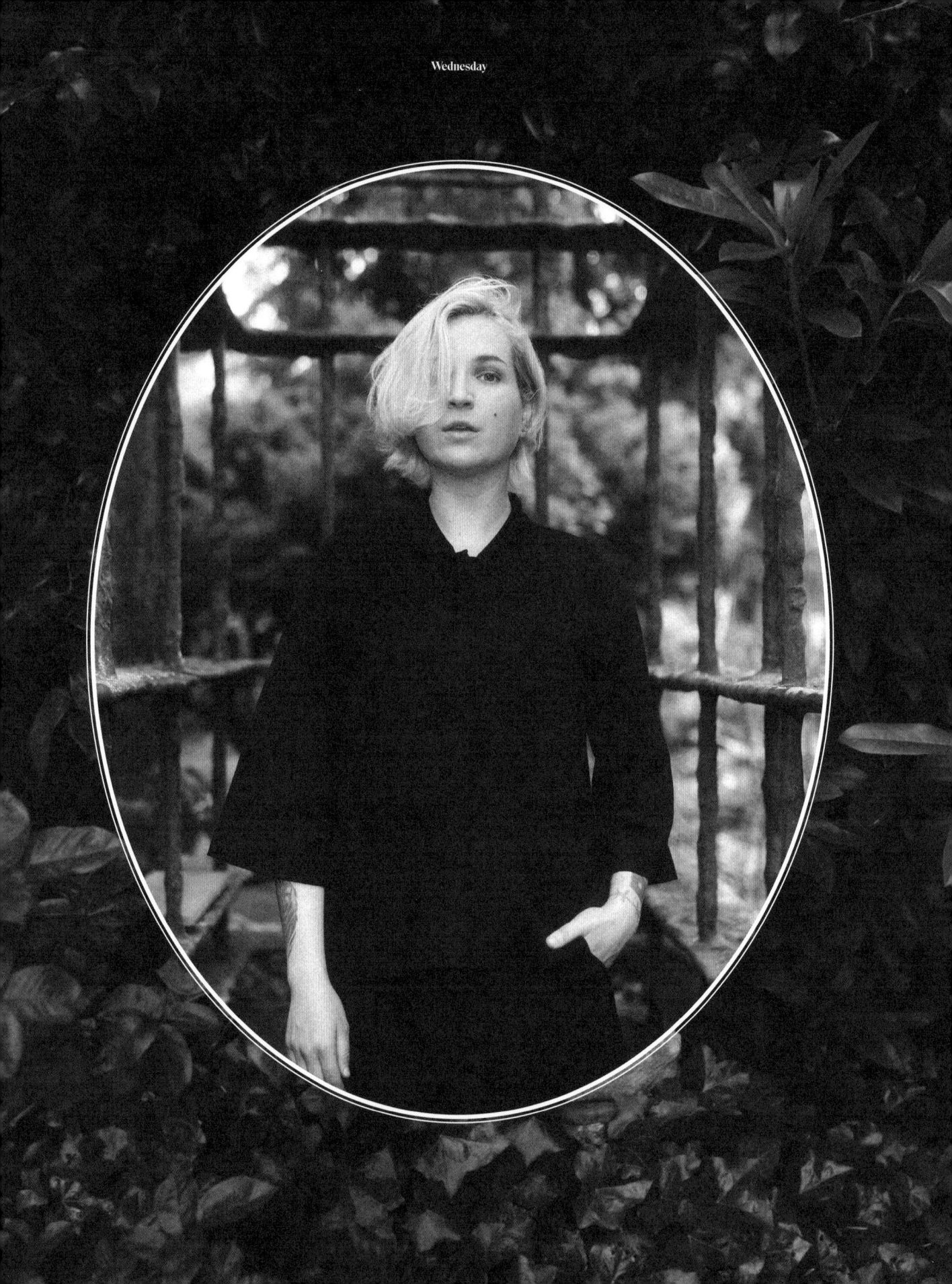

Claude Crobatia

In Death's Embrace

—

Death, the great enigma, is often cloaked in fear and silence—
too unsettling, too taboo for many to confront. Yet facing
the end of life doesn't have to be filled with dread.

Across history and cultures, death has been viewed not as
a finality but as a transition—a passage to another realm or
state of being. These perspectives offer an alternative to fear,
embracing dying as a natural, even meaningful, part of life.

This outlook is at the heart of Claude Crobatia's work.
A death-positive advocate, death awareness coach, and grief
counselor based in Amsterdam, Claude helps people navigate
the often-overwhelming terrain of grief while encouraging
a deeper understanding and acceptance of mortality.

Wednesday spent time with Claude to explore the
complex nature of death—and how we might find
peace, even purpose, in life's final chapter.

Words *Kenzie Barrena* / Photographs *Svenja Petersen*

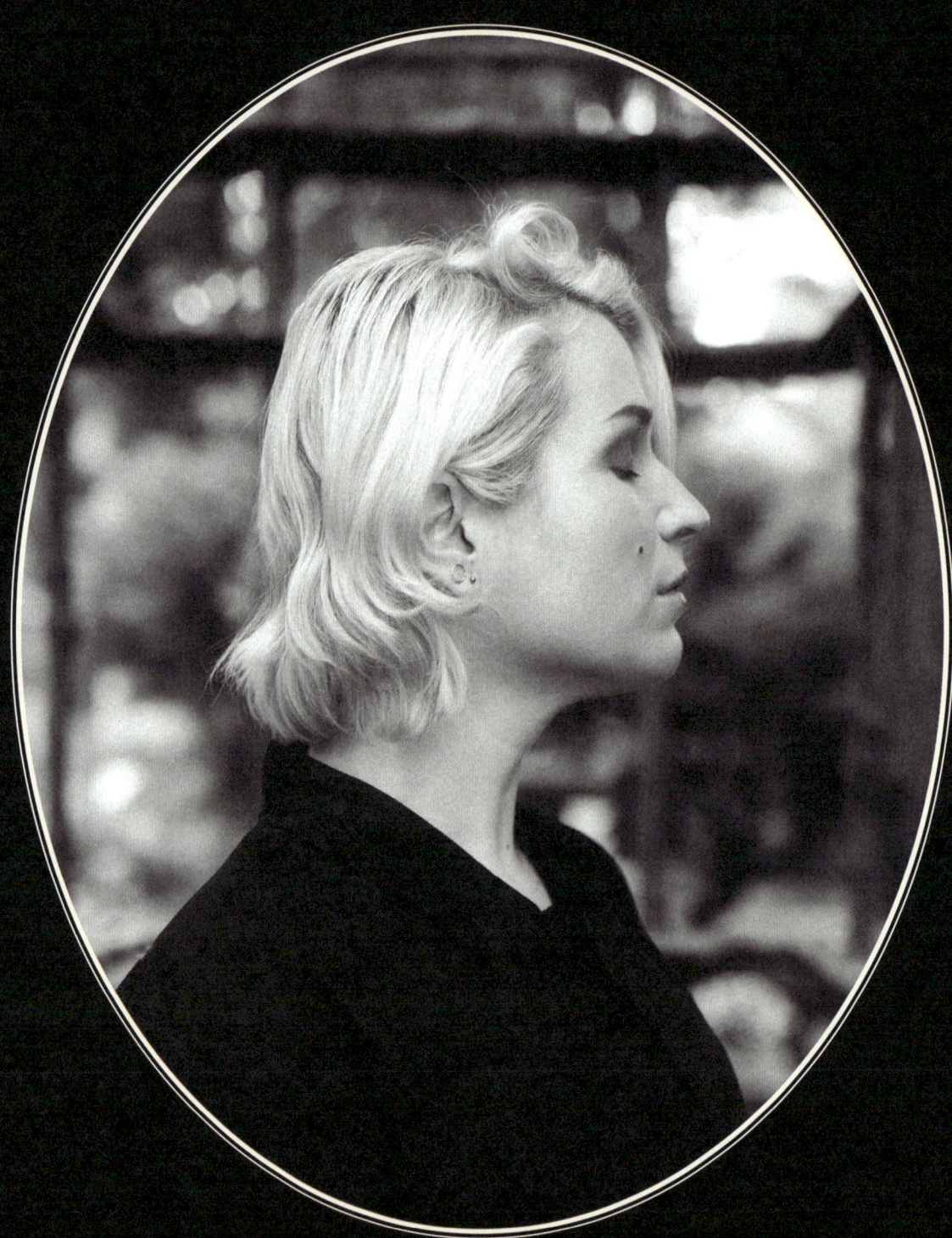

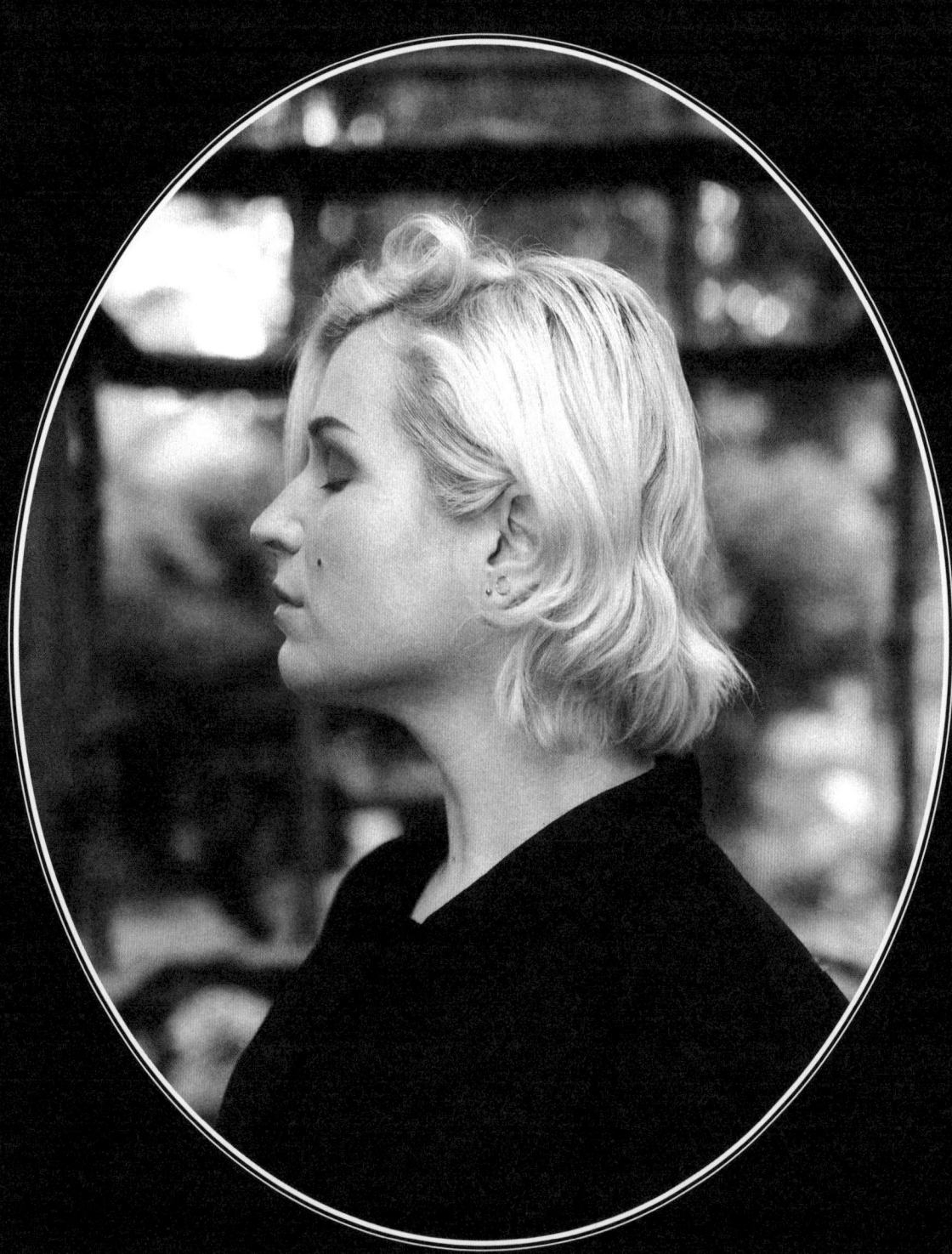

"I perceive death as a transformative journey, not a finality."

W What inspired you to become a death awareness coach?

C A series of personal encounters with death, including the passing of my father. Being present during his passing not only exposed me to the raw reality of death but also the collective denial that surrounds it. My relatives found it hard to acknowledge he had passed and would avoid any conversations surrounding the topic. This phenomenon, which anthropologist Ernest Becker coined "death denial," inspired my work. I wanted to help these individuals embrace mortality as a natural part of life and transform societal perceptions surrounding its taboo stereotypes. This journey culminated in creating my platform, "A Course in Dying," dedicated to exploring and promoting acceptance of mortality. Complementing this endeavor, I published my first book, *Als de Dood*, in 2022. However, reflecting on these achievements, I noticed how I missed the personal connection with those who could benefit from my insights. So, as a response, I established a grief counseling practice in Amsterdam.

W What do you hope people take away from your work?

C Many believe that facing mortality is inherently depressing, and it should be left for the elderly or life's morbid fatalities. In reality, grappling with mortality can yield profound benefits for individuals at any stage of life. I hope to inspire people to find the beauty and wonder in this process instead of fear.

W In "A Course in Dying," you publish a series of cemetery reviews. What is the most interesting one you've visited?

C It's hard to pick one, as all cemeteries are fascinating. I used to be a bit of a snob, only wanting to visit the ones with elaborate monuments, but I've come to appreciate them all. I enjoy Hollywood Forever Cemetery in Los Angeles, California, for its beautiful monuments and palm trees—a stark contrast to the gray skies I'm used to here in the Netherlands—and Teutonic Cemetery in Vatican City, Rome, a hidden burial ground adjacent to St. Peter's Basilica. It's almost like a secret garden—absolutely stunning.

W Can you discuss any cultural differences you've observed in attitudes toward death and how they influence our understanding of mortality?

C A striking cultural contrast is seen in attitudes toward death between Western and non-Western societies. In many Western cultures, there's a prevailing tendency to conceal death, often to the confines of hospitals and funeral homes. This medicalization of death has resulted in a loss of personal connection to the dying person and the dying process. Consequently, death has gradually become a distant and taboo subject rather than being recognized as a natural, integral part of life.

This contrasts sharply with cultures like those in Tibet, where sky burials openly embrace death as a part of life. Sky burials entail leaving the deceased on mountaintops for vultures, a practice deeply rooted in Buddhist beliefs about the cyclical nature of life and the body's role in death. While offering a body to vultures may seem straight out of a horror movie, it is viewed with reverence and compassion in Tibetan culture.

These cultural disparities profoundly shape our perceptions of mortality, influencing how we approach or evade the reality of death. In cultures where death is regarded as a communal event, there appears to be a greater acceptance and integration of the life cycle, fostering a more holistic and less apprehensive stance toward mortality.

W Do you view death as an ending?

C I perceive death as a transformative journey, not a finality. To me, death frees the body, the ego, and all facets of the self—a liberation of pure consciousness.

W What advice do you have for those with death anxiety?

C Create a comprehensive death plan that outlines personal preferences for funeral arrangements and specifics surrounding the dying process. This can be profoundly impactful as it instills a sense of control and ensures one's wishes are understood and respected. Additionally, engaging in open discussions about these preferences with loved ones serves to demystify death and integrate it into the fabric of life as a positive and normal aspect. ∎

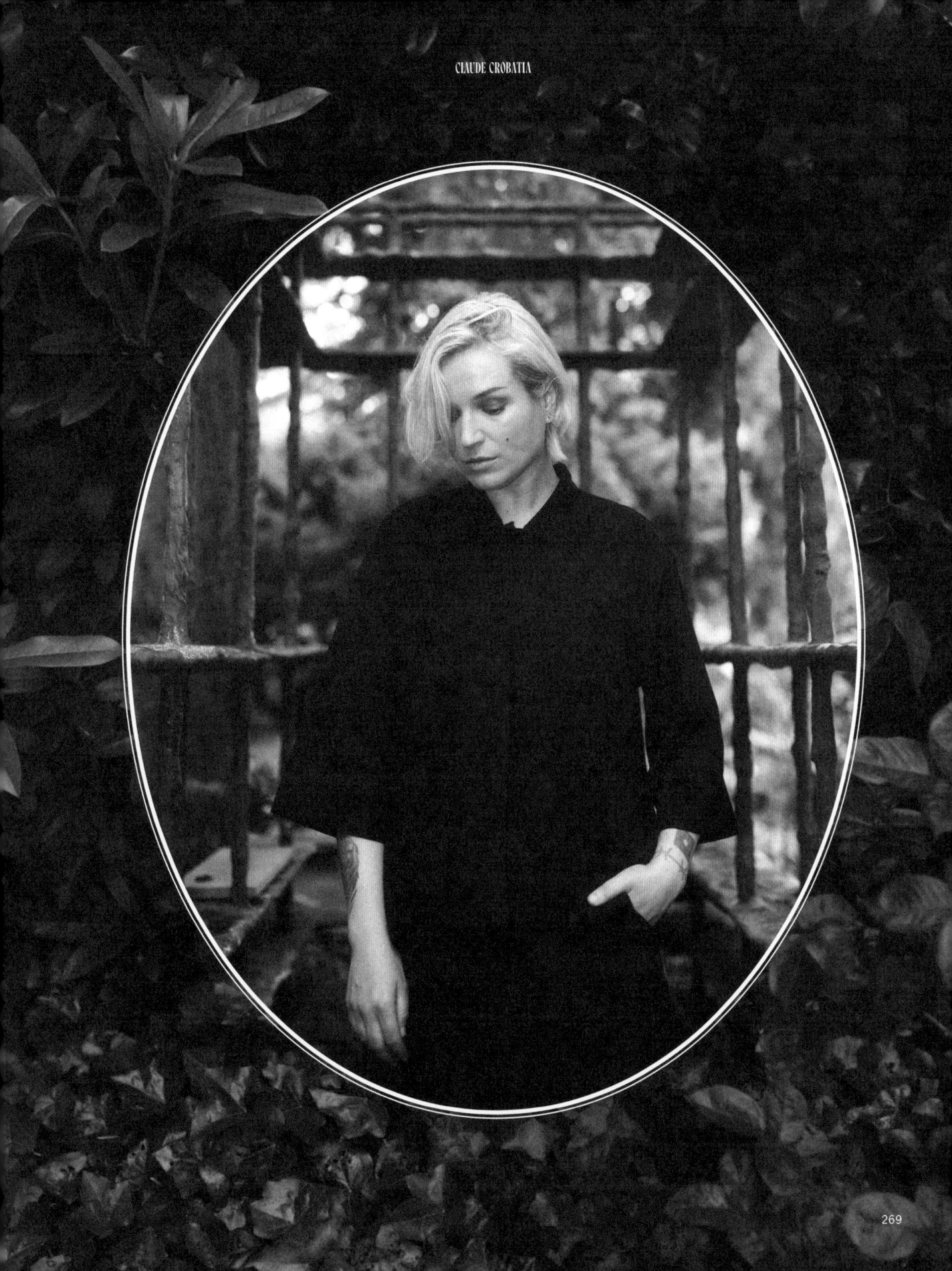

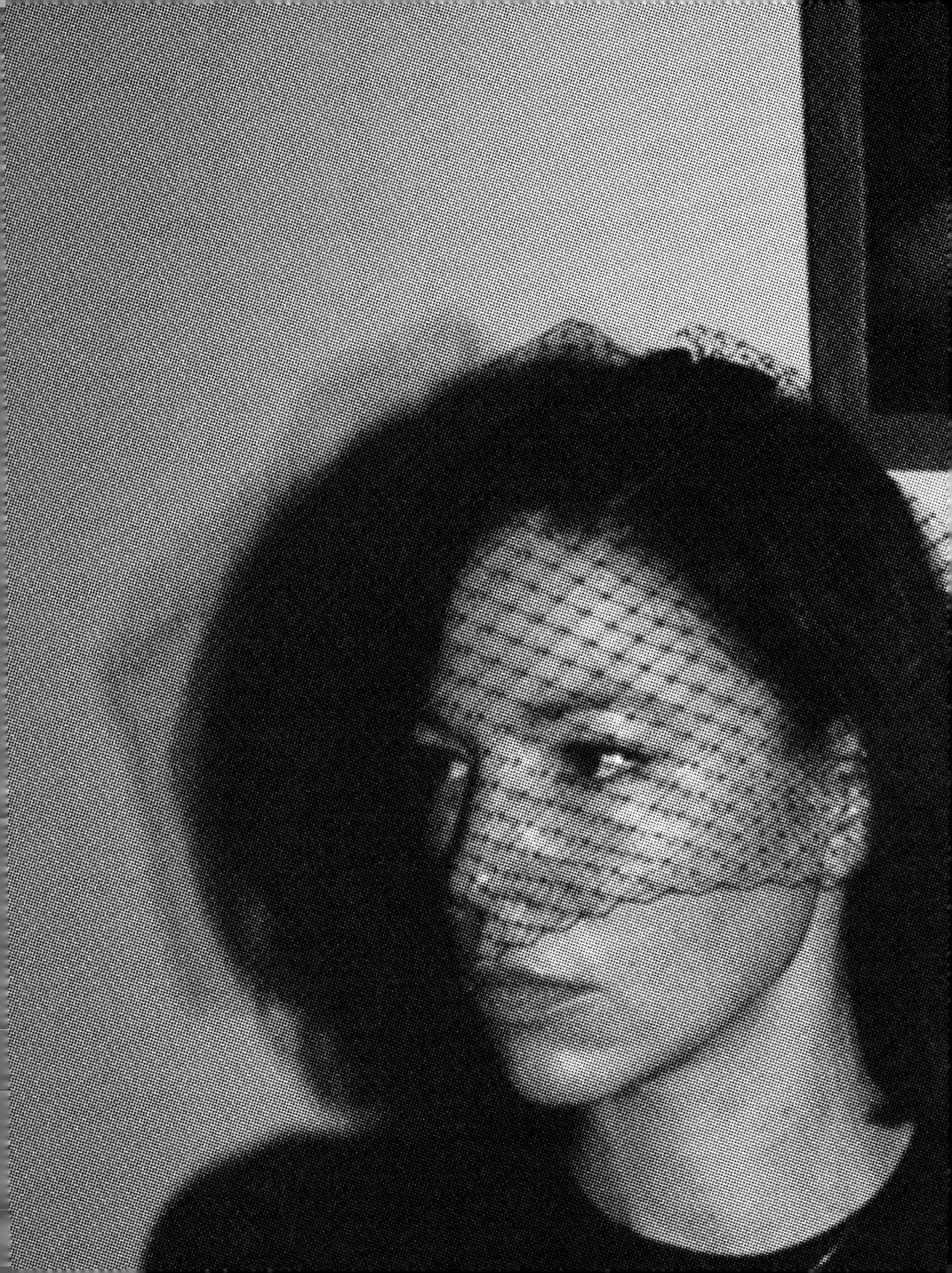

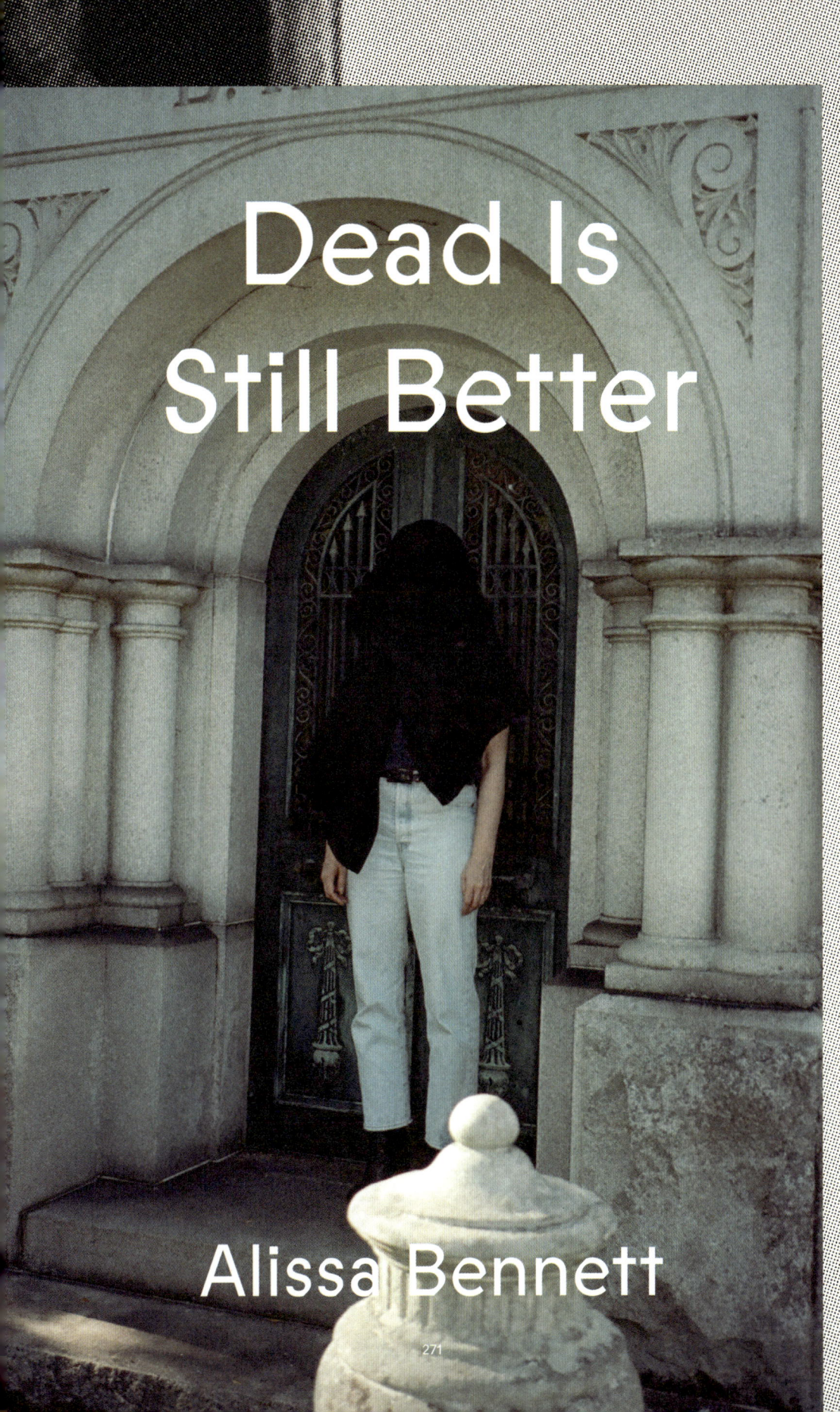

Dead Is Still Better

Alissa Bennett

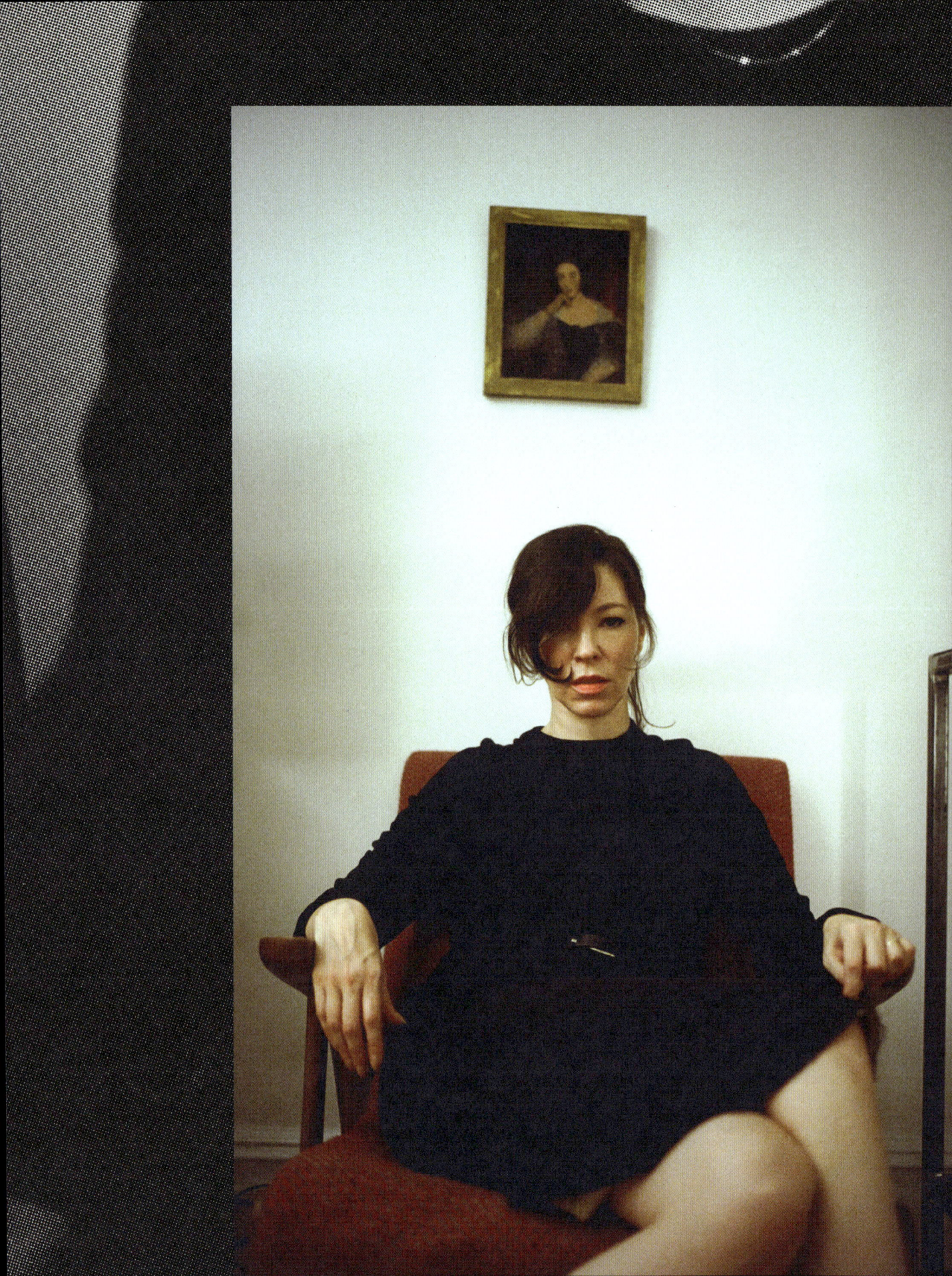

By Laura Albert

Photographs *Leigh Ladare*

The herd tends to move on too quickly, but Alissa Bennett instinctively knows, or fears, that something was missed—something critical and desperately needed. She cracks open the crypt, redirecting our attention to the importance of a person, an artist who was here. And she allows rest to a soul who, like an unjustly punished child, had their voice silenced.

This trajectory defines all her creative work: her zine *Dead is Better;* co-hosting with Lena Dunham the podcast *The C-Word;* audiobook narrator, from my JT LeRoy story "I Don't Go There Anymore" in the audiobook of *The Heart Is Deceitful Above All Things* to Ursula Parrott's cult Jazz Age novel *Ex-Wife* (for which Alissa also wrote the Foreword in the McNally Editions reissue); Director at New York's Gladstone Gallery, where she organized the eye-opening exhibition *The Secret History,* inspired by the 1992 Donna Tartt novel; writer for *The New York Times, Texte zur kunst, The Paris Review;* teaching at Yale University and Sarah Lawrence College (where her next course will be on writing creative nonfiction); anthologizing her essays in her debut book *Taxidermist's Handbook;* and her current project, a screenplay about author Edith Wharton.

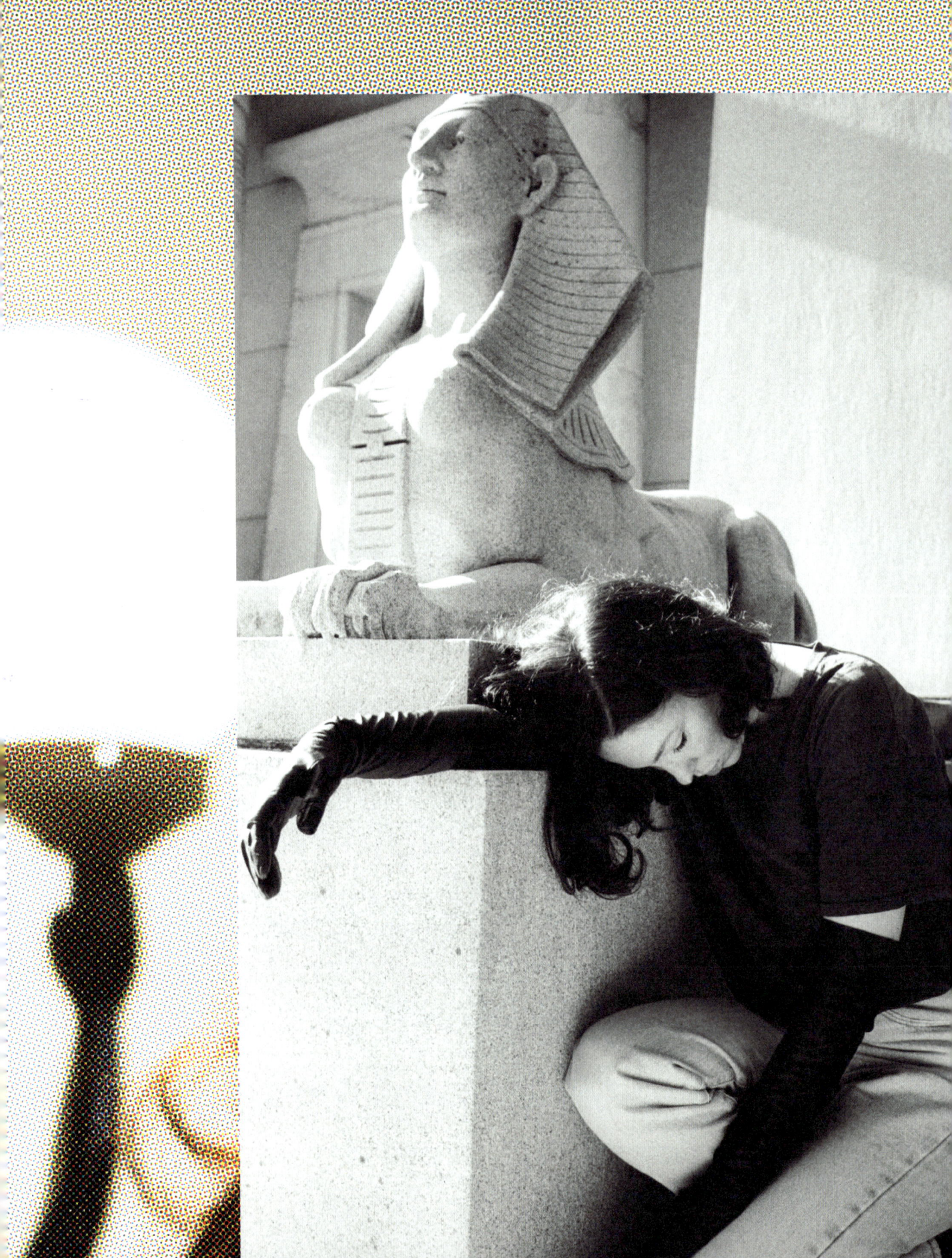

L You are this absolute curator, saying what happened and reconstructing it, knowing exactly where to look.

A The research doesn't happen because I'm attracted to a subject. The research happens, and then if it goes far enough, I'll have enough material to write about a person. But I don't pick a person and then research them. Toward the end of an essay, I'll understand exactly what it is that I've related to about them. And it becomes about myself as well, which is something that I intentionally tried to measure out from when I first started writing those types of essays. I didn't want to ransack someone's life and not measure-for-measure it with, you know, humiliations from my own life.

L Hilary Mantel, the author of the *Wolf Hall* series, went to the Tower of London because she was writing about Anne Boleyn. And when I did a private tour of the Tower, the guy there and I were discussing Hilary. They were up in the cell where Boleyn had been, but he had to let someone else in, so he left her for a while. When he came back, he apologized, but she said, "Oh, no, I've been deep in conversation." With Anne.

A I 100% believe it. As a writer, as a person, or an artist, or whatever, I think you either have the propensity to intuit where that porosity is and access things that are not in the world of material things, or you don't.

L I feel that everyone is born with it, but I think we're also trained to ignore it. I do think there are some for whom it's more highly attuned. For me, when I go to a graveyard, I'm very interested in reading the tombstones.

A Well, I'm a great graveyard enthusiast, but when I go to a graveyard, it's usually to see someone specific within my research. Once a year, I go and see Barbara Hutton's grave at Woodlawn, or if I'm in London, I go and see Lizzie Siddall—I teach a class at Yale about her. She was the great pre-Raphaelite muse, the model for Millais' *Ophelia* painting, and then she married Dante Rossetti. But she was also a writer and a poet. She got subsumed under Image, and I became really interested in this myth of the muse and what she represented and what her life was actually like. She was a laudanum addict and an anorexic; she had this very complicated life that has gotten reduced into pure Image. She's sort of real for me; she's like a North Star. I have a couple of figures in my work who come up again and again and again, and she's one of them. She's at Highgate in the Rossetti family plot, and when I first started to try to go see her, it was so overgrown that you couldn't get to the plot. And then you watch as history corrects itself, and now her plot is completely clear. I definitely am also a casual graveyard wanderer, but usually it's to see a person. And when I get to the grave of that person, I do feel—know they're not there, but there is some... It's like a charging port. I do often feel there's some kind of communion.

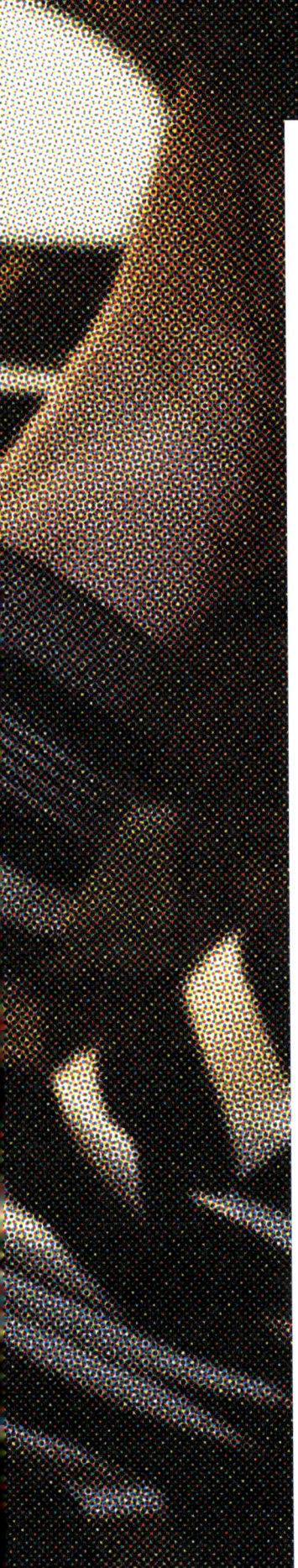

L   When I went to Oscar Wilde's grave in Paris, I did feel that.

A   Right. I do believe increasingly that there are these kind of elective affinities between you and whoever it is that influences you or who you're connected to intellectually or spiritually. You can attract these remote figures and have communion with them.

L   When you go there, do you ever talk out loud, or is it talking in your head?

A   It's usually talking in my head. I'm working on this Edith Wharton project; she's the last one that felt really incredible to me. *Ethan Frome* is the novel that everyone in America reads in seventh grade, and they hate it. But she based it on a true story about a sledding accident that happened in Lenox, Massachusetts. I went into the records and found out the name of the girl who died in the accident and where her grave was. And when I was at her grave, it felt like a flash of lightning, like when your navigator says you have arrived. I just kind of say in my head, I found you.

L   When you write about a person, the way you go in is like a saving of someone, an invitation to hold space for them.

A   I also really believe in ghosts. I really believe in being directed by things that you can't see. I feel often that I'm led to things. There's like a little channeling that happens.

L   When was your first ghost experience?

A   I was in my twenties and living in Brooklyn. I'd never seen the spectral evidence before. But I came home one night and opened my front door, and I saw a man walk across the staircase and into the wall. And I thought, what a horrible sentence to have to live out your eternity in a shitty tenement in Williamsburg. But my experience with ghosts is less spectral, more receiving signs or indicators that confirm things. I've always had that.

L   What type of things?

A   I'll tell you my most recent one. My mentor died in June, right before I opened a show that I organized at the Gladstone Gallery, titled *The Secret History*. I was on a plane to New Orleans because I had another friend who died, and I was going to clean out her apartment. And a friend of mine who goes to a very fancy celebrity psychic texted me. He didn't know what I was doing, but he said, "I just talked to my psychic about you. Do you want to know what she said?" I told him yes, and he said, "First she said she sees you packing a lot of boxes, and it's gonna be really hard, and you need to take breaks." And I was like, okay, that's weird. Then he said, "She also said that Barbara is really proud of you, and she's going to leave you a sign, and it's going to be so straightforward that you won't be able to miss it. You'll know it right away." I got to New Orleans, and I went to this friend's house. We had to pack up her things, and I started at the bookshelf. The first book was in a cardboard folio; I couldn't see what it was. I slid it out of the folio, and it was a reprint of a book from 550 AD called *The Secret History*.

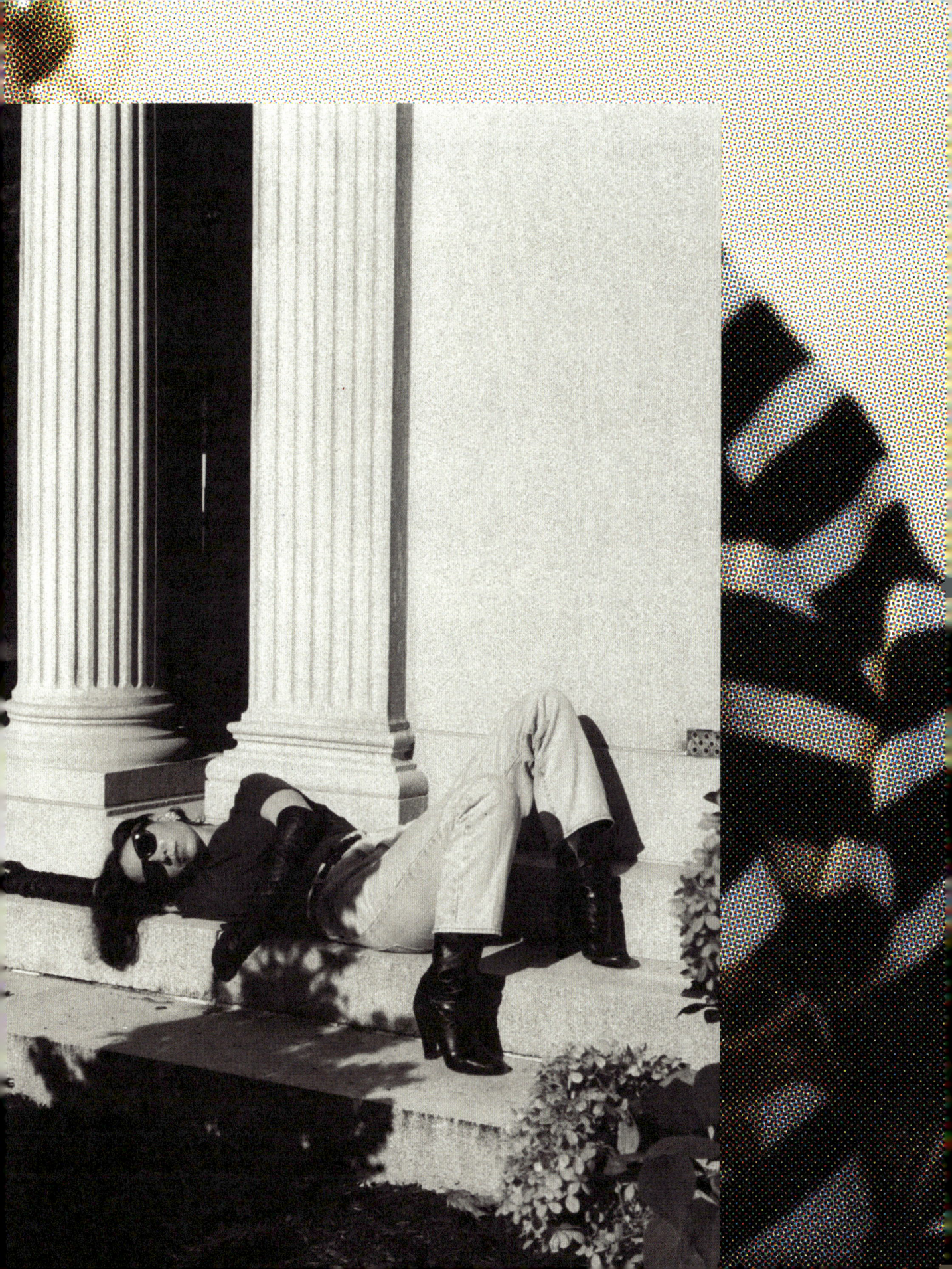

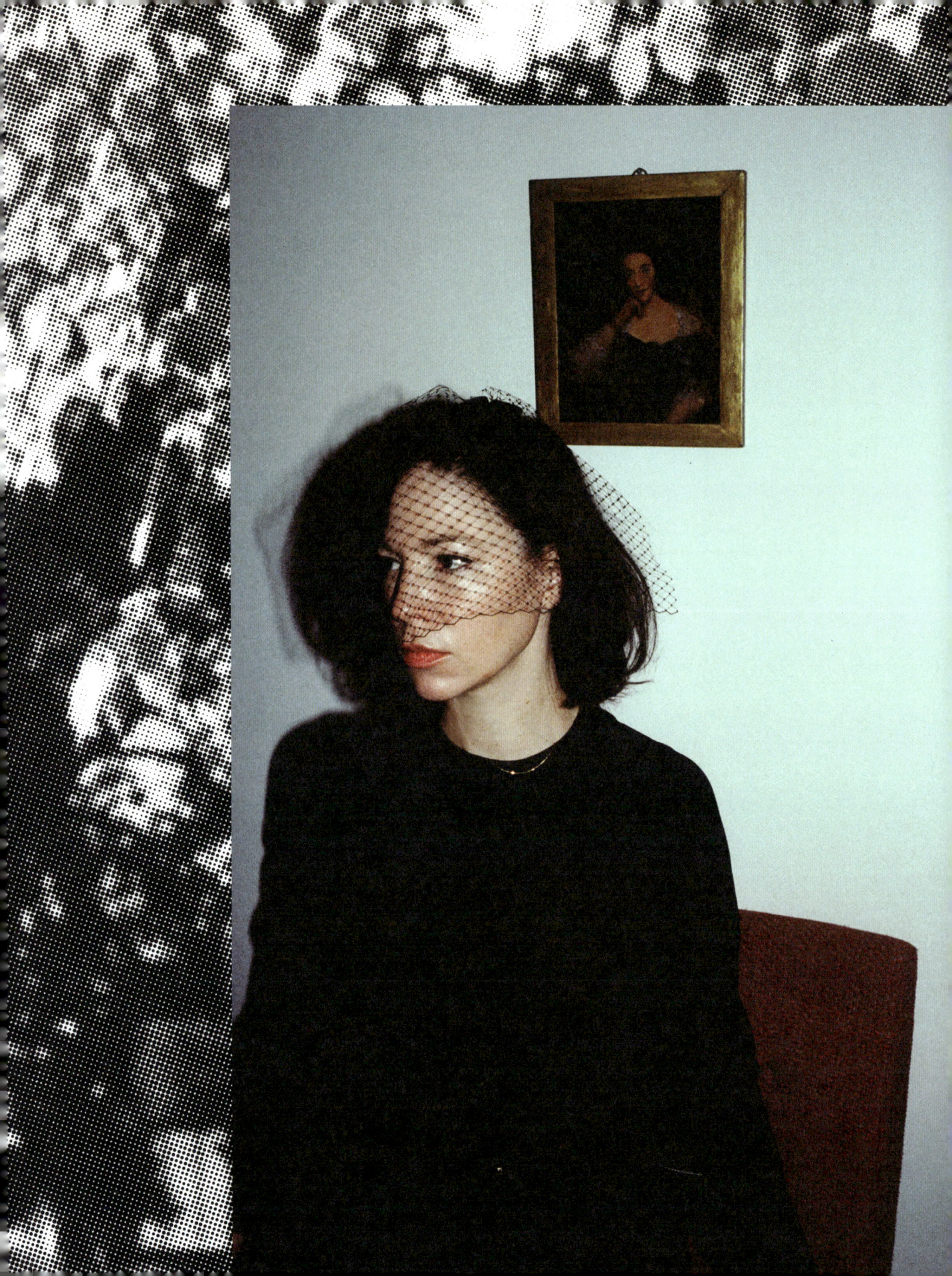

L Oh my God.

A It was weird, but also so confirming for me. It made me feel such relief and comfort. It reaffirmed that, when people die, it's not a complete vanishing act. Something comes next. And I had little things like that the whole weekend; it was maybe a week after Barbara died. That sort of thing happens to me quite often. Also, I'd written a novel, probably from 19 to 22, but I had no copy of it. And I found what is probably the last existing copy in this same apartment in New Orleans.

L You're such a truth teller; you'll say things about controversial subjects which are so flat-out obvious and honest but no one will say.

A I'm always like, why don't you say it? As much as I believe in ghosts and Jean Harlow tapping me on my shoulder, I also believe in rationality. And I often feel like, if you make a habit of being honest and saying rational things, even if other people don't want to say them, eventually the public is kind of inured to it, and they expect it. I think that people like my candor, even though it is a little bit loose-cannon-esque. I'm not a very self-edited person. I'm not self-censored. I don't worry in my writing about who's going to read it.

L My great interest in life, what is survival for me, is storytelling. And I've used visual art and music in combination with other voices—there's a way that music can elicit with greater immediacy than any visual medium.

A I have to tell you, one of my dark secrets is that music is often too painful for me to engage with. I don't listen to a lot of music anymore because I feel it's like a slideshow of the past.

L Oh my God. Oh my God. I'm the same way about music.

A And like, I can't. If I'm going to listen, it has to be like Schubert or something. I can't, it makes me too sad.

L Yeah, I recently found this band that excited me. And I saw they were playing here soon but I just was... It disturbed me so much because it felt too much like loss, you know?

A Yes, I do. That's exactly what it is. It feels too much like loss. A hundred percent. Yes. Yes.

L I was in a band called Daddy Don't Go and have all these old CDs, but I don't listen to them anymore. I'm listening to podcasts.

A Same. That's what I do, too. Or books on tape, I like.

L Were you ever in a band?

A Yeah, I had a girl band in high school.

L Were you a singer, or did you play?

A I was a singer, of course. I didn't have any attention span to play an instrument, but we had like a little punk rock little-sister girl group.

L What were you called?

A First we were the Quagmire Quirps, and then we were Anal Fixation. It was fun, but it's like a different life. Russian doll.

L To have that command of an audience and walk away from it is hard.

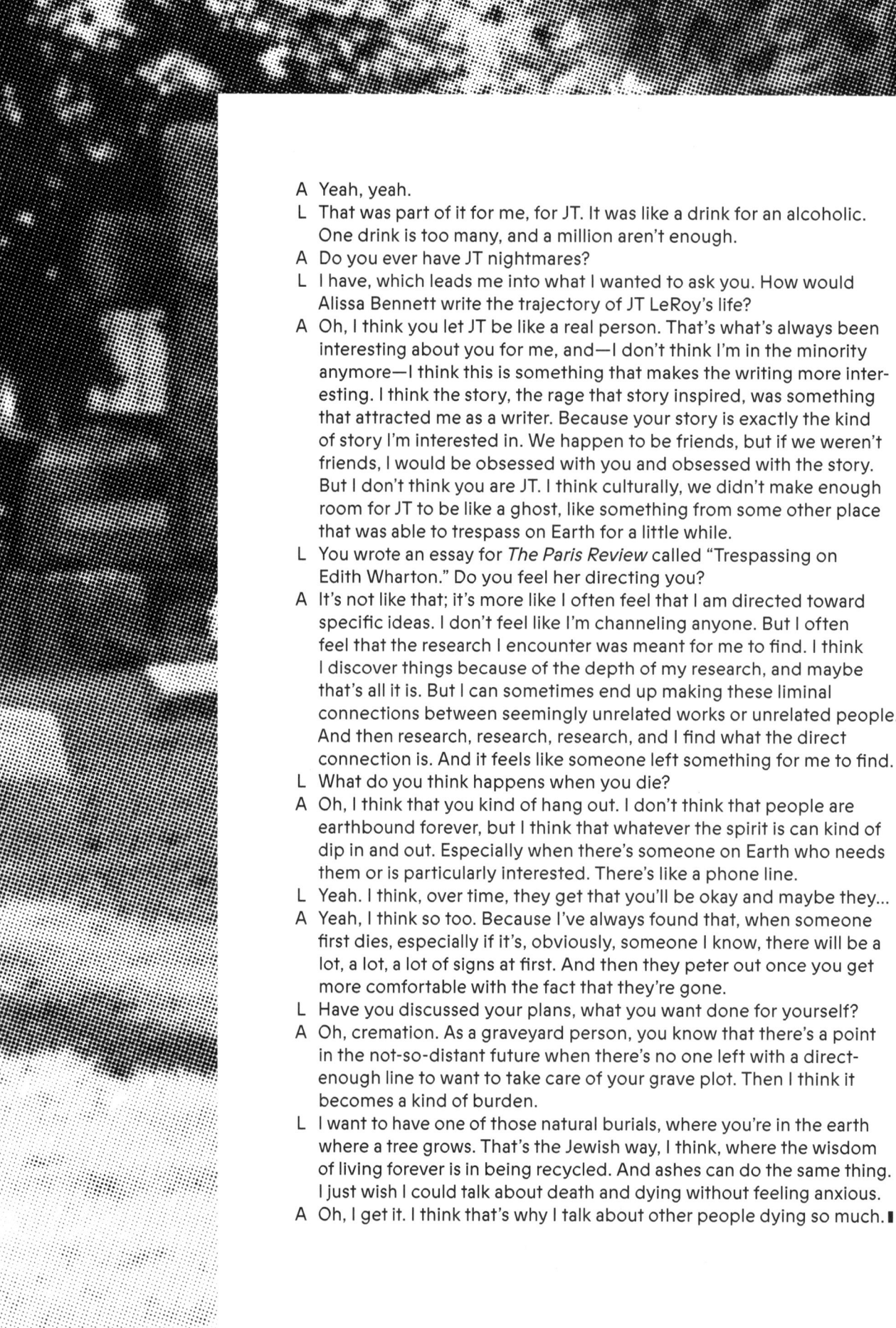

A Yeah, yeah.

L That was part of it for me, for JT. It was like a drink for an alcoholic. One drink is too many, and a million aren't enough.

A Do you ever have JT nightmares?

L I have, which leads me into what I wanted to ask you. How would Alissa Bennett write the trajectory of JT LeRoy's life?

A Oh, I think you let JT be like a real person. That's what's always been interesting about you for me, and—I don't think I'm in the minority anymore—I think this is something that makes the writing more interesting. I think the story, the rage that story inspired, was something that attracted me as a writer. Because your story is exactly the kind of story I'm interested in. We happen to be friends, but if we weren't friends, I would be obsessed with you and obsessed with the story. But I don't think you are JT. I think culturally, we didn't make enough room for JT to be like a ghost, like something from some other place that was able to trespass on Earth for a little while.

L You wrote an essay for *The Paris Review* called "Trespassing on Edith Wharton." Do you feel her directing you?

A It's not like that; it's more like I often feel that I am directed toward specific ideas. I don't feel like I'm channeling anyone. But I often feel that the research I encounter was meant for me to find. I think I discover things because of the depth of my research, and maybe that's all it is. But I can sometimes end up making these liminal connections between seemingly unrelated works or unrelated people. And then research, research, research, and I find what the direct connection is. And it feels like someone left something for me to find.

L What do you think happens when you die?

A Oh, I think that you kind of hang out. I don't think that people are earthbound forever, but I think that whatever the spirit is can kind of dip in and out. Especially when there's someone on Earth who needs them or is particularly interested. There's like a phone line.

L Yeah. I think, over time, they get that you'll be okay and maybe they...

A Yeah, I think so too. Because I've always found that, when someone first dies, especially if it's, obviously, someone I know, there will be a lot, a lot, a lot of signs at first. And then they peter out once you get more comfortable with the fact that they're gone.

L Have you discussed your plans, what you want done for yourself?

A Oh, cremation. As a graveyard person, you know that there's a point in the not-so-distant future when there's no one left with a direct-enough line to want to take care of your grave plot. Then I think it becomes a kind of burden.

L I want to have one of those natural burials, where you're in the earth where a tree grows. That's the Jewish way, I think, where the wisdom of living forever is in being recycled. And ashes can do the same thing. I just wish I could talk about death and dying without feeling anxious.

A Oh, I get it. I think that's why I talk about other people dying so much. ∎

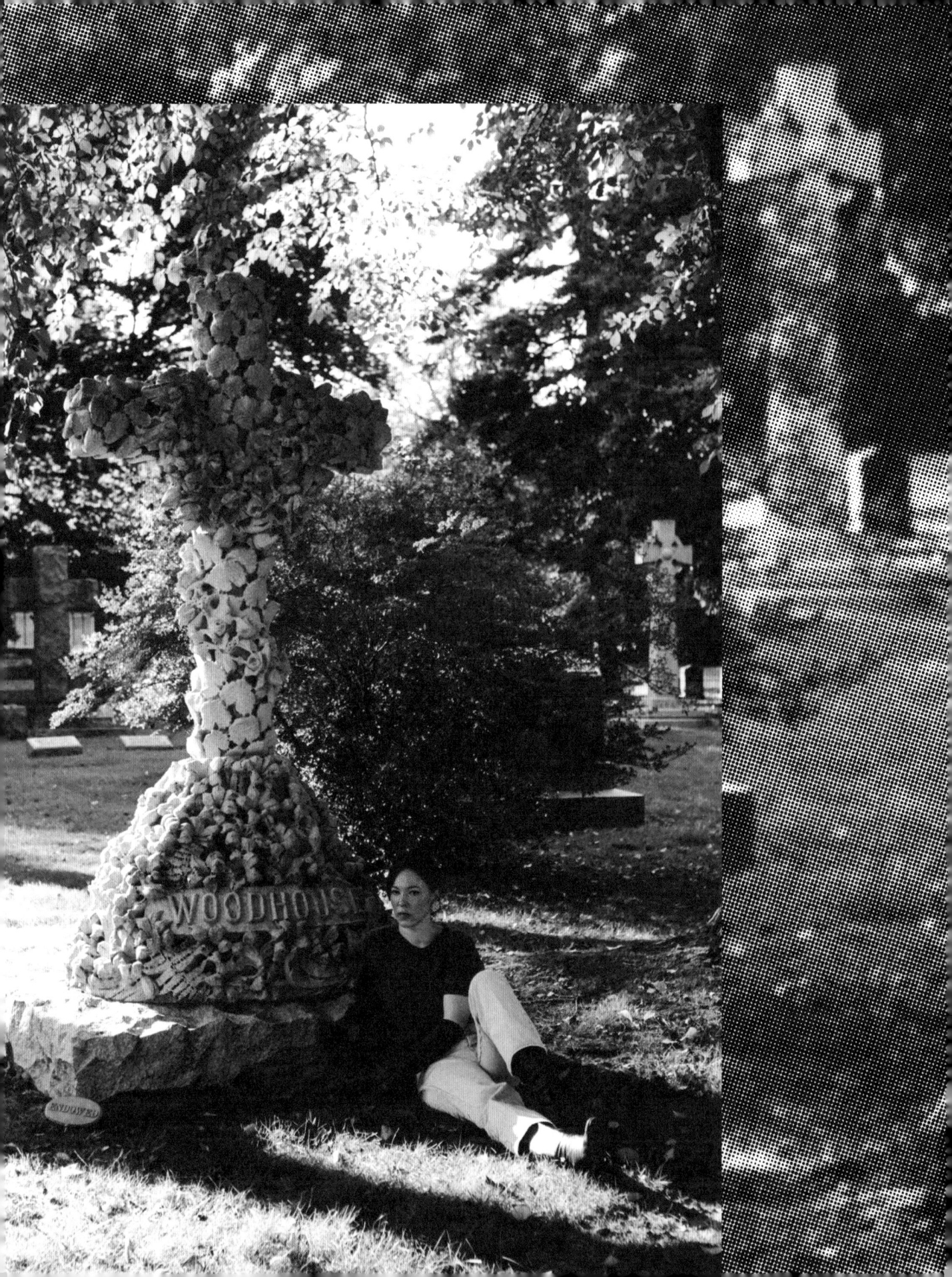

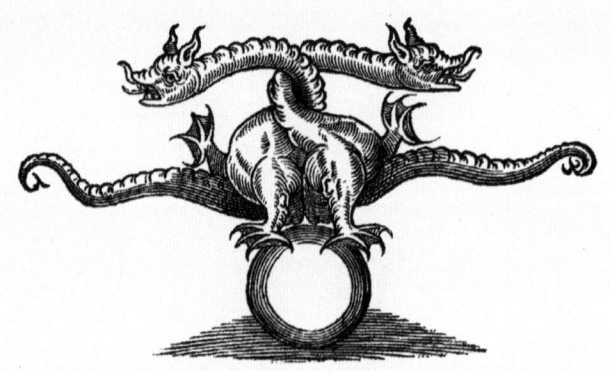

Volume 1, Number 2
2025

The Editorial Coven

Editor-in-Chief,
Creative Director
Kevin Grady

Creative Director,
Art Director, Editor, Designer
Adam Larson

Design Assistant
Leanna Waldron

Editor-at-Large
Laura Albert

Music Correspondent
André Obin

Photographer-at-Large
Matthew Reeves

Endpapers
Simon Ungless

Divider Copy
David B. Olsen

Black Cat-in-Residence
Vandal

Founder
Black Plastic

Contributors

Gustave Doré
Sébastien Biache
Sadie Liebo
Ascii Disco

Writers

Richard Herstek
Ian Sattler
Christopher Stella
Dylan Wolfram
David B. Olsen
Britt Collins
Kenzie Barrena
David Moynihan
Charles McEnerney
Roger Rueff
Jason O'Toole
Brittany Raglin
J. Bennett

Photographers

Tarek Mohamed Mawad
Rebekah Campbell
Leigh Ladare
Heather McGrath
Jordan Hemingway
Allard Bovenberg
Ian Allen
Alejandra Guerrero
Svenja Petersen
Mitch Tobias
Corinne Schiavone
Steven Piper
Stephen Rutterford

Styling, Hair & Makeup

Anika Ladero
Karen Jiménez
Laila Hayani
Jennifer Corona

With Gratitude

Stump Mahoney
Calissa Grady
Lara Grady
Mo Hy
Darenzia
Charles McEnerney
Deborah Ayerst
Porscha Michelle
Rhys

Inquiries

info@wednesdaymagazine.com
+1 (303) 378-1706

wednesdaymagazine.com
@wednesday_mag

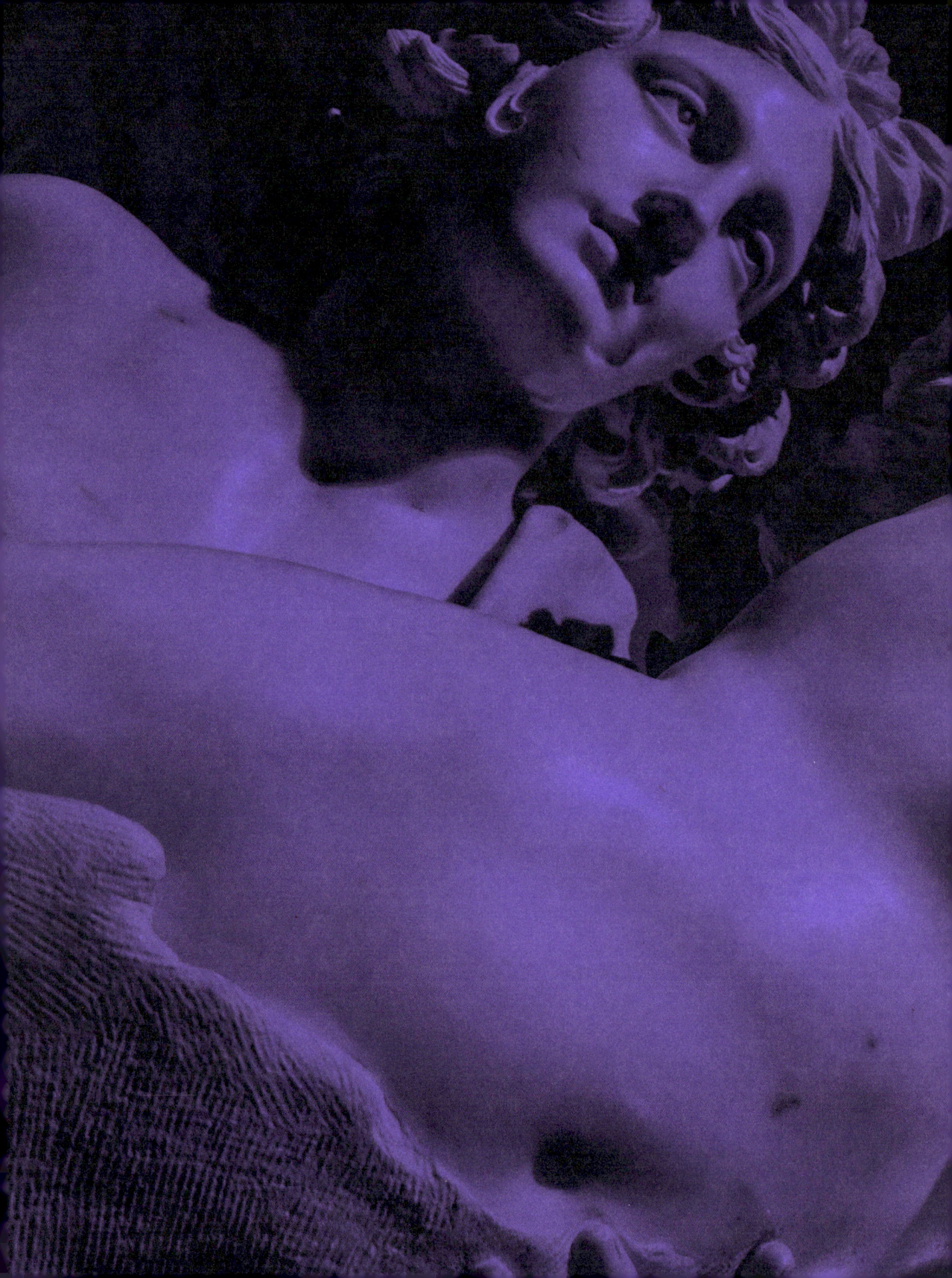

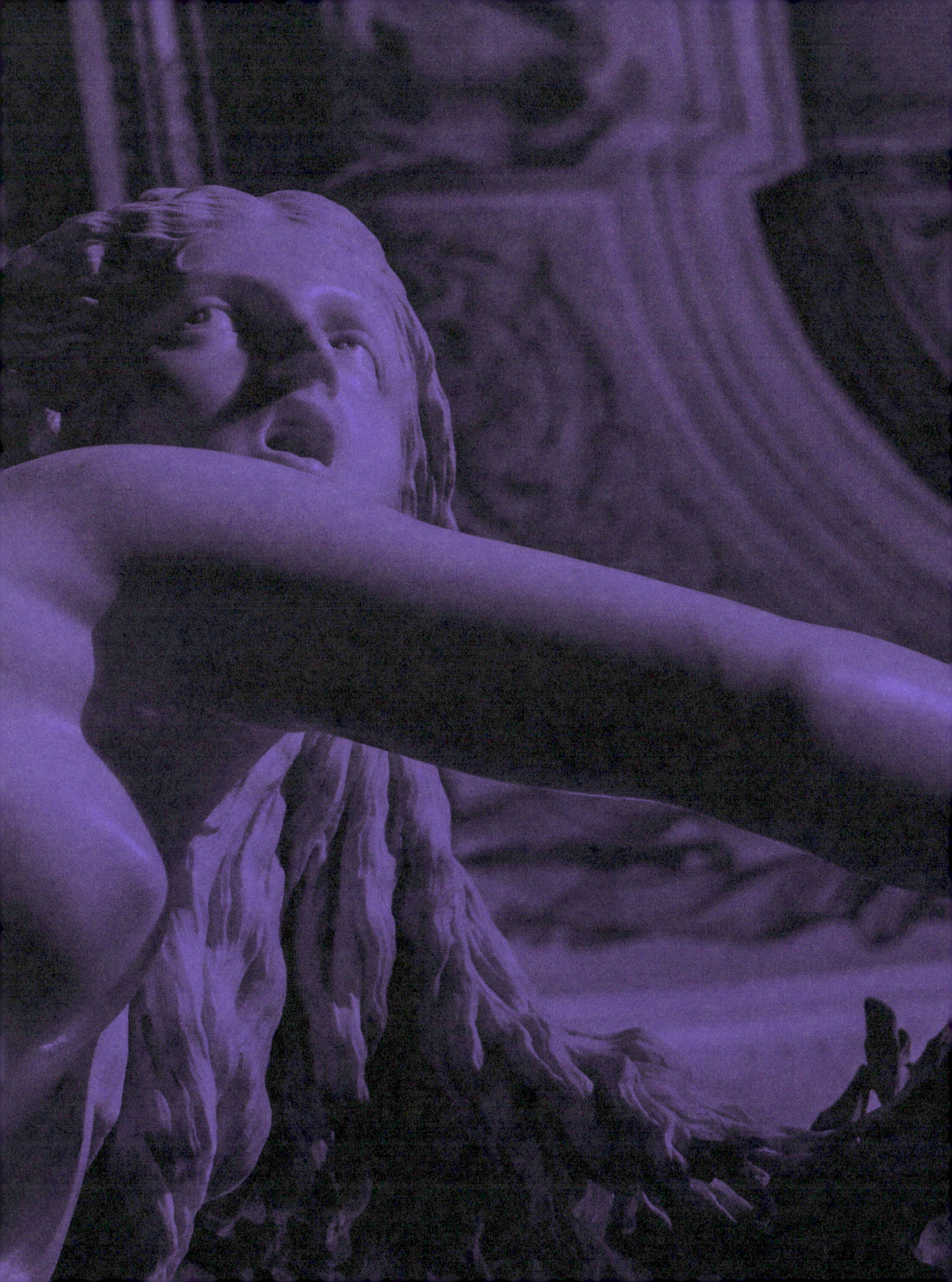